TO LIZ

Look Mummy I'm Dancing

NOT IN YEARS.

AN OLD FRIEND OF LONG STANDING

LOTSALUV

Bob (Malcc)

A catalogue record of this book is available from the British Library

ISBN: 978-1-84375-333-9

To order additional copies of this book please visit:
http://www.upso.co.uk/robertmarlowe

Published by: UPSO Ltd
5 Stirling Road, Castleham Business Park,
St Leonards-on-Sea, East Sussex TN38 9NW United Kingdom
Tel: 01424 853349 Fax: 0870 191 3991
Email: info@upso.co.uk Web: http://www.upso.co.uk

Look Mummy I'm Dancing

by

Robert Marlowe

'In Africa – when an old man dies –
A library disappears!'

Quote – Hampate bé.

'In England too!'

Quote – Robert Marlowe.

Alternatively to quote the opening lines of "Chicago"

'Welcome, Ladies and Gentleman, you are about to see a story of Murder, Greed, Corruption, Violence, Exploitation, Adultery and Treachery – all those things we hold near and dear to our hearts.'

Jenny

Nina

This book is dedicated to Jenny Vance and Nina Brown. My consecutive dancing partners who, with their skills and dedication helped me to climb the ladder of success in the theatrical profession.

Contents

To Dear Bob,
a friend and Mentor.
lots of love
Bradley
x

FOREWORD

I remember telling some fellow comics that I was thinking about going to Cromer and appearing in an end of the pier show. "Are you mad?" came the answer, "it's a backwater, go and do Blackpool or Torquay or maybe even Yarmouth, you're wasting your time".

I had a gut feeling that it was the right thing to do. Well thank god I had guts, because I had three fantastic years starting at the bottom of the bill and working up to top of the bill. It was like having a three-year crash course in stage schooling and my singing teacher, dance teacher, acting teacher, and stage craft teacher and director was one man.

Three summer seasons at twelve weeks per season (that's 36 weeks) under the guidance of the brilliant Bob Marlowe. Bob taught me everything I needed to know, he was hard but fair and encouraged me to be brave and try things like tap dancing or singing, which I had never done on stage before. He built my confidence to such a height within my first week I felt like I had always been on a theatre stage.

We have since become great friends and he regularly regales me with stories about an era, which I had just missed out on.

Bob is a genuinely funny and warm man with so much experience, I am sure once you have read Bob's book you will want to get up and be in showbiz, that's if you aren't already.

The industry is a much brighter place because of people like Bob Marlowe and without his help and guidance I don't think I would be where I am now.

God bless Bob, I say!

Bradley Walsh

Bradley Walsh

Purchasing Barbara Windsor's book, she inscribed it with the following dedication, which she permitted me to include in my own biography when I met her at the Lady Ratlings Ball "Stomping at the Savoy" 7 May 2006. Barbara was guesting, as president of her charity, to accept the Lady Ratlings contributory cheque, which the ball was in aid of.

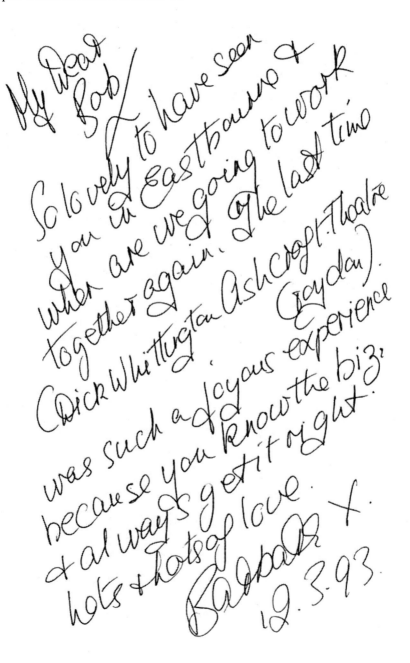

ACKNOWLEDGEMENTS

Throughout my career friends have urged me to record my memoirs. Although I kept every programme, contract and newspaper cutting, I was very reluctant, fearing I would not have the writing expertise to carry it through. Ghost writers were suggested. But how could they express my memories and thoughts satisfactorily? However, the watershed of my own fifty glorious years in show business coincided with the Queen's coronation celebration in 2003 and I decided to 'have a go, Joe!'

As I had always been praised for writing a good letter, I decided to take that tack in my autobiography – as though writing to a friend, ie the reader. Taking six months between engagements, I had to collate all the relevant details, venues, managements, dates, etc. Finally, putting pen to paper in longhand, I commenced. I had never learned to type - no time for that - and I had never had ambitions to work in an office. I will not mention computers - I'm a dodo where they are concerned. Too old a dog for new tricks.

My friend Claire Waters typed my first attempts and encouraged me to continue. Unfortunately, her circumstances changed and she was unable to continue, so I had to find someone else to take on the task -Rosemary Tyler, née Waters - by a strange coincidence, the same surname as my friend Claire, but not related. I felt this was a good omen.

Rosemary was 'mistress of the robes' for top Triumph management and commanded the repository of the largest wardrobe of costumes in theatre-land. We had known each other for years, through the Richard Stone period until he sold out to Triumph, with whom I then worked for a further number of years. I had known Rosemary's daughter since she was a baby. Catherine was secretary to a consortium of doctors, and possessed typing skills, so I asked her to take on my autobiography, to which she dedicated herself in her spare time. Even though she was never in showbiz herself, her interest came through her mother, who had been a classical ballet dancer, whilst her father was a stage manager. There's nothing like keeping it in the family.

Finally I wish to pay tribute to all my showbiz friends who encouraged me to continue when I flagged, fearing my ability to continue.

Whilst recollecting the past can be exhilarating, it has trauma attached in equal portion, especially when reliving odd moments - some exceedingly odd - as readers will discover. The one truism I have realised is that authenticity is essential, and in that I cannot be faulted.

I hope you will find it an interesting and enjoyable read - about times, unfortunately, gone forever.

THE REASON

'Oh no,' I hear you murmur, 'not another showbiz biography!'

The aim in writing mine is to chronicle the theatrical state-of-play from the 50s, when I entered the profession, up to the present day. Momentous changes have occurred during those 50 years, which in my opinion have changed the face of theatre-going irrevocably. During the 50s I actually rehearsed on the building site of the television centre in White City and realised that this was going to alter, perhaps even damage, live theatre in the foreseeable years.

The Queen's coronation, filmed and replayed to the public on an exceedingly small screen in their own homes, made the television a desirable possession, which quickly proliferated until the present day when most homes contain any number of sets, which can almost do the housework, if one could only fathom the controls! With so much entertainment available within the home, why should the public travel distances, pay - in some cases exceedingly high prices - to view live entertainment, which may sometimes not live up to their expectations. In live theatres it is not possible to fast-forward or change channels.

This has resulted in theatre companies producing ever more lavish and highly technical effects to persuade audiences away from the box. Which in turn makes ticket prices rise extortionately to cover the production cost of such enticements, thereby making theatre-going a special occasion only, in many cases for a particular celebration. The cost of presenting musicals, probably the popular choice for most people when contemplating a theatre visit, is now more often in millions rather than thousands of pounds. This escalates continually.

I fear many smaller companies can no longer compete and are being made bankrupt, or going out of business before they do. My autobiography shows the reasons and events that have closed more theatres, until now even the largest towns and cities scarcely support more than one or two. Back in the 50s even small towns had a music hall and a weekly repertory theatre for plays. This gave wannabe entertainers and actors the chance to perfect their arts in semi-obscurity until ready to reach out for that hoped-for fame. This is no longer a possibility. Most theatrical aspirants now require training in schools and colleges, in the words of Victorian music halls 'at enormous expense', to even try to enter the profession.

I was fortunate at the beginning of my career to work with small entrepreneurial companies with exceedingly high standards. People who loved the business so whole-heartedly that they took enormous risks, even bankruptcy, in pursuing their dreams. Most, though, succeeded because they knew their profession so thoroughly, having also been performers in their youth, in many cases achieving fame. These people have departed this mortal coil and the theatre companies, where they exist, are now in the hands of executive accountants, who tend to disband when the bottom line of profit is not met. The depressing fact, therefore, is that love of profit exceeds love of showbiz. However, I digress. Back to the reason for putting on record my own experiences - I wish to leave historical fact when it's time to 'pop my clogs', as we say in showbiz.

Trained as a dancer in all facets, I quite swiftly climbed the theatrical ladder to become a choreographer. Most dancers have this desire but the opportunity to do so is often denied them. I was lucky and when the chance came I grabbed it with both hands, or should I say feet. As an experienced choreographer, fortunate to be in demand through the 60s with all the top companies, the next career move was to direct. My guardian angel ensured that for me. Engaged to dance and perform Slave of the Lamp in the Cole Porter musical 'Aladdin', also to choreograph, I was asked halfway through rehearsals to take over direction. Although I jumped at the chance it was with a certain trepidation, for there were three comics in the leading roles - Tommy Trinder as Abanazer, Charlie Chester as Aladdin and Reg Dixon as Widow Twanky. All went well and the season held the financial record for quite a number of years for that theatre.

This made me at the time one of the youngest director/choreographers in the profession, and over the years I have been honoured and privileged to direct more famous names than one can shake a stick at, not only directing but in many cases playing opposite them. Yet another privilege. Many of these artistes are no longer with us and whilst I have intimate knowledge of their backgrounds I deplore the present 'warts and all' approach in most biographies. Therefore I record only fond anecdotes.

I have no wish to soil or destroy the fan base of the artistes I include in my memoirs and I trust my book will remain of historical and factual interest for theatrical aficionados. It includes sections devoted to many fast-disappearing areas within the profession, including summer season shows, which are now almost non-existent, yet were the mainstay of English seaside resorts in the not too distant past. Companies with famous names, which were their own record of excellence - 'Fol-de-Rols', 'Out of the Blue', 'Starlight', 'Twinkle', 'Gaytime' and many more, all with high standards, helping to turn performers into experienced professionals.

Pantomimes used to occupy theatres in the 50s for three or four months, becoming the main financial stay for the year in many cases. Whilst pantomimes still endure, they are fortunate if they can maintain six weeks, whilst many can only run during the school holiday. In the past they never opened until Boxing Day. Now they open at least a couple of weeks before and schools bring parties prior to Christmas. pantomime is an English phenomenon which must endure, if only to bring children into contact with live performance for the first time.

I am also in a position to elucidate the ever increasing entertainment on cruise ships - the rise in cabaret, full revues and musicals. I was fortunate yet again to work with my partner on both the original Cunard Queen Elizabeth and Queen Mary. Both of them exemplified the excellence of British craftsmen, unlike today's *plastic* examples of a different 'excellence'. My view is that every area where show business has a niche must be recorded for posterity and historical fact, and written by people who have been there.

Finally, as a dancer in the earliest part of my career I was able to experience probably one of the last big tour musicals, with a cast of over sixty company personnel performers, technicians, and musicians, travelling from city to city by private trains. The contract demanded a code of dress on leaving and arriving at new venues, due to publicity in local press. Showgirls were required to wear day dresses, stockings, high heels, hats and gloves. Males smart clothes and ties. All in the cause of glamour and publicity for Bernard Delfont's 'Folies Bergere' shows, direct from Paris via London. This is what is missing in today's climate, where scruffiness is endemic – more's the pity.

I, of course, name drop unashamedly, for the theatre-going and interested public will expect nothing less. However, no sex or dirt, which will make my reminiscences unique by today's standards. I surmise that I will by now have convinced you that I do not have the answer to the problems I am trying to portray within the profession. My hope is that I can leave a record of what it has been like in a now-distant past.

Hope springs eternal, and I await the decision to allow casinos to operate, in the hope that they will regenerate shows, as Las Vegas and Reno have always maintained in the States. This could be a much needed lifeline for British resorts and leading cities.

As the long suffering husband Amos in 'Chicago' says, 'Sorry for taking up so much of your time.'

PROLOGUE – IN THE BEGINNING

It was hot. Regent Street in late May, the stench of traffic hung like mountain mist. However I floated on cloud nine way above the thronging pavements, and my feet were now on the first rung of the show business ladder.

It had been a hard haul, but love of theatre and determination had reaped its reward. Suddenly panic stopped me in my tracks. I had an appointment at 2pm with an agent in an office near Piccadilly Circus. Glancing at my watch it was 1.45 and in my euphoric state I was now approaching Oxford Circus. At that moment I could have broken the world record for running. Arriving at the door in Panton Street, the agency presided over by Renée Stepham, and covered in perspiration, I clambered up the stairs to almost collapse into the outer office. An assistant showed me into 'the presence' and I stood before an elegantly dressed and coiffed lady who was to become instrumental over many years in helping to place my feet more surely up that ladder.

The morning had started with a lie: I was working pro-tem in a job which I had no intention of continuing. My Uncle Bill was a grocery assistant who had elevated himself to become one of the elegantly attired, morning-dressed floorwalkers at Fortnum and Masons in Piccadilly. He had used his influence to obtain me a temporary job in a South London high class grocery shop, where biscuits were displayed in glass fronted boxes to be measured out, and butter was patted with wooden spades into the required amount permitted by war time rationing, which was still in operation in 1953. The manager of this emporium was a thoroughly miserable old man who made life equally miserable for his underlings - another incentive to get out, as if I needed it with my show business ambitions.

The lie was that I had a dental appointment, which was essential, and I needed time off which he reluctantly conceded. My audition was for 1pm in Cambridge Circus, London and I was in a perspiration of rush and fear to get there, having no idea of the location which was added anxiety. Eventually I found the venue located by the side of Alkit, the gentleman's outfitters, on the corner of Charing Cross Road opposite the Palace theatre. Descending a circular staircase to what seemed to be the bowels of the earth, I found myself in a none-too salubrious nightclub. Under cover of darkness it may have appeared glamorous with the smell of expensive cigars but by day the stale smells, threadbare carpets and shabby décor were all too apparent.

Gazing apprehensively around I noticed about half a dozen other boys in practice gear limbering up. More apprehensively I noticed a rehearsal pianist with about six pints of beer balanced on the piano top, two of which were already empty; the third only half full. Should I turn and scoot off? My false courage was deserting me when a stentorian male voice bounced off me, barking 'Come on, we haven't got all day!' This was Frank Adey, a director of great repute who had been production manager for Bernard Delfont, the theatrical guru everyone wished to get on the books of. Frank had now become a freelance director, famous for the 'Ocean Revue' in Clacton on Sea; the importance of which I was soon to discover. Hurriedly changing into my rehearsal gear, which included a brand new top bought especially for the occasion, hopefully to bring me luck, I took my turn in my very first audition. I had come prepared to tap dance, which was the requirement, and had chosen 'Miss Annabelle Lee' a well-known tune of the period. Shaking like a jelly I gave my sheet music to the pianist, now quite the worse for wear, with only one and half-pints of beer left on the piano top.

Suddenly, half way through my audition there was a crash and no further music. I 'la-la-ed' my way to the end in abject misery, trying to execute the big finish required by my dancing teacher and failing. Totally humiliated, I stumbled my way to the dressing room to change into my outdoor clothes. Returning up the spiral staircase, the stentorian voice suddenly bellowed, 'That boy there, where do you think you are going? No one leaves my audition until I decide.' Slinking back, I stood silently whilst the last boy finished his audition piece and we were then asked to line up. Mr Adey viewed us penetratingly whilst reviewing his notes, and lined us up in order of height. Finally he selected a rather short boy call Billy and then me. It appeared that we were to be a height match for the dancing act called the 'Edorics' starring in that year's production. Two boys, and a girl well established in the dancing world. I have never ceased to believe that I was picked for height alone, after the escapade I concluded minus accompaniment.

Later that afternoon I returned home to inform my parents that I was going into show business that very same weekend. Although I had kept quiet about the audition they were not too surprised, knowing that from the age of five I had been besotted by the glamour and excitement of the theatre, and they supported me whole-heartedly until they passed on. The brand new top had indeed brought me luck. Theatrical crimson is still my favourite colour. The following morning I cycled to work to inform 'old misery' that I was leaving the grocery job that following weekend, happy in the knowledge that I would never return to that trade.

When Saturday came there was no pay packet. 'Old misery' had informed me that he was retaining it in lieu of notice. I didn't care; being sure I was on the show business ladder at last and convinced that I was going to succeed.

ACT ONE – THE FIRST RUNG

You may well wonder at the title of my autobiography. Apparently, as my mother affirmed, when I was about three or four I had the habit of putting my arms above my head and revolving on the spot until I collapsed with dizziness whilst proclaiming, 'Look Mummy - I'm dancing!', to which she would reply 'Well stop it, you're rucking up the rugs.'

At five years of age I started infant school, as there were no play schools at that time. Screaming, I tried to clamber out through the windows until my mother made a quick return, smacking my hands and pushing me back into the classroom. Astonished at my mum's response, my tears turned to smiles when Miss Sylvester, my first teacher, gave me crayons to colour pictures.

That first Christmas I was chosen to play a Christmas Cracker in the first school production, and I can still recall the costume that an auntie made with a frilly skirt and collar which scratched, all finished with a Father Christmas face fastened on my tummy. My first words on the stage were, 'There's something scratching my neck', to which a senior boy playing Santa Claus replied 'It's a motto'. I was none the wiser. However I've remained crackers about showbiz ever since.

During the Second World War I decided to help the war effort with charity theatrical performances by becoming an impresario. One Saturday afternoon whilst my parents had gone shopping I was left in charge of a snoozing aunt and uncle. Taking a saw from my father's shed I stripped the veranda from the front of a summerhouse at the bottom of the garden, thereby creating a platform. Purloining curtains from my mother's airing cupboard I fastened these on drawstrings at the front of the little platform, creating my first theatre at the grand old age of eight. Borrowing costumes from the cooperative headmaster of my school, I dragooned all the local kids, including my very reluctant brother Peter, to perform supporting roles to my leads. Amongst the costumes was a rather resplendent crimson velvet cloak with a white fur collar, which I always wore no matter what the parts required. I hasten to add this idiosyncrasy did not follow me into the profession.

I still have the receipts from the British Red Cross Society to which my mother sent the proceeds after I had forced pocket money from local children and any adults that I could muster to watch my performances. I even designed and painted the sets. Tickets and lavish programmes did not escape my attention either - for extra revenue, naturally.

Every Christmas, even during wartime, was always a big family occasion. Food rationing did not deter my parents from creating the most magnificent feast. We lived in a fairly large Victorian house in Thornton Heath, between Streatham and Croydon, south of London. There was ample room for guests, whilst Peter and I were excited to sleep on the floor -, a useful acclimatisation for my early years in theatrical touring.

Boxing Day was always the long awaited event for me. My parents were not theatre-goers on a regular basis. However, at Christmas, pantomime was an integral part of the festivities. Boxing Day matinées in London became a double whammy. London always was, and still is, an exciting place to be. The combination of history and theatre, even at a young age, was exhilarating. Even at my advanced age, it still weaves its magic. And those pantomimes, wow! If anything watered my theatrical garden it was those, fostering my ambition even more.

While most of the traditional stories were endemic, my favourite visit was to see 'The Land Where the Rainbow Ends', a Christmas show hardly ever presented nowadays. Drama, romance, patriotism, ingredients that even today remain pertinent in my logicality. Based on the St George and The Dragon theme, with music composed by Roger Quilter and star-studded casts.

Like youngsters, even today, who demand repeats of their favourite stories, so with myself. I always wanted to return time and again to this production; made even more perfect by seeing Anton Dolin as St George and Alicia Markova as the Spirit of the Lake; famous ballet stars who later created the festival ballet. How I wish this musical play could be revived. But would it survive now in our cynical age? I doubt it. Nowadays, schools foster more interest in the Arts than in my school days, which consisted only of a Christmas production of a fairly indifferent presentation, by semi-interested teachers forced to comply with filling in time until the holiday break.

However, I was fortunate in moving up into the class of a Miss Lloyd, a rather severe and formal looking lady who seemed very old to a seven year old. Terrified by stories from other pupils about this teacher, which ranged from Cruella de Ville to the wicked Queen in Snow White, I developed a nervous rash in an effort to avoid returning to school after the holidays. It was true that her appearance didn't help the image. Dressed always in sombre attire with jet black hair, very severely cut with a fringe, she appeared to represent every child's nightmare. However appearances belie, as I discovered very early on. From my original fear of meeting this gorgon, I developed my first innocent love affair with someone who wasn't my mother.

A strong bond existed between us, a bond forged by love of the Arts in all their aspects. Looking back in retrospect, she was an infant school teacher and was possibly in her late teens or early 20s. However, she was the first person to recognise my love of all things artistic and informed my parents that she thought I would eventually make my mark either in the theatre or a related area of the Arts. How perceptive she proved to be. She was a major influence in my life, and years later I tried to find her, without luck, to tell her how important she was for me in my kindergarten years.

Moving up eventually to the senior section of the school, I encountered another teacher, Mr Hurst, a carbon copy of Mr Chips who also became another influence in my life. Every week on a Friday afternoon he encouraged his class with play readings, mainly the classics. Shakespeare I have never really cottoned on to, whilst recognising his major influence. Oliver Goldsmith, who I liked for a certain bawdiness and rude words, though not as rude as today's 'no holds barred' phraseology. But that's another story. Those Friday afternoons developed into small ad-lib performances, encouraging the pupils' individual talents. Guess who was a prime mover on those occasions? No prizes. But oh, such happy days.

Because I had been so happy, I could not envisage leaving the safety of my first school, and to that end destroyed the letter given to all pupils by the headmaster about future education possibilities. At the age of 11 we took entrance exams for secondary schools, colleges, etc. By withholding this letter from my parents I imagined I could remain where I was. What stupid naiveté that was. On the day that the exams took place I sat with a few other pupils whose parents obviously didn't or couldn't afford to finance their children to higher education, reading to my heart's content in the small kindergarten library.

If you didn't sit entrance exams it was assumed that your parents wanted you to continue at the local elementary school. I was due now for much trouble and dismay. My parents heard too late about the exams and a furious situation developed, whilst my mother sought an appointment with my headmaster, the outcome being that there was no option other than the Lanfranc School in Mitcham for me. Horror of horrors, this school had a reputation in that area of 'Bang 'ole', whether justified or not. I quickly learned the facts of life in no uncertain manner. Coming from infant school of mixed sexes I was now deposited in an all male environment, and rough at that.

In the 50s there was no such thing as sex education. Teachers assumed that parents would deal with that aspect of life and most parents were too embarrassed to even broach it. So you got your information from the older boys in a somewhat rough and ready way. Of course I did know the physical difference, having persuaded a little girl who was inquisitive to see my private parts that I would show mine if she would show hers first. To my everlasting shame I also demanded a small brooch she wore, which her parents had given her when they had taken a pre-war holiday in Switzerland. This brooch had minute dangling Swiss boots, which at six years of age I coveted. She agreed and I remained more impressed with the brooch than the other aspect of the exchange.

However at 'Bang 'ole' my education was completed when an older boy informed me of the true reason for the differing organs. I totally denied it and he taunted me with the fact that my mum and dad must have done it to get me. Of a non violent disposition, I broke my clean record and sloshed him. Although older than me, he was smaller. Of course, I never ever broached the subject with my parents, which was par for the course in those far off days - how different to the climate today.

My parents' dismay that I was in this school gave me an obligation to sit an entrance exam for the Stanley Technical College in Upper Norwood, which I duly did. On leaving school in those days there was never any discussion about the future, so one was dangling over a chasm of uncertainty. My Father was an engineer so, wanting to please him, I agreed if successful to take up that occupation.

Examinations took place in the college and almost 200 boys were sitting it. There were only 30 vacancies and I became dismayed to hear that a boy living in my road had in fact achieved a place, whilst I had heard nothing. One morning after my parents and I had given up hope, a letter came through the door telling me that due to someone dropping out, a place was available for me. For my parents a decision was taken to cut some corners, because it was a fee-paying college and they were not wealthy. So I was enrolled for three years in the Technical College.

I have always felt a certain guilt, because frankly I had no real desire to follow that path through life, hankering as I always had for a theatrical career. My mum, however, got a certain pleasure in relating to friends and neighbours that out of 200 who had taken the exam entrance I was in the 30 vacancies available. She never explained that actually I was the 31st. Well, she deserved some pleasure.

Three years later, my course completed, I left college. Whilst I had loathed the engineering, I had enjoyed the draughtsmanship and carpentry aspects of the training and my mother always treasured a fruit bowl which I had turned in oak, the only bonus of those years, which on her passing was still being used in the family home. My father's influence within the trade had obtained me an apprenticeship in a cabinet making firm with an acquaintance of his. This unfortunately turned out to be a catastrophic move.

THE LEARNING CURVE

Moving into a truly adult world after the 'little gentleman' approach of college and being the only apprentice, I became the butt of bullying by men old enough to know better. Sending me to make tea they used to trip me up deliberately, so that I had to go through the whole process again. When I became physically upset they then found further ways to make what they considered 'fun' out of me, even resorting to striking me with planks of wood, seemingly by accident.

Finally with the fear of what they would do next, I was diagnosed with a nervous breakdown by my doctor, who told my parents that it would be a serious setback to my recovery to return to what I now considered a hellhole. I have never forgotten that extremely short period in my life which illustrated man's inhumanity to man, or should I say boy. Today when everyone reads of bullying in schools I get murderous feelings towards the perpetrators, and I am not a violent person.

Out of employment now, a neighbour of my mother's had a brother who was a dental technician, and was seeking an apprentice to train. As I had always liked model making, mainly theatres of course, my parents felt that this might prove a more congenial situation. Mr Kettle, for that was his name, had twin sons Peter and James who had attended that same kindergarten school as myself, although slightly older, therefore not in my class. This proved to be a very happy time. Working from his home Mr Kettle treated me more like family and the model making aspect of dentistry was creative enough to satisfy me. By now though I was more determined than ever to follow my dream. But how? That was the question.

Readers this far may well wonder why I decided to enter show business through the dancing profession. Retuning now to my kindergarten days, I became the shining light at six years old in country dancing. Partnered with a little girl of the same age we were taken from our classroom to demonstrate to older pupils these skills, which gave us an exaggerated idea of our own importance.

Leaping forward yet again to my adolescent years, and whilst serving my apprenticeship in dentistry, I took up ballroom dancing by way of gaining a social life. Persuaded by my teachers to further my skills by entering medal classes I achieved bronze, silver and gold medals in the national ballroom teachers examinations, all within eight months. So from being a hobby it had become a way of life, opening up further doors.

The films of Fred Astaire and Ginger Rogers, always high on my list of favourite, fostered my ambition with their ballroom tap dancing skills, so tap dancing became my next hurdle to leap. Realising that I now needed private instruction with the best teachers that I could afford on my apprentice's wages, I asked the advice of the principal of a local theatre school.

Mrs Grandison-Clarke whose pupils had entered the theatrical profession advised me in words that I didn't wish to hear that I was far too old at sixteen to even consider such a career. Her advice only compounded my ambition to succeed. I approached yet another local ballroom dancing school, which had encompassed tap dancing in its curriculum. This was due to a trend gaining much popularity with adults, who also nurtured secret ambitions to be Fred and Ginger.

Kathleen Prengle's School in Norbury, Surrey engaged a peripatetic teacher for this branch of her school. This led to me meeting Dorrit Maclaren, one of three sisters who ran the Euphen Maclaren School in Knightsbridge, London, behind Harrods. In *my* estimation the school became far more important than the store. Miss Dorrit ran the tap and modern branch whilst the eldest sister, Miss Euphen presided over the classical ballet teaching.

Even her advanced age, rumoured to be well into her 70s and ascending, did not prevent her from extending her leg in the second ballet position and holding it higher than many of her teenage pupils. A truly amazing and charismatic teacher she proved to be for me. The youngest sister, Miss Alison, was a choreographer who was involved in presenting 'Hiawatha' every couple of years at the Royal Albert Hall with massed choirs and dancers from the school.

My excited ambition was spurred on when Miss Euphen invited me to take part in the 1953 production planned for that summer. My idea of stardom dissolved with the information that boy dancers were always in great demand, providing they had reasonable height and two legs. How the tables have turned in the new millennium, with a new found respect for not only ballet but 'River Dance' and 'Tap Dogs' performers. It's no longer perceived as a sissy occupation, with audiences admiring the agility and technical skills required for success.

In the film world Gene Kelly was responsible also for a change in styles during the 50s to rival Fred Astaire, and now in our present time the choreographic skills of Matthew Bourne are bringing new audiences into the theatre firmament.

My excitement at the prospect of dancing in 'Hiawatha' at the world famous Royal Albert Hall was however never to materialise. Miss Euphen had asked all pupils taking part to each contribute a couple of biographical lines for the programme. At a loss as to how I could present myself, this being my first appearance, I wrote that I was at 16, probably one of the youngest dancers taking part. I then received one of the most important pieces of advice in my entire career.

Calling me into her office Miss Maclaren told me never ever to put an age in a biographical note, her reason being that should I gain a successful show

My first professional photograph, age 17.
Taken when performing in an amateur revue.

21

business career in, say, ten years, I would be 26 and with years passing rapidly, rivals might claim otherwise and pile on years to claim that I was past it. This was my first intimation that bitchiness existed and could claim me as a victim. How true this was to be proven much later, but that's quite a way ahead. At that particular moment in my life I took this information on board, and nowhere in any biography did I ever put an age. I never lied, only avoided it. Readers can work it out for themselves if they read any further into my life. But heck, it's ability and talent that really count.

I have now brought you forward to my very first audition in that seedy nightclub in London.

CORONATION 1953
MY FIRST THEATRICAL YEAR

The year 1953 was the Queen's Coronation. Travelling on Sunday to Clacton on Sea in Essex, I commenced rehearsals on Monday the 1 June, only to discover that Tuesday had been declared a national holiday, therefore no rehearsals.

Coronation Day dawned with pouring rain, which never ceased. However I had set myself a task occasioned by the first day's rehearsal. The choreographers had set the opening routine, which required a double spin, which I had not as yet mastered in my training. Fearing that I would be dismissed during the Wednesday rehearsals for incompetence, I had resolved to practise until I dropped.

My first ever digs were with Mrs Dorset, a mad Irish lady, not literally, but great fun who had sort of adopted me for the season. Her husband ran a taxi service, which was in permanent use on that disastrously wet day. Mr Dorset said that as the garage was empty, I could use that to practise in. Slithering and slipping in spilled oil, I practised and fell time and again. However by the day's end I had mastered my double spins and was not sacked on the Wednesday, as I had feared.

In retrospect I never imagined in my wildest dreams on Coronation Day, slipping and sliding about in a garage to the accompaniment of ferocious rain on a corrugated iron roof, that fifty years on I would be invited by the Queen to attend the first ever Sandringham garden party.

However back to the future, Frank Adey the director appeared awesome to me, but I learnt so much from him during that season, which was to stand me in good stead for the rest of my career. Giving me a small part in a sketch as a goalkeeper with a speech impediment - something that would not be tolerated in today's climate - I was an immediate success during rehearsals with the rest of the cast who fell about with laughter.

The comic however did not appreciate my new skills, and on my first night, whilst waiting very nervously in the wings for my speaking role, he looked me straight in the eye and muttered 'Just remember I am the comic,' as he made his entrance. Chastened, I followed him and was nowhere near as funny as in rehearsals. First lesson learned - never upstage a comic.

In 1953, Britain was in recovery from the war years and rationing was still in place although about to come to an end. Holidays abroad were not yet in vogue. Most people took their annual holidays around the British seaside resorts. Clacton on Sea in Essex, already a favourite with Londoners, had four theatres, the largest and most popular on the privately owned pier which housed the well-known 'Ocean Revue'.

The company was large by today's standards, with the comedic team headed by the principal comic. The three team dancing act was supplemented by 2 male and 12 female dancers, supporting a male and female singer and two double speciality acts, comedic and musical.

Completing the company was a ten-piece orchestra with a baton conductor. The show also had a great reputation, reinforced by lavish settings and costumes. On the first day of the week queues stretched all day long from the box office and up onto the promenade and by Tuesday all seats were sold out in the 800 seat theatre. The season ran for five months including a three week tour to the Hippodrome theatre in Ipswich at the season's end. I took to showbiz like a duck to water and confounded the seasoned performers with my enthusiasm for performing. It was my first experience so I hope they forgave me for being a bore.

When the season ended I feared that I would never get another job, which I soon discovered was, and still is, a universal fear of most professional theatrical performers. During that season an agent friend of the director came talent spotting and sent me a message to contact her on my return. Izna Roselli had been a well-known dancer in her day and had a thriving dancing school and agency in Archer Street, behind the Windmill theatre in Soho, London.

Her school was above the musicians union building, and I recall every Monday when musicians packed the street meeting with their mates and seeking work with the fixers who had jobs to offer. Of course variety theatres were still in evidence at that time, requiring musicians to augment their pits or even to go on tour.

It was the only open-air agency as I recall, and the chattering musicians always disturbed the ballet classes taking place in the Izna Roselli studio above the union offices on the ground floor.

Making contact and meeting Miss Roselli she signed me to her books, even giving me free lessons to keep in trim. In return I would do odd jobs looking after the office and taking messages. Even helping to decorate the studio, which was in need of a lick of paint. Her business partner was Leslie Branch who had originally been a singer. He now gave tuition and coaching for auditions, even helping me to discover a voice, although I would never call myself a singer. Nowadays though it is essential for any show dancer to train in singing, which needs to be as expert as their dance ability. It's truly much harder to get into the business and there are fewer jobs on offer. Still the schools turn out wannabes and only the truly skilled and talented have a chance for longevity in their chosen career. However no words of mine could, or should, deter anyone with a yearning, burning desire. But one has to be prepared for a hard struggle and possible failure in the end. It's a hard world.

For the first time in my life I was now signing on for the dole, a humiliating experience made even more so when altercations broke out between clerks made belligerent by out of order signees, which on occasions became violent and needed restraining. In those far off days, one was required to sign twice weekly. I was always glad when I left the office, usually on the Friday, clutching my 35 shillings.

Not looking forward to this ritual I placed an advertisement in the theatre newspaper 'The Stage' as an experienced dancer. To my surprise I received a letter from the proprietor of a stilt-dancing act seeking replacements for his company. Replying to his letter I was requested by return to travel up to Northampton to be interviewed. Which I duly did. Eddie Field and his wife Elsie were appearing at the variety theatre and although, as I was on a day return ticket, I did not witness their act, he explained his situation exactly.

It appeared that he had a contract to perform in a long running pantomime in one of the country's premier theatres the Alhambra, Bradford. His act known as 'The Seven Romas' had a big problem, basically only he and his wife. Therefore he was seeking to recruit three more people, preferably male. I had only been on a weekly salary of 7 pounds 10 shillings in the summer show. Therefore I was totally seduced by the offer of 12 pounds a week, especially as I had no other offer of work at that moment and it was a long run. Agreeing on the spot, I returned exhilarated back to London telling my parents that I was back in show business. The contract duly arrived and on a foggy December day, I headed up to a foreign destination, Manchester! As a southerner, whose furthest distance from London had been Clacton that summer, can you wonder at my trepidation?

The steam train rattled further into the unknown and I became more apprehensive. What was I doing heading so far from home to do something I had never thought of doing, dancing on stilts. Eddie assured me that in show business it paid to have many strings to one's bow. Well, he would, wouldn't he? He was desperate to recruit three others to join his act.

That desperation became evident on the Monday morning in rehearsals. However I am jumping briefly ahead. Arriving in Manchester my parents funded me to get a taxi, another luxury. I headed towards Salford, at that time not the prettiest part of the foggy north, although the fog gave a certain charm.

Eddie had supplied the accommodation and I was to meet the other two boys who were to join the act.

The cab driver deposited me at my destination and I walked up a rather long garden. To describe it in retrospect, I can only liken it to the house in 'Psycho', especially shrouded in the fog. Meeting up with both of the other lads, I was happy to learn that neither of them had walked on stilts. What a relief, we all started on an even wicket. These two boys were from Birmingham and were not in any way experienced in theatre skills. Andy had just left school, and George was the eldest of us all, having been working in an office or factory and deciding he needed to get out. I was in total sympathy. We were all booked together in one freezing cold bedroom. Three for the price of one, we agreed. But as Eddie was paying for us in this initial week, we suffered.

After my happy accommodation during my summer season this really brought me to earth with a bump. However it in no way diminished my ambition for the life of a gypsy, as American dancers are labelled. Looking back, those digs were probably the worst I ever had to experience. The whole house was a shambles. One night we ventured up to an attic area and on opening a door, were horrified to see a skeleton suspended from a beam. Later, musicians at the local theatre enlightened us by explaining that the landlord had studied to be a doctor, but for some misdemeanour had been struck off the register. Hence the skeleton in the loft. Well, one thing's for sure - we were all on the learning curve of life as lived by others. My education was being quite violently brought up to date.

Staying in the house also were two rather sleazy girls appearing in the revue that week at the Hippodrome. These girls were strippers in the quite awful nude revues that toured the country during that period, helping to close and finish variety forever. These shows were continuous and men, usually in long macs, would come in for the first performance at 2pm, and remain until it finished at 10.30. During that week we all decided to stay on to see the first show. We only rehearsed in the mornings for obvious reasons.

That show was the most depressing non-event I have ever seen. Nudes were not allowed to move a muscle, and only posed in a thong. And posing in the most inartistic tableaux, these caused us to collapse in stifled laughs. Nobody in the audience was aware of mirth, being extremely busy under their macs. We beat a hasty retreat as the male singer, who couldn't sing either, intoned in a decidedly camp voice the next fabulous tableau about to be revealed.

One of the strippers staying in the house discovered during that week that she was pregnant and with the help of her friend and a copious amount of cheap gin, induced her abortion in a hot bath one night. We all agreed that she should not seek help from the landlord. That week became a university course in sleaze and was completed one evening with police at the door seeking that abortive girl. Apparently they were after her boyfriend - for what we never knew or asked. We'd had enough and were excited at being picked up on the Saturday to head for Bradford and the start of the pantomime rehearsals.

Once again the accommodation had been arranged by our boss, although we were all individually responsible for our full board which was, as I recall, 4 pounds a week.

That was then considered quite high when the theatre digs list had prices ranging from 3 pounds. However it was such a relief to be in clean and warm surroundings with excellent meals and only five minutes from the theatre on the run, and we ran every day after oversleeping and a hurried breakfast.

We were all on strict instructions from Eddie Field not to reveal a word about the previous week in Salford Hippodrome for reasons you are about to discover.

My first pantomine – Bradford.
I'm the 3rd down from the right with the eyes barely visable through the mouth.

FIRST PANTOMIME – NEW TALENTS

Monday morning dawned after a rather disturbed night's rest due to excitement and a small amount of fear as to what I had let myself in for. As I recall it was bitterly cold so we all wrapped ourselves up against the northerly winds and headed for the theatre. Entering the stage door to the accompaniment of a carillon of bells ringing in the hour from the town hall clock tower playing a known tune, which I now cannot recall. Appropriately it should have been the Entry of the Gladiators for George, Andy and myself as we scrambled up stone steps to be ushered into a rather grand boardroom by the stage door keeper.

Francis Laidler was the producer/director who inspired all who came into his presence Now in his 90s his pantomimes had commenced in 1902 with stars of the Victorian era. Mainly a northern producer his Bradford and Leeds theatres were a byword for his excellent pantomimes. His fame spread and in 1932 the West End beckoned and he presented 'Mother Goose' at the Daly's theatre in London, going on to present 'Babes in the Wood' in the Victoria Palace. During the Second World War his pantomimes were presented at the Royal Opera House and the London Coliseum, where Mr Laidler actually slept in a corridor during the Blitz.

We were now actually face to face with this great man. This meeting I have never forgotten although ignorant at that time of his fame. I was nevertheless overwhelmed by the sheer magnitude of his organisation, the like of which I have never experienced since, in spite of working for many top pantomime companies in the intervening years.

I had auditioned and been accepted to join a stilt dancing act known as the 'Seven Romas', and felt humbled to discover later the act had third billing, although ignorant of such refinements at that time. Mr Laidler presided over the first meeting of the company in the boardroom of the Alhambra theatre in Bradford.

A venerable, white haired, Victorian, gentlemanly figure although quite frail as I recall, he was attended by his wife, Gwladys Stanley, a well known principle boy in her day, still with commanding presence aided by enormous gold rimmed spectacles. The whole company was seated at designated places around an enormous mahogany table, dominated at the far end by a large model stage.

Before each place was a folder containing a script, appointment lists indicating to each artiste when and where they would be required for costume fittings, vocal sessions and rehearsal schedules all timed to the last second. As the script was read aloud, the stage manager revealed the sets on the model stage manipulating the moving sections into their changes whilst the electrician illuminated it. During this action, sketches of the various costume changes were handed round. Pausing for a coffee break, waitresses in black and white, reminiscent of Lyons Corner House 'Nippies', passed around refreshments.

At the conclusion of the read-through Mr Laidler addressed the company wishing all a happy season which was toasted in crystal glasses with I think champagne, although I was far too young to have ever tasted it before. The subject was 'Jack and the Beanstalk' starring Bunny Doyle as Dame Durden and Betty Dane, Billy Dainty's sister as Jack. The boss of the 'Seven Romas' act, Eddie Field, played the giant and the rest played the giant's children. I was proud to be given the additional role of the back legs of the cow, being told I should start at the bottom!

The stilt act proved to be a baptism of fire, for three of us joined the act only one week prior to the commencement in Bradford. In that week we were trained to dance on graduated stilts by Eddie and his wife Elsie at the Salford Hippodrome in Manchester. This required great secrecy as Mr Laidler had booked the act as known and seen. Stumbling across the stage clinging to the dust laden legs and boarders we had the added hazard of wearing huge giant papier-mâché heads with visibility confined to only peering through the mouths. Youth triumphed though, because after only a week of morning-only rehearsals we were passed off as a facsimile of the original act.

Nowadays one is lucky to have 12 dancers in pantos consisting of 6 senior and 6 junior girls, but in those far off days we fielded a chorus of 12 John Tiller Girls and 12 of the famous Francis Laidler sunbeam juveniles. Augmented by 12 local girls recruited to fill out the crowd scenes, these plus 6 singers totalled 42 on stage, plus principles, unaffordable today.

Another interesting anecdote is that Eddie Fields' father and his brothers were partnered in a famous stilt-walking act known as 'The Pender Troupe'.

Whilst playing the Bristol Hippodrome during the 1920s they were visited by a father and his stage-struck son seeking an entrée into showbiz. As the troupe were about to fulfil an engagement at the Chicago world fair this boy was engaged to go with them. His name was Archie Leach, more famously known eventually as 'Cary Grant'. Each Christmas he would visit his widowed mother in Bristol and kept in touch with Eddie throughout the years. We were thrilled that he had attended a performance at Bradford whilst we were there.

In conclusion I reiterate that, never since, have I been involved in such a lavish and long running pantomime which extended until Easter.

Unfortunately an incident on the first night, which was Christmas Eve, brought fame by default to our act, although there were only 5 of us on stilts, because we were called the 'Seven Romas' 2 others from the company were co-opted into the act, the assistant stage manager and the smallest juvenile.

The act commenced with the juvenile first entering to the strains of the 'Teddy Bears Picnic', wearing a large head with visibility only through the mouth. She in turn beckoned on the assistant stage manager who then brought on the first stilt walker. This progressed until we all joined the stage in ascending heights, with Eddie our boss the final one on the tallest stilts almost touching the proscenium top. This brought great applause during the act's progress.

We formed other line-ups which brought amazed gasps. However the biggest gasps came towards the end. One of the stilt walkers on the lower stilts moved at the wrong moment. He caught his leg between the next walker, which in turn put his leg in mine and we finished in a heap on the stage, bringing down both the bosses. Eddie on stilts that took up to about 14 feet managed to grab the proscenium.

The curtains were quickly closed and for the first and only time in my long career we heard the well-known phrase 'Is there a doctor in the house?' Fortunately there was no damage done. However, once a walker is strapped securely onto mechanical stilts it is impossible to rise until the leather straps are released.

The outcome of course was that our act had hit the headlines in the press, bringing fame through notoriety. I think the box office was inundated with audiences longing to receive a similar treat. They were disappointed; it was a one off accidental attention grabber. After the show Eddie made us all get up again on to the stilts, for he feared that the novices, whose first stage appearance it was, might lose their nerve when it came to the Boxing Day performances. He was a good boss and didn't berate the culprit.

THE FOLIES BERGERE – FIRST TOUR

It was now Easter 1954. I headed back to London after my first professional pantomime engagement, secure in the knowledge that I could return to Clacton for a second year during that summer if I wished. However after listening to the other 'pros' I became determined to try my luck and get into a big scale musical. I heard via the grapevine that the current French 'Folies Bergere' production 'Paris to Piccadilly', after a long run at the Prince of Wales theatre in London, was about to embark on a country-wide tour of all the No.1 theatres.

Bernard Delfont was the producer and passing his palatial offices one morning, on impulse I entered into a vast vestibule with an imposing reception desk on my right. Boldly taking my courage in both hands, I approached an even more imposing receptionist who enquired my business. Gulping I replied 'I want to see Mr Delfont'.

She coldly asked, 'Have you an appointment?'

'No, but he will see me,' I squeaked.

'Not without an appointment,' she replied, icicles now forming.

My courage rapidly departing, I turned to leave, when a lift in the opposite corner opened to reveal two smartly dressed men, one of whom I recognised as Bernard Delfont. Well, 'fools rush in where angels fear to tread', so without another thought I rushed across and stopped him in his tracks, saying swiftly, before he could brush me aside, 'Excuse me, Sir, but I am a dancer seeking work. Have you any vacancies?'

I don't think too many confrontations of this nature had occurred before, even though he was No.1 on most artistes' hit lists for work. Slightly taken aback, he paused then said, 'Go up to the office and speak to my secretary'. Turning on his heel he departed with his companion, leaving me gasping for breath at my temerity.

Triumphantly I returned to the reception desk to enquire as to which floor his office was on, knowing full well the receptionist had witnessed the scene. I still believe she thought I had special access to the great man. Entering the office and sinking into the carpet pile, I boldly said 'I have just spoken to Mr Delfont who has sent me up regarding the 'Folies Bergere' Tour.' They took down my particulars which, although brief, I was able to embellish by quoting that I had just finished pantomime as a member of a well-known act.

Without even auditioning I think that my bold approach had reaped its reward and I was signed for a long running tour which was commencing within a few weeks' time. The show was still running in London and my parents booked seats to see what I had let myself in for. The Folies Bergere revues were a direct import from Paris with French leads but obviously English comedy stars and this one topped Frankie Howard at the height of his fame.

Closely watching the dance routines I soon realised that they were basically quite simple, and I relaxed knowing full well that I would not be out of my depth. I realised also that the shows were basically set and costume productions with spectacle as the main thrust.

Hazel Gee was the choreographer and a couple of weeks later we started rehearsals actually on the stage of the Prince of Wales theatre. Many of the West End company also were going on the tour as a continuation of their engagement. It was now well into the spring and London was basking in the early sunshine with the parks covered with daffodils and crocus.

Journeying north we witnessed almost a return to winter, the weather was decidedly colder and en route the flowers of London and the south regressed to barely opening buds the further north we travelled. Finally arriving in Glasgow on our first tour, winter was back with a vengeance.

When the train arrived the company were met with a barrage of photographers and reporters. The company manager organising photo opportunities. Whilst the whole company was expected to maintain the high standing of this top theatrical company, an extra responsibility was on the shoulders of the females. They were contractually required to present a glamorous presence to uphold their reputation as the most beautiful girls in the world. As the train approached its final destination this meant a frantic repair to their make-up, digging out their high heel shoes, gloves and smart hats to maintain their images. Even the men were required to wear smart outfits with ties. This was obligatory in the 50s.

Train calls are now a thing of the past with most artistes driving themselves on journeys and claiming back travelling expenses. Even stars tend to depart the theatre dressed in jogging outfits and trainers, indistinguishable from their audiences. Sadly, from my point of view, we have lost the theatrical magic. I can recall some years ago seeing Marlene Deitrich on her farewell tour, leaving the theatre in my home town, dressed as glamorously off stage as she was on it. The agent who represented her told me that she demanded special lighting on the stage door so that her exit was as perfect as her performance. That was true stardom.

FOLIES BERGERE 1954 'PARIS TO PICCADILLY' COMPANY PERSONNEL ON TOUR

Jewish cockney comic Hal Monty. Of some renown who, I was informed, had originally been partner to the impresario Bernard Delfont in a dancing duo way back in their theatrical beginnings. To the young dancers in the show that was difficult to envisage. Guess it's always been the same twixt youth and age. However, even the famous have to start somewhere.

French leading lady Claudine Cereda. Quite the most dazzling beautiful blonde I had ever seen. So chic, so French, so Folies Bergere.

French leading man Paul Mattei. Tall and darkly handsome with pleasant baritone singing voice.

Paddy Lyndon. English soubrette and principal dancer.

The Barbour Brothers and Jean. A well-known act who danced on extremely high stilts. Having already danced on stilts myself, I really appreciated their fantastic skills.

Eddie Vitch. Continental comedy artiste.

The Trio Cotta. An adagio act who performed their acrobatic feats in a pirates hold scene which caused problems with the notorious watch committee when we played Birmingham. The boy dancers as pirates whipped the slave girls. Whips and bare flesh were anathema to the burghers of Birmingham. We were banned and had to rehearse an alternative routine.

The main attractions of the Folies were of course the fabulous set pieces, which cost thousands even in those days. Costumes of such lavishness with hundreds of ostrich plumes, fox furs and sequins by the mile. All adorning the bodies of the chorus. Basically the show's mainstay. The company was enormous by today's standards, consisting of the following:

10 semi-nude showgirls 5'9"–6' tall. When costumed in high-heeled shoes and head-dresses, on occasion topping 3' they appeared to be over 10 feet in height. 12 dancing girls 5'4" who never appeared nude.

4 dancing boys 5'10"–6' never nude, but occasionally brief thongs. 6 female nudes average height, bust size depending on fashion, which in the early 50s was Parisian and rather flat and boyish in my opinion – not that I was an expert!

Interestingly the dance mistress auditioned the nudes and speculation was rife amongst the company males as to what the audition consisted of. Mini G-strings and nipple caps, which consisted of a few sequins, were their only bodily adornment, though fantastic headdresses and jewelled boots somehow made them sexier. A working man's dream.

The performing company numbered forty including principals. However this required a large backstage crew in each individual theatre, which was placed under the control of the permanent staff travelling with us.

Company manager in overall control George Cross who wore a dinner suit for the show. A custom then, but not one I have ever encountered since, in my long career. A stage manager, first and second assistant. Chief electrician and assistant. Chief carpenter and assistant. Touring productions of this magnitude always had repairs on the vast sets. Property master and assistants, to keep props in pristine condition.

Finally and most importantly – the musical director and his lead musicians for each orchestra department, ie pianist, strings, brass, woodwind, etc.

Equally important was the wardrobe department who always had renovations and laundry to attend to. This in the capable hands of a wardrobe mistress and two permanent assistants supplemented at each theatre with a local team to act as dressers.

As you can now see, a vast company in total of almost 100 to present this glamorous revue.

Touring with the Folies Bergere during the 50s was an experience second to none. 'Paris to Piccadilly' had finished its London run at the Prince of Wales theatre, which in London had starred Norman Wisdom. I've already explained that my parents had taken me to see the current show in London 'Pardon my French' which starred Frankie Howard and Cilla Black. This was to experience what I had let myself in for and to this day that lavish spectacle was an inspiration which followed me through my career, until I was in a position to devise/direct and choreograph my own productions. But more of that later.

After the Second World War these shows were a welcome relief for audiences long starved of such glamour and spectacle during the post war dreariness, that seemed to endure forever. Strangely, there were more hardships after the war as I recall than during it, with sweets and bread rationing and general shortages. Even the harsh winter of 1947 seemed to be against the conquering heroes. It's small wonder that the 'Folies' shows became a popular escape for their eager audiences.

After 'Paris to Piccadilly' finished its long run in London it was taken to South Africa including many of the original cast. On its successful return a long tour of the British Isles was planned and this was my excited appearance on the scene. Rehearsals were held in the Prince of Wales theatre mainly in the bars and corridors.

The accommodation off Sauchieall Street in a typical Glasgow tenement was all granite steps and dark, small windows. Rather depressing but I was happy as a pig in clover being a member of this famous show.

On a bitterly cold Monday morning the company assembled at the Empire theatre. It was I believe the largest theatre in Scotland and known as a comedian's graveyard first house on a Monday during the variety days. It took a couple of days to get the sets into place so we were on hand to make sure of our costumes and props etc, then recalled for a Wednesday rehearsal and opening that evening. This enabled the company to get acquainted with our surroundings and change digs if unhappy with what we'd booked at a distance. Although bitterly cold, my room sharer and I decided to remain. We could have got worse accommodation.

The vastness of the backstage area in the empire was necessary to accommodate huge sets, including glittering staircases, always a feature of the Folies. London buses could have been accommodated in the wing space, which became a useful storage area for some of the showgirls' costumes. Lavish crinoline skirts which could not find space in the dressing room were suspended on wires and hauled high up into the flies until required. stage crewman would lower them onto the girls standing below whilst dressers fastened them in. One particular set had chandeliers contained in the dress framework. Delighted electricians had to dive under the girls' legs to connect the batteries and light them up. There were many sharp intakes of breath when over-zealous 'electrics' got their come-uppance with a sharply placed shoe, as the poised showgirls swayed on for their applause-getting entrance.

Glasgow in 1954, due to its drinking laws which closed public houses at 9pm could be a wild place. During one Saturday night performance one of the boy dancers dislocated his nose during an energetic routine. I offered to accompany him to the accident department of the local hospital after the show. Waiting whilst he was attended to, I was horrified to see a policeman escort a girl whose face had been slashed to ribbons and was bleeding profusely. A second policeman followed, manhandling a handcuffed drunken male, screeching words I had never heard used so picturesquely. I discovered a Glasgow Saturday night was a place to be avoided if possible.

Leaving the theatre after our last night residence was a tour de force of organisation. Railway carriages were transported through the streets to the stage door, lined with dress rails to accommodate costumes, head-dresses and props. Once packed they were trundled back to the sidings to be attached on Sunday morning to the official train, which carried banners proclaiming 'Folies Bergere on Tour'. This attracted local newspaper interest both on departure and arrival at the new venue. As I have already explained the cast were contracted to appear smartly attired for these train calls to uphold the glamorous image of the show. That was show business personified. Today's loss.

Our next stop was Edinburgh where we were resident for a month. Having just finished a six-week stay in Glasgow we welcomed the more refined atmosphere we found ourselves exploring, even climbing the beauty spot of Arthur's Seat after the show one night when the bright moonlight revealed the magnificent beauty of the city below.

I have just realised I am writing in the plural which happens when one is part of a company, especially such a large one - almost a family, with its likes and dislikes.

After Edinburgh we left Scotland and travelled down country playing to packed houses in all the No.1 theatres. In these large towns and cities our residence varied between two or three weeks. For me, on my first tour, it enabled me to explore not only the town but the surrounding countryside, stately homes and museums en route.

The main drawback was the search for accommodation after arriving on the Sunday. Old hands had their personal digs list whilst the newcomers only had the Equity and Actors Church Union accommodation lists, vetted by recommendations. This could be a hazardous exercise lasting from arrival until late night. Most did not have a car so it was a case of 'shanks's pony.' On occasions when two or three large companies converged on the same town it was a case of first come first served.

I can recall arriving in Nottingham when the Royal Ballet Company were already in residence and all available accommodation was taken. I teamed up with a couple of the girl dancers and the young second electrician searching by taxi to find a place to stay. We finally found a large house in a none too salubrious district, and gratefully booked into a couple of rooms. Unbeknown to us this turned out to be an extremely active brothel. Throughout the night, noisy comings and goings ensured little sleep. By the light of day we discovered that American service personnel were stationed in the area and this was their favourite venue. Trying to find other accommodation the following day proved to be fruitless. Neighbours informed us the ghastly old woman in charge was a convicted brothel keeper so we made sure our doors were locked and barricaded for a couple of weeks.

On the Sunday we were due to move on, the second electrician told us to gather as many farthings that we could muster. He then instructed us to remove the bulbs from the light fittings, place the coin in the socket and replace the bulb. We crept around after a meagre breakfast finding any available socket to sabotage. We hugged ourselves with glee during the journey to our next venue as we relished the knowledge that with nightfall as each lamp was switched on it would plunge the brothel into darkness and the old 'madam' may well have had difficulty finding an electrician. Revenge was sweet.

On yet another occasion – this was Birmingham – a few of us combined to rent half a house and look after ourselves for a couple of weeks. At the theatre on the Monday when leaving our address with the stage door keeper he gleefully told us that the owner of that house was in trouble with a rival gang. Apparently his wife had run off with another gang leader who had threatened to fire his house. This was a smart area of Brummie-land. We all made sure the upstairs windows were unlocked and practised knotting sheets. We certainly breathed a sigh of relief as we escaped unscathed two Sundays later.

Thankfully most theatrical accommodation was a family affair going back for years into the days of music halls etc, and artists would return happily time and again, almost like extended family. Sadly as the old folk passed away these places became few and far between and are now non-existent. As most performers now have cars, it's easier to move around. Back in the 50s though, cars in a company were as rare as hens' teeth, except for the stars, who could also afford hotels.

My first tour, however, was coming to an end in the autumn of 54 and it terminated in Brighton. We all bade tearful farewells vowing to keep in touch and departed our separate ways – hopefully.

It was estimated, by accountants that any new Folies Bergere show presented in Paris took at least five years playing to packed houses of foreign visitors to break even financially. Times change however and these theatre shows no longer attract audiences even in Paris. A few years ago the doors were closed on the Casino de Paris, the spiritual home of the famous choreographer Roland Petit and his equally famous ballerina wife, Zizi Jeanmaire.

Little did I realise my association with the Folies Bergere was destined to be sooner rather than later. Casting around in the spring of 1955, I was seeking a job to fill in until my contract with 'Out of the Blue' commenced. Frankie Howard's Folies show 'Pardon My French' was finishing its long run at the Prince of Wales theatre in London and embarking on a countrywide tour. Miss Roselli's influence with the Delfont Company and my previous track record obtained me a short term contract filling in the awkward gap before the summer season.

I was delighted with the opportunity to observe Frankie's skills first hand for he was riding high in the comedic field. Every 'Oooh' and 'Aaah' was assiduously rehearsed, his timing immaculate to gain the guffaws. His pianist was a Southend housewife, Madame Blanchie Moore whose very ordinariness made her the perfect butt of all his derogatory remarks. Another butt for his sketches was Sunny Rogers, a bubbly blonde of indeterminate age.

One day during a first house and very uncharacteristically, Frankie decided to pep up the Customs sketch. This had all the requirements of the Folies with one of the very tall beautiful showgirls removing nearly all her clothes, being confiscated by the customs officer because she couldn't pay the duty. At the start of the sketch Sunny was discovered waiting for Frankie to pass her case with his customary chalk cross. Winking, preening and posturing at the audience in her usual OTT manner, Sonny grabbed the case to saucily exit swinging it triumphantly in one hand. Not this show. As Sunny always rushed on stage at the last moment, Frankie filled her case with stage weights used to hold scenery in place. Sunny couldn't move the it one inch. Frankie watched straight faced, not offering any help. Eventually, Sunny hauled the case to the floor with an almighty crash and exited, dragging the case between her legs. Fortunately the audience had cottoned on to the joke, and, joining in with the cast waiting in the wings for their next big scene, the laughter was hysterical. A comic's dream.

After exiting and being the pro she was, Sunny returned to take a bow to tumultuous applause. Frankie never repeated that joke, however Sunny always got in place early to test the case before the scene opened.

Another spectacular act took place in the tavern starring a Scandinavian act 'Los Likajos'. Two men and a girl. The men were expert sword fighters and fought a duel up and down winding staircases which collapsed at given moments most convincingly. The girl they were fighting over ran screaming all over the set. We, the chorus, dressed as wenches and peasants, also ran screaming as the swords got too close for comfort. The scene finally blacked out with the victor winning the girl and the opponent dead at his feet. Phoor! They don't make 'em like that anymore. This is a prime example of what the Folies stood for - unexpected spectacle.

With my personal contract coming to an end I bade the company farewell to take up my summer season contract. Frankie Howard was an extremely complicated person, friendly one moment, distant the next, but always kindly. Throughout the years we met up occasionally and he always showed an interest in my career.

One day walking up Charing Cross Road in London's West End, I noticed a shambling figure ahead. Even from the back it had to be Frankie. So, catching up, we briefly chatted. On departing, I had an uncanny premonition we would not meet again. Sadly I read of his death a few weeks later. A unique talent had departed. There must be laughter in paradise now.

CHRISTMAS 1954
WINSTON CHURCHILL'S SON-IN-LAW

My friend Izna Rosseli had used her influence to get me into the pantomime 'Old King Cole' which was being presented in Birmingham at the beautiful Victorian theatre Royal, which sadly was destined to be demolished and replaced with a local Woolworth's store. Local authority vandalism in my view!

'Old King Cole' even then was rarely used as a story line and never heard of since. However its star had played the role many times. His name was Vic Oliver, a comedian well known during the war teaming up on radio with Bebe Daniels and Ben Lyon, American performers cheering up wartime listeners during their darkest days.

Vic was also famous for being married to Sarah Churchill, and therefore Winston Churchill's son-in-law. Sarah, now divorced, had made her name as a serious actress. A striking redhead with real style.

Mr Oliver, as I soon discovered, had some exceedingly strange quirks. Nowadays referred to as dysfunctional. I have promised not to dish the dirt and other biographers have exposed him. So I will only refer, as incidents.

The other stars of this Emile Littler production were Harry Shiels, well known in the Midlands, who played a 'mumsy' dame with great charm and warmth. The principal boy Sylvia Campbell, a well known singer. Last but certainly not least, Vanda Vale. Little known but very important in this particular story line.

My own role was as one of the Fiddlers Three, as the nursery rhyme decrees. I was also contracted to play the part of the young Prince Cole in the prologue. This necessitated the swiftest costume change I have ever encountered before or since, to transform in only seconds from elegant courtly attire as the Prince into multi-buttoned uniform as a Fiddler and join the other two Fiddlers in leading the chorus in the spectacular opening scene.

Vic Oliver always surrounded himself with young girls, more especially if they slightly resembled his ex-wife. He was however what is now widely known as a control freak. Any male in the company found trying to get friendly with a young girl met with his disapproval and was sanctioned.

The father of one young dancer turned up at the stage door during a matinée

41

and removed his daughter from the company after she complained about Mr Oliver's attentions. The exact details we never discovered but rumour and scandal was rife.

Sylvia Campbell, who I became friendly with, was a charming principal boy with exceedingly long legs and a beautiful singing voice. She owed her allegiance to Vic Oliver because whilst appearing in the chorus of his West End revue 'Starlight Roof' he elevated her into prominence due to her singing quality.

Our paths were to cross later under totally different circumstances when Sylvia successfully escaped the 'golden' cage. Almost worthy of a Barbara Cartland yucky storyline, but a true romantic ending. The aforementioned Vanda Vale was playing a fairy and astonishingly resembled Sarah Churchill in looks, if not talent.

Received information was that Vanda had been a 'chosen' chorus girl and been transformed with elocution and deportment lessons, Titian hair colour and wardrobe makeover until she bore a truly uncanny resemblance to Winston Churchill's daughter.

At that particular moment in time she was leader of the entourage that assembled each night after the show at the stage door waiting for Mr Oliver to lead them out, receiving accolades from waiting fans before driving off in a chauffeured car awaiting them. All the dancers were of the opinion that Vanda was not particularly talented and would indeed have had difficulty making the chorus ..... meow!

If the 'look-alike' culture now creating its own market had surfaced at that time, Vanda could have had a nice little earner as Sarah Churchill.

'Old King Cole' had a long run playing to twice daily acclaim and I was particularly thrilled to be in my very first television excerpt when the BBC programmed it on a Sunday afternoon during the run. My parents dined out on that for weeks.

Further information has come to light recently and highlighted situations that reveal even further Vic Oliver's quirky character. Fortunately for him he is no longer on this planet otherwise in today's climate his career would be in shreds. Years ago newspapers would not reveal news that would assassinate a national treasure's character. That position was firmly held by audiences who admired Vic Oliver. He was indeed a funny comedian and furthermore a gifted musician and orchestral conductor of classical music.

It's on record that Winston Churchill hated his son-in-law and did everything in his power to put paid to his daughter's marriage, which eventually happened when Sarah could no longer tolerate Oliver's habit of playing the field, especially with teenage girls, and divorced him to her father's delight.

The aforementioned now has resonance with an incident that I had close knowledge of in the 'Old King Cole' company. During the early rehearsals a young dancer actress Mary Forbes had been contracted by Vic Oliver to play a small part. She was young, pretty and very ladylike, the sort Mr Oliver had a predilection for. She was sharing a dressing room with the current favourite, Vanda Vale, which was adjacent to the star dressing room of Vic Oliver. One day certain suggestions were put to Mary of a rather lewd sexual nature which involved voyeurism. Her refusal was instant and vehement. The following day on arriving at the theatre Mary found her dressing room had been changed far from the favoured position near to the stage. She now had to traverse steps galore up into the roof area.

Refusal of expected favours resulted in banishment to the back of beyond. However Mary kept her dignity and continued in her role within the pantomime. To have her sacked would have caused a scandal. My own innocent attitude to life was losing ground big-time. My vocabulary of words that needed a dictionary to define was getting heavier by the show. Perversions had now joined with how to achieve an abortion in a hot bath with the aid of gin. It was welcome to the real world.

I was able to help Mary, in compensation for her hard time, by introducing her to a company I was involved with later on, as a dancer, which she achieved with great skill and charm. A useful lesson learned – always stick to your guns in situations you find abhorrent.

MY GREATEST BREAK

Returning to the parental home from pantomime and the security of a salary, I viewed with dread returning to the dole queues at the labour exchange. Determined as I was to remain in show business and prepared to do anything except return to stilt dancing, I scanned all the theatrical papers and haunted agents' offices.

Little did I know that my next move was to be the most important and far reaching of my whole theatrical career. In retrospect my guardian angel was working all out on my behalf, and yes I do believe in guardian angels but more of her later.

Whilst between jobs I took advantage of the free classes offered by Miss Rosselli to keep me in trim for auditions. Classical ballet in my belief is the basis necessary for all dancers to have a certain achievement in. It's the fountain from which all dance forms sprout. The barre exercises also strengthen the whole body. Back in the 50s football clubs experimented by sending their members to partake in these classes, strengthening their thigh muscles and agility in swift movement. I decided to extend my abilities with classes in Pas de Deux and lift work. Working in class with a girl partner we quickly reached acrobatic standards; especially useful in the line of work I was aiming towards–musicals.

The girl I worked with, Margaret Hurst, rang me one day asking if I would mind partnering her in an audition that she had been put forward for by her agent. The company was a well known management specialising in summer shows. Ronnie Brandon and Dickie Pounds, a husband and wife team, they had been performers in their youth and now had numerous companies working under the collective banner of, 'Out of the Blue'. They were seeking a principal girl dancer of high balletic standard and Margaret wanted to also display the advanced lift work we had been perfecting. I readily agreed to partner her and on the appointed day we presented ourselves at the well-known Dinely Studios off Baker Street near Madame Tussaude's famous Waxwork Museum.

Entering the studio there was a long trestle table at one end behind which sat four people with scribble pads. Margaret danced her point solo and then introduced me explaining that I had agreed to partner her in a Pas de Deux introducing classical lifts. This studio, one of many, was mainly used for singers who had been heard previously and the floor was not particularly useful for dancers, being highly polished. However, we managed to complete our routine without breaking a limb or landing in a heap.

The four executioners were scribbling furiously and I had retired to the far end of the studio when Mrs Dickie Pounds suddenly requested, 'We'll hear the song now.' Margaret was rummaging through her music case, whilst I stood back relieved that my participation had successfully ended. Suddenly that same voice bellowed, 'Come on boy! We've others to see yet!' I started to stutter that I wasn't auditioning when the lady pianist hissed, 'Don't turn down a chance to be heard,' and invited me to look through a few pieces of music she'd brought with her.

Margaret by now was auditioning her song, whilst I stood sweating glumly. Should I make a dash for the door? In my head I heard my mum's voice proclaiming her mantra when I was scared of school exams 'Do your best. They can't kill you.' I wasn't so sure on this occasion. But resolved, I handed the only piece of pop music I vaguely knew to the pianist who smiled and whispered encouragingly 'Good luck'. The introduction seemed exasperatingly short, however. I screeched 'I wanna say hello, I wanna see you smile!' Huh, fat chance.

Halfway through I thought, I am a dancer not a singer … I'll go for a big finish. At that time many of the top American teachers were giving classes in the latest dancing gimmicks and I had studied with George Erskine Jones at the Joan Davies studios in the West End. I had proudly perfected knee slides where one had to take a long running glide until dropping onto one's knees and hopefully sliding as long as possible to a successful conclusion. It was now mercifully reaching its conclusion and I had positioned myself into my running drop, continuing the slide on my knees right underneath the table the directors were sitting at. That blasted polished floor.

I was gazing up at the underside of the table when Mrs Brandon's head suddenly appeared over the edge. 'Thank you, Duckie,' was her only response as I crawled out and hurriedly vacated the studio. No! I didn't take a bow!

Margaret tried to console me over a cup of coffee 'It really wasn't that bad,' she giggled as I attempted to cut my throat with a blunt teacake knife. Wishing her luck for the audition she had successfully concluded, I decided to stay in town and take some evening classes. No, not singing ones. Catching the final Green Line coach from London back to Thornton Heath I arrived home around 12.30am. My mother, being an owl, always watched the white dot fade on the television set whilst awaiting my return to share a coffee and hear of my escapades. She was sure in for a treat that night.

However, she had news of her own to impart. She informed me that a man had rung many times during the late afternoon and evening asking for me. Finally he said no matter what time I returned I must ring him, and left his number. I protested that it was now almost 1am but did as asked hoping that my mum had heard correctly. The phone was answered by an exceedingly cultured and resonant voice enquiring, 'Am I to understand that you appeared at my private audition in the Dinely studios?' I could hear the police car screeching down the road to arrest me. The man continued 'Brandon and Pounds want me to contract you as their principal male dancer, so if you agree can you call into my office later today to sign the contract?'

Could I? I was almost on the doorstep when the office opened in case they had all had second thoughts. The agent was Robert Layton of Long Acre in the West End. He was mainly an agent for singers, now there's a laugh. In his prime he had played leads in the West End musicals. Bet he had never done a knee slide though. I asked him whether my friend, Margaret, had got her job but sadly she wasn't quite what they were looking for. Our friendship survived. After all, that's showbiz.

There's a postscript. During rehearsals later in the summer, Dickie Pounds asked me if I could sing. I proudly proclaimed 'Well, you auditioned me,' to which she replied 'I know, Duckie'. She called everyone Duckie as I recall. She continued, 'I looked up my notes but where I usually write my comments I'd put only *nice smile*. Was I relieved as I told her 'I can do a nice knee slide though.' However I was given songs within the show, so can't have been too awful. Nobody threw anything.

My summer season now ensured, after signing my contract to become principal dancer for Brandon and Pounds 'Out of the Blue' revues, it was imperative to find a fill-in job until the rehearsals commenced in the early summer.

I abhorred the prospect of signing on at the Labour Exchange. Once again taking advantage of Miss Rosselli's kind offer of free dance classes to keep in trim I also asked her to agent for me in any interim engagements available.

Attending a tap dancing class one day I came into contact with another young man who had just finished his national service in the RAF. He had by chance met up with my brother Peter during service in Egypt. Peter had signed on for further service as a transmitter engineer and well remembers sharing a tent on a camp with Anton Rodgers – for that was his name. Anton was working on a radio network show and hosted a children's programme where he was known as Uncle Christopher. Peter also recalls Anton being totally immersed in seeking a theatrical career on his de-mob, which he has achieved with phenomenal success.

However, back to the spring of 1955 and my first meeting with Anton. One morning Miss Rosselli called us both into her office. She had been approached by a wealthy black American producer who was seeking two male dancers to partner his female protégé. We met and were interviewed by Donald Heywood, for that was his name. He explained that we were to partner this young dancer/singer in a trio act. He had dates lined up in southern France and Italy in smart nightclubs that summer to finally polish and work the act. Then that autumn we were to fly to New York to star in a Broadway theatre.

Whilst this all sounded so exciting and glamorous I was very dubious and suspicious at the same time – it seemed too good to be true. Mr Heywood told us that he had discovered two American girl dancers that he had promoted to stardom, one of whom was married to Gower Champion. Although I had heard of Marge and Gower Champion in Hollywood musical films I was still not convinced that all was above board.

However, my only selfish intent was to fill in time until my contractual obligations commenced. The prospect of a month's rehearsal money was attractive instead of the dreaded labour exchange dole queues. We were to rehearse in Miss Rosselli's studios so were on familiar ground. I was to partner the prospective starlet in balletic routines whilst Anton, whose tap dancing skills were much in evidence, partnered her in the American Vogue sweeping London at that time, thanks to Gene Kelly.

We were sent to Hornes the outfitters in Piccadilly Circus to be measured for coloured bowler hats and boaters. Also suits with one of the top theatrical costumers. So far so good. However, come Saturday no rehearsal pay and I was having to dip into my meagre savings for the travel and lunches. Miss Rosselli told us we would be paid next week as Donald Heywood was awaiting a bank draft. My suspicions were gathering pace and one day I told Anton I was going to ring Equity, our union, to see if they had any information on Donald Heywood. Surprise, surprise, they certainly did. My contact told me to drop the situation like a hot brick.

Apparently Mr Heywood was known as an American entrepreneur who during coronation year, 1953, had assembled a large company of black and white performers to present a revue called 'Coffee and Cream'. This was due to be presented in the huge Stoll theatre in London's Kingsway – sadly now no longer in existence. The assembled cast had been paid no rehearsal money so Equity called the shots. The company was disbanded and Mr Heywood fled the country.

So with my suspicions made concrete I told Anton I was not prepared to remain. Readers may well believe that I was hardly playing the game by using the situation as a stopgap until my contract started with 'Out of the Blue'. However, all's fair in love and war, and showbiz can on occasion be a war zone, with winners and losers.

Anton decided, as he had nothing concrete, that he would take a chance and remain. Unfortunately the whole episode came to naught. That's showbiz. However, readers will know, Anton went on to achieve great fame in the films and theatre, gaining many awards and partnering some of the most famous names in the business, his latest role in 'Chitty Chitty Bang Bang' gaining yet more acclaim.

We have met up on a few occasions when I visited him backstage in the star dressing room of various West End theatres. A thoroughly nice guy who I'm proud to have contact with although we only worked together once as extras on a film set starring Michael Denison and Dulcie Gray, a long time ago now.

First Out of the Blue Company – Felixtowe

OUT OF THE BLUE

The expression 'out of the blue' can be interpreted as an unexpected surprise either for good or bad. In the early part of my career it turned out to be the most amazing opportunity to come my way and led me down a path that I would not have dared to dream about. However I am jumping the gun, another odd expression.

Production companies in the 50s used the same titles for all their summer shows no matter how many they had. Brandon and Pounds had five, as I recall, spread around various seaside resorts. Other well known companies competing for resorts were Cyril Fletcher's 'Masquerade', Greatrex Newman's 'Fol-de-Rols', Sandy Powell's 'Starlight', Hedley Claxton's 'Gaytime' - a title that today would cause sniggers - Eric Ross's 'Dazzle', Wilby Lunn's 'Bouquets' … I could go on as there were many of these companies around. However, these will suffice to make the point. This was the summer resort shows during the 50s and onwards which helped young aspiring artists to perfect their talents, me included.

Readers who have travelled this far with me may recall the audition I attended back in the spring of 1955. Now was the time to prove I was worthy of the management's unexpected belief in my talents. Rehearsals commenced in a large studio in the gardens of the Dinley rehearsal studios where I had given what I thought had been the most disastrous audition piece ever placed before a beady committee. Meeting the full company on the first day turned out to be the beginning of some life long friendships which is fairly unusual in such a peripatetic profession. However as many of us were young and impressionable it was fallow ground on which to sow our ambitious seeds. Enough of this wallowing, back to reality.

Mr and Mrs Brandon, our bosses, had a highly respected company. Before their marriage they both had single success within the profession, Dickie Pounds as a dancer/soubrette and Ronnie Brandon whilst at Cambridge University with the famous 'Footlights' revues. Our respect for the 'bosses' grew when we discovered that during the Second World War 'Out of the Blue' had actually joined up with ENSA touring the war zones of Egypt at the height of the desert war.

ENSA, the Entertainment National Service Association, stood for all artistes taking part in entertaining the troops, bringing a brief moment of relief to the war zones. Rather unfairly, but given the sardonic sense of humour, the troops referred to ENSA as 'every night something awful'. This was only said jokingly as they were always vociferous in their praise and applause for these gallant entertainers, who could have opted for a 'softer' war. They had not been conscripted.

Being a child during the war and living in London through the Blitz, sleeping in Anderson shelters and seeing one's home destroyed by a bomb dropped in a neighbour's garden, I became totally in awe of Ronnie and Dickie and their bravery in opting to take the entertainment actually into the fighting zones.

Most certainly I have discovered the truth of the adage, 'it's not what you know, it's *who* you know'. This is more true, possibly, in the theatre than any other profession.

However I now had to prove that I had the talent to support my position in showbiz and further it. I had experienced during my brief chorus days a couple of occasions when there was a decidedly snobbish divide between principals and chorus. We were instructed to speak only when spoken to. Being in the business only a couple of years I was still considered a beginner. However, I was appalled by this attitude and resented it.

Throughout my career I have always considered my dancers as individual artistes, not underlings. We all fight for survival in an overcrowded and difficult profession and that deserves respect on every level whether onstage, backstage or front of house. 'Out of the Blue 1955' was now my opportunity to gain equality with my fellow performers as a principal artiste – a magic word which opens further doors as a soloist.

The company consisted of: principal comic Felix Bowness, who went on eventually to play major characters on television in 'Dad's Army' and 'Hi-De-Hi'; Ravel, a musical clown; Rey and Rongy, a clever and well established sister act, known on the music hall circuit still presenting variety bills; Doreen Lavender, a well known soprano who became a particular friend of mine throughout her life, which sadly finished a few years ago, far too young; Cyril Crook, principal male singer, darkly handsome but so terminally afraid of catching a cold and being 'off' that he always wore an overcoat and scarf, even in the beautiful summer of 55; Ronnie Sowton and Isobel Swan who were basically straight actors, perhaps I should say legitimate but it always sounds so stuffy, although it does still divide artistes into opposite groups - unnecessarily so, as I have directed both legitimate and musical artistes in my career. Both groups need commitment and dedication to survive in an overcrowded profession. Ronnie and Isobel's straight acting in the sketches brought a greater veracity for the comics to bounce off, in getting essential laughs.

The musical accompaniment was provided by two pianos and drums, par for the course in summer season shows at that time. On the grand pianos were two extremely pretty girls, Elizabeth Ball and Josephine Scott, who went on to perform in music halls and on concert platforms. Eventually they split up when marriage intervened - Josie to Hugh Lloyd, who later found fame with Terry Scott in the TV sitcom 'Hugh and I'. Hugh and Terry had met in another 'Out of the Blue' company where as individual artistes they had been teamed in sketches and developed a working charisma. Elizabeth married a tennis professional but sadly both marriages ended in divorce. Josie still continues a lucrative career and I last saw her when she was musically directing and performing in '70 Girls 70' in Chichester which transferred to London's West End. Hugh Lloyd is now a stalwart of the Royal Shakespeare Company playing character roles.

Finally the company was completed by four girl dancers, proficient in all styles of dance and with singing ability.

A tall and handsome young Canadian actor, who had trained at RADA, was assistant stage manager to Ronnie Sowton's dual stage manager role. Both were required to appear in the sketches and musical ensembles. Last but certainly not least was our boss, Ronnie Brandon who still enjoyed treading the boards. This then was the entire company numbering 18 in total, quite normal at that time in the smaller resorts.

As Doreen, Howard and I were the new kids on the block, all the others having worked in previous 'Out of the Blue' companies, we especially bonded. Howard and I eventually, besides being good friends, also became business partners in a 16th century restaurant in Sussex. However, that's a long, long way into the future.

1955 was the company's second season in Felixstowe, which I regard still as one of my happiest in a long stream of summer productions, some much larger with star studded casts. However it was for me the first step to greater opportunity, and I still remain indebted to Brandon and Pounds, now no longer with us, who helped so many artistes to glittering careers.

There's one member of the company I've left out, quite deliberately- Caramel Fudge - quite the most disgusting, whitish poodle anyone had ever seen. Only his mother and father could have loved him. He ruled the roost in Ronnie and Dickie's estimation. They treated Caramel as the substitute child they never had. Caramel strutted through the theatre as if he owned it, and lifting his leg whenever he felt the urge, which was frequently. Bad tempered, he would even turn on Dickie, especially when seated on his own chair in the aisle where Dickie directed the show from, seated at her trestle table covered in important papers to which she constantly referred. Dear Caramel also referred to them by chewing. When chastised verbally by Dickie, he attacked her, much to her embarrassment in full view of the company.

We all quickly learnt the truism 'love me, love my dog'. However, the whole company, whenever an opportunity occurred, would take a covert swipe at the little beast, but only when the Brandon's were not in view.

My own chance came one morning in rehearsal whilst I was waiting in the wings for an entrance. I had previously noticed Caramel walking stiff legged towards the side steps onto the stage from the auditorium. As I knew he favoured urinating on the house tabs and being such a snob only velvet sufficed, I waited unseen. As he lifted his leg I gauged his position and from behind the tabs gave a sharp kick, right on target. With a loud yelp he dribbled off the stage into Dickie's welcoming arms in the stalls. Her consternation he rewarded with a vicious biting attack. Two-faced, I also showed consternation but keeping well away.

The company were delighted that the piddling poodle had received his come-uppance. I also was delighted that the bosses never discovered the culprit - I would have been sacked on the spot. Caramel ruled. Thank goodness he couldn't give evidence.

Throughout the years Dickie Pounds had always choreographed her shows, bearing in mind that these had commenced back in the 30s and still paid lip service to the dance styles of Jack Buchanon and Elsie Randolph. In retrospect, I recall being embarrassed dressed in white tights and black velvet tunics flitting through a fairy bower where a sylph statue came alive and we danced a love duet in the moonlight. With dawn breaking I was required to collapse heartbroken at the foot of the pedestal on which the statue retuned to stone. Oh yuk! Remember this was now 1955 and I had studied with the American dance experts such as Richardina Jackson of the Harlem City Dance group and George Erskine-Jones who taught me to knee-slide. I was ungratefully embarrassed when friends came to see my debut and fell about with laughter, teasing me unmercifully. Modern choreography had advanced tremendously with the advent of musicals and films such as 'Oklahoma' and 'Annie Get Your Gun' with the stunning dance arrangements of Agnes De-Mille.

However, a stunning opportunity was literally about to come 'out of the blue' for me. Almost into October, the box office needed a special boost to attract the local punters now the holiday makers had departed. The management had devised a tradition which had proved popular with all their long running shows. This was to let the monkeys run the zoo. In other words for one night only in the final week the cast were free to create their own spots.

I approached the sister act, Rey and Rongy, and suggested devising a gutsy dance routine for the three of us inspired by the ballet 'Slaughter on 10th Avenue' danced on screen by Gene Kelly and Cyd Charisse. I worked out a routine with Rey as my girlfriend and Rongy as a seducer who vamped me into drug taking - in this instance whacky baccy. Whilst under the influence she stole my wallet and in an adagio frenzy she was to shoot me dead. A risky endeavour considering the audiences had been spoon fed such 'itsy-bitsy' fey routines in the past.

Whilst rehearsing on stage in the morning the other dancers would creep into the stalls to watch and eventually asked if I would enlarge the concept to include them. I was really excited to agree and co-opted the other men in the company by persuading them that I would keep it simple but effective as they weren't trained dancers but could all move reasonably well. Howard had found an unused backcloth in the theatre which fitted the bill perfectly. It was a New York skyline viewed through the archway of a bridge which with murky lighting was absolutely perfect. How spooky was that? My guardian angel and destiny were on a collision course. Would you believe I even persuaded Isobel, the straight actress, to play a posh lady about town and carry the piddling poodle. Dickie was thrilled at my kindness. Little did she know it was my revenge because he was unable to soil the tabs.

With the enlarged group I was able to be more ambitious. Rongy was now a night club stripper whilst two of the girls joined me in getting embroiled with drugged cigarettes in a frantic trio. With Rongy being an agile acrobat, I was able to create spectacular lift work. When she stole my wallet I worked in a strangulating struggle which terminated with the sleazy night club owner shooting me dead. As we had a gun used elsewhere in the regular show we were able to borrow it. The extremely loud retort was matched with startled shrieks from the audience. A further grisly effect I concocted by using a toothpaste manufactured at that time. It was blood red – very appropriate for my purpose – and was manufactured to colour the gums thereby making ones teeth appear white.

I had secreted a large segment discreetly upstage and on being shot, staggered and fell nearby which enabled me to retrieve it unseen by the audience. Stumbling to my feet I rubbed the paste into my white T-shirt and dropped to my death with the sound of police sirens and rotating lights offstage as it blacked out. Slaughter on 10th Avenue was on the billboard of a newsboy as he sauntered across the stage.

After a stunned silence the audience erupted. They had never had such a dramatic ballet in their summer shows before. The lights slowly came back up as the whole company took their bows. The tabs closed but the applause continued louder so the stage manager pushed Rey, Rongy and myself back through the house tabs. Rushing excitedly back to our dressing rooms we were recalled by Ronnie Brandon as compare to return yet again. Totally stunned at the response we raced back to prepare for the finale.

After the show, a message came through the backstage Tannoy asking me to go to the office next morning. The following day Ronnie and Dickie were effusive in their praise for the success of 'Slaughter on 10th Avenue' the previous night and offered me the chance to return the following year to their No.1 company in Southend-on-Sea as principal dancer and choreographer in my own right. I have always been appreciative of the great opportunity that Mr and Mrs Brandon gave me to have a choreographic career not only throughout England, but eventually the world. Many talented dancers aspire to become choreographers. However, it's being given the opportunity that is by far the greatest gift.

In my first show in Southend-on-Sea for the 'Out of the Blue' Company I created a dramatic ballet legend of the Incas in which I took the role of The Sungod. This photo, taken by a skilled amateur photographer, John Pascoe, won him 'Photographer of the Year' beating all the top professionals and was displayed in an exhibition in Mayfair, London to great acclaim

THE FLETCHER YEARS

In the theatre the greatest truisms are 'being in the right place at the right time' and 'it's not what you know but *who* you know'. True as these are, talent and ability must come into the equation if one is to succeed.

Back in the 50s, young dancers never considered going to an agency when auditions could be found every week in 'The Stage' newspaper. Why pay ten per cent of your wage to an agent? At that time there were tours galore, some large scale musicals on long contracts, whilst others could be quite tatty music hall revues. These were graded as were the theatre circuits, ie first to tenth rate! As were the managements who produced them.

Every town and city had more than one theatre. Croydon, the nearest large town to my parental home, had four. The Empire Variety theatre, the Grand which housed a weekly repertory company, the Davis theatre, one of the largest in Europe and a civic hall which staged concerts, etc.

In 1956 the Bolshoi ballet company of Russia did a sell out season in London's Opera House in Covent Garden. Its only other venue in England was a short run in Croydon's Davis theatre, a 3,000 seater, also a sell out.

A young dancer friend of mine, Barbara Willoughby, who later I was to partner, obtained a job as an usherette purely temporarily just to be able to watch the performances. Barbara was a trained classical dancer who had appeared with the festival ballet and this was an enterprising chance to view what every dancer considered was balletic excellence. Young dancers today are in a totally different ballgame. Companies are generally much smaller and singing ability of a high standard is a must. Years ago in larger companies there was a back row of the chorus where aspirants could perfect their skills in front of an audience whilst hoping for promotion to the front row. Next stop a soloist position. One expected training on the hoof at that time whilst being paid.

Nowadays in auditions dancers come prepared to sing, in some cases with their own backing tapes, and it's this skill that cements their position in a dance group. Thirty years ago when I held dance auditions I selected my dancers by their ability in ballet, tap and modern styles and then asked them to group sing, where the only requirement was quantity, not quality. Invariably either 'Happy

Birthday' or 'God Save the Queen' sufficed, which did not require a backing tape, only the pianist.

In the olden days, which most of my readers will consider my writings to be about, there was a camaraderie amongst dancers which evolved into lifelong friendships in many instances. Dancing involves group learning far more than either singing or acting. It demands co-ordinated movements which cannot be ragged or untidy so requires a total mindset of conformity. Auditions, which were held mostly in London, involved meeting with other applicants in friendly competition. As there could be a glut of auditions girls would travel to London staying for a few weeks with friends or in the well known theatre girls club in Greek Street in Soho. As this was a slightly insalubrious area this club was very strictly run with rules which had to be obeyed if one wished to remain. How impossible does that sound in today's climate?

I have digressed so let me take you back to 1960. Howard Eastman and I had met first in 1955 in Brandon and Pounds 'Out of the Blue' company. That company spawned many friendships which continue to the present day. Howard and I remained with 'Out of the Blue' for three more years. Unfortunately, due to differences with the producers, we decided to go separate ways towards higher goals. Howard became a stage director with the famous 'Fol-de-Rols' company, whose summer shows took long country-wide tours at all the No.1 theatres after their resident seasons.

I decided to further my embryonic choreography career with other companies to widen my scope and was fortunate to get a contract with the famous 'Catlin Follies', a northern theatrical company of high renown. Also to get a foothold in the burgeoning television companies that were proliferating throughout the regions. This was the time when television started to rival live theatre for supremacy and although we in the profession where innocently unaware, started the death knell for regional theatres, which could not compete.

My 'Catlin Follies' summer revue, which was in north Wales in the beautiful resort of Llandudno terminated and I was back in London seeking a Christmas engagement. Howard Eastman was now stage manager for Cyril Fletcher's production company and introduced me to Cyril who engaged me as choreographer and principal dancer for his pantomime 'The Queen of Hearts' at the Arts theatre in Cambridge. Cyril Fletcher was a well known comedian whose speciality was his self written 'Odd Odes' which brought him to fame in the 30s and 40s. As a small child I can recall being taken by my parents to see the famous 'Fols-de-Rols' revue at the White Rock theatre in Hastings. This starred both Cyril Fletcher and Arthur Askey. I also remember being terrified when Mr Fletcher recited a rather spooky odd ode bathed in a dark green spotlight. Now I was to actually work for his production company. Besides presenting quality pantomimes he also produced summer shows under the title 'Masquerade'.

It became traditional for known comics to set up their own companies enabling them to have total control and exploit their own talents without hindrance. These shows became academies for newly discovered talent enabling young artistes to perform and perfect their skills in out of the way resorts until ready to try and make a break for the 'big time'. Many stars of today owe their position to these companies, which with the passing of the time are almost non-existent, more's the pity.

Attending the dancers audition to help select girls for 'The Queen of Hearts' pantomime I was very impressed by the standard of the auditionees, which was not surprising when I realised they were all pupils of the Royal Ballet School. Likewise the singing chorus were culled from the Royal Academy and other top singing institutions. Looking back on the programme I found the names of artistes who went on to fame from humble beginnings. Amongst the dancers Elaine McDonald and Elphine Allen. Elaine went on to become principal ballerina with the Scottish Ballet and Elphine studied to become chief notator of the Royal Ballet Company, an onerous and respected post which preserves original choreography of ballets worldwide.

My association with Cyril Fletcher's company extended over four years in both pantomimes and summer seasons. I recall a young singer in the chorus of 'Sleeping Beauty', who went on to achieve worldwide fame in both opera and musicals. Her name – Valerie Masterson.

Mr and Mrs Fletcher certainly knew talent when they saw it – happily for me also. I was now able to introduce a young dancer I had first partnered in 1958 working in pantomime for Elkan and Barry Simon's 'Aladdin' at the Grand theatre in Swansea. Barbara Willoughby had danced small roles with the festival ballet company formed by Anton Dolin and Alicia Markova during the festival of Britain, which celebrated the end of the Second World War. A slender, pretty and bubbly girl who went on eventually to marry Kenneth Earl, partner of Malcolm Vaughan. Barbara and I danced together in both pantomimes and summer shows not only for Cyril Fletcher but also in 'Out of the Blue' companies over the next four years. Whilst these were seasonal shows we separated for fill-in work in between, mainly television productions.

Following my first pantomime with Cyril Fletcher's company he asked me to choreograph and appear in his forthcoming summer season, which was to be split between Yarmouth's Windmill theatre and the Essoldo theatre in Brighton. The Essoldo had been the inspiration of Jack Buchanon and Bobby Howes way back in the 30s but used mainly as a cinema ever since. In the summer of 1960 it was decided to re-open it with a lavish revue, which was to be presented by Cyril Fletcher's production company.

He brought together a company starring himself and his wife, Betty Astell as principal singer. To bring an up-to-date touch he engaged the young pop singer

Craig Douglas to appeal to younger audiences. Backing the show and also appearing was the Eric Delaney show band. I was partnered by Barbara Willoughby and a dance group of 8 girls known as the 'Ballet Robaire'. Cyril had engaged Pamela Cundell the comedienne who also partnered him in sketches along with Jack Stanford the eccentric dancing comedian. A four male singing group. Also in the company a young actor known as the utility man who had to take part as required in sketches etc. His name – John Noakes, who eventually became famous on children's television for a number of years especially with his dog 'Shep'.

Completing the dancing ensemble were Bob Cole, and Rey Seton, Rey and I had met up in my first 'Out of the Blue' company five years previously when she was in a double act with her sister known as Rey and Rongy. Rongy had married and retired early. Rey eventually married Denny Willis famous for his hunting quartet, which was known worldwide.

This show was very lavish with beautiful costumes and sets. During rehearsals I discovered a walkway right round the orchestra pit which had not been used since it opened in the 1930s. The stage manager uncovered it to discover it was made of glass and still had coloured lights in working order. It made for a quite spectacular effect when the dancers paraded round it during the scenes bringing them into close contact with the audience.

Eric Delany's orchestra were stunned when I presented them with the band parts for the act Barbara and I were performing. I had devised 'The Sorcerer's Apprentice' which was to classical music by Dukus and not the type of music usually played by Eric's musicians. However as some also doubled instruments which they never used much, flutes, piccolos etc, they were quite delighted and used to get into the pit early to practise. It was a great success and the whole performance, pit and stage received rave reviews, especially as it was an unexpected item in a revue. The opening night was a star studded event. Brighton was a favourite residential area for show business folk with its proximity to London. In the audience were Elsie and Doris Waters, Gilbert Harding, Max Miller and the actress Ann Todd, along with other local luminaries.

Unfortunately after the successful opening with good press reception the business was not overwhelming. The Essoldo had not been used as a theatre for years even though it was in a prime position in the centre. Furthermore the Theatre Royal which housed all the big touring musicals and shows excelled themselves that summer with a star studded cast we could not compete against. Topping the bill was Frankie Vaughan who had just returned from filming in Hollywood with … wait for it … Marilyn Munroe, and the film was due for release. Also supporting was the most expensive cast list it was possible to present. Singer Adele Leigh, the Ryan Twins, and an assortment of variety speciality acts that through the fog of time I can't now recall. It certainly was strong competition. But that's showbiz – some you win and some you lose.

I am now in 1961 and still working under the 'Masquerade' banner of Cyril Fletcher's company. This summer I was to begin my love affair with Eastbourne

'The Sorcerer's Apprentice' created for Out of the Blue Company.

in Sussex, the beautiful Victorian resort nestling in the shelter of the South Downs. It boasted four theatres. Two Victorian - the Royal Hippodrome and the pier theatre, an Edwardian one - the Frank Matcham designed Devonshire Park, and a brand new Congress theatre with the largest seating capacity. The Winter Gardens venue hosted other activities such as tea dances and had staging capacity for smaller travelling shows etc.

Cyril's show was destined for the perfect little jewel, The Royal Hippodrome. These shows were usually presented elsewhere for a couple of weeks prior to the resident season. Most theatres throughout the country were usually council owned and the opening night was a civic occasion before an invited audience or should I say jury, therefore a polished performance was a necessity for the production company to ensure their contracts for following years.

In the 60s summer shows enjoyed long runs, 16-24 weeks not unusual sometimes with a follow-on at the end by a further month elsewhere to test the water of other venues who might be looking to make changes for the future. It was a hotly competitive world for bosses as well as performers.

Following the season which was a long one I didn't have much time to fill in before the pantomime rehearsals began. Television was occupying more airspace now and musical shows which required dancers were a useful stopgap. Frankly I did not enjoy working that medium as much as the theatre. Pre-recording was not yet in place and many TV productions were live, with attendant problems. However that's another area which I will elucidate later.

I was about to encounter someone who was to be instrumental in opening up a world of possibilities undreamed of previously and frankly not even contemplated. The time was ripe. I had selected the dancers for the pantomime of 1961 which was to be 'The Queen of Hearts' again in the Arts theatre in Cambridge. As before pupils from the Royal Ballet Schools were auditioning. One young, dark haired, pretty girl caught my eye not only for her dance skills but her personality, something not always encouraged in serious ballet schools who preferred their dancers to have serene expressions – some would say po-faced. Jenny was her name and she was contracted to be one of the team. Fate, or as I believe my guardian angel, had decreed that this was the girl I would eventually team up with in a dancing duo that spanned the world and made us one of the most successful acts in the profession of that period.

During the run of 'The Queen of Hearts' I experienced one of the most traumatic experiences of my whole career. Cyril Fletcher did not bother with understudy rehearsals and all went well generally. However during this run fate intervened. One Saturday with two performances in view he had awakened with

Opposite: Jenny was only in the chorus when we first met. She is top centre at the back dressed as a Jester – very appropriate whith her wicked sense of humour!

no voice whatsoever, not even a croak. Panic stations prevailed and Cyril was for cancelling the performances. However Commander Blackwood, the administrator of the theatre Trust would not hear of it. He had two sold-out performances and as pantomimes could re-balance most theatres' financial year, another solution had to be found.

I was staying with friends who owned a restaurant, 'The Waffle' in Petty Cury much patronised by the University undergrads. Suddenly the door opened and in came the company manager having had a meeting with the powers-that-be, including Cyril, apparently writing his proposals. The decision was that I would be the one to take on this role as I was only performing in a non speaking part, usual when one is principal dancer.

I was panicked. With absolutely no rehearsals I was to be flung into the titular role without a safety net. Hurriedly scanning the script it was surprising for me to discover that certain scenes had gone into my subconscious via the dressing room Tannoy during the weeks we had been performing.

Cyril had suggested that I should carry the script. However this was impossible as the role required a great deal of physical action. Fortunately the role of the King was in the capable hands of Billy Tasker an accomplished actor who helped me with obvious ad libs when I lost the plot. Which brought me back on line. Another problem was the costumes, as Cyril was hardly ever 'off' during the show his many changes of costume had to be accomplished in the wings. The dressers stood by to pin me into the frocks and bundle me back on. They had to use safety pins galore as I was only half the size of Cyril. With relief I reached the interval and praise from the rest of the cast helped tremendously to get me through to the end of the matinée.

Going out before the evening performance to get a breath of fresh air I went via the front of house and saw a special notice had been posted hurriedly bearing the following words: Cyril Fletcher is unable to give his unique portrayal at today's performance due to indisposition. Patrons can either transfer their tickets to a subsequent performance or get a refund from the box office.

Underneath however in letters that required a magnifying glass was the apology: At this performance his part will be undertaken by Robert Marlowe.

How encouraging was that? I returned to my dressing room to be told that Commander Blackwood had invited the entire company for a celebratory drink after the show in the theatre restaurant and was apparently delighted with the matinée's reception. Encouraged, I relaxed and the evening's performance flashed by with a rewarding response at the final curtain.

At the reception in the restaurant, champagne was the reward for the whole company and Andrew Blackwood told me that only four people had asked for their money back and those tickets were resold on the door. Success!

The stage crew had actually taped the evening's performance so I have a

64

Look Mummy I'm Dancing

souvenir of the only time I ever played Dame, by default of course but very enjoyable in retrospect. Cyril recovered over the weekend and the season continued to the end with no further setbacks.

Jenny who I had auditioned and selected to appear in the 'Queen of Hearts' had proved her place in the company and was invited to join the team for the 1962 summer season in Eastbourne. Jenny's sense of humour would not have been welcome in a serious ballet company and it would not have suited her being a swan, or in her words 'a dying duck'! She has such an expressive face that even pretending to be serious made audiences laugh. A perfect gift for her in the lighter branch of showbiz where her skills, waiting to be developed, were always in demand with the comedic stars who relished her natural ability to encourage laughter. So Jenny had decided that a Royal Ballet career was to be jettisoned in favour of the traditionally lighter side of show business. During this season a friendship developed between us that has lasted to the present day. We've shared laughter and tears over the years as we have travelled this exciting road together. However, in 1962 it was in the embryonic stage. Watch this space.

I'm finding it difficult to keep dates in the correct sequence so now I must revert back to 1960. Following the summer season Cyril asked me again to choreograph and appear in his 'Sleeping Beauty' pantomime this year in the King's theatre Southsea.

Cyril obviously starred as the Queen whilst his wife Betty played Beauty, Billy Tasker a well known actor played the Lord Chamberlain whilst an even better known character actor played the King – Wally Patch was a stalwart of British Films in their 1950/60 heydays, mainly cast in cockney roles as policeman or service men.

Dennis Martin, a well known singer, was cast as the Prince. Dennis became one of the prime movers in the Players theatre which presented authentic Victorian music hall in the theatre underneath the arches of Charing Cross in London for many years, a great favourite of tourists to the city.

Once again Elaine McDonald, still a student at the Royal Ballet School, was in the dance group – her talent gaining her a role in the Harlequinade. I was partnered by a talented young dancer Joanne O'Hara. In this production I had devised an act by dancing on stilts whilst manipulating the dancers as puppets on strings. This I brought back into practice, when as a newcomer into the business, I joined that stilt dancing act back in 1953. My very first pantomime. I used this skill many times when I needed to inject an innovative novelty into my own productions. Lesson learnt – any skills are a plus in showbiz.

When the pantomime finished its run I made a decision to form a dancing act, as there were many opportunities around at that time. Jenny was my natural choice especially when I discovered that we both lived near each other in Surrey, which made it convenient to work together on creating a couple of speciality acts which I hoped we could sell to production companies. Whilst I had the experience to create the acts, Jenny's contribution was to know a friend who had a dance studio which she loaned us gratis.

That summer of 1962, I was returning to Eastbourne's Royal Hippodrome theatre, and had the chance to work Jenny in as a principal in presenting one of the acts we had worked on. Cyril and his wife Betty were obviously the stars and once again Pamela Cundell was the comedic feed to Cyril along with Jack Stanford. Julian Jover, who had been in the Cambridge pantomime, was also engaged to act as feed in sketches with Cyril. Julian came from a well known theatrical family and was married to Kitty Bluitt an Australian actress famous for playing Ted Ray's wife in the long running radio show, 'Ray's a laugh'.

Kitty was not a company member but became part of the family atmosphere, regaling us all with anecdotes and photographs of her Hollywood years, when she was courted by Burt Lancaster and others. She was not popular with the management however. Too famous? 'Nuff said.

Other new members were Peter Hudson, a young tenor with a great voice who later found fame as a comic and finally Eric Garrett, a baritone who joined the company having already signed a contract for the coming winter season with the Royal Opera Company in London. He went on to operatic fame as the principal baritone playing opposite the world's most famous female singers. I was in the audience for Joan Sutherland's final performance with Eric in a major role opposite her. As I've already stated Cyril Fletcher always surrounded himself with highly talented performers, a wise move for any artiste, some already stars and others in embryonic stage who went on to prove the maxim.

During the season an unaccountable atmosphere had developed within the company, which was hard to define, strangely. I harboured the suspicion that Cyril had not been too happy that I had undertaken his role of the Queen of Hearts for two performances in Cambridge the previous Christmas. This of course had been at his instigation, and at least there had been no cancellations. There of course had been no understudy pay and only scant recognition from the management that I had saved the day. To say I was disappointed is putting it mildly; after all I was totally unprepared and given no option. However the show business mantra prevailed – the show must go on, and it did.

There had been uncomfortable instances during the run for other company members. I'm not in the business of tittle-tattle. Suffice to say that after the final performance Mr Fletcher's agent came round to the dressing rooms and informed us that as all the contracts were terminated at the fall of the final curtain, we had half an hour to vacate the theatre. A sad finale, in particular for me after four years of loyal service. However, in showbiz you pick yourself up, brush yourself off and start all over again!

ASHTON COURT – THE COUNTRY CLUB

During the season I had been approached by a London agent enquiring whether I would be interested in presenting cabaret. Theatre had always been my first love but with the atmosphere during that season I was open to any offers and made an appointment with Percy Silk whose office was in London's Park Lane, a most prestigious address.

The offer was to present a floor show of three months' duration in the Ashton Court Country Club, Failand, Bristol. This was owned by a local millionaire, John Ley, well known for the Caroline Tea Shops. The permanent company was to consist of 4 girl dancer/singers, 2 showgirls, myself as principal and guest artistes booked weekly by the Percy Silk agency. The only drawback being that a weekly change of show was required. I considered it and decided to accept as I've never refused a challenge. With only another few weeks to go of the summer season and due to the aforementioned atmosphere I knew that a pantomime with the Fletcher company was out of the question on both sides.

As a choreographer I obviously relished creativity so decided that each show should have a theme using a combination of location and colour, together with an act that complemented the production. I approached Berman's, the top London costumiers and liaising with one of the directors they agreed to supply from their vast stock and even make, if necessary, what I required.

With the contract now firmly in place I needed to find the permanent group. Naturally Jenny was definitely involved. The pier theatre in Eastbourne also had a similar show to Cyril Fletcher's. This was presented by another well known comedian, Sandy Powell of 'Can You Hear Me Mother?' radio fame. Watching their matinées which were on different days to ours I had spotted a couple of girls who had the required talents and offered them the season which they accepted. The fourth one I asked to complete the group had worked with me in a previous company. A trained dancer she also had a strong singing voice, a double asset. The two showgirls were to be recruited from a Bristol agency who specialised in fashion show models and therefore local.

Accommodation was a problem. Being a country club it was naturally isolated with no guest house or bedsits in the area. John Ley suggested that he could tarmac an area in the woodland near the club, installing a water supply and getting a firm to supply caravans which we could rent for a nominal sum. We accepted – Hobson's choice actually – and it seemed a good idea at the time. So fuel burning residential caravans were towed in ready and waiting when we arrived in mid October. The Autumn was sunny and mild with no need for boiler fuel. However hell was waiting just around the corner.

Rehearsals occupied the days from 10am until 4pm, when we could avail ourselves of the club's bathrooms, before relaxing and getting dressed to have dinner in the club, which was part of the contract, and to mingle with the club members prior to the floorshow.

As the club was popular with 'hooray Henrys' and their would-be society gal friends, I made a decision to help my team of dancers by suggesting a dress code so that they didn't feel the need to compete. As the little black dress was essential with the fashion pundits, I felt this should be a uniform which they could explain away to the quite obviously well-off club members - it was their director's command. I suggested to the girls that they could tart it up with jewellery, scarves, stoles, etc to maintain their individuality. They weren't working for 'flumpence' but this relieved them in the financial stakes with the perfect excuse that I was to blame. My shoulders were broad.

Whilst their contracts had clauses that required them to mingle with the members, I had assured them that it was not the consummation clause popular on the continent, where girls were required to 'be nice' to the customers and we all know that hidden agenda. As we had a deadline to prepare for the floor show I had arranged with the manageress that we all occupied the same table in the dining room for dinner at 7 o'clock without delay. This enabled us to digest our food, get on the 'slap' and quite elaborate costumes, in time for the performance.

In such a situation as this there are strict preclusions which one has to enforce to maintain standards and be successful, the two main ones being - drunk or incapable, and being found in a compromising situation on the club's premises. One strike and you're out. Obviously this job demanded girls with looks, figures and personality, a magnet for the guys. Ah well, nothing changes. All completed the contract and we were praised and admired.

As the Club was closed on Christmas Eve and Christmas Day we all decided to travel back to our various homes for our first break from a punishing schedule. John Ley had very kindly given permission for us to borrow the large club people-carrier, and our musical director John Brucker, a brilliant pianist and arranger, offered to drive us all to various pick-up spots en route. As most of us had homes in the South East, it was a long journey. We eventually got back on Christmas Eve, arranging to be picked up where we had been dropped off. The nightmare was about to begin.

Snow started falling after nightfall on Christmas Day, which had been threatened, and Boxing Day dawned with a heavy fall still progressing. Starting

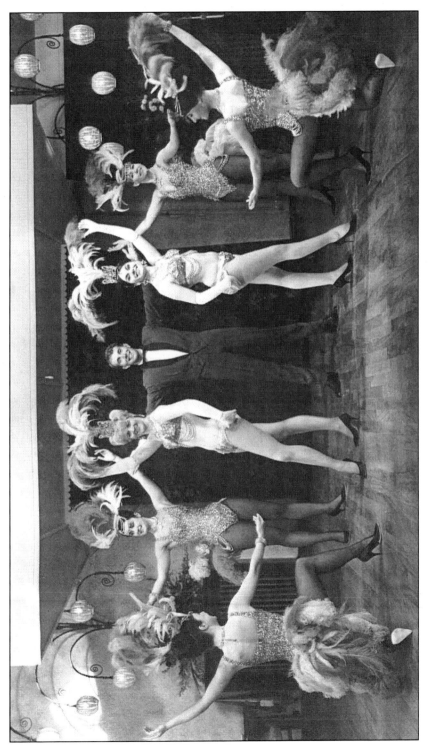

Cabaret Floor Show in The Country Club in Bristol

off earlier than expected, John picked everyone up and we headed back for Bristol and our Boxing Day performance. It was the most hazardous journey we had ever encountered but we made it. After all the hassle our reward was only about a dozen patrons who braved the steep hills in what for the remainder of our stay was reminiscent of the Canadian Rockies, which I had experienced about five years previously. However, England was totally unprepared for what turned out to be the worst winter in living memory for the West Country, a total whiteout.

Relying on Coalite for our fuel-burning caravan fires, we had previously collected it in the club van from the docks. This road was now cut off so we were reduced to raiding the club's coalhole and surreptitiously scuttling back with a few shovelfuls to stay alive. Unfortunately caravans in a wood cool to freezing when the meagre coal burns away, and we found ourselves imprisoned in the morning when, on opening the doors, we found icicles from roof to ground which we had to break before regaining our liberty. Fortunately, as we had to rehearse every day for the following week's show we were in the centrally heated club and exercising our frostbite away. Dancers do have compensations at times like this.

The shows were proving very popular with patrons and I now understood the need for a different production each week to keep the customers coming, hard work as it was for us. I became more ambitious with the shows using the club's facilities for scenic effects, one time borrowing from a travel agent a large model aeroplane which was suspended on wires high in the ceiling, and with sound effects traversed the length of the floor with the spotlight following. This blacked out to astonished applause. to reveal a South Sea island setting with palm trees, etc and our guest artiste for that week, Nat Gonella the well known trumpet player, singing 'The Only Man on the Island'. The dancers in hula-hula skirts sashayed round him whilst wolf whistles resoundingly forced Nat into full throttle.

Nat was such a popular performer both with club members and all the artistes that John Ley retained him for two more weeks, along with the other pre-booked acts. This not only extended the show time-wise but increased audiences and bar takings. Nat was such a happy personality to have around and work with. When he left he was missed and remembered as a great guy. What more can a performer ask, except money?

The problem left when creating a spectacular show is that one is expected to top it next time. Quite difficult on a limited budget. However, fortunately for me Mr Ley was also caught up with the roller-coaster syndrome and went along with my ideas.

With the November celebration of Guy Fawkes night I had devised a show around the famous plot. Obviously fireworks would have to come into the equation. As there was a large set of windows above the working area I realised rockets, etc could still be viewed in safety by the audience from inside. The costumiers made saucy beefeater costumes for the dancers and I devised a routine with swirling silver banners for inside, whilst I risked my life as Guy Fawkes by scaling the roof outside and choreographically setting off the rockets and set pieces, once again to the audience's astonished applause.

This was the first time that the club had ventured into full scale floor show production ensembles and I found myself hoist by my own petard. However Mr Ley was delighted with the results and fully supported me. Once again many of the staff were co-opted to help and enjoyed working with us, joining in its success.

The local showgirl models, Yvonne and Peggy, had enthusiastically joined in with the production ideas and helped to increase club membership I'm sure. I recall one occasion when the Young Farmers' Association had booked in a huge party. We were all very wary when these events were mooted for they were renowned for drunken bawdiness, especially when pretty showgirls in skimpy bikinis were seductively parading around. One particularly drunken young la-di-da farmer staggered onto the floor encouraged by his equally drunken friends and made a lunge for one of the models. Very high-heeled stiletto shoes were all the rage at this time, no good for dancers but perfect and sexy for showgirls. I don't know which of the girls got clutched at and if I did I wouldn't say. Suddenly a loud screech hit the air and the young farmer collapsed to the floor clutching his foot. A well placed stiletto had reached its target. The routine continued with all the girls exhibiting larger smiles than usual and the target being dragged unceremoniously from the floor. The club was not a rowdy establishment, quite the opposite, and this sort of behaviour was frowned on, rightly so.

We were now coming towards the end of our contract and as the weather was still abysmal we could not wait for the end. On the final night we all decided to combine in my caravan which was the largest, mainly to celebrate and more importantly to keep warm with body heat, having no fuel whatsoever left.

Morning arrived and we bid our farewells, vowing to keep in touch and put the whole escapade down to experience. The resilience of showbiz people can be quite awesome. It's what kept us going, that and the love for our profession.

One has to believe in guardian angels and I do. With no prospects in view for the summer season I had previously approached probably one of the most important and influential people in show business. Richard Stone was agent for almost every top star in England and America. It's always been my belief that if one has the guts to approach business gurus with something to offer they respond favourably. I had invited Richard Stone to come and view the shows I was presenting in Bristol with a view to engaging Jenny and myself for one of his summer productions. There is a maxim in showbiz that hell will freeze over before an agent or management will come out of London to view anything.

Surprise, surprise! I received notification that both Mr and Mrs Stone wished to see the show during that autumn which had turned into an Indian summer. Richard had married a charming and delightful West End star, Sara Gregory. Now retired from performing due to family commitments she nevertheless supplied the artistic input for her husband's productions. Meeting with them after the show we were thrilled to be offered to join one of their productions for the summer of 1963.

LET'S MAKE A NIGHT OF IT

Colonel and Mrs Richard Stone had travelled especially to Bristol in the autumn of 1962 to view my productions. This visit resulted in a contract for their famous summer shows, which was eventually to extend over four years. Rehearsals began before Easter 1963 in London and for the first time in my career my birthday on 19 April was celebrated. As I've explained previously, summer season shows had a generic title applied to all their productions. Richard's was 'Let's Make a Night of it'.

Being a newcomer in this company I was to meet many members already embedded within the management hierarchy. Naturally I was viewed by some with wary suspicion, being the new kid on the block. However, that's par for the course in showbiz, and up to me to prove my position. I'm happy to record that friendships developed which have endured for over forty years both onstage and within the management.

The costume department was in the capable hands of Una Choyce, whose husband Jeff was Richard's production manager. The wardrobe supervisor in charge of the production I was choreographing was Rosemary Waters and we developed an ongoing friendship up to the present day, with Rosemary costuming many of my subsequent shows with other managements.

The comedy personnel in my first show were a well-known duo, Gordon and Bunny Jay, blood brothers in a very high-octane act. Their comedy co-star was Billy Burden, the West Country yokel comic. A perfect foil for Gordon and Bunny to bounce off in sketches. Billy was very laid back and his appearance generated instant warmth within the audience. Many of his gags were well tried and known, which guaranteed the audience joyfully finishing the tags with him and culminated in an even louder response – a study in getting the audience to work for you. I always told him he initiated community gagging, as opposed to singing. However, he possessed a powerfully rich baritone singing voice, which he would finish his act with unexpectedly, and to great acclaim. A well-loved artiste both on and off stage, unfortunately no longer with us.

Gordon Jay was the director and I found myself quite wary of him. His personality could be described as loud and abrasive. However a warm and friendly heart beat within his breast, as I was to discover. His brother, Bunny, was a totally different character off stage but on stage they were like peas in a pod. A very funny pod and slick with it.

The season was seven months long with before and after visits in other resorts. This particular show was destined for the Pier Pavilion theatre in Worthing, Sussex. However, we opened as a tryout in the beautiful Little Palace theatre in Westcliff on Sea, Essex -a period gem now struggling for survival in today's ethos 'if it isn't making money, close it'.

Back in the 60s with holidays in English resorts still in vogue most theatres were crying out for special fill-in weeks prior to their main seasons. A choreographer needs to foster accord with the director and vice versa. I quickly learned to give as good as I got, so when Gordon asked 'How're you doing you old tart?' my quick response was 'OK you old poof,' which evoked much amusement amongst the cast. All comics appreciate laughter, no matter at whose expense. Not that I was casting aspersions.

Gordon and his wife Margaret produced their second son during that season and all the male members in the company were presented with a cigar in celebration. Mine has remained in my theatrical make-up box ever since as a good luck token. I never smoked anyway.

In the cast that season were an Australian husband and wife singing duo, Arthur Downs and Valerie Grey. Arthur either could not be bothered, or had a word hang-up, because on certain numbers he would position word cues at the footlights. All went well until someone switched them around. I had never heard so many la, la, la's in my life but it is amazing how many audience members never even noticed.

Today's songs are so repetitive one doesn't need to memorise them, just let the audience sing along remembering you get paid for it, they *don't*.

The musical director Ken Flower, had created a singing group well known on radio as The Kentones, now disbanded. He was an excellent MD. A speciality act Julius Nehring, a wizard on the xylophone, and the Ten Pavilion Lovelies completed the cast, led by Jenny and myself as principal dancers and speciality act.

'Pavilion Lovelies' made the dancers squirm even then, for it sounded so coy. Much later groups with titles like 'Hot Gossip' proliferated, suggesting a more saucy or even risky content. I recall a few years ago an agency promoting an act entitled 'Cunning Stunts'. This was quickly dropped when disc jockeys with a couple of pints on board were in danger of breaching the obscenity laws. Who knows what the future holds? The mind boggles, especially with celebrity chefs now sprinkling their menus with the F word.

Show business is the most peripatetic occupation to enter, especially the variety section because one can find oneself working for many differing managements within the space of a single year - fill-in jobs, for example filming, modelling, teaching, even set and costume designing, which I was able to turn my hand to throughout my career. All of these talents can be interlinked in an artistic world. But ... one has to be prepared for good and bad years. Many dancers had office skills and were able to fill in awkward spaces between summer shows and pantomimes by temping.

Unfortunately today many trained performers are finding the temporary jobs of longer duration than their theatrical engagements. A few years ago I could give my regular dancers ten months in a year engagements, with summer seasons of five to six months duration and pantomimes of three months. A few cabaret weeks could offer a fairly full date book. Not any more I'm afraid.

Shipping lines are now one of the main sources of long runs, even presenting full-scale musicals. I've already described the expertise now required by all performers for a successful career in our shrinking profession. Most ambition is concentrated on television soaps with their long term contracts which generate stardom in other areas like pantomimes at Christmas, where even walk-ons can lay claim to fame, ironically. However that is another story.

Back to my remembrances of the Worthing summer season of 1963. Even today when meeting up with other performers in that company certain occasions are recalled from our many social engagements during that run - some fabulous, some embarrassingly awful and some hysterical.

Towards the end of the season we were all invited by a council member to a farewell party in his home - no names, no pack drill. Arriving after our evening performance we encountered a large and elegant double fronted house in a leafy Sussex road. The driveway accommodated quite a few cars. Imagine our amazement to find ourselves escorted into a replica olde country pub, complete in every detail with beer pumps and optics, etc. However, no menu or price lists! It was a party and a very generous one. Obviously our host was living out his frustrated dreams and desires from a more prosaic workaday world, even though he occupied quite a high and important position in the local community. This pub was full of surprises causing stifled laughter which, actors all, we successfully kept from our host.

My attention was brought to a replica period fireplace whose chimney piece kept frantically changing colour with a concealed flywheel, usually only found in the wings of a theatre. Must have fallen off the back of a truck.

Last and by no means least, we were all assembled in a vast conservatory in total darkness. With a flourish our host pulled a switch and illuminated the garden. We all gasped at the riot of colour, a plethora of out-of-season, *plastic* flowers whose garish form and vivid hue were all the rage in the early 60s. To say we were surprised is putting it mildly. Like a vast stage set, but not one that Colonel and Mrs Richard Stone would have allowed anywhere in their elegant and tasteful shows. However, I and others have dined out on that anecdote for years. That, my friends, is showbiz.

With the season now coming to a close in late autumn I had decided to travel for the second time to Canada and America for the next six months, with two objectives. Firstly my greatest ambition to travel the world and secondly to try my luck at exploring any theatrical possibilities on offer.

As Jenny and I were assured of the summer season in 1964 with Richard Stone's company, we separated until the spring. Jenny obtained a pantomime, playing her first principal role as the Fairy in 'Dick Whittington' in Southampton starring Richard Hearne as Mr Pastry.

In the theatrical world, making decisions and taking chances can be tantamount to gambling. Some you win, some you lose. Whilst I have never gambled my hard earned cash, fearing to lose it, I would always go for an estimated gamble with my career, and fortunately always won. Once again, credit to my guardian angel.

Leaving England in late autumn on the Queen Elizabeth for New York, I travelled through the American south and was in New Orleans the day President Kennedy was assassinated. A tragic and historic period to be in America, sharing their shock and grief. Briefly, I was able to secure various television chat show appearances but more of that later.

Returning to England in the spring of 1964, Richard Stone had guaranteed a certain number of weeks in the summer season, which was to be Weston-Super-Mare. As this season was shorter than the previous year he had arranged a variety tour for Jenny and myself, prior to our resident season. Variety was now a dying art, television was wreaking its revenge and acts were either leaving the business or seeking work on the continent where variety performers were still in demand.

Renée Stepham, the agent I had encountered when signing my first contract in the business had booked the short tour on Richard's behalf, starring Norman Vaughan, Mrs Mills the sing-a-long cockney pianist, Billy Burden the yokel comic, plus Anna Lou and Maria, a performing dove act. Jenny and I opened each half of the show. By tradition dancing acts always occupied those spots, which were required to be bright, breezy and colourful, settling the audience down for what was to follow. An onerous position.

In my childhood, my parents treated my brother and myself to occasional variety bills playing the Croydon Empire. I can recall seeing the musical act of Ted and Barbara Andrews, during their act introducing daughter Julie, who can only have been about 10 years old. She stood on a chair to reach the microphone and displayed the crystal quality that was to rocket her to fame and stardom in the years to come. Other performers such as Tommy Trinder and Teddy Brown, the vastly rotund xylophone exponent, also Ernie Lotinga who always brought his touring revue company and packed out the theatre. His shows were considered to be downright suggestive with saucy and smutty schoolboy humour, which delighted me and my brother. Our parents were broad minded and laughed as loud as we did. I would memorise the sauciest bits and repeat them to my schoolmates who were less fortunate and had not seen the show. This made me briefly popular and envied, until the teacher found out.

However, my abiding memory of the Empire was the electric boxes on either side of the proscenium, which flashed the number, in bulbs, of each act. There were no compères so the audience would look up in their programmes to see who was next on.

Imagine my delight years later playing the Lyceum theatre in Sheffield to discover that they still used this method of identification with Jenny and myself lit up as No.1. That was worth more than money – well, almost!

The short tour only occupied four or five weeks and I was thrilled to spend a week in the Alhambra theatre in Bradford, scene of my first pantomime in 1953.

Returning to London we went straight into rehearsals for the summer season and met up with the cast which starred Ivor Emmanuel, the Welsh singer who popularised the Sunday television show 'Land of Song'. This also starred his beautiful wife, Patricia Bredin who was a star of many films and had first come to notice when playing the lead in the musical 'Free as Air' in the West End, eventually replacing Julie Andrews in 'Camelot' on Broadway. She was a delightful member of the company totally natural and un-starry.

The comedy was literally in the hands of Terry Hall who manipulated the children's favourite Lenny the Lion. Chris Carlson, a stand-up comic, completed the humorous aspect. A family act The Gaytones, mother, father and two exceedingly pretty daughters, skilfully played trombones and trumpets, etc. Jenny and I, together with The Knightstone Lovelies – ugh, that title - not the girls I hasten to add, for I had hand picked them in auditions previously - completed the cast. Once again the musical direction was in the capable hands of Ken Flower. Richard was very loyal to the performers who reached his high standards.

The beautiful summer that year ensured the show's success. Visiting the resort recently, I was extremely disappointed to discover that the local authority had allowed the charming theatre, which is situated on a promontory, to fall into such a state of disrepair, that the only solution will be to pull it down. This now seems to be the predicament across the entire country. Who do I blame? Television. People who still prefer to holiday at home stay in hotels and guesthouses with TV sets en suite, and prefer to catch up with their favourite soaps. Personal choice of course, but a disaster for any summer shows unless they have the financial pull to engage television names whose agents' asking price can be through the roof. Lecture over.

My third season under Richard's banner in 1965 was in my view the nearest approach to a West End production one could hope for in a summer season show. This was being presented in the Cliffs Pavilion theatre between Westcliff and Southend, Essex and the Premier theatre in the same county. In my view the former sadly represented an aircraft hanger with steel grey predominating, and from an audience point of view quite gloomy. Apparently the fashion for designers at that period of time. Very recently I visited the theatre and the manager kindly showed me round for old times sake. I was really delighted to find a total makeover had restored it to theatre crimson with the original grey walled auditorium now glazed, flooding in light during the daytime. Top marks.

The cast of 1965 starred Jimmy Edwards whose fame was in impersonating a headmaster with the catchphrase of 'sit up at the back there' and in making rude noises on musical instruments. He could be difficult, as I was to discover. Co-star was Joan Regan the singer who had been proclaimed one of the world's beauties in a weekly TV show some years previously. Even today she remains a beautiful and charming lady and still a delight to work with, as I did recently. Third top was Arthur Worsley, a unique ventriloquist whose dummy Charlie Brown did all the talking, even berating Arthur for being so stupid. Arthur was a quiet and gentle man whose fame had encompassed all the London theatres from the Palladium down, even enchanting America on the well-known Ed Sullivan chat show on TV, to which he was invited to return over 14 times. Truly an international star. With Arthur you never saw his lips move - unlike the American ventriloquist Edgar Bergan with Charlie McCarthy whose main claim to fame was that he was perfect for the radio!

Also making up our company were the stilt dancers Jean and Peter Barbour who I had first encountered in the Folies Bergere in 1954 when they were a trio with Peter's brother Roy. A singing group 'The Southlanders' were a 4 guy black team, one of whom was the father of Gary Wilmott, a West End star in his own right, performing in 'Me and My Girl' and quite brilliantly in the Old Vic production of 'Carmen Jones' when he sang the Harry Belafonte role of Joe, which having seen it I can vouch for. The last time I had seen him he was about 9 years old. What a transformation. A chip off the old block.

Jenny and I were particularly thrilled to be a part of this distinguished company leading, yet again, the 'Ten Pavilion Lovelies' – no comment – presenting our own unique acts which by now we had perfected worldwide.

Musical direction was in the extremely capable hands of Jack Pebardy, husband of England's top jazz singer Betty Smith who fronted her own quintet. Readers will now see by the aforementioned that my claim of West End standards was fully justified.

After opening night Richard Stone approached the producer David Croft and myself asking why Jimmy Edwards and Arthur Worsley were not included in the first half finale along with all the other principals. This was a tricky moment because Jimmy had refused point blank to do so. Richard was insistent, and I was instructed to request the stage manager and company to attend a special rehearsal next morning to include Jimmy and Arthur in the hoedown routine, which frankly was extremely simple. At 10 o'clock the next morning the company and the musical director were present on stage but no sign of Mr Edwards. Going to his dressing room to politely request his presence I was informed by his chauffeur/stooge Ernie that Jimmy had no intention of attending, although he was in the theatre. My reply was that Ernie inform him it was my duty to do as our employer requested and I intended to proceed, with or without him.

Going onto the stage Arthur Worsley was ready to comply so I partnered him with the head girl dancer, whilst telling Joan that she would partner Jimmy if he deigned to turn up. As the rehearsal continued I noticed Jimmy secretly observing from the wings although not coming onstage. What a big girl's blouse. Eventually Joan approached him and persuaded him to take part, which he did with poor grace. That evening the whole company took part and Colonel Stone was satisfied. What a stupid fuss though. Photographs displayed outside of the theatre showed Jimmy together with Prince Philip in polo clothes and the company pondered as to whether simple punters expected to see His Royal Highness also in the hoedown. They were in for a right royal disappointment.

Another fiasco caused problems the first time it occurred. Jimmy Edwards' final spot was prior to the lavish finale, which was always a tour-de-force of spectacular setting and costumes. During the weekday performances Jimmy's act was scheduled to run for 15 or 20 minutes, giving the cast ample time for their costume changes. However, Jimmy had his private plane at the local airport and piloted himself back to Sussex at the weekends. As the curtain fell his chauffeur Ernie had the Rolls Royce waiting at the stage door to whisk him off post-haste.

Imagine the panic the first time Jimmy shortened his Saturday performance to less than 10 minutes and the stage manager's voice screeched through the Tannoy with the 'on stage' call. Half-dressed dancers hurtled down the stairs dragging on their costumes and head-dresses en route, to stand breathless in their elegant positions exhibiting sickly smiles. That only happened once because all the company made sure they were in readiness for the finale immediately after the final production number prior to Jimmy's act. We were never caught out again. Although Jimmy could get the audience into hysterics with his trombone-playing finale, he was unfortunately not the most popular person in the company. He should worry though!

Jenny and I had a quietly satisfactory incident one particular Saturday. With

Jimmy ready to make his usual dash for the airport we had friends that we had made whilst performing in cabaret on the Queen Elizabeth to see the show. They had driven from Bournemouth where they lived in a brand new, coffee and cream, 1965 Rolls Royce and had promised to drive us back to London after the performance. As we exited from the stage door, our friends were waiting whilst Mr Edwards quietly seethed, as Ernie could not get into his usual position for their quick get-away. We bade him a cheery farewell as we quietly slid away. One-upmanship triumphed.

After the usual growing pains of any company getting together for the first time, the season reached its successful conclusion and I reiterate it had all the slickness and spectacle of a West End show in every aspect. The 1966 summer season was destined to be the last one I would choreograph and, together with Jenny, perform in for Richard Stone.

We commenced rehearsals in London mid June and we opened on the 24th at the Grand Pavilion, Bridlington in Yorkshire. Two years previously Jenny and I had done a week's variety in this theatre with the popular singer Ronnie Hilton and we were once again re-united as he was the star of 'It's a Grand Night' co-starring Lenny the Lion with Terry Hall, and Norman Collier an extremely funny comic whose sketches were hailed as masterpieces. One in particular when he duetted with himself in a parody of Jeanette McDonald and Nelson Eddy, simply by changing hats, had the audience in stitches.

Other company stalwarts were Tommy Wallace and Beryl, now known as the Plummers after Tom's father Sid Plummer, the brilliant comedy xylophone player passed away. Tom and Beryl, whom I already knew, were also skilful xylophonists combined with many other talents. Beryl has a super singing voice, also an accomplished tap dancing technique. They are both fine examples of an all-rounder in its truest sense, and they joined Jenny and myself in the production scenas together with – you've guessed it - The Pavilion Lovelies. Eventually when I was in a position to form my own dance groups I never insulted them with such a naff appellation, even though they *were* lovely.

Myrna Rose, an American singer now married to an Englishman, completed the cast. musical director was Will Fyffe Junior, son of the famous Scottish comedian.

It was during the first night's performance that the most incredible accident took place. All the dancers, except for the stars but including the speciality acts, were assembled behind the house tabs ready for the grand opening routine. The overture completed, we were poised ready for the house tabs to rise. Imagine our horrified gaze as instead of rising, they started to fall. We were engaged in a staring match with the audience. We all froze – it looked like Madame Tussaude's waxworks.

The stage manager realised, too late, that the wrong button had been pushed.

As it was a mechanical operation we watched and waited as the bar holding the tabs was put into reverse. We all hysterically waved to the audience who waved back, also in fits of laughter. What an opening – bet the comics were livid. Will Fyffe began the overture once more and as the curtain rose we performed the routine to thunderous applause. The comedy team took great advantage of the situation and the opening performance was a wow from start to finish. That has never happened again in my experience. It could not be deliberately repeated for it was the total unexpectedness that made it so hysterical.

It was during the first night party that Jenny was to meet her future husband. Other summer season performers had been invited and John Lawrenson, the singer well known for radio's 'Friday Night is Music Night' was singing with the Edwin Harper Orchestra in the Floral Pavilion for the summer. For John it was love at first sight though Jenny confesses she was more anxious to get to the buffet and mildly irritated at the attention she was getting from this stranger. However, persistence paid off and romance blossomed during that long, cold summer.

When it's cold in Yorkshire, it's cold. I only once ventured onto the beach that year. The sun was shining brightly and my boxer dog Jet loved the beach and water. Stripping off hopefully to get a tan I quickly realised my mistake. Clouds formed and Jet huddled close beside me. Even his teeth were chattering. We beat a hasty retreat, never to go again during the run. No wonder people were going abroad for their holidays where the weather was more dependable. On one occasion the company were invited to take the boat trip up the coast to Flamborough Head. Well, we all thought the end was nigh! We praised the sea god when we arrived back on dry, but cold, land.

Jenny's romance was flourishing and during the season she told me she and John were to get engaged and she would quit the business to start a family eventually. I was pleased for her in one way but sad that our act was to terminate. However, we had pantomime already booked for Derek Salberg in the Alexandra theatre, Birmingham. It was 'Goody Two Shoes' and Jenny was to play the titular role. An opportunity too good to miss – more of that later.

The season was now drawing to a close. On stage we were performing a variety show. However, off stage it was more like a Whitehall farce – so many doors opening and closing. I've promised not to dish dirt and I won't. Let's just say for the onlookers it was most entertaining.

On the final night the council announced that it had been the most successful show to date playing to 68,000 people as opposed to 54,000 the previous year. Seat prices were 7/6d, 6/-, 5/- and 4/- all shillings in old money. Twice nightly, so we all worked hard for our shillings.

That season was to be the last of four very happy shows under Richard Stone's banner. Eventually he was to drop all shows which he had originally promoted for his wife Sara's artistic talents and to further her theatrical interests whilst raising her young family. Richard then concentrated on his agency of all the top names both in English and American show business.

Finally just a brief footnote. I returned to Bridlington in 2003 to direct pantomime in the council's Spa theatre. Back in 1966 this theatre housed a repertory company. I searched high and low to find the Grand Pavilion where the summer season had performed, without any luck. Returning again to direct pantomime in 2004 I was determined to solve the mystery of the lost theatre. My remembrance had been of a flight of steps rising to the vestibule and box office, then descending into a quite large auditorium. I was directed to an area that my memory was totally unfamiliar with and search as I might, the whereabouts of the Grand Pavilion eluded me. How do you lose a theatre, especially a large one?

Back in 1966 my impression of Bridlington was as the Blackpool of the East - brash, gaudy and chips with everything! In the intervening forty years much has changed and Bridlington is smart, refined and genteel. A tribute to its Victorian past. With climate changes occurring right across the country my recent visits were unexpectedly warm, with clear skies and sunshine in December.

The Spa theatre is soon to become the jewel in Brid's crown with a makeover to carry it forward into the 21st century. Together with forward-looking council administrators and the young, enthusiastic backstage crew I feel sure it will be successful.

If this were a letter I now have a postscript. The Grand Pavilion has been found, though not by me. My impresario friend Paul Holman who produces the pantomimes was taken recently to view the theatre, now long closed and in need of a transformation to house a 2006 Christmas production, even if only briefly. Maybe packed houses and laughter will bring a renaissance and create an entertainment use once again. As in 'Peter Pan', belief in fairies may yet restore a theatre.

A HAPPY RETURN

1967 loomed without a summer season in view. However, as Jenny and I were now a well-established dancing act and summer shows still proliferated we remained undaunted. Casting my mind back 13 years and with the happiest memories of my first summer season as a chorus boy in the Clacton 'Ocean Revue', I decided to drop a line to Frank Adey who was still producing his shows in the Ocean theatre. My Guardian Angel came again to the rescue. Mr Adey was indeed in the market for a dancing act and I was engaged to choreograph the show also.

Topping the bill was a young comedian Johnny Pace, who had won Hughie Green's television show 'Opportunity Knocks' where he had been awarded the most votes ever recorded for a TV show – television again rearing its head.

Comedian Billy Burden shared top billing and the rest of the case included Bruce Allen, a young talented mime artiste, Gwen Overton and Clive Stock, a well established singing duo, and Tony King an accordion artiste.

Tony's act encompassed an electronic accordion of which there were only 6 in the entire country. He had boasted of a big finish to his act and we were all agog during the dress rehearsal to witness the novelty. During his final number the stage lights started to dim. As he reached the crescendo his legs lit up! We all stared in disbelief – was this it? Falling about with laughter we realised this indeed was his 'big' finish, as the stage lights returned to full up. Investigating later we found he had wrapped fairy lights around his legs to achieve this effect. He could have electrocuted himself! We had heard of an electric chair, but this was a new dimension. Had someone been taking the mickey? No, it was his own idea. What bravery, risking his life for his art.

This was a typical line up for summer shows in that period. The dancing chorus were under the collective title of 'The Monte Carlo Girls'. A decided improvement on Pavilion Lovelies.

Besides presenting the acts that Jenny and I had perfected on worldwide cruises on board the Cunard Queen Mary and Queen Elizabeth, I also persuaded Frank Adey to let me produce the 'Slaughter on 10th Avenue' ballet that had originally gained me my first choreographic engagement 13 years previously, in Brandon and Pound's 'Out of the Blue' revue. This was now re-titled 'The Happening'.

I am now going to boast proudly by quoting the Press reports. Forgive me – it was my first show as choreographer.

> *Highlight of the show which had the audience spellbound was the modern ballet 'The Happening' depicting the fast moving world of today. Charged with expressive action the ballet largely concerned itself with the effects of drug taking and took place against the background of a strip club and disreputable discotheque. The choreography arranged by Bob Marlowe is a masterly display of originality.*

Towards the end of the season, Clive Stock, who was eventually to form his own production company with great success, suggested introducing me to Sandy Powell. I had worked in Cyril Fletcher's summer show in Eastbourne where Sandy now resided, and was known as 'Mr Eastbourne' for his well known productions on the End-of-the-Pier. Although I knew of his fame we had never met. This introduction resulted in an engagement for the summer of 68 which came at a most convenient moment in my career. Jenny was retiring to marry John Lawrenson and the Clacton show was her swansong, therefore I was reverting to being a solo artiste for the first time in 6 years.

THE OVEN DOOR

It's my belief that fate is predestined for everyone and the summer season of 68 was about to prove a shining example.

Back in 1955 I had first met Howard Eastman, the young Canadian actor in the 'Out of the Blue' company. During the intervening years we had kept in touch and I had even travelled to America and Canada with him and met his family. During the following years he had forged a successful career as stage director with the famous 'Fol-de-Rols' company. Eventually tiring of the endless travelling he had become disenchanted and decided on a drastic change of profession. He had always nurtured a talent for cooking and decided to train as a chef, with a view to owning his own business. Studying with friends who owned a restaurant in Ely, Cambridgeshire, he quickly scaled the culinary ladder and was ready to venture forth. Not having the capital for going it alone, Jenny's brother Michael and I decided to go into a non-working partnership and financially backed Howard as chef-in-charge.

Finding a delightful Elizabethan restaurant in Uckfield, Sussex trading as 'The Oven Door' we entered into a lease and Howard quickly gained a reputation, especially for his home made cakes and pastries which eventually gained him an Egon Ronay recommendation of excellence. His fame spread and customers living in London would ring in advance to order picnic hampers, which they would pick up en route to nearby Glyndebourne during the summer operatic season. Even the opera singers would travel to Uckfield to sample lunches or afternoon teas.

We had covered the walls with signed photographs of the many famous names we had both worked with and this became a talking point amongst customers. The Oven Door became known as the 'showbiz caff'. A health farm in the vicinity also attracted may show business folk who would break the rules whilst undergoing treatment, to sneak out for forbidden cream teas. On one occasion the Beverley Sisters arrived for tea and Howard cunningly placed them in the window seats. Their instantly recognisable flamboyance – they always wore matching outfits – stopped the traffic and clogged the streets. The restaurant had living accommodation above and my summer show in

Eastbourne being only twenty miles away enabled me to have free digs for the summer.

This was helped by the fact that the musical director of the show Colin Tarn also lived in Uckfield with his family, so I was able to cadge lifts too. What a fortunate set of circumstances. In return I also acted as ticket agency for Sandy Powell's show by encouraging our patrons to visit the pier show. Having now explained my extra curricular business venture, it's a case of on with the show.

Howard Eastman – A long-time friend and business partner

STARLIGHT

I had seen Sandy's shows 9 years previously, when I was appearing in the Royal Hippodrome with Cyril Fletcher's rival company, so I knew the format. For a number of years Sandy and his business partner both on and off stage, Norman Meadows, a brilliant feed, starred with Sandy's wife Kay White in the pier show.

They now had retired from their own shows although in my first year Sandy and Kay were now working in a star-studded cast at the Royal Hippodrome. A real turnabout for all of us. Sandy's company was known as Southbourne Productions but the generic title was Starlight and in this my first year I was delighted to discover that the comedy leads were Don Smoothy and Frankie Holmes, both of whom I had worked with in previous companies. This is always an advantage as there is no 'getting to know you' hang ups from day one.

I had met the musical director when I had seen the previous year's production. Colin Tarn was an exceedingly talented composer/pianist and we

Sandy Powells 'Starlight' summer show – 'American in Paris'

formed a friendship, which has lasted through to the present day, working together for many differing companies.

I had brought my own team of dancers and had introduced a new young dancer as my partner. She was a beautiful girl of Icelandic parentage named Thorey. Sandy had asked me to include a young girl he had met when he was guest artiste in the famous Fol-de-Rols and she was a dancer. Her name was Nina Brown and she was destined to eventually become my second permanent dancing partner. Fate was yet again playing its hand.

The rest of the company consisted of operatic soprano Anne Verity together with Tommy Wright a well established, very butch singer, who always had girls waiting at the stage door after the show. A double musical act The Excelsiors completed the company. No one waited at the stage door for *them!* Colin Tarn on piano was the musical director accompanied by Peter Durrent on a second grand piano and completing the trio Sam Bryant on percussion. The company consisted of 17 in number, unheard of nowadays. Where summer shows still exist less than half that number form a company today.

My engagement as choreographer and principal dancer enabled me to introduce ideas I had previously devised, with certain success. That, I guessed would be the taste of the audiences attracted to Sandy's shows. These ideas elevated me to actually direct the productions for the first time with a well-respected company. Never again would I sign a contract that did not include directing.

I'm now going to tell tales, as many of the culprits are no longer with us who were involved. The wardrobe department was in the capable hands of Madame K Dunbar. In her prime she had performed in the music halls dressed as a man in immaculate evening dress. She sang, very basso profundo, I was informed. She was a lovely old duck with a racy sense of humour and we got on like a house on fire. Sandy's wife, Kay White, in her youth had been one of the London impresario Charles B Cochran's young ladies, renowned for their style and beauty. Once these young ladies were past their sell-by date, they were abandoned. However Kay had the good fortune to meet Sandy Powell, who in the 30s along with Jessie Mathews was the highest paid performer in England. They married so Kay's future was secured.

Sandy along with Kay were honoured more than once to be included in the Royal Variety shows where Sandy's well known ventriloquist act always was a great success and much enjoyed by the Queen whose preference theatre wise has always erred on the side of music hall, rather than the classical theatre. King George and Queen Elizabeth always took the princesses to their local theatre, the Victoria Palace, to see the Crazy Gang shows, which they enjoyed hugely. Princess Margaret grew out of this type of entertainment, for classical dancing, when she became the patron of the Royal Ballet Company.

Kay had through the years taken artistic control of the costume department, much to the private disgust of Peggy Meadows, Norman's wife. Kay would not throw anything away, no matter how old, and many costumes looked as though they had started life in the 30s.

One night after rehearsals, with the company now departed, Peggy asked me to help her down in the wardrobe. I say down because we were right over the sea. Madame Dunbar and Peggy had plotted to get rid of a ghastly set of old sequinned leotards that Kay insisted still had life in them. My assistance was required to lift a large trap door in the deck which was disguised by a huge carpet. Heaving the door up, the sea was lapping only about three feet below. Madame Dunbar and Peggy, chortling with laughter, heaved this ancient set of costumes through the gaping hole into the darkness with a resounding splash. I slammed the trap door shut and we replaced the carpet – good riddance! We three all danced our way off the pier gleefully conspiratorial, vowing to keep the secret for ever.

The following morning I was with the company for the 10 o'clock rehearsals when Peggy called me into the stalls to tell me that Kay, who always appeared about 9 o'clock, had been accosted by one of the outdoor attendants with a mysterious package. Guess what was in it? Right - those awful frocks dispatched into the sea the night before. Kay was totally mystified but fortunately they were beyond recognition. Being from the 30s the sequins were the ancient sort that congealed into a solid mass, or should I say mess.

We conspirators had thrown them overboard onto an incoming tide, instead of outgoing, which would have taken them across to France. Well, we were all landlubbers. Kay would occasionally ponder on the mystery but that's what it always remained – until now.

Sandy and Kay were now starring at the Royal Hippodrome theatre. A rather strange anomaly to be in the same town and being paid by our boss who was in direct competition with us, with his Starlight company in the Pier theatre.

In these circumstances, I had to succeed – it was friendly warfare. However, Eastbourne has always attracted crowds of visitors and still does. Its sunshine record is well nigh unbeatable, being in the shelter of the South Downs with prevailing winds mostly from the West, and bad weather firstly hits Winchester where it veers eastward, finally making its impact in Norfolk, mainly on the coastal resorts. I'm detailing this because it has relevance later when I was contracted to complete 20 years in that area. However back to Eastbourne and the 60s.

Four large theatres could comfortably achieve 'house full' boards equally with all the hotels and guesthouses. To have the edge on profitability competition was fierce with the emphasis on top-of-the-bill artistes and the style of production. The world was my oyster and I felt obliged to seek the pearl on behalf of

Southbourne Production. To be rivalling my own boss was something I relished especially when I contemplated the powerful array of music hall stars in the Hippodrome show. Old time music hall was enjoying a strong revival and the original stars of that genre were in their prime.

Elsie and Doris Waters, famous for their Gert and Daisy warring sisters routines, were sisters in real life to Jack Warner, famous for portraying policemen in 'cops and robbers' situations where his catch phrase was 'Evenin' All'. He caught on with the public, even to the present day. The film 'The Blue Lamp' starring Jack has gone into the annals of history.

Gertie Gitana was well known for her male impersonations in immaculate evening attire or military uniforms. She was rumoured to be in her 90s, but never ask a lady her age – young or old, they all lie, still do. Also men, although they avoid it, rather than lie and hear guffaws.

I was particularly honoured when one of the artistes performing in Sandy's show contacted me asking if I would teach him the currently favourite American tap dancing vogue sweeping London, which I had updated my own tap skills to encompass.

Leslie Sarony had, back in the heyday of the music halls, partnered Leslie Holmes in an act known as 'The Two Leslies'. Leslie Sarony was now a solo performer of indeterminate age whose long career in music halls obviously placed him well into his 70s. However, he could still cut the rug with his 'Jake the Peg' routine where he impersonated a man with a wooden leg, frantically tapping with one foot whilst beating the time spasmodically with the other. It always brought the house down with thunderous applause. I was in awe. Leslie suggested that as our shows had matinée performances on the same day it would be favourable to work out between our evening performances. When he arrived for his first instruction I demonstrated to him the different style required and he was extremely quick on the uptake. The lessons always culminated with anecdotes about famous music hall stars of 40 years previously, which I was privileged to receive first hand from someone who had been there. Almost a theatrical degree course and I was spellbound.

As the season was now drawing to a close, like Arabs in the night all the theatre folk were folding up their camps to depart. At our last meeting Leslie handed me a rolled-up scroll tied with a ribbon. He explained that he would not insult me with a monetary offering. I thought to myself, try me! However what he had given me in my view was worth far more. During his career he had composed music hall songs that were pertinent to the period. His own composition that he always encompassed in his act was 'I Lift Up My Finger and I say, Tweet Tweet,' which even I had heard. In my hand was now an original song, which is still in my treasure chest. Any cash remuneration would have quickly dispersed, but not the manuscript. The song was entitled 'Grandpa's Old

Soft Shoes'. I never incorporated it in any of my later routines; as it was too dated for someone my age - don't ask – to even contemplate. However, it remains one of my treasures to this day. Maybe I should bequeath it to the Theatre Museum in London. It's a virgin copy and there aren't many of those around today -virgins of any sort, sardonic but true.

During the long running season on the pier I had incorporated a more modern approach to the production scenas, which has been well received by the public. Even the management agreed it had brought a breath of fresh air into the equation. The principals were all seasoned performers and like all good pros had moved with the times joining in with my production ideas with enthusiasm. The final night was agreed by all to have broken the mould and been a new triumph. I was personally rewarded with the offer of a continuing contract and given carte blanche to create and further modernise the future of the theatre on the pier. This was heralding a new dawn for all concerned.

Sadly fate had determined a tragic situation, which was to engulf this Victorian treasure eventually. However fate also mitigated the threat by giving me a year's breathing space before striking the death blow. Read on.

The Christmas pantomime that year was my third one in Birmingham's Alexandra theatre for Derek Salberg's 'Aladdin'.

The summer of 1969 was all too soon upon me. The contracted company consisted of Frankie Holmes, topping the company as principal comic because he had been very popular the previous year in the secondary role. Charlie Noble was to back Frankie in the comedy stakes. Also Richmond and Jackson, a well established comedic act. Betty Jackson amazed me with her acrobatic contortions. Singer Donna Douglas was making a strong name for herself on television and in recording studios. Niven Miller was her male counterpart, a Scottish singer who was eventually to ask me to direct his one man show 'The Life of Harry Lauder' at the Royal Albert Hall in London. Once again the beautiful Thorey, who had been my partner the previous year, joined me again in fronting the 6 Starlight dancers. I was further pleased and grateful to have Colin Tarn as musical director of a three-man team. His musical skills were, and still are, second to none.

I had decreed to the management that I was determined to top the previous year. As a moon landing had been on the books to take place in early summer I decided to gamble my growing reputation for modernising by creating a show opening which used this projected worldwide lunar landing as my muse.

My plan required two distinctive settings scenically and Vic Friendly who I had worked with previously in other management companies was again contracted to Sandy's company, much to my delight. He had always approached his work in a modernistic style, which I admired, even though occasionally it could be a little bizarre and had to be reigned in. Vic was fortunately on my wavelength mostly, and I carefully explained what I wished for in this daring opening scene.

Firstly I needed a space station, which was to be manned by a crew preparing the rocket to project into space heading for the moon. Secondly I wanted a moon landscape. Not as easy to design as shots taken were still to come. My own idea was a landscape of valleys and mountains all crystallised and glittering white and silver with the space rocket in situ after a safe landing. Vic came up with a quite fantastic interpretation of my ideas. The space platform showed the rocket ready for launch through a glass dome. Inside was a row of desks in futuristic style with control panels etc. The second design was exactly as I had envisaged. The old quote that great minds think alike was now proving itself most flatteringly right.

Costumes required needed a great deal of thought. The girls had to look like an efficient crew but also glamorous in a theatrical way. It was after all only a summer show trying hard to look authentic. My ideas which I discussed with the wardrobe department called for a white cat suit over which was a modernistic silver tabard, short to show the girls legs. Knee high silver boots and a silver helmet completed the astronaut effect. Imagination on all sides was needed. It was carried through to perfection as photographs taken show.

The shape of the routine was to show the dancers manning the controls whilst the singers fronted the set singing 'Fly Me to the Moon'. How more obvious than that can you get? However, rule of thumb in shows like this, it is essential to retain familiarity. This scene faded with countdown to a total blackout whilst sound effects flooded the theatre with rushing winds and futuristic musical chords. Finally the lights came slowly up to reveal the breathtakingly silver setting with the rocket safely landed. Slowly the door opened and the entire cast entered, finally bringing on the comic, Frankie Holmes, now topping the company.

The reason why I have explained this opening in detail is because a bombshell was about to drop. I had invited Sandy Powell our boss to attend a full dress rehearsal to get his views. After all, this was quite a turnabout from his usual show, adventurous and daring. The company pulled out all the stops to show it off to perfection. I was so proud of them. Sandy and his wife Kay were most impressed, especially as the actual moon landing was anticipated for our opening weekend. After a thoughtful moment Sandy suddenly dropped the bombshell – literally. 'What happens if there is a tragedy and they are all killed?' Silence … as we all took this on board.

No one, not even I, had contemplated such a disaster. Quickly thinking on the wing I said, 'OK, we will quickly run up scanty silver dresses. With fishnet tights and high heeled silver shoes, and replacing the helmets with little red velvet hooded cloaks, we could change the whole concept. The males only need

The Operational Centre for the Moon Landing

Vic Friendly's excellent set design – The Luna Landing

a red shirt with their white trousers. Scrap the first scene and using the lunar landscape minus the rocket, replace it with a large decorated Christmas tree, the company singing a series of carols and Christmas songs. Re-title the scene 'Early Xmas' – tra-la-la!

Everybody looked disconsolate. But desperate stakes need desperate measures. We all held our breath and prayed for a miracle, which I'm sure would have echoed the sentiments of everyone in the world for the crew of the spaceship.

All our prayers were answered and there was much rejoicing especially for the safe landing of the adventurous astronauts breaking new boundaries. None more so than in Eastbourne's Pier theatre. We opened on Saturday with the packed audience hardly believing their eyes that we could be so topical.

When I first entered show business old pros would tell me that timing was everything. How true that is. The rest of the show lived up to the new approach modernity and again I was contracted to present for a third year a revolutionary style show to compete with changes now happening in the other three theatres in Eastbourne.

Going against his grain, Sandy Powell had decided that he needed even bigger names to head his show. I was asked to enlarge my dance team - yippee! - including boys also to rival Dougie Squires' dance groups.

Dougie had made a huge success with his various teams like the Young Generation and now I was set to emulate his success. Strangely, whilst Dougie and I had never met I had followed him into various companies and situations in which he had preceded me. Brandon and Pounds Out of the Blue company for one, also various pantomime companies. So you can well imagine I was thrilled to be offered the chance to emulate and hopefully rival Dougie in friendly competition, for I had always admired his work.

During the autumn, Sandy kept me informed of the company he was forming for the 1970 season. Ronnie Hilton the pop singer was to top the bill, whilst comedy was in the very capable hands of the West Country comic Billy Burdon. Also on the bill was the popular 'Kitten on the Keys' artiste Kay Cavendish. This, together with my new dance team led by myself was the nucleus of the show, to be completed with a couple of speciality acts yet to be contracted. I was by now getting excited with the prospect of summer 1970. It was not to be. The bombshell I have already alluded to was about to explode.

SUCCESS INTO TRAGEDY

Back in 1955 when I was performing in my second pantomime 'Old King Cole' in Birmingham, starring Vic Oliver, I first heard of the Salberg saga. The Salberg family, used throughout the year basically as a repertory company famous for weekly plays, privately owned the Alexandra theatre. Its main claim to fame was at Christmas when Derek Salberg, son of Leon, presented very lavish pantomimes with long runs of three or four months. Derek had taken over the reins when his father died and was determined to continue his legacy. In 1955 I had seen the pantomime, which starred one of the most famous principal boys Adele Dixon, and I was enthralled. Two legends in one day. Moreover I was overwhelmed by the lavish splendour of the production and wrote a letter to Mr Salberg praising his show and enclosing particulars of my meagre experience in panto. It was after all only my third year in the profession.

At that moment I was working for Tom Arnold, also a well-known impresario, in Birmingham's No.1 Theatre Royal playing my first solo role out of the chorus. 'Fools rush in where angels fear to tread' and 'faint heart never won a fair lady' - in this case, man - both adages that sprung to mind and prompted me to write the first of many yearly letters to Mr Salberg, who always replied personally. However it took 14 years before my letters bore fruit.

During those years, with many different managements, I had also gained my laurels as a well-known choreographer and my CV had gained stature. However, Mr Salberg was very loyal to his workforce and Madame Lehmiski had been his choreographer for many years, with no sign of retiring. My yearly letters had strangely formed a distant friendship and Mr Salberg's were now signed 'Derek' with the comforting promise that one day he hoped he might be able to offer me a position with his management. Yet another adage - 'patience and persistence bring their own reward'.

In 1966 I was working in the Princess theatre in Torquay, playing Slave of the Lamp in 'Aladdin' with my partner Jenny as Genie of the Ring. Sending my usual letter to Derek and expecting yet another reply similar to the previous 14 – promising, but not getting - I went into the theatre one Friday to collect my pay packet to find the usual Alexandra theatre stamped letter awaiting me.

On opening it I stared incredulously and had to read it half a dozen times before it finally sank in. Derek was inviting me to a meeting with him in Birmingham. After all these years we were finally to meet. My hands were shaking with excitement. Madame Lehmiski was retiring after the current Christmas season and Derek was in the market for someone of my calibre. Once again my guardian angel was working overtime on my behalf. With my panto season now drawing to its close I took the first available appointment and travelled to Birmingham to meet face to face with someone I had come to think of as a friendly pen pal.

It's odd how in imagination a person of great theatrical stature is contemplated as being also of great physical stature. Not so. Derek was quite diminutive but such a gentleman in every sense that we had great accord from the first moment of meeting. He sat on the boards of just about every important organisation it was possible to be on, including within the cricketing world which was his fervent hobby - almost as important as his first passion - or was it second? - the family owned Alexandra theatre.

I was now in his hallowed office, my target at last, as I had always hoped. Was it a bull's-eye? Derek had employed just about every famous, and I do mean famous, person in my profession. I was flattered to hear he had followed my career assiduously through the years, helped by my constant letters I'm sure. We both needed to know nothing further about each other. It was now a fait accompli for signing a contract, the deal being that I was to choreograph the pantomime of 1967, taking on Madame Lehmiski's dancers, which I was happy to do as her reputation was high in the dancing world.

The subject was 'Goody Two Shoes' which was rarely done and had not previously featured in my repertoire. However, I was further excited to be breaking new ground. Jenny was to play the titular role of Goody, incidentally her last role in the profession as she was marrying the singer John Lawrenson in the spring and wanted to start a family. Show business and marriage do not always combine well if each is intent on a career. Jenny and I had seen many examples to prove this point, unfortunately.

I was to be cast opposite Jenny as the evil Demon King – type casting? - and I left Derek's office and floated sky high back to London. Mission accomplished. It had taken 14 of my years but worth every one.

'Goody Two Shoes' starred the well-known Dame of Fol-de-Rols fame, Jack Tripp along with his partner Alan Christie. Fay Lenore, of some renown, played the principal boy most elegantly and in swashbuckling style. Our sword fight at the end was quite a terrifying experience, as she was well known for possessing the killer instinct. I had my work cut out to outdo her, which no villain is allowed to do. For the audience, kids and grown ups, only death will suffice.

I was also to come into contact for the first time with the renowned curries waterfalls, which Derek always encompassed in his pantomimes. He would probably have put them in his repertory plays also except there's not much opportunity. Bet the straight actors were relieved. However, with skirling highland pipers and drummers leading the entire cast all marching over the top of the falls it certainly brought the first half finale to a triumphant conclusion. Unbeatable. The second half focused on beating the power of the villain – me - with my death a certainty. The only time in showbiz when the term 'I died tonight' could be classed as success, and not a comic's graveyard, which it usually implies.

Now to bridge the gap between the Salberg pantomime and Sandy Powell's summer show. My contract with the Salberg Company continued over the next four years and I now bring readers to the 'Aladdin' production of 1969.

Sandy's 'Starlight' had finished late autumn and with my dancers we all re-assembled in December. An added bonus for me was that Colin Tarn; Sandy Powell's musical director, had accepted a contract to join the 'Aladdin' company also.

We were well into rehearsals with only four days to go to the opening night on Christmas Eve. Relaxing on Sunday in our digs over breakfast, I was suddenly called to the phone. I instantly sensed that something was wrong – intuition? My mother had unexpectedly suffered a stroke the previous evening. My father had called the doctor against my mum's wishes, and the doctor instantly called for an ambulance. During the journey she had suffered a further stroke and now was dangerously ill.

When you are young you think your parents will live forever, death is not in the equation. My dad was imploring me to return home. Wild Horses would not have kept me away. I rushed to the railway station for the first train back to London, thankfully quite frequent even on a Sunday. Howard, my Canadian friend, met me and we drove directly to the Croydon General Hospital. My parents had offered Howard a home 17 years previously, and emotionally adopted him, so he was equally concerned and worried by the situation unfolding. With my dad we stood helplessly by the bedside.

A young Indian doctor tried to comfort us saying she would come through and with help gain the use of her limbs and lead a near normal life. We were fearing the worst and frankly felt he was doing his best to break things gently to us. We decided to go back home for some tea. Mum was not even stirring. We found out later she had sunk into a coma. Returning again at visiting time, for hospitals were not open all hours as they are today, we found the situation unchanged. We held her hand, whispering encouragement, to which there was no response. A large black nurse stood on the other side of the bed. She had such a kind, sympathetic, gentle face and I asked her whether Mum would recover? She whispered softly 'I think it better to prepare yourselves and think otherwise.

We stood silent, each of us kissing her brow and whispering 'Good Night'.

Blinded by tears we left. Once at home the whisky bottle took a thrashing. What else was there to do?

The next morning my dad had gone to buy his paper trying hard to follow his usual routine. Suddenly the phone rang and I was gripped with panic knowing in my heart it was all over. The almoner told me she had passed away quietly a short while ago and could someone come in to sign the necessary papers. I waited for my dad to come back. The worst day of my life was unfolding.

I decided, even though I had no experience of the aftermath of death to relieve my dad of the arrangements and went with Howard to the hospital where the almoner told us of the procedures required. In the world of show business when anything of this nature occurs we have a comforting belief that 'Doctor Theatre' will help. This was certainly something I was about to discover.

Although heartbroken I went to the undertakers my father wished to handle the funeral. This was Monday 22 December 2005 and I was anxious to get the arrangements over before Christmas, for everyone's sake. I also explained my own situation. We all have the imperative that no matter what, the show must go on. I know that my mum would have echoed that also, for she was so overtly proud of what I'd achieved.

The undertaker understood perfectly and with a bit of re-arranging booked the funeral for 10.30am on Christmas Eve. With heartfelt thanks we returned home and I had to dash for a train back to Birmingham in time for a 6pm dress rehearsal that evening. Howard remained with my dad, helping him phone relatives and friends telling them of the arrangements.

My train journey was a lonely, silent affair but once back in the bosom of my theatrical family, sympathy was very apparent and quietly supportive. However, there is a job to do and a contract to fulfil. 'Doctor Theatre' does take control.

With concentration foremost I got through the performance. No time for tears - save them for later. Derek Salberg came up to me after the performance and said, after commiserations, 'Go home tonight to be with your family and we'll see you again on Christmas Eve'.

I will finish here by saying the whole family gathered and dispersed after the ceremony back to their Christmas arrangements.

On the train back to Birmingham I had a couple of strong gin and tonics and concentrated on the job in hand, which opened successfully for all. At times like this the theatrical profession is the greatest in the world, which I had been told and had now been proved.

Christmas passed and with no performances on Sunday – unlike today – I headed back to be with my dad. In the afternoon with my brother and his family we viewed the flowers in the cemetery. As we left I explained to my dad that I would never return there again. I wanted to keep the memory of my mum more alive than a cemetery plaque.

I only ever returned once and that was to combine my dad's ashes with mums under a dedicated white rose tree. I firmly believe in an afterlife, so no problem. Even death had not dimmed my love of theatre – re-affirmed it in fact. 'Aladdin' was playing to packed houses and friends made special journeys offering their support.

However, fate had another shock waiting round the corner. One evening after a matinée I was called to the backstage telephone to find Sandy Powell's' business manager, Norman Meadows on the line. He quietly asked if I had seen the television news – I hadn't. The next blow was about to be delivered as he told me that the theatre on Eastbourne's Pier had been totally destroyed by a maniac who had deliberately set fire to it.

Unfortunately, he went on, the contract for the summer season was now null and void. After commiserations, I replaced the receiver totally bewildered by such incomprehensible actions. What on earth was going wrong with the world? However, there was a show to perform, rant and rage later.

Further news revealed this madman had been employed to do odd jobs. This had to be his oddest. Apparently a few days earlier he had mysteriously reported a small fire, watching from a distance whilst firemen dealt with it. This is also part of a perverse enjoyment in their mad, bad world. On the day he had decided to fire the theatre for real, there was a fierce wind which swept flames through the beautiful gold and crimson Victorian theatre, where the great actor Henry Irving and his company had performed the classic plays of Shakespeare, etc. Now gone for ever – a travesty.

At the culprit's trial it was further revealed that he had fired his own home whilst his children slept. They were rescued thankfully but he was finally committed to Broadmoor for life. Which hopefully he will be forced to serve. However, although revenge can be sweet, I was still without the summer season I'd already started to plan and my dancers had lost their jobs as well.

Now for a truly happy, happy ending. Obviously now without a summer season I had made it known around the profession that I was available, together with my dancing team, and open to offers.

On the final performance of 'Aladdin' I was removing my makeup when a knock came on my dressing room door. Opening it, I discovered Frank Adey, the first director I'd ever worked for way back in Clacton in coronation year in 1953. Congratulating me on my performance he continued, 'I understand, lad, you have lost your summer season. Are you still available?' Was I? Not 'arf! 'Good, he replied 'go to Renée Stepham's office on Tuesday, she will sign you up'.

'Can I bring my dancers also?' I asked.

'Bring who you like.' We hugged, shook hands and the deal was concluded.

After he left I rushed to the girls' dressing room with the news – such rejoicing. Drinks flowed in the bar that night. We were all back in business – show business, God bless it.

On the following Tuesday I presented myself in Renée Stepham's office in the West End and it was officially signed and sealed. It was in Renée's office I had signed my very first contract in the profession so I was back where I started but with 18 years' experience behind me now. So on with the show.

NINA BROWN

1970 was the key that opened the door to the next 12 years and my second long term dancing partnership which was to extend over 13 years – unlucky for some, but certainly not for Nina and myself.

Nina's mother was the principal of a large dancing school based in Southsea, Hampshire. She had been a professional dancer in the Sadlers Wells Ballet which eventually became the Royal Ballet and obviously both her son and daughter were destined to be professional dancers with such a background. Paul, Nina's elder brother entered the Royal Ballet where he was soon elevated into principal status dancing opposite Rudolf Nureyev in 'Romeo and Juliet' amongst others. He married Biddie also a dancer with the 'Royal' and after starting a family both quit dancing. Obviously a loss to the classical world of ballet.

However, Nina carried on the tradition and when she hung up her dancing shoes in the professional theatre, partnered her mother in the Southsea school. When her mum joined the big heavenly dance school, Nina continued as principal and trained many pupils to the required standard so that they were able to train in the royal ballet schools. Quite an illustrious background. Which helped her pupils into ballet companies world wide.

However I have jumped ahead quite a bit. Nina had first joined my team in Sandy Powell's 'Starlight 68' after being a member of the famous 'Fol-de-Rols' where very strong classical ballet standards were demanded by their choreographer, Thurza Rogers. In 1970 she was still a member of my group of 6 girls but circumstances were about to change.

Frank Adey had generously taken on my dance group after the Birmingham panto 'Aladdin'. I had held out for the girls' salaries as agreed by Sandy Powell for the 1970 season which was above the Equity minimum. However he had taken advantage of my situation and not agreed to the financial terms that I had entered into with Sandy for the aborted season. However, more of that situation later.

Commencing rehearsals the company consisted of: comedian Ronnie Collis and his goat (really, live!); Pat Hatton and Gloria, a well known magic act that Jenny and I had first encountered when we were dancing on the cruise ships - Gloria was particularly worth her weight in gold for her performance in sketches, one especially when I had to portray James Bond and she vamped me – hysterical for the audience *and* me!

Chris Edwards was second pianist in the pit but was elevated to first during rehearsals. I'm not naming the MD pianist out of sympathy for his predicament. He nervously couldn't start the proceedings which obviously was frustrating for all concerned waiting for the tabs to rise on the opening. Consulting with Frank we decided to elevate Chris, who played organ, to MD which he had done before in the business. Once again, all's well that ends well. The demoted pianist still remained and played in the pit. I think the poor guy was relieved. We could still be waiting for him to start to this present day.

Halfway through rehearsing, Frank invited me to have lunch with him and his partner, Betty Martin, a talented soubrette in her time, in a little country pub, a favourite of Frank's. The day was warm and sunny and after lunch we were taking coffee in the garden when Frank gruffly said 'I'm really pleased with what you are creating and I've raised your pay packet to what you asked for originally'. I was overwhelmed by his kindness. After all he did have me over a barrel in the situation I had been placed by the Eastbourne disaster. A real gentleman and regarded by all who knew him with great regard and affection.

With my dancing team – Clacton

I still remember watching him during rehearsals in 1953. My first show, glitter dusting a set of bowler hats for an Irish scene which were not sent as he required. Being in awe of him, that was a lesson I took to heart. Even top of the range directors should be prepared to muck in to realise their vision. During my career I had worked with some so-called directors who were as useless as tits on a bull, and wondered how they reached their position.

I was always prepared to help when hard pressed stage crew where short staffed. However, I can recall a certain occasion when a particularly 'bolshie' stage manager, intent on political correctness, threatened me with strike action unless I abandoned a brush I was sweeping a filthy stage with to prevent my dancers from ruining their costumes during a strenuous routine. I've remained wary ever since but fortunately that situation has never arisen again. I have a particular dislike of 'grand' directors who hide under their position and when push comes to shove are generally totally incompetent. In show business, particularly with its total deadline of opening night, directors are in no position to cancel.

I won't go into recent West End musicals where such situations, usually stage set complications have resulted in cancellation which completely throws into chaos the box office staff. That of course is the penalty of top managements trying to emulate films with their sweeping capability. I've side tracked myself so back to the plot and Clacton in 1970.

During the run, Frankie Holmes, the comedy magician I'd previously worked with, had brought my name to the attention of John Bullock the entertainments director of Folkestone District Council. John was casting around for a creative director to present summer seasons and replace the company that had been engaged for a few years and unfortunately, in the council's view, had lost the plot. Fortunately for me Frankie's suggestion was taken up and Mr Bullock contacted me to arrange a date to view my work.

During the show I had presented a couple of classical ballet routines, one of which I particularly wanted Mr Bullock to see. This was called 'Autumn' in which I had given the lead role to Nina. Unfortunately the date chosen by the director of entertainment from Folkestone did not include this particular routine so I asked Frank if I could substitute the 'Autumn' ballet. He refused saying, 'Why should I help you to leave my company for another?' I saw his point though was disappointed.

I enjoyed working with Frank but wanted to get south again and nearer to my flourishing 'second fiddle' business, my restaurant in Sussex.

On the day that Mr Bullock and his partner were due to arrive Frank said 'OK lad, substitute the ballet you want, I understand your reason.' God bless him! He had been my guru ever since I had entered the profession through the door he opened for me. I had taken many of his ideas on board and they had served me well.

Two or three days later I received a letter inviting me to Folkestone to discuss the future which was eventually to stretch over the next 12 years.

FOLKESTONE 1971

During the spring I was invited to lunch to discuss my ideas for the summer show. I had not even met John Bullock when he travelled to Clacton to view my work. He had returned to Folkestone immediately after the performance. I had in fact never visited the resort at all. This was virgin territory to me. However the Leas Cliff Hall was a most impressive building set on the famous Leas which in Victorian time thronged with the haute monde strolling and listening to military bands playing in the rotunda. Large Hotels facing on to the Leas were packed with visitors and after 6pm only the gentry who dressed in evening attire were allowed to promenade before dinner. Errand boys on bicycles and low life were turned away by official wardens unless they were suitably attired to mingle with the refined atmosphere. A long lost age ago.

John Bullock was an extremely tall, quietly spoken man with military bearing due to his wartime service. We were instantly on a mutual wavelength and I chatted over lunch about my ideas for the summer season. The Leas Cliff Restaurant had views stretching across the English Channel to the French coast. On really clear days it was possible to see cars traversing the French coast, not so on this particular day.

After lunch John and his side-kick accompanied me down to the Marine Pavilion. 'Down' and 'marine' were the operative words for it nestled on the shingle beach. So this was the place where the shows were actually presented. I well remember my horrified introduction and I was initially prepared to refuse the contract. It was not at all what I was used to. In the winter months the Pavilion did service as a roller skating rink. It was crowded with loud mouthed, scruffy louts. Dusty, even dirty. I was appalled.

John assured me that a total transformation took place before rehearsals began to turn the building into a 'dome of delight'. Oh yeah?

On returning to the calm of the Leas Cliff Hall for some tea – I needed more than tea to change my mind – John brought out some photographs of the transformation, which were not too impressive. However, further conversation started me thinking that with the carte blanche I was being given it could be quite a challenge – something I've always relished. Thank goodness I didn't resist for what was about to happen would stand me in good stead for the next 35 years. Sounds ludicrous doesn't it? You wait.

With the contract signed for the Folkestone show which was to be entitled 'Show Time', it was time to get various departments together that are needed for the making of a production. Vic Friendly who I had worked with for a number of years with other managements, was contracted to supply the sets, his studios in Hastings being well placed for consultation. Also contracted was my friend Rosemary Waters who was to supply the costumes. I had worked with her for a number of years when I was directing for Duncan Weldon and Paul Elliott's Triumph Organisation. Rosemary had access to the vast wardrobe department of that company which she controlled on their behalf.

Things were starting to fall into place and I was happy to have dancers who had worked previously with me. Nina was officially contracted as principal dancer for the first time, teaming with me. For that first season, however, Jenny had expressed a desire to return to the business, especially as her husband John Lawrenson had been signed as the principal male singer. He was a star name after all his appearances as principal baritone on 'Friday Night is Music Night' on the radio and television. I had also appeared on the television programmes as a

This was a classical ballet excerpt from 'Copella'.

dancer, occasionally with John. Then my old friend Billy Burden as the comic. It began to look like a family affair when Colin Tarn the musical director, who I had first met in Sandy Powell's show, joined the company. Everything was falling into place with uncanny success which augured well for the future. Nevertheless, we still had the hurdle of the first night to overcome.

In retrospect 1971 was about to be cataclysmic for me on a personal level. For the first time in my career I was not under the comforting umbrella of a professional theatrical organisation. This was my first encounter with local authorities and their appointed officers who were for the first time entering show business with all its ramifications.

I welcomed the rescue operation of local authorities intent on keeping their venues open for light entertainment. The traditional companies who specialised in summer entertainment were going out of business due to rising costs and dwindling audiences for English coastal resorts, who were intent on seeking sunnier climes for their main holidays. What I was not prepared for was the vaunted ambition of locally elected councillors to be impresarios, who could not organise a booze-up in a brewery in my view. Once again, more of that insidious intervention later.

I was now preparing to work with John Bullock, the entertainments director of Folkestone Corporation. Whilst we were virtual strangers at this moment I soon came to gain much respect for him. He never interfered and was happy to leave the production in my hands, and with the assembled company, I was very confident that it would work.

Alas, confidence is not sufficient in the embryonic situation I was about to enter. The show's construction was a major consideration, not only to display the company's talents but also to appeal to the prospective audiences. With my experience of lavish productions and large financial budgets, I now needed to 'temper the wind to the shorn lamb', not that Folkestone Corporation were mean in that department. Fortunately, the set designer and costume supplier were friends of long standing who I had worked with previously in other companies and were prepared – no, eager – to produce visually what my artistic vision had in mind.

With all the local newspaper hype about the new styled production being put into place by the corporation there were obviously going to be two channels of thought, for and against. Nevertheless I was undaunted, believing that my previous experiences enabled me to have a clear vision of what was needed for rounded productions that could appeal to all audiences.

I found that walking around the area and speaking with the locals gave me the insight necessary to realise the style of show I was about to produce. Not in any patronising manner but more exploratory, by staging ideas from across the whole theatrical spectrum.

Firstly I needed to stage my own good luck symbol within the first show. This was my ballet, 'Slaughter on 10th Avenue', which I had created 16 years previously. It had then gained me my choreographic crown and I regarded it, rather superstitiously, as my lucky talisman.

For the first and the only time, both my dancing partners Jenny and Nina were together in the show and I shared equal status between them. Especially in the 'Slaughter' ballet where their differing styles were superbly displayed. After two weeks of intensive rehearsals the whole company had gelled into one cohesive unit – all for one and one for all.

For the very first time I had overall control, no star name producer on their ego trip to whom I was obliged to meekly co-operate because he or she paid the salaries. It was an opportunity I relished, not for my own ego but because I entertained a fervent belief in what I anticipated audiences would enjoy.

Now with my dream team in all sections in place I was about to embark on the most exciting 32 years of my entire career. This was to culminate in a personal invitation from Her Majesty the Queen to the first ever garden party at Sandringham for my services to the variety theatre. Being a fervent royalist this was more than I could ever have dreamt of.

However, back to the first night of Folkestone's first corporation production, 'Showtime 71'. On with the motley – 'Overture and Beginners" – curtains up and on with the show.

At the first night party given by the council, all the local celebrities, bigwigs and hangers on were vociferous in their praise and congratulations. In his welcoming speech the chairman forecast that the show would break all previous records which on reflection, I recalled seeing headlines in a newspaper report for the previous summer stating 'Seaside Spectacular makes spectacular loss'. So we had little to beat. However as another belief of mine is that 'self praise is no recommendation', I shall desist and merely quote from the showbiz report in Folkestone's premier paper the Herald on Saturday 5 June 1971 by Ron Green.

JOHN DOES IT HIS WAY … AND HIS SHOW IS A TRIUMPH

'I did it my way' is a line from a song in Folkstone's new summer show. It fits the bill as far as the corporation's entertainments manager, Mr John Bullock, is concerned. Mr Bullock may well feel like singing. He played a key role in presenting Showtime 71, which is undoubtedly a triumph for him, the cast and the town. If it doesn't make a profit, Folkestone may as well not bother to have a summer show in future.

It is already being acclaimed as the best summer show the town has had for many years – if not the best ever. After seeing the first night on Saturday, I go along with that. Quite frankly I think Showtime 71 is better than a seaside town like Folkestone should expect to have for the limited resources available.

What is more, the backstage story is just as entertaining as the show itself. It has all the ingredients of those old Hollywood musicals ... judging by the first-night, there really is no reason why it should not be a resounding success. It is a sparkling mixture of entertainment designed to please the palate no matter what the taste of the audience. Just as any seaside summer show should be.

Costumes, scenery and lighting are colourful, imaginative and constantly changing. The cast obviously has a lot of talent and works very well together. What lifts it out of the category of previous summer shows is that it is vibrant and so highly polished that it glides smoothly along. Probably the man most responsible for this effect is producer and choreographer Robert Marlowe. Folkestone Corporation was lucky to get him. Robert spent two years with the summer show in Eastbourne – and if the Pier theatre had not burned down he would still be there. It was his idea to introduce a short, modern and highly effective ballet.

Most of the cast join in the scene, which has a simple little moral - drug takers get hurt.

It is not the only movement of sobriety. There are classical songs from baritone John Lawrenson, of Friday Night is Music Night television fame and Diane Marie Lally, as well as a delightful Pas-de-Deux from Robert Marlowe and Nina Brown.

The farmyard humour of top-of-the bill comic Billy Burden, the droll Dorsetshire bumpkin who has the smug, cheeky look of someone who has been dragged through a haystack by the milkmaid, was in fine form. There was also musical comedy from Rod King who combines jokes with some remarkable playing on a steel guitar, and Glyn Evans and Kathy Downey, who between them seem to play enough instruments to form a band. Supporting them are the six Showtime Dancers who have figures to display their costumes to the full.

For me the evening's high spot came when everyone joined in a colourful, riotous cockney sing-a-long. It was nicely updated by the use of some more modern London numbers from recent films, such as 'Oliver'.

Full marks must go to musical director Colin Tarn, who wrote some of the material especially for the show. This glittering package is gift-wrapped in a Marine Pavilion that has been cleverly converted from a five-a-side soccer rink to a sophisticated nightspot. So there it is, probably the best summer show that Folkestone has ever had. Even if this kind of revue is not up your street.

The show is a damn good 45 pence worth. In fact it is too good to keep for the holidaymakers – so go and see it for yourself.

This was the verdict on the previous two weeks' backbreaking endeavours. Attending the first night party the whole company exhaled and basked in the vociferous praises being showered on them by the guests. With only Sunday to recover the whole company were given the rehearsal call for Monday at 10am to commence rehearsals for Showtime 71, second edition.

The really hard slog was about to begin with the daily rehearsals topped by the evening shows. However we were floating on cloud nine and game for anything.

That a wise director will not put all his eggs in one basket was advice I took on board at an early stage in my career. Happily the second edition of Showtime 71 was received with equal acclaim and we were all heading for a moneymaking success, which boded well for the future.

The problems with a success though are manifold. Firstly; when one is an unknown quantity there is little expectation. Once you have unveiled your ideas and ability much is expected for the future, which puts extra pressure on how to follow and capitalise on the first success. Therefore the second season is the true testing ground.

THE NEXT DECADE OF SHOWTIME

Once my contract was signed and sealed for the summer of 1972 it was imperative to discuss casting of the personnel. Due to the previous year's fantastic success, agents and managements were rushing to get on the bandwagon, sending in their clients' details and CVs for perusal. As comedy is essential in the making of any production this has first priority.

Felix Bowness had been the principal comic in my first Brandon and Pounds 'Out of the Blue' season in Felixstowe in 1955. He was very experienced in the style of shows we were embarking on so was contracted to top of the bill. Other signees were: ventriloquist John Bouchier; Gwenfron Hughes and Brian Kemp, classically trained singers but versatile in all styles; and a fabulous wizard on the xylophone Julius Nehring, with whom I had previously worked. Finally the Showtime Dancers, many of whom had worked with me previously. They were led by Nina Brown, my second dancing partner who was destined to remain with me for the next 12 years until she left the profession to become principal of her mother's well respected dance academy. The indispensable Colin Tarn was again responsible for the musical arrangements, so on paper it looked set for a successful second season. Wrong! The old proverb that chickens should not be counted before they hatch was about to be proved correct.

Unfortunately, during rehearsals, Felix Bowness had asked John Bullock if he could present a give-away interlude at some point during the show. Apparently he had a contract with a company, which toured the country during certain periods giving away small articles in a question and answer game show. Really only a disguise for an advertising gimmick for much larger electrical appliances.

To say I was horrified by this suggestion would be putting it mildly. In my scheme of entertainment it had no place. Such rank commercialisation … However, Felix was very determined and persuaded John that it would be an advertising gimmick and encourage people to participate for small gifts in the style of 'Sunday Night at the Palladium' on television. Obviously John was wary of upsetting the top of the bill at this stage, so conferring with him I suggested that it might be sandwiched after the opening of the show into a 10-minute spot and finished with. After that it would be on with the show. I remained a very unhappy bunny. This was nothing I wished to have my professional acumen linked with.

As the first night approached I became more apprehensive when I discovered extremely large boxes containing electrical apparatus such as stoves and refrigerators, etc in an area of the theatre not in use. Try not to imagine my fury arriving at the theatre one morning to find the box office covered in posters proclaiming a give-away show and the aforementioned electrical items blocking the entire area. It resembled an ideal home exhibition rather than a summer variety theatrical production.

I immediately rang John Bullock's office requesting him to come down as soon as possible to view what I considered would be a deterrent to anyone wishing to book for the summer show. John hurried down ad was equally dismayed and demanded that the Pavilion manager remove the offending apparatus. Naturally Felix Bowness was quite upset that John refused to allow the box office to be cluttered in this manner. Later, a compromise was reached in which John agreed Felix could do just a ten-minute spot after the opening of the show, which I had originally suggested. This enabled the contract that Felix had with the manufacturers to remain extant.

Unfortunately the atmosphere within the company was to say the least downcast at what most of the pros felt was blatant commercialisation. The whole situation deteriorated even further when the ten minutes agreed 'give-away spot' extended to over half an hour. Although Felix could be a likeable and funny

'Kings Rhapsody' by Ivor Novello

112

comic, his timing could be erratic and after this episode, John Bullock withdrew the give-away gimmick altogether.

Unfortunately other incidents occurred during the season, which cast a shadow over the company for the rest of the run. A complaint was made by Felix and brought to the council's attention. Over-officious elected councillors, anxious to flex their muscles, rushed to convene a meeting in an attempt to condemn the actions of the entertainments director John Bullock. Oh, the arrogance of these self-important posers. Only a year before they were effusive in their praise of John, for bringing a successful season into fruition. As director of the summer show I attended the meeting and furiously supported John whilst condemning the coterie who had conspired to cause trouble. Unfortunately a sticky atmosphere prevailed. Not however within the show as presented to the packed audiences attending the performances. We were after all dedicated professionals and the show must go on – if only to earn our salaries.

I have never encountered this situation again. Furthermore I never encountered Felix Bowness again, although he went on to perform in various cameo roles on television such as 'Hi-de-Hi' and others.

The season finished and we all went our separate ways. Nina and I together with the dancers were engaged for 'Babes in the Wood' in the beautiful Richmond theatre for the Triumph Organisation, with a truly star studded cast.

In retrospect, after the quite phenomenal success of Showtime 71 in Folkestone, I was relieved when the season of 1972 terminated due to the atmosphere generated by certain disturbing elements bent on personal battles. It only takes one lousy apple in a barrel to contaminate others.

Please forgive me if I now mount my soapbox. When I first entered show business in 1953 true theatrical impresarios ruled, professionals who had come through the ranks forming their own companies and in certain cases like the Salbergs and Popplewells even owning their own family theatres or having extremely long leases on others. With the coming of television and holidays abroad many professional theatres became victims of a decreasing market and many smaller showbiz companies went sadly into liquidation. With many theatres now under the control of local authorities some were becoming white elephants and an expensive liability.

A new era was about to surface when entertainment officers, under the control of locally elected councillors, were encouraged to embrace the professionals and enter the world of showbiz. The wise ones contacted professionals with sound theatre backgrounds and proven ability thereby, ensuring as far as possible a certain success. Readers who have followed my path through the profession will realise by now that I have a certain disdain for elected councillor, not all I hasten to add, but the Johnny-come-lately's -

business people who put themselves forward to promote their standing in the community - the chain wearers, first in line for the freebies.

Show business has always been a magnet for amateurs in all walks of life. Now councillors viewed themselves as impresarios with power. I do not take kindly to butchers, bakers and candlestick makers lecturing me about my own profession. It has always been my baby and I will fight ferociously for its survival. I will now descend from my soapbox hoping I've not bored the pants off readers.

However, proof of what I have just expressed will be evident a few years ahead, when a certain gentleman, I use the term loosely, took personal revenge on me, which he engineered successfully, but in retrospect did me the greatest possible favour. Biter bit!

The season of 1972 was thankfully now behind me. It had not been a particularly happy situation due to all the hassle initiated by certain company members. However, being a thoroughly professional group any disarray was kept under wraps as far as the public were concerned. The success of my first production in 1971 was sustained and the show of 72 had achieved high ratings with the audiences, again financially viable for the corporation. I was contracted to produce the season for 1973.

Meeting with John Bullock in the autumn we agreed that we needed to be more scrupulous with regard to the casting, especially the top of the bill. Using my previous knowledge of artistes that I had worked congenially with I suggested Frankie Holmes. I certainly owed him a favour, as it was his introduction that had brought my work to the notice of John Bullock initially.

Frankie has great charm and warmth, even to the present day, and more importantly is extremely funny. He had been principal comic for the Clarkson Rose companies and knew exactly the formula required for seaside shows. Having worked two seasons with him in Sandy Powell's' seasons of 'Starlight' in Eastbourne I had never known him to fail. He was a sure fire hit with audiences. Once his contract was in place it was necessary to find a second comedic support.

Agents contacted proffered their clients and John booked George Meaton as top support to Frankie. Kathy Downey and Glyn Evens who had been so successful in my first production were engaged for their second season. A musical instrumental act, they were extremely versatile and useful in the production scenes. Kathy also had a beautiful singing voice.

I have always favoured classically trained singers and dancers which I firmly believe gives an excellent foundation to their talents and a greater ability to work across the whole spectrum which is necessary in variety productions. I have also always favoured open auditions, which allow performers to sign their own contracts, thereby avoiding commission to agents - dancers especially, as they were usually the hardest worked and lowest paid, unless they were principals. I always remained loyal to my girls and many remained with me until they left to get married. I was generally able to get them year round work with long running pantomimes, revues and summer seasons. I still remain in touch with many to the present day. Some went on to play leads in musicals in the West End and I am so proud of their achievements.

The singers contracted for Summer 73 were a pretty soprano Christine Lion and a Spanish tenor Valerio Martinez, darkly handsome to set female hearts fluttering. Nina and I were to present new acts and ballets and to work throughout as foils to the comics. As I have previously stated with smaller companies, everyone had to muck in – no passengers. Some of my dancers even discovered a singing talent they never realised they possessed.

The musical director was again Colin Tarn. We had by now formed a close cooperation and his exceptional talent for composing was a most useful asset. If we couldn't find suitable music for certain situations – easy peasy – he wrote it. With the whole company now in place I turned my attention to the theme I required to hook the show on.

I decided to commence with an airport scene with the company embarking on a worldwide trip encompassing Spain, Greece, France, Holland and even Scotland. We engaged for this scene, a Highland piper, leading the entire company over a waterfall, dressed in kilts and colours of all the clans which

This was a ballet I created based on 'Alice in Wonderland'.

delighted all the Scots in the audience and led them into the bar for a wee dram during the interval. A clever business ploy for the bars.

Rehearsals usually started after Easter and were an extremely concentrated two weeks to get the show ready for the opening night. One of the oddest situations occurred on the first morning, which had never happened previously in my career, or since. More of this later.

I am now going to explain to readers the formula needed to get an original production up and running. The whole company is called the first Monday for 10am and prompt timing is essential for the whole period. With only two weeks to rehearse every minute is precious. All concerned are absolutely professional but in many cases called to perform in situations that are totally alien. The first call enables all to meet over a coffee and also to be greeted by the various local authority bigwigs and press officers to gain advance publicity for the first night.

Once this is over the dancers are sent to the wardrobe department for costume fittings, which hopefully will do just that – fit. All performers will have been sent costume measurement forms well in advance for outfits that were being made from scratch, whilst others were being hired. A combination of both.

The principals are taken by the musical director to acquaint them with the musical numbers they will be involved with during the production, setting the keys to enable the non-singers a comfortable chance to participate without embarrassing themselves - very necessary in a small company of only 12 to 15 artistes. Most complied, happily relishing the chance of extending their individual talents. However a setback was lurking just around the corner.

The working day involved 8 hours with an hour for lunch and refreshment breaks mid morning and afternoon. Breaking for lunch on the first day I expected all to be back at 2pm to start putting the production scenes together. Whilst most of the company were enthusiastically back early trying to memorise the words of the songs, one person was missing. I waited patiently for George Meaton, the support comedy act to return – no sign of him. Eventually I rang the office, making enquiries as to whether he was there. Still no sign. Eventually I was informed he had done a bunk and we never saw him again or since. Apparently he had not anticipated the cooperation required in the production scenes and had broken his contract. Obviously he wasn't used to the summer show ethos where everyone did everything. A most useful academy of paid theatre training for even experienced performers, now sadly lost forever with the gradual demise of these type of shows – never to return.

At least Mr Meaton had bunked on the first, not the last, day of rehearsals when he would have really set the cat amongst the pigeons.

We now had to find a replacement quickly. Frankie suggested someone he had worked with previously and thought would be an excellent asset to the company, so Bernie Landy was contracted and proved to be a most congenial and useful member with his comedy act. As Shakespeare wrote 'All's well that ends well'.

Bernie was also an amateur filmmaker. He devised a working script during the summer and the whole company cooperated and we filmed a short film around the show. Shooting outdoor scenes throughout Kent, even the local vicar Peter Cole allowed us to use the parish church tower to double as a castle for 'The King's New Clothes' scene which was featured in the summer show. This had the combined effect of very good publicity when holidaymakers joined the throng watching the outside shots being very professionally engineered. Even the backstage crew joined in on the technical side acting as 'gofers', etc. A very happy experience for all concerned and I still have a video as the only record, visually, of the 1973 show.

Incidentally I never did find out what George Meaton's act was all about.

With 73 up and running my job of devising and directing was basically finished apart from keeping an eye on maintaining the standards. That's not a problem when working with dedicated professionals.

Whilst I do need to substantiate the success of each show there is only one way to do that. By the unsolicited reports of the theatre critics in the local press.

The Herald
Saturday 2 June 1973
Ken Hamer

SHOWTIME IS SET TO BREAK ALL RECORDS

You can have too much of a good thing. That is an old adage based on the frailties of human nature. But there are exceptions to every rule and Showtime, Folkestone summer entertainment for the third successive year, is one of them. Before a critical first–night audience on Saturday the cast of 14 flung that saying into a backstage rubbish bin at the Marine Pavilion after two seasons of success. Showtime has not gone stale for Folkestone.

Indeed the 150 minutes production is good and thousands of holidaymakers and residents will feast on its special brand of fun and gaiety. Whilst Showtime 73, again splendidly devised and produced by Bob Marlowe, disproves one old saying it demonstrates the accuracy of another, that things come in threes. The first of the successful Showtimes set new standards in Folkestone entertainments. The 1972 was even better.

The current production gives indications of breaking all previous records. Showtime has all the traditional ingredients of summer entertainment;

glamour, dancing, singing, zany humour and music stirred together with a large dollop of exuberance and team work.

The final mixture is a smooth, fast moving, family show. It's a personal triumph for Bob, who is also the talented choreographer and for Folkestone's entertainment director John Bullock, who stake their professional reputation on its success. From a team of 14 it is difficult to single out anyone for a special mention. All contribute to its success. But the star is Frankie Holmes. A comedian with an inborn sense of fun. A goon with a spontaneous wit.

I will stop there before you become too bored to continue. However, the final sentence bears out my view that the most important members of any show have to be the comedians. If the comedy fails the show struggles no matter how good the supporting cast may be. All performers believe their particular talents - singing, dancing, etc - to be most important, and of course they are, but only in the overall context.

Rule No.1 – no comedy, no show.

Working directly for the first time with a local authority, I realise with hindsight that I should have insisted on a contractual arrangement of a certain period rather than the year-to-year agreements in place back in the 70s. When a devisor/director has a period contract it allows for pre-planning which has benefits all round. For instance one can budget for costumes and sets, always expensive, which can be utilised in another form in following years. Little did I realised in 1973 that on the yearly system my tenure was to continue for a further 9 years.

Being engrossed in my professional responsibilities, I was quite unaware of the major local authority changes already planned and about to go into operation. Suddenly, my mentor John Bullock the entertainment director was no longer around. His place was now occupied by his assistant, Nigel Stewart but only temporarily until a new entertainment director could be appointed. Folkestone Corporation no longer existed, having been amalgamated into a larger area to be called Shepway District Council. Oh dear, more councillors with bigger ideas?

I was freelance and concentrated on my commitment to the shows although I did ponder that 'new brooms sweep clean'. However, with three years accomplished, the shows were now strongly established and almost attaining a cult status. 'They' wouldn't dare – would they?

Later during the summer I had a request to meet a Councillor Brown, Chairman of, …….. I didn't know what. During proposals put to me during the meeting I decided he was chairman of the 'dirty ideas' department.

With Showtime so popular and attracting large audiences, his idea was to muscle in and take advantage by presenting a late night Saturday cabaret show using the company in a cut down version of the original but – wait for it – bringing in strippers to go the whole hog. He excitedly went on that if it was to prove popular it could be extended to further nights. The air around me turned blue, the right colour for his ideas in my view. He was astonished that I was so vehemently against his lucrative money–making ideas. In his defence he brought up the knowledge that he had garnered from my biographic details that I'd spent a couple of years in the Folies Begere. It was no use trying to explain that the Folies was so extravagant and beautifully presented attracting visitors worldwide. Not the sordid titillating spectacle he wished to present in Folkestone.

Refusing completely to even consider such a move I threatened that I would report him to Equity, the showbiz union, for suggesting even altering our contracts which still pertained.

The question never arose again and I had far superior areas of entertainment already formulating for future productions, which were to achieve praise much higher than I could have anticipated.

I must defend my ideas as I certainly never intended to belittle certain areas where 'risky' ideas were desired. However in presenting any show one must take into account what goes where. There are certain towns and resorts where I would not dream of doing the sort of show that I had presented in Folkestone, Eastbourne, etc. Places like Blackpool, Yarmouth, Glasgow need a brasher more rumbustious style.

I'm not being patronising, but it's a well known fact that one must adapt to differing areas and resorts. In the comedy stakes certain comedians work better south than north and visa-versa. Likewise when music halls were still around comics would change their acts according to the audiences. In fact comedians face the hardest task of all, for what can make one audience roll around hysterically can find another sitting po-faced, using the identical joke. It's a mystery which comics face consistently, and that is why they are usually the highest paid performers in any production, deservedly so. For they sometimes pay highly for good jokes. directors also tend to specialise in certain types of production which they become well known for. I had decided, once I was able to pick and choose to target, the production companies that I wanted to work with, and I quickly learnt that persistence does bring its own reward.

In the latter part of 1973, a new entertainments director was appointed, Derrick Blackburn, and his wife Norma together with his daughter and son set up home.

It was now a case of 'the king is dead – long live the king'. We formed a good relationship. Derrick was a London boy, as was I, and he remained right up until I departed 9 years later. Which was rewarding for continuity. Derrick had previously held his position in a London borough booking variety bills, etc so had knowledge of the sort of artistes suitable for Showtime, a great advantage.

So there ended the summer of 73 which broke all expectations both artistically, and more importantly, financially. Once again we all packed up camp and departed for our winter pastures new. 'Gypsies' as the American theatrical profession labels showbiz folk. Nina and I, together with my team of dancers were heading for our Christmas contracts in pantomime.

With the spring of 1974 coming into full bloom, the planning stage for the summer show loomed. Derrick Blackburn, the new entertainment director for Shepway was now preparing to put together his first summer season for Folkestone, together with myself.

Top of our list were of course the comics. Acting on my suggestion, because I had worked with them in 1963 in Richard Stone's show in Worthing, Derrick engaged Gordon and Bunny Jay. They are one of the best comedy acts in the business and should have been recognised nationwide in my view. They could certainly hold their own amongst the likes of Morecombe and Wise, The Two Ronnies, and Little and Large, had they ever been given the opportunity of their own TV shows, which was a necessary benchmark back in the 60s/70s. However they never stopped working, so, fame enough in our profession.

Recently I was present when they performed their hand bells act during a festival of music halls and variety in Weston-Super-Mare. This was before an

This photo with Gordon and Bunny Jay was taken in 2004 at a special celebration dinner – they were my longest standing comedy act in my various shows.

audience of mainly fellow professionals and they were given a standing ovation, praise indeed. Fellow pros are not usually so generous.

Derrick also engaged a young, up-and-coming ventriloquist Tony Venner to fill the second comedy spot. The musical vacancy was filled by a famous trumpet player, Joan Hinde. A great gal with a wicked sense of humour, which she used to great effect feeding Gordon and Bunny in their wealth of funny sketches.

The singers were soprano Diane-Marie Lally who I had worked with previously and tenor Louis Brown. With Nina and I leading our team of dancers the casting was complete. Colin Tarn was once again the musical director, adding to his audience popularity with Sunday morning music entertainment in the Leas Cliff Hall.

As before Rosemary Waters was supplying costumes and Vic Friendly, the set designer, in charge of creating the effective scenery, which made a small stage appear to have the capacity of the London Palladium. Also he created the theatre décor which turned a virtual 'shed' into a glittering showcase palace, brilliantly.

With my dream team in place we were all set to go. As I have already detailed the process of rehearsals, there is no need to reiterate the unchanging plan of action towards the civic reception opening night. This was now becoming the eagerly awaited fixture in Folkestone's social calendar when the haute monde turned out in their fineries, not forgetting their chains of office, naturally.

With this being the fourth production I had devised, the show was yet another resounding success on all accounts. A headline emblazoned on the editorial page of the local paper stated:

GO AND SEE IT FOR YOURSELF

The outcome, as seen on the stage of the Marine Pavilion, is a summer spectacular more worthy than any show the town has seen for years – if ever.

It is a show Folkestone is lucky to have – lucky because it has the man capable of getting it together, lucky because for the limited budget available it is better than one can reasonably expect. And if you don't believe it is that good – go and see it for yourself.

With the season of 74 triumphantly coming to its conclusion we all enjoyed a last night party and went our separate ways.

The problem attendant on growing success is that it can come perilously close to being a poisoned chalice. With expectation high there's no room for smugness or self-congratulation. During the show my mind was exploring possibilities for 1975. This could prove to be wasted effort if my services were not required. However, as the council's decision came before the last night and was positive, my ideas were back into play in 75. With pantomime now bridging the period between summer and winter, my attention was focused on the job in hand so the following summer show was on the back burner.

Returning home in February 1975 after enjoying a truly mild winter down in Devon, where Nina and I had appeared with a host of 'Carry On' stars in 'Babes in the Wood' at the Princess theatre, Torquay, my attention turned to the casting of Folkestone's fifth production of Showtime.

Howard Eastman, my Canadian friend and partner in our Sussex restaurant, who you may recall came to England in 1953 to train at RADA, was still a devoted theatre-goer with interest across the whole spectrum - opera, ballet, musicals, etc and would frequently draw my attention to an artiste he surmised would be perfect for one of my productions.

He had attended a show in Hastings, starring Jack Tripp supported by a young comedian Des King, and entreated me to see him working. I did and was very impressed, so when the season of 75 was again my responsibility, I made sure that Folkestone secured his services as the top of the bill. It was a very successful and happy decision. Second top was trumpet player Bobbie Stewart, an all round entertainer.

I had decided to try an experiment in this, which I had toyed with for a couple of years and then lost my nerve. Harking back to the 60s and 'Sunday Night at the London Palladium' on television, I recalled the audience appreciation when classical interludes of ballet and opera were presented by stars of that genre, especially when included within a variety bill. The contrast was received quite excitedly and I had concluded that it flattered the audience's intelligence.

I was eager to try out an excerpt from a well known opera as a total surprise. Nina and I had danced classical par-de-deux and entractes, together with the girls who were all classically trained, and discovered that interludes of this nature, kept brief, were admired and appreciated. I hasten to add I was not being patronising, it's just that I believe all branches of entertainment should be able to cohabit.

I recall as a child being taken by my parents to see a variety bill in the Stoll theatre in London with famous comics and singers. One included item was a table tennis display of skill starring Victor Barna, a champion player. I was confused but fascinated, and held the belief that any skills expertly displayed could be entertaining. Which I believe to this present day.

Conferring with Derrick Blackburn I persuaded him to hold auditions to engage four operatically trained singers. A classical training does not limit performers to one style alone. Singers, like dancers, encompass all the skills - jazz, pop, and the latest musicals. However, classical training gives an extra edge.

Announcing auditions in the profession's bible 'The Stage', we were inundated by singers and had to extend the period booked for the studio. No one was to be turned away before auditioning. After about three hours of recalls we finalised on a married duo who had sung in the D'Oyly Carte Opera Company. Soprano Joan Lawrence and baritone Alan Lloyd. Completing the quartet were mezzo soprano Shirley Rayner and tenor Anthony Menary, both experienced in opera and West End musicals. With all the vocal requirements they all possessed that other desirability – good looks. They were definitely eye candy for the audiences.

For the season of 75 I needed three dancers to complete my group. Dancing auditions are always inundated with hopefuls. With infinite choice it is truly heartbreaking to have to turn so many away, especially when the standards are extremely high.

I was disappointed when Colin Tarn, my musical director for five years decided on a change of direction. His talents required other avenues of exploration. Working with Bernard Miles Mermaid theatre in London and the Edinburgh Festival, he achieved great success in this other realm.

So we had to find another MD for Showtime 75. Enter Maurice Paige who had worked extensively in Australia and New Zealand and was now seeking work in his homeland. His skills in musicals, jazz and opera secured his contract and completed our casting. During rehearsals the company gelled instantly and

This scene represents a Mississipi Showboat

a happy atmosphere helped to smooth the concentrated and strenuous period always par for the course up to the opening night. I have to confess that certain nosey parker councillors calling in during the rehearsal period expressed doubts about the opera content. I remained undaunted and determined, having the complete support of the performers whose distinctive skills were being positively exploited.

The set required for the Rigoletto quartet was a double one requiring both interior and exterior of a tavern and Vic had produced a stunning design, likewise the costumes by Rosemary. With fingers crossed I eagerly awaited the first night.

The quartet was scheduled for the second half and hopes were high that it would be received favourably. Favourably was not the word, rather sensationally, enthusiastically was more to the point. Calls of 'more' and 'encore' resounded through the Pavilion. I'm sure Verdi must have been revolving with delight.

Opera goers never call for an encore knowing full well it isn't going to happen. However an operatically innocent audience have no such scruples – they did not get an encore. The response had been so overwhelming that I included an operatic spot in every following production, which became an expected custom amongst the audiences. I had been fully vindicated in my belief that classics and pop could co-exist in the same shows providing it's performed by artistes with expertise. Once again I will let the expert critic give account.

Gazette
Drew Smith

I say, I say, I say, this Showtime is another winner. Showtime 75 is one great big birthday cake. There is a layer of Hollywood, a layer of Gilbert and Sullivan and one of comedy, and in the end it's one great big, extravagant, colourful, show business success...

Mainly thanks to Bob Marlowe who devises, directs and choreographs. But this year was to be different – a breakaway from the tried and trusted formula.

Showtime 75 is a nostalgic kaleidoscope of musical memories...... it opens with a wow and the Showtime chorus sings... There's No Business Like Show Business... then on bounces Des King who teases the audience into life with such classics as We've Got An Orange Tree In Our Garden – It Took Me Six Months To Paint It. Back to the roaring 20s with excerpts from No! No! Nanette and a little magic with a glass and whisky bottle from Des King... The first half ended with all the differing parts coming together like a clash of symbols in a rip-roaring cycle of songs and dances from Oklahoma. Everyone obviously enjoyed this routine, not least the Showtime Girls. The second half opened with songs from 'Oliver'. Followed by what was, for me, the high spot of the evening, an extract from 'Rigoletto' sung by Anthony Menary, Alan Lloyd, Joan Lawrence and Shirley Raynor. At once they managed to stamp the magic of opera on the small theatre. They slipped almost naturally from the frivolous fun – making spirit into serious emotional mood which had the audience crying for more at the end. No encore was allowed and Bobby Stewart, guest artiste trumpeter arrived to take up the reins. By this time the battle was won. The show was a winner all the way. The routine from the 'King and I', the tribute to Ivor Novello were preaching to the converted......... What a winner. What more can I say?

Des King and I shared a dressing room and from day one instinctively bonded, forming a strong friendship which survives today. During conversation I discovered that I had worked with his first wife – Jenny Maynard, back in 1958. I had been engaged as choreographer since gaining my laurels in 1955 as a competent dance arranger.

Jenny was playing Aladdin, the titular role and I was the Slave of the Lamp in the Grand theatre, Swansea. Jenny eventually starred on television in the impressionist show 'Who do you do?' Stage struck Des had met and married Jenny whilst working on a farm. But with ambition to enter showbiz himself. Sadly the marriage failed. I never asked questions, they divorced.

Needing to find three replacement dancers for Showtime 75 I held auditions and selected the dancers with the qualities I required who were to continue in my group until they left to further careers. Their names were Vivienne Law, Margaret Sheffield and Cherith Towler, I have named them deliberately because they have all become important players in my life since. Vivienne auditioned with an ulterior motive. She had worked as a dancer elsewhere the previous year when Des was the comedy lead and decided he was the one for her. Obviously I had selected Vivienne for her dancing skills and appearance. Viv together with Maggie and Cherry were all to become players in my own life's tapestry.

Des always took a long time after the show, changing and getting ready to go for a drink or meal and Viv waited impatiently drumming her heels. I was the audience for this unfolding scenario, which was to end a few years thereafter in tragic circumstances.

With my contract already confirmed for 1976 I put the show out of mind until after the pantomime which Nina and I were heading towards. This was an exciting new venture for me because I had been poached away from the Triumph Organisation by the Howard & Wyndham company, to the beautiful and historic Theatre Royal in Newcastle. Howard and Wyndham Limited were mainly a Scottish based company. To have one of their shows was certainly a feather in the cap of any director/choreographer.

They were also a publishing company – WH Allen - with palatial premises in Mayfair. The head of production Herbert Donald invited me to lunch in the magnificent headquarters and I took the lift up to the private apartment at the top of the building, meeting with Herbert Donald for the first time. This was also to meet the stars Mike and Bernie Winters, who I had never previously worked with. Whilst chatting over a gin and tonic, Herbert's secretary rang to say that Mike and Bernie were waiting down in the vestibule.

Interestingly I was about to witness power supremacy working full on. Herbert, with a wink in my direction, told his secretary to offer them a coffee, purely, as I discovered later, to let them know who was the boss.

After I had satisfied him about my own modus operandi Mike and Bernie were brought up in the lift and we all enjoyed another drink before the housekeeper summoned us to a splendid lunch, which enabled me to get acquainted with the stars.

I was also to play the role of Blackbeard the pirate whilst Mike and Bernie were Bosun and Mate. Playing the ship's captain was a dear friend of mine, with whom I had previously worked, Pat Lancaster, a famous Principal Boy with a super singing voice. The Dame was Old mother Riley, alias Roy Rolland, the well-known understudy to the original Old Mother Riley, Arthur Lucan.

Arthur was a star unfortunately well-known for a drink problem and Roy told me that he would very frequently take over the role for the second half of the variety show when Arthur was unable to continue. The changeover was never detected by the audiences, so perfect was the transformation. In fact Roy had to be in transformation form right from the start of the show just in case Arthur didn't even make the interval. How very sad.

I have a personally signed photo of Roy when he was interviewed on the Russell Harty television show after Arthur had departed this world and all was finally revealed.

The original act was known as Old mother Riley and her daughter Kitty. However Kitty McShane was in fact Arthur's wife and his foil in the crockery smashing routine which had the audiences convulsed with laughter. Arthur and Kitty were a facsimile of George and Beryl Formby. Both wives ruled the roost – and how! The crockery scene in this pantomime was performed exactly as the original with Laverne Kari Grey playing Polly Perkins, joining in to help create the 'bull in a china shop' effect which continued to convulse the audiences.

Nina my dancing partner was the Fairy of the Sea and my dancing team from the summer season were again in the show along with Viv, Cherry and Maggie, my Three Musketeers. I came out of the character to perform my stilt act in a specially created gold oriental statue outfit, working the puppet dancers on strings also in oriental costumes, which created a novelty moment in keeping with the subject.

Bernie Winters could be quite awkward at times but Mike, who I became matey with, poured oil on troubled waters when necessary. At the very first meeting of the whole company, Bernie informed me that *they* didn't need to rehearse as they knew what they did, always. Whilst I never intruded on well known comedy partners I insisted that I expected their involvement with the other characters that was integral to the plot.

One scene, which had been presented previously in the show, consisted of a special set with revolving doors and traps, which required the comics to be the fall guys. Watching the rehearsal I felt uneasy with the fact that this act had originally been created for a team of acrobats, which we did not have in our present production. Combined with Bernie's reluctance to rehearse, I informed the office that I felt the scene should be abandoned, especially as the show timing was stretching beyond what had been stipulated. It would certainly help to remove the scene completely. Herbert Donald agreed. Rather oddly, going privately to Mike and Bernie's' dressing room to quietly inform them that the scene was to be cut, Bernie went ballistic. He bellowed at me that if anything of theirs was to be cut out they were leaving. I calmly said, 'That's up to you but it's the management's decision as well as mine, so don't bother with the costumes because the set won't be there.' I left the room immediately. It wasn't up for discussion.

Obviously they didn't leave and Mike later confessed his own gratitude that they were relieved of the whole potential disaster. During the run, I was approached by the manager of the theatre, who confided in me that the council were not going to renew Howard and Wyndham's contract, which they'd had for a number of years, and would I be available to direct the following year's pantomime for the council instead?

I was surprised that they were behaving so indiscreetly and just passed it off saying, 'Contact me later in the year.' Out of the loyalty to my employers I informed Herbert Donald. Forewarned was forearmed. On the final night Herbert Donald gave me a specially inscribed copy of Margot Fonteyn's biography, which the publishing house under the name WH Allen had just brought out.

Fate had already decreed that I would return, however, for now I headed south to prepare for Folkestone's sixth production of Showtime.

Turning my attention in the spring to casting, I found to my surprise that the decision had already been taken on who was to top the bill. I have emphasised time and again that the first decision of casting any show is to get the comedy element correct. I did know the person contracted and was rather uneasy about the booking. Show business is a tightly observed community and word of mouth speaks volumes. However, I am not going to name names in this instance because I have no wish to prejudice anyone's future. So I will refer to him as

Mister X. I had never worked with him in the past but we were in rival seaside shows. His credentials as to his past were solid, knowing who he had worked for. However there are many other considerations to take into account when getting a company together. So Mr X was a fait accompli – time would tell.

I confirmed my desire to continue the operatic interlude that had proved so popular and successful, and to that end I wanted the 4 singers back again. Joan Lawrence, Allan Lloyd and Shirley Rayner from the previous year were contracted along with baritone newcomer Raymond Scally from the English National Opera company who made the quartet. Also in the company was impressionist singer Barry Daniels, tall, handsome and oozing charm to break the female hearts. Nina and I led our regular team of girls which completed the company.

A new musical director Stuart Buckton joined us and was to stay for a few years. With him in the pit was Julian Scott on drums and percussion in his third successive year. He was eventually to exchange the pit for the stage with great success. I decided to stage 'Carmen' for the opera interlude, which enabled the dancers to participate in the excerpt with flamenco choreography. Once again I'm leaving the theatre critic to boast on our behalf.

The Gazette
2 June 1976
Dave Routhorn

SHOWTIME IS A SURE FIRE SMASH HIT!

It seemed far too mundane a setting for magic – Folkestone's seafront on a quiet Saturday night. But it was there, ask any one of the audience who packed the Marine Pavilion to cast critical eyes over Showtime 76. A show handicapped by inevitable comparison with its five record breaking predecessors.

Within minutes of the opening drum role it was obvious that producer Bob Marlowe had not only done it again but had scaled a peak of perfection that few would have thought possible.

Make no mistake. This Showtime is a cracker – the Entertainments Committee needn't bother about Showtime. It will be a success. It will smash records and it will be remembered when other shows are forgotten. It is sheer magic.

From the opening number, 'Masks and Faces', it is patently obvious that the dancers are well rehearsed and moving with Bob Marlowe inspired precision. The singers are in perfect harmony and that anything they attempt is going to come off.

There is something for everyone with extracts from the Arcadians, Doctor Dolittle – with animal costumes which defy description – Kismet, Fiddler on the Roof, Camelot and a string of Strauss melodies. The Showtime Dancers are all that we have come to expect them to be and musical director Stuart Buckton and young drummer, Julian Scott are as effective as a full blown orchestra.

Don't take my word for any of this. Go and see it. I shall certainly be going again – and I'll willingly pay for my tickets.

Greater love hath no critic.

Every morning when the box office opened it was inundated with queues for seats. The company became socially involved by opening fêtes and bazaars throughout the season, taking part in the Autumn in the torchlight carnival parade by entering a float. This attracted large crowds from across Kent and Sussex, contributing greatly to the various charities.

Showtime had an unfair advantage with access to all the glitter and jazz enabling us to gain first prizes, until the committee of the carnival society requested us to participate but stand down as far as the judging was concerned. We did gracefully, allowing other floats their chance of a first prize. However, we did gain top place for getting our charity bins filled before any other groups.

Also we gained because the show was cancelled on this one night and we all went on to a party afterwards whiling away the rest of the evening and joining in with the fireworks display.

This occasion always signalled the approaching end of the season and the farewell party night bade us all goodbye and 'see you next year'. Showtime 76 was history – successful history as the box office had broken 75's record.

Readers who have travelled this far with me now know how a show is assembled and the working mode necessary up to the opening night, so I will dispense with any further explanations. Casting any show takes forethought to ensure the compatibility essential in forming a happy group of performers, which shows across the footlights.

Frankie Holmes who had proved such a success in 1973 was again booked for 76. Barry Daniels from the previous year was re-engaged and the two worked extremely well together, bouncing off each other to great effect. Only one singer remained from the previous year, Raymond Scally, so auditions were held for operatically trained performers. As always supply exceeded the demand and I selected Graham Trew, a member of the Chapel Royal Choir and always visible during Royal occasions on television. In fact I had to give him a day off during rehearsals to attend the Queen's Jubilee celebrations in Westminster Abbey which the company watched on TV back in Folkestone. A historic moment.

Carole Gibb, a soprano from the Welsh National Opera and Australian

Frances Carr-Boyd from the Sadlers Wells Opera company completed the quartet. I needed two new dancers to join my stalwarts, Maggie and Cherry. Auditions brought in Lesley and Helene. Helene eventually fell in love and married the stage director Laurie Jones, keeping it in the theatrical family.

On the classical level, which was proving to be popular and expected, there were to be excerpts from the opera 'Madame Butterfly' and the ballet 'Sleeping Beauty'. Both were received enthusiastically. This was an essential contribution alongside the more modern music of Abba, the Beatles and the Rolling Stones, which created variety in its truest sense. As 77 was the Queen's Jubilee, I decided on a tribute for the finale. In glittering red, white and blue costumes against a dazzling silver set it was a truly loyal celebration for the royal couple, from Folkestone's Showtime company. As before I will now let the professional critic have his say.

The Herald
June 1977
Dave Routhorn

SHOWTIME SMASH
BRILLIANT BOB DOES IT AGAIN

If Bob Marlowe ever decides to take his talents elsewhere, Shepway District Council should nail his feet to the Marine Pavilion. Alternatively they could offer him a permanent job as resident miracle-worker. Either way his particular brand of production magic is something for which the ratepayers of Folkestone should go down on their knees in gratitude.

All of which means that the Maestro has done it again. Showtime 77, which opened at the Marine Pavilion on Saturday, is at least as good as last year's record-breaking spectacular, and that is saying something.

After the overture by Stuart Buckton and Peter Durham it took all of 10 seconds for Showtime to win back its special place in Folkestone's heart. There was something inevitable in the way that the audience responded as that man of many talents, Barry Daniels, strode forward for the show's opening song. You could almost feel the affection crossing the footlights. Showtime was back where it belonged. Everything slotted into place, with the lavish costumes giving additional glitter to as talented a troupe as the town has ever welcomed.

Comedian Frankie Holmes, back after four years, produced his inimitable brand of inspired lunacy which soon broke down any vestige of reserve in the audience. Comedy, magic and ventriloquism that has to be seen to be believed. All come alike to this natural clown who could well make insanity fashionable. He is ably backed by Barry Daniels who proved such a favourite last year, when his baritone voice and rugged good looks set female hearts fluttering, while his brilliant impressions and easy banter make him such an asset to this well balanced production.

As always the show's successful formula owes much to its musical content. Raymond Scally is back for another season and he is even better than before.

His red shadow in the rousing Desert Song sequence would make John Hansen think he was hearing echoes. There are three new vocalists. Graham Trew ably demonstrates how he won the gold medal at the Guildhall School of Music, but I wish he would relax more. He is good. Girl singers, Frances Carr-Boyd and Carole Gibb should prove great favourites during the next few weeks. Both are talented and attractive.

They did much to the impact of the ragtime sequence The Pyjama Game extract and the Song of the South. Carole's One Fine Day from Madame Butterfly was a showstopper on Saturday night. It was followed by a ballet sequence which almost brought the house down.

Bob Marlowe and his fairy footed partner, Nina Brown, danced the awakening scene from the Sleeping Beauty – a masterpiece of choreography which saw the talented duo at their incomparable best, backed by four very attractive dancers, Margaret Sheffield, Cherith Towler, Lesley Houlden and Helene Todd.

The appropriate finale, Land of Hope and Glory gives the show a Jubilee touch.

Twelve months ago, I wrote: 'How do you follow a smash hit? You come up with a second smash and start wondering how you are going to cap that little lot another year.'

Bob Marlowe was the man with the problem. He has solved it. I can say no more.

This write up I have left in its entirety, as soon there were to be rumblings from certain elected councillors to remove my services in spite of the audiences' response at the box office. Certain people, who wanted control, with no theatrical know-how whatsoever!

I still survived for a further five years with help from my council supporters. However when the end came it was messy. But in retrospect the best thing that could have happened. Not only for me but for all who had been loyal to me throughout.

In the Autumn of 77 I travelled with Folkestone's entertainments director, Derrick Blackburn, up to Leicester to see the work of Les Wilson, a comedian who had a great reputation and following in that area. It was not a wasted journey for he was very, very funny with a different approach and we agreed he must be engaged for the show of 1978. First things first, we now had our leading comic and to support him a young performer, comedy impressionist, Bobby Bragg was contracted.

As none of the singers were available from 77 it had to be a clean sweep for 78. Holding auditions in the spring I selected from a well attended audition held in the Wigmore Hall rehearsal rooms, Freda Farnworth soprano, Alexandra Denman mezzo soprano, Simon Masterson tenor and Patrick McCarthy baritone. By holding auditions on the premises of the Wigmore Hall it ensured that classically trained singers attended, usually en masse.

Patrick had achieved fame when, as a young student, he attended a promenade concert given by the London Symphony Orchestra conducted by André Previn. During the television concert the baritone collapsed and an appeal was made to the audience for a stand-in. Patrick volunteered as he had studied the role in college and knew it. He stepped in, to great acclaim and fame in the national press. A case of the right time and the right place. His career blossomed.

He also had proficiency in playing the violin which prompted me to present operatic excerpts from 'Orpheus in the Underworld' a romp by Offenbach which requires Orpheus to drive the other gods mad with his violin playing. When the gods descended into hell I had them strap hanging as though on an underground train and finally arriving in the underground station of Hades, which amused commuters used to strap hanging during rush hours on the London underground, also hell.

This was a scene depicting the world of pantomine –
all the guys are dames and the girls represent every principle boy

Les Wilson went on to consolidate our belief in his comedic skills by proving a hit with the audiences.

The 78 season went on to break the previous year's attendance figures which appeared to be par for the course, though smugness must never enter the equation. Once again my contract was renewed for the following year.

As I have mentioned previously great expectations bring great problems in their wake. Council show finances are always a struggle within the local authority and the entertainment director will always have a fight on his hands. Some councillors reading of record attendances and therefore increased revenue believe, ignorantly, that there is a crock of gold waiting to be raided. How thoughtless is that?

There are other considerations to be taken into account such as once a comic, usually the highest paid member of the company, is an outstanding success, he or she demands a much higher fee for any following contract. Rightly so, if they have put bums on seats.

Other aspects of a production, costumes and sets, also need to be as spectacular as the previous season, if not more so. Audiences are greedy especially if seat prices rise for the forthcoming season. These present enormous problems on limited budgets.

Folkestone was fortunate - once I had decided to take on the responsibility of presenting the show, I introduced Rosemary Waters to them. I had previously worked with Rosemary, when choreographer for Richard Stones company and we formed a close friendship over the years. Richard eventually sold out to Duncan Weldon and Paul Elliott's Triumph Theatre Organisation. Rosemary carried on with the new management and was the chatelaine of the vast costume stores now owned by Triumph. We had access to one of the largest costume repositories in showbiz. When London musicals flopped after a short run, the Triumph Organisation would snap these barely worn costumes up, adding to the thousands already in their warehouse.

With access to this treasure trove my imagination could run riot. The set designer, Vic Friendly, was also an institution and his different style worked admirably well considering the very limited area we had to work in. Three dimensional became the name of the game. So with 79 now in the bag it was time to bid farewell to 78. The last night, always a packed house, applauded enthusiastically when the leader of the council announced that Showtime was returning the following year. We all departed glowing with the success in which we had participated.

Nowadays it has become a cliché country wide, everybody asking on New Year Eve, 'Where did the year go?' However the backroom people and myself knew where it went - planning and devising the forthcoming year's summer show.

Des King had made such an impression in the 75 show it was time again to return him after many of his fans had almost besieged the council with requests to do so. In the 75 season he had met up with Vivienne Law and they married in 78, so they returned as husband and wife.

The second comedy support was David Andre, the son of Victor Seaforth, now an agent, and his wife Suma Lamont, sister of Johnny Lamonte a very respected oriental act. David had an original style of presentation which went down well, in perfect contrast to Des King. Singers Freda Farnworth and Alexandra Denman returned for their second season, joined by Graham Trew who returned after a year's absence. Newcomer Paul Arden-Griffith completed the quartet of classically trained singers, with the added advantage that I was aware of their capabilities when designing the production.

My decision was to divide the quartet, giving the girls one show and the boys the other. The girls Freda and Alexandra were scheduled for the first show, singing the Barcarolle from the Tales of Hoffman, complete with gondola and light effects creating a Venetian canal. Graham and Paul in the second show sang the famous duet from The Pearl Fishers in a jungle setting with a ruined Aztec temple, very atmospheric. With these experienced performers both these offerings were rapturously received by the audiences, proving that talent will out, even if it's not your bag.

I decided on presenting a different type of classical ballet segment just to show the many types within the genre. This was 'Les Patineurs' with Nina and myself together with Maggie, Helene, Viv and Paula, a new recruit to my team. Paula had studied as a child in Nina's mother's school, going on to train for two years with the Royal Ballet School so was more than qualified to join the team. A very beautiful girl who remained with us for a while, going on to work in Paris. Now she lives in the South of France with her French husband and her family.

Les Patineurs requires dancers to simulate ice skaters. Dressed in beautiful velvet costumes with snowflakes gently falling. it was received with enthusiastic applause. Audiences were beginning to realise that ballet did not consist only of fairies on tippy-toes floating around. Obviously aficionados of classical dance knew this but I was aiming it towards an audience that would not dream of visiting a ballet performance. Hopefully some might get hooked after attending a small, seaside summer revue. We were not being patronising, far from it, just introducing samples from our profession in all its aspects. I felt totally vindicated in bringing the classics to an otherwise boisterous summer show, proving that variety is the spice of life.

A new musical director Martin Turner had been introduced to me by Colin

Tarn who had worked with him in the Mermaid theatre's Molecule Club. Yet again with excellent local praise from Press and public, the show moved forward to beat the previous season. An ever spiralling upwards success.

Des King had surpassed his previous summer in 1975 and his popularity with David Andre took the comedy stakes to a higher level. I had persuaded Des to go into drag for the first time ever, imitating Carmen Miranda in a fabulous frock that was still trailing on as he exited on the other side.

Whilst he was not too comfortable wearing female attire he comforted himself with the knowledge that if it was too awful I would cut it. What he didn't realise was that his sheer awkwardness added comedically to the impersonation. By the end of the season he relaxed and added touches to the hilarity. So much so that he went on to play Dames in pantomime with great success, with top stars in all the No.1 theatres.

As you can see now these smaller theatres allowed artistes to experiment and hone skills not possible in the larger shows where if you fail in experimenting you fail in the profession.

I can give you an instance of this. No names, but some years previously, a young comedy impressionist in Showtime was spotted by an ITV talent scout who was impressed by his talent and eventually was given his own show, together with publicity praising the birth of a new, upcoming star. I watched the show, willing him to be a success. Sadly, it was a disaster. He later told me it had been flung on without enough time available to perfect the presentation. He became so disillusioned that he left the profession and with his marriage disintegrating, left England emigrating to Australia. A sad loss to the profession because he possessed a great talent. I have not heard from him since. The lesson, surely, for anyone with ambition - don't run before you can walk.

Finishing on a positive note, in the local press appeared the following headline.

BBC CHIEF PRAISES SHOWTIME

High praise for Folkestone's Summer Show at the Marine Pavilion came from one of the BBC's top executives. In a letter to the Herald Mr Roger Race, Producer of BBC's Light Entertainment wrote: I would like to say how much I enjoyed Showtime. The comedy was excellent and the whole company seemed to enjoy themselves as much as the audience. Congratulations on a fine show, such good family entertainment.

With the final night's applause ringing in our ears we parted company, secure in the knowledge that we would all work together somewhere, sometime. True friendships were formed which exist to the present day.

Showtime had become a pioneering enterprise. Returning after pantomime in the beautiful Georgian Theatre Royal in Bath, the summer show of 1980 in Folkestone was next on the planning list. Sadly this was the one show, in retrospect, I wish had never taken place.

Derrick Blackburn the entertainment director, without consulting me had contracted Mr X for a return engagement. I don't blame Derrick because we had returned comics in the past and obviously he felt he was on safe ground – not so. In 1976 the first time Mr X was proposed I was wary. We had not worked together but some years earlier I had worked in a rival summer show and heard certain rumours about his attitude. These I dismissed as should be all rumours. When he had been put in the frame I agreed to give him a chance, not even voicing my doubts. That season passed relatively quietly but Mr X's attitude did not win him many friends in the company which now in 1980 was about to be proved in aces.

Other artistes booked for the show were Syd Wright, who I had worked with before - a quiet, unassuming but terrific xylophone player who shared top billing. Returning from the previous year were singers Freda Farnworth and Alexandra Denman with newcomers Paul Arden-Griffith tenor and Bronislaw Pomorski baritone. Musical director Martin Turner returned fro his second season and was joined for the first time by Jimmy Tagford, now grandly titled percussionist. My dancers Maggie, Helen and Paula were joined by newcomer Kim Ellen, another product of Nina's mother's dance academy in Southsea, always reliable additions to any show with their training.

One quite spectacular scene was a three-dimensional setting, designed by Vic. The banqueting hall of Hampton Court in the time Queen Elizabeth I with magnificent costumes from Rosemary, which brought gasps and instant applause when the lights came up on a frozen picture.

Nina and I, paying tribute to the classics, danced the Rhapsody On a Theme by Paganini. The singers where indulged with lighter tributes from the music of Cole Porter and Sigmond Romberg. Music from more modern musicals pleased younger audience members. I had always believed in a totally rounded show with something for everybody, which had turned Showtime into a cult.

Now for the problem, which was to cause so much trouble. Southern Television had finally decided to turn the spotlight on the show which had taken Folkestone by storm throughout the previous nine years. About time too!

Local TV stations did not have financial resources to compete with their national big brothers and being eager for the publicity, the whole company agreed to being paid a nominal sum of £100 to take part, this included musicians and backstage staff, and was in thanks to Shepway council for providing work for performers throughout the previous years.

Fortunately the director and cameraman, in spite of the fact that we were in a rehearsal situation for the show's opening, were very compatible in working together and it went smoothly.

One morning going down to the theatre, the box office manageress told me that Southern TV had left a message for me to ring them as soon as possible. I rang and was astonished at what I was hearing. Apparently Mr X had rung them demanding that he was the star of the show with all the responsibility and wanted more money than the agreed amount we were all due. If not forthcoming he threatened to refuse permission for it to be aired. So finally his true colours were coming to light. I was staggered but not surprised, so ringing Derrick's office I lobbed the ball back into his court.

As the dress rehearsal was planned for 2.30pm that afternoon I decided to go onto the beach for the rest of the morning. It was a hot sunny day and I needed time to myself to reflect and to get as far away as possible from the theatre, especially as should I encounter Mr X, I was in the mood to annihilate him once and for all. I stumbled my way along the beach to Sandgate. How dare this b.....d ruin nine years' work. As I've said it was unusually hot, and fuming over the situation and exhausted emotionally, I fell asleep. Little did I realise that the company had alerted the office that I was missing and they were searching for me. Awakening when the pebbles became too uncomfortable, I realised with horror that it was past 2.30pm when the dress rehearsal should have started. I was more upset now that the incident had reflected so badly on my professionalism.

Derrick comforted me with the fact that he had argued the point with Mr X and it was resolved, thankfully for all concerned. In spite of the inner tensions the company were all true professionals and the audiences had no knowledge of any problems, which is what we are all paid for. The shows yet again broke attendance records.

On a personal note Nina and I had chalked up 1000 performances as the longest serving members of Showtime, of which we were inordinately proud, and the Council had thrown a fabulous party with many past members invited to return for a reunion in celebration.

On the final night of the season a packed house responded enthusiastically on being told that I was to continue into my eleventh year of creating Showtime. I had still spiralled upwards, and creating new ideas was what excited me the most. On the other hand I was disturbed by the knowledge that certain members in the council were desirous of achieving more power and influence in the presentation of the show. How dare the butchers, bakers and candlestick makers pretend more knowledge than the professionals?

However whilst I still had a majority of support within the council I needed to be aware of the dissidents and one incident gave me much pause for thought. Towards the end of the season one council member who owned a small private hotel in the centre of town invited the entire cast to supper after the show, explaining that his guests would be thrilled to meet us. I'm not going to name him or his hotel. He has since died and out of respect for his family I do not wish to point a finger and upset them.

This is a necessary illustration of power struggle, which is endemic throughout the land. Arriving after the show, we were all ushered down into what could only have been described as a cellar, with that unmistakeable odour that always seems to linger. With the over-loud addition of a turntable, and a stack of flashing lights blazing and moving in dizzy circles, it resembled a low-life disco. All the guests were seated expectantly around the walls, like a dentist's waiting room. Our host led us to the buffet where tired old sandwiches, curled up at the edges like a ruff because of the longevity of their stay, were accompanied by bottles of warm white wine – ugh. What a repast for performers who do not eat before a show, but are starving afterwards.

Clasping a glass of wine I had no intention of drinking, I contemplated with Nina as to how soon we could escape to the nearest 'chippy'. Suddenly our host bounced over expectantly with a toothy grin. He enquired, 'When's the show starting?' I knew exactly what he was expecting but obtusely I said, 'We've just finished it.' He gaped. I continued, 'We don't do second houses.' End of story.

The cast had mingled with the guests only to discover that most hadn't seen the show.

A finale of Showtime – Des King a discovery of mine starred
and has gone on to world wide fame since.

In the late 70s most seaside hotels and guest houses were on this scam of keeping guests on the premises to booze away during extended licensing hours with the added promise of disco dancing and possibly a local amateur entertainer. Our host had obviously promised much, much more. Expecting to exert influence by being on the entertainment council, he'd promised his guests – us. Wrong.

We left en masse, heading for our favourite little café in the old High Street where our friends Bill and his Italian wife Franka kept open hours for us after the show, turning every night into a private party with the most delicious home cooking, in convivial surroundings that were just like home. So ended our foray into no-no land. Only one person had remained at the other débâcle – guess who?

Although I was returning for the season of 81 the odd rumblings were getting to me. I had worked hard for ten years to bring the shows to success undreamed of at the beginning. Yet as I've already explained there were one or two dissidents working against me.

I needed to protect my own back now so pencilled a memo to myself to contact Richard Condon, an impresario gaining enormous stature in the theatrical firmament. Dick, a personable Irishman had rescued the Norwich Theatre Royal from a dismal period and turned it into a resounding success. I was determined to acquaint him with my work in creating Folkestone's Summer Shows with a reputation equalling his in East Anglia.

To my surprise I received a letter almost by return. Surprised, because in our profession many letters remain unanswered, no matter who one writes to. In this case though my reputation had gone before me and Mr Condon was well acquainted with my work and success rate. He was very interested to meet me although he wasn't in the market at that particular moment to change his own arrangements. On the other hand neither was I. After all, my future was already contracted for the following year. However, I was planning ahead as does everyone in my position.

Visiting friends up in Leicester that Autumn I decided to travel home via Norwich making an appointment in advance with Dick Condon. Arriving in that beautiful city, an area I had never visited previously, we met up in the Theatre Royal for the first time face to face. He was a charming man with charisma and I liked him instantly. We shared the same sense of humour, always a useful link. This meeting was to prove one of the most important in my whole career, but at this very moment it was to remain on hold. Whilst I had been invited to lunch, Dick excused himself, having a meeting to attend. In his place I was to meet his current director who was to escort me to the theatre restaurant.

Enter Yvonne Marsh, who I knew via the grapevine was not only director but also girlfriend. She was pleasant and we enjoyed lunch. However, as Dick's staying power in the romantic field was dubious to say the least, I had the feeling that she was suspicious of my appearance on the scene. During lunch I consoled her with the fact that my continuing contract in Folkestone was intact and she visually relaxed.

Christmas of 1980, Nina and I were performing in 'Robinson Crusoe' at the Congress Theatre in Eastbourne, my third pantomime in the theatre directing, choreographing and performing, although on this occasion as Anita Harris was starring, she demanded that her own choreographer Denise Shaun be contracted, whilst Duncan Weldon wished me to continue choreographing for him. I had done this for the previous eight years to acclaim, also directing and performing, but due to certain contractual difficulties with Anita's manager, her husband Mike Margolis, Duncan was over a barrel and had to agree.

I concurred. However with my own contract sealed the previous spring I refused it being amended, demanding the fee as agreed for all three positions, directing, choreographing and performing. This hiccup did not spoil my relationship with the Triumph Organisation and I continued working with them for a further four years until I wanted a change myself. One can get in a rut.

Denise Shaun was charming and talented and we had a most congenial relationship. Sadly she was to die a while later – far, far too young.

Spring arrived and casting for Showtime 81 was too soon on the agenda. Two young comics were engaged to share top billing, Jeff Stevenson and Chris Lloyd. Jeff at the age of 14 had appeared in the 'Bugsy Malone' film with many child actors taking on the adult roles. Chris also had started as a Butlins Redcoat. Quite a baptism of fire for a teenager just out of college but one that teaches rapport with all age groups - another plus when dealing with theatre audiences. The only singer to return from 80 was Freda Farnsworth who was popular with the audiences. It's always useful to have a continuing line - audiences like to have familiarity with performers they like. Thank goodness for that as Nina and I were now into our eleventh season.

Auditions brought forth singers Julian Forsyth and Paul Weakly. I had decided to forego the fourth singer as I wished to introduce a male dancer into the choreographic equation, a young dancer who had worked in two previous pantomimes with me. So Sean Lydon joined dancers Paula, Maggie and a newcomer Siobhan O'Kane.

We had also to hold an audition for a new musical director. I was taken aback during the audition, attended by half a dozen pianist MDs at pre-arranged timings, when the door opened to admit a burly guy in black leather looking rather like a navvy. As the previous auditionees had not been particularly outstanding Derrick and I were despairing and this one didn't look musical at all. His very presence and gait were not hopeful. We explained that we needed someone with a classical background.

Seated at the grand piano he rippled a few notes to relax his fingers, then swooped into the most amazing classical performance. It was as though a musical angel had descended. We gasped and offered him the job on the spot. His CV indicated his training at the Guildhall School of Music, a most prestigious training ground, even forming his own opera company which had performed 'Marriage of Figaro', 'Cosi Fan Tutti' and 'Paliacci' amongst others. He had also specialised in current musicals. It just went to prove one should not judge by appearances, but just wait for the talent to out.

Percussionist Jimmy Tagford was in for his third season - we were complete. I will now let the professional critic have his view on the production.

The Herald
Dave Routhorn

SHOWTIME SAGA IS A NON-STOP SUCCESS TALE

Once upon a time, in the far-flung outposts of the district now known as Shepway, the citizens were much distressed by the plague of tellyitis, which confined them to their homes worshipping the devil box called Goggle.

There was much wailing and beating of breasts as the cruelly–afflicted populace cried: 'Save us from the telly peril … prise us from the dreaded cathode ray tube.'

And it came to pass their pleas fell on fertile ground.

The clarion call was answered by a strolling player, one Robert Marlowe, known throughout the kingdom of theatre land as Sir Twinkletoes.

'There is only one cure for the plague of tellyitis,' he cried. 'Sheppey must have an injection of live entertainment.

'Bring on the clowns, the song and dance men, the musicians and the dancing girls. Let the citizens laugh, sing and be entertained.'

HUMOUR

And that, children, is how Showtime came to Shepway in the year of deliverance 1971 and why, 11 years later, Sir Twinkletoes and his merry band are still presenting their star–spangled brand of mirth and music at Folkestone's Marine Pavilion.

All right, the story of Showtime isn't really a fairytale, but it certainly has all the ingredients of one.

With seaside shows struggling against recession, apathy and lack of potential customers, Showtime has managed to chalk up one successful year after another.

The format is simple – give the public what it wants.

The 'something for everybody' cliché has been done to death, but that is what Showtime offers.

Belly laughs and ballet ... pop and operetta ... show songs and gospel numbers. The permutations have been endless, with producer Bob Marlowe invariably hitting the magic formula that signals success.

Over the years, Showtime has become the shining diamond in Shepway Council's crown. Delighting locals and holidaymakers alike, it brings a constant ray of sunshine to a sometimes bleak corner of South–East England.

Its popularity can be gauged by the number of devotees who make seat–booking the first priority of their holidays. At least one regular spent every night of her holiday in a Showtime front row seat – and made countless other day trips to see the show. You don't get that sort of loyalty without earning it.

Bob Marlowe and his long–time dancing partner, the delectable Nina Brown, are the only ever presents in Shepway's long–running spectacular, but old favourites like Frankie Holmes and Barry Daniels have had the habit of reappearing over the years.

This year's No 1. show is a musical world tour, with comedians Chris Lloyd and Jeff Stevenson popping up at the landing stages with their entertaining brands of humour.

Freda Farnworth, Paul Weakley and Julian Forsyth blend their voices with the harmony that Showtime addicts have come to expect and the Showtime Dancers, Margaret Sheffield, Paula Rowntree, and Siobhan O'Kane are joined by Sean Lydon, a talented male dancer.

Musical director, Stuart Barnham and his noteworthy accomplice, Jimmy Tagford, provide the melodies for a show with more zip than you'll find in a giant's trousers.

Last year, Sir Twinkletoes and company celebrated their first decade.

If the people of Shepway have their way and the District Council knows a good thing when it sees it, the show's golden jubilee should be a sell-out in the year 2040.

The above somewhat Hans Anderson fairy tale style of the writer nevertheless showed that the success yet again surpassed the previous year. Eleven years of spiralling achievement.

I feel now that I should record the final exit of Mr X from my life. Some years later when his name came up for consideration with another company to which I was very securely connected, I told them, it's him or me - the choice is yours! As my feet had been successfully under their table for a number of years I had no hesitation in issuing this threat. I won in the end.

Back to Folkestone's summer season planned for 82. Eleven years previously I first visited the town and found to my dismay that the Pavilion was hardly in the most salubrious area of the town. However, with the show's ensuing success and glamorous yearly make-over of the Marine Pavilion it had survived.

The new channel port and a large hotel had helped in tidying the area, also advertising the Pavilion's presence. However the area towards the west had been taken over by a local entrepreneur who had established a noisy funfair and a Sunday market. This attracted large crowds but also a different type of clientele, not necessary theatre-goers. Was the end of the Marine Pavilion nigh?

The Leas Cliff Hall up in the town centre was mainly Folkestone's showplace set on the spectacular Victorian Leas Cliff Gardens Boulevard. This venue staged concerts, both orchestral and variety, with top star names. The council had decided to revamp it and stage the summer season there.

I am now going to reproduce the press report announcing the stages, which states far better than I can what was planned.

NEW REVUE SET TO REPLACE SHOWTIME

Showtime is dead - a new summer production called Top of the Town will be born in June. The old Showtime revue as it has been known over the last 11 years is buried. In its place Shepway District Council has a new baby, which I hope will be more 'up market' and sophisticated. With a change in venue from the Marine Pavilion to the 'top of the town' at the Leas Cliff Hall, there are new things in store for Folkestone's summer season show.

And the new approach includes getting a 'big name' star to centre the production on. This year the council's entertainments department has signed up impressionist and comedian, Peter Goodwright. Peter was in town last week to meet the show's producer Robert Marlowe, entertainments officers and to take a look at the re-vamped Leas Cliff Hall.

He was last seen at the venue in his own show last year, which was a great success with the local audience.

The hall's general manager said Peter is an ideal choice for the new show. He explained that after spending £1.7 million on the hall it was felt that it would be 'nice' to put a summer show there. With a change in venue it was also the perfect opportunity to completely re-arrange the annual show.

However, Folkestone cannot compete with other top class summer show resorts like Eastbourne and Bournemouth. There are financial limitations involved because it is a council entertainment, he said. But we wanted to 'put a bigger name into the show'.

Peter Goodwright has worked for them in Sunday variety concerts and has always done very well.

Top of the Town is a new venture. It will involve making alterations to improve the Leas Cliff Hall's stage for the type of production it is.

'We pride ourselves on the fact that the show is family entertainment. It doesn't offend and it is not the run of the mill, end of pier summer season production. It is slightly sophisticated and not corny.

This year there will be something, which the residents of Shepway will like. 'We have always had a good residential clientele. But with the new show we feel it could attract even more local people.'

Producer Robert Marlowe, who has been with Showtime since it started, is very enthusiastic over the latest venture. For the Top of Town he envisages a Palladium style show centred round the top of the bill, Peter Goodwright. It won't be an entertainment where the star does his bit and that's it, with disjoined acts and sketches.

There will be one item left in for the Showtime fans but the main bulk of entertainment will touch on the disco style of dancing and new trends. He has recently been following through on fashion, getting to know what teenagers are wearing. This will be the style for the show's costumes.

But, because there are a lot of elderly people who come year in and year out to see Showtime these will of course be 'glamorous.' 'That's the way the usual audiences like things,' he added.

Robert has designed a stage set, which is being made up at the moment. The stage itself will soon be altered for lighting and other technical equipment to be used.

Peter Goodwright is also very enthusiastic about the new show. Many people will recognise him from umpteen television appearances. His first broadcast on radio was in 1958 but he broke through into showbiz when he appeared in the BBC series 'What Makes a Star'.

With the summer of 82 in the bag it was time to concentrate on the pantomime, my tenth for the Triumph Organisation. This was 'Jack and the Beanstalk' presented in the New Palace theatre in Plymouth. Titled 'New' it was hardly that. In fact a very old theatre situated in the red light district, which is usually a feature of every port. A comfort zone for sailors.

It was in fact to be the last one ever presented there, as millions were being spent on the beautiful Theatre Royal which I was privileged to be shown around, wearing a hard hat because it was still a work site prior to being opened by Princess Margaret in the early summer. A fabulous, innovative design, with a cantilevered ceiling which could be brought in and locked onto the dress circle, thus enabling plays and other presentations requiring a smaller, more intimate atmosphere to be of appropriate seating capacity. Likewise when musicals, usually launched to try out before going to London, required more seating, it was there at the touch of a button. Also a boon when musicals toured after their London run, for eager audiences in the West Country awaiting their turn.

Anyway, 'Jack and the Beanstalk' unfortunately was destined for the ornate but tumbledown New Theatre in red-light land.

Nevertheless, it had a first rate cast as was usual for a Triumph panto. It starred Basil Brush with Billy Boyle, Mark Wynter, Jack Tripp, Anthea Askey, Richard Murdoch, Allen Christie and Beverley Adams. In fact the cast was almost a replica of the previous year's production in the Congress theatre in Eastbourne, with Nina playing her usual fairy role and myself, as well as directing and choreographing, playing my usual role of the Baddie.

It was just as well that the cast were already familiar with the show because a total freak snowfall on the day we all had to decamp for Plymouth caused havoc with the trains, hours late arriving at their destination, whilst road travellers were unable to get down to Devon, in some cases even a couple of days later.

It certainly did not help that the theatre was also freezing cold, hardly used throughout the year and with a dodgy roof, in some places open to the elements. It was in a death row state – sadly, because in its heyday it must have been quite splendid with ornate gilt plasterwork, now dropping off in chunks.

So cold also that at the dress rehearsal I had to abandon it half way into the first half, the performers, costumed and covered in topcoats with teeth chattering and children in tears with the freezing conditions. I had asked the company manager to contact Equity. Although not a staunch unionist, I felt these conditions were not acceptable. Armed with the knowledge of work conditions which temperature-wise was way below requirements, I contacted the

A special celebration of all past members who returned for Nin's and my 1,000th performance in 'Showtime' Folkestone

theatre manager and demanded commercial heaters be brought in, sending the cast off to defrost and get something to drink. As we also had a full orchestra whose wind instruments had gone totally out of tune it had definitely been a no go situation. Even poor old Basil Brush's teeth were chattering.

With rapidity the heaters were installed. Like blast furnaces they heated the whole place within a couple of hours enabling us to return and complete the dress rehearsal, ready for the opening night.

Fortunately with audiences attending throughout the run, the theatre was obliged to maintain the required temperature, which was obligatory council wise.

As most of my scenes were with Basil I had become quite used to the fact that I was playing opposite a glove puppet with personality. It did present problems though, when Basil, seated on his plinth with his partner Ivan concealed inside pinching my ankles when I got too close. Being a dancer I nimbly escaped taking revenge by insulting 'Basie' who played hurt. I was the Baddie after all.

Ivan, Basil's mentor and creator was a joy to work with. A modest man, he never allowed himself to be photographed with Basil for publicity purposes, wanting Basil to remain a performer in his own right for the children's sake. Therefore an actor was always employed to partner Basil, in many cases becoming as famous as Basil. In my collection of photographs I have one of Basil signed 'To Mr Bob, a great producer and a gentleman, may we work together again sometime. Best wishes, Basil Brush,' and signed with a paw mark.

As Ivan was so liked by the company, I had found a Royal Doulton plate with a fox on it and suggested that if the company liked to contribute we would present it to Basil on the last night. Asking Jack Tripp if he would present it, he refused saying he did not like last night speeches. However, on the last night, after taking his walk down in the finale he took centre stage, unbelievably, to deliver a few well-rehearsed words. He justifiably was considered one of the finest Dames in the business but at that moment, in my eyes, he had demeaned himself irrecoverably. I had worked a few times with Jack, but found it impossible to forgive him for such selfishness. Basil Brush had top billing in the pantomime hierarchy and I knew Jack resented his third position on all advertisements. But hey - how sad is that?

When the curtain fell and before the company left the stage I stepped forward and gave the plate on behalf of the company to Ivan, who was visibly touched. A modest man, who only wished to perpetuate the myth that Basil Brush was a real character for the children's sake. Pantomime is ostensibly for children and one should encourage their wide-eyed beliefs, even if it's a glove puppet.

In my view the management got it right. As our pantomime was the only one in Plymouth it did excellent business keeping up the Triumph Organisation's reputation for excellence. At that particular time they had pantomimes in every large No.1 theatre in the country on their listings and I felt really privileged to be in demand with them.

Fortunately there were no further snowfalls and the West Country regained its warm climate reputation. Now it was all systems go in preparing for the new look Folkestone Summer Show in the revamped Leas Cliff Hall. A very exciting project.

There were my stalwarts from Showtime, Freda Farnworth, Graham Trew and Maggie Sheffield my ever dependable head girl, and Julian Scott who had commenced his career with Showtime in 1974 returning again in 75 and 76 as percussionist. Now in 1982 he had met and married a dancer/singer Diane, forming a musical vocal act, and they were featured in all the production work as well as their own acts. Plus a novelty act Rip Van Wonkle and Nikki, an unusual rather bizarre act, totally different, which added to the 'new look' production.

I auditioned for three new dancers to join the group and this year we had extended the musicians group when Freda's husband Peter Collis joined us for the first time as musical director, although I had previously worked on two London productions with him, the Seven Deadly Sins and Godspell and knew of his excellence in the musical world both at home and abroad. Jimmy Tagford was back again on percussion, then George Sketcher a multi instrumentalist trained at the Royal Marines School of Music proficient on clarinet, saxophone and violin. The quartet was completed by Ray le Her, yet another military trained musician from Kneller Hall, again proficient in clarinet, saxophone and guitar. Peter on keyboards was also proficient on the synthesizers, now becoming indispensable in creating almost any orchestral instrument including organs to give grandeur. It was for the very first time the most solid backing for Folkestone's Summer Shows I had ever had.

Once again I will let the professional critic speak for us all. There had been many doubts expressed about the wisdom of moving up to the major venue so Folkestone was agog for its first glimpse and verdict - here it is.

Pip Clarkson

PETER TOPS THE LOT IN SUPER SUMMER SHOW

The Leas Cliff Hall was packed, the stage set ready for curtain up, performers waited quietly in the wings but the burning question in everyone's mind was, Is the change of venue going to turn Folkestone's new look summer show Top of the Town into a glittering success?

It's a hit thanks to the life-blood of the new show's top comedian Peter

Goodwright. The show kicks off with a flurry of action, a blaze of colour and a stack of talent. The effect is stunning.

Peter Goodwright appears next, relaxed and promising the audience lots of summer-time fun. He is followed by singing duo Diane and Julian - a very bright, up to date, harmonic couple, geared to modern entertainment. American stars, stripes and songs provide the company with its next burst of entertainment. Freda Farnworth has her first solo spot, and as every year, is in excellent voice. Then Peter is on again proving his opening burst is not a flash in the pan, cracking a stream of jokes.

The joke enjoyed most was the one about Folkestone's new Sainsbury's supermarket building. I thought it was a detention centre for delinquent housewives, he said, adding that he would not mind a job cleaning its windows during the day.

Novelty act Jock McLog and McNikki are great. These two pseudo-Scots offer bags of humorous entertainment. I especially like their persuasive way of gaining audience participation.

Old favourites, Bob Marlowe and Nina Brown, a woman who seems to get younger as the years pass, delight the audience with their singing and dancing spots.

Peter Goodwright performs his main slot towards the end leaving the audience laughing. Throughout the show there are full company scenes including a tribute to Gracie Fields and excerpts from the musical Oklahoma. Bob Marlowe can certainly give himself a pat on the back for directing what is a superb show. AND THE AUDIENCE SAY IT'S A HIT!

Shepway District Council Chairman Claude Poll
'Terrific. If it does not take off, nothing will.'

Folkestone Mayor Peter Poole
'It's entertainment for all ages and is great value for money.'

Chairman of Shepway's Amenities Committee Councillor John Hallett
'I'm thrilled with the show. It's of a highly professional standard.'

Councillor John Jacques
'I think people will come just to see Peter Goodwright'

Councillor David Pratt
'The success of the change of venue will not be known until the end of the season, but nothing ventured nothing gained.'

Leas Pavilion Theatre Boss Charles Vance
'Superb. It's about time the council realised it needed a star for the summer show.
The Leas is becoming the entertainment centre of the town and will draw crowds from all over the place. Top of the Town is top of the pops.'

Producer Bob Marlowe
'Peter has style and class and has made the show.'

Peter Goodwright
'A jewel is set better by its setting.'

With the applause ringing for the show's success in one ear I was hearing different things in the other. Undoubted rumblings from a certain councillor who wanted to get the praise and glory for himself. Jealousy rearing its ugly head with one in particular masterminding the process. No wonder councils find themselves in a mess when they don't work together for the common good. The chief culprit was the gentleman I had crossed swords with at the end of 81, he of the warm white wine and stale sandwiches who demanded a free floor show for his guests. His small mind now sought revenge, but little good it did him in the end.

Changing venues can be a risky affair as most people are creatures of habit, however the box office bells were ringing and the bookings taking off with praises all round.

As the end of the season approached I awaited the council's decision on the following summer show of 83. Peter the musical director promised that he would attend the council meeting when it was being decided. Unfortunately the meeting coincided with all performers preparing for the show, which prevented my attendance. Peter arrived back for the overture telling me that my services were no longer required. It was exactly as I had surmised, I was particularly disappointed that Derrick Blackburn had not offered a word of support for my position. Surely I could have expected a year's notice of intention to enable me to plan ahead?

For twelve years the council policy had kept me dangling over a chasm of uncertainty. Now it was a case of 'over and out'. With one month left before the show finished. I hurriedly placed advertisements in the theatrical papers inviting managements of my availability for 1983 to view the production before it closed in a month's time.

Fate intervened and the adverts, due to printing problems, only appeared after the show had closed. An expensive exercise with no results. Little did I realise it but destiny was to deal me a winning hand in the fullness of time.

On the last Thursday, our pay day, Derrick arrived before the show with our final pay off cheques, together with a reminder that the company had an invitation for a final drink together on the morrow in the council chambers with the Mayor. I told him that I would not be attending. He begged me, saying that the rest of the company in sympathy had also refused. I had only told Nina of my decision but walls have ears. Derrick argued but I was adamant. With the overture and beginners call in place he pleaded. This was the penultimate show so I agreed, promising that I would ask the company to concur for my sake and attend - but - I warned Derrick to prepare for a bumpy ride when I met up with my detractor.

Friday dawned and I prepared for battle. The die had been cast and I sought revenge. Confronting my opponent I quietly told him what a turd he had proved to be and departed. He did not follow to remonstrate, thankfully, for I was in the mood to floor him.

The last night's performance was a sell out and was now over. Nina and I already decided to exit quickly and quietly by the back doors not wanting to be involved any further after twelve years of devotion to something we fervently had belief in - in retrospect very successful years. When the news spread that I was not returning there was quite an outburst from members of the public. Below is a typical example.

Eric Whittlesea-Webster
Lord Wakefield Club of Hythe Chairman
Friday 1 October 1982

BOB'S FAREWELL IS FOLKESTONE'S LOSS

It was only on Friday last that I had the opportunity of visiting the Leas Cliff Hall and seeing that much-discussed show The Top of The Town. The occasion was an evening's entertainment for 42 members of the Lord Wakefield Senior Citizens Club in Hythe, and each and every member thought that show was excellent.

With only a few days to run one might have expected to see some drop in the early or high season standard, but such was not the case, as the cast appeared as fresh and keen as if it were the opening week.

The show was beautifully dressed and the costumes were still in perfect condition. The choreography and production generally were of the highest order and Peter Goodwright and the whole company were sparkling.

I am at a loss to understand any criticism of the show. The Leas Cliff Hall was packed and the audience was a complete cross-section, ranging from some of my own club members in their 80s, right through the spectrum to a party of youngsters.

In my opinion the show provides a delightful example of good wholesome family entertainment, and I sincerely trust that the powers-that-be will have very serious second thoughts about dispensing with the services of Robert Marlowe, a very hard-working, talented and likeable person.

If he does go it will be Folkestone's loss and I feel sure that many of the company will remain loyal and follow him to a new venue.

If I were a district and not a town councillor, I would not be in two minds about accepting a free ticket for the final performance. I would be first in the queue.

Francis Golightly, a show producer from Clacton in Essex came every year to view my productions, virtually ignoring me in the bar after the show with just a nod in my direction. He was of course befriending Derrick Blackburn quite obviously with an eye to the main chance. However this is showbiz and all's fair in love and war. I'm sure I don't need to ask who got the contract for 1983. The following says it all in the local rag.

NEW LOOK SHOW FOR FOLKESTONE

Talks are under way to sign up veteran comedian Harry Worth to top the bill of Folkestone's 1983 summer show.

The revue is to be known as 'Cascade 83' and a new producer replaces Robert Marlowe to mould it into shape.

Shepway District Council's entertainment department is negotiating with Harry Worth's agent and a deal is expected to be tied up very soon.

The Council has chosen Harry Worth because he has a name, commands a price it can afford and he is a very 'clean' comic.

The Council wants to improve the standard of the show it is providing. Last year it tried an up-market scheme by moving the revue from the Marine Pavilion to the newly refurbished Leas Cliff Hall.

Now it has replaced producer Robert Marlowe after more than 11 years of shows, including the long running 'Showtime', with Francis Golightly, a man who has been producing light entertainment shows for more than 20 years. 'Cascade 83' gets under way with an opening night at the Leas Cliff Hall on Saturday July 9 and will run until October 8.

This incensed former members now working in London who replied with the following.

DEDICATED MARLOWE

Sir, With regard to your report on Folkestone's new summer show, (January 27) we were most surprised to read the comment that 'the Council wants to improve the standard of the show'. This implied slight on producer Robert Marlowe, named in the report, after 12 years of dedicated service to the town, needs refuting immediately.

Those of us lucky enough to have worked with Robert Marlowe know that he would not allow anything on stage under his name which does not achieve the highest standard possible - a view shared by the general public who returned time after time to see his productions in the years up to 1982.

Singing and playing at Folkestone last season, we were able to view with distaste the petty infighting in the Shepway Council 'corridors of power'. They in their wisdom have decided on a change of format for their show. This, they think, will save them having to take their heads out of the sand, and admit that the falling number of tourists is due to their own lack of imagination in the planning and promotion of their amenities.

Graham Trew, Peter Evan Collis, Freda E Famworth, Cockpit Theatre, Gateforth Street, Marylebone NW8 8EH.

This was the final production of my 12 years in devising, directing and choreographing, also appearing as a dancing duo with Nina. The star was Peter Goodwright, the first time the show was topped by a television personality

Postscript. In the autumn of 83 Nina and I were persuaded to see the show that had taken over from me. Not wanting to be observed I requested seats at the back of the circle for anonymity. You can imagine our horror to find it was virtually empty and we both stood out like a sore thumb. Harry Worth, as we had heard, a brilliant performer, had stayed too long at the fair and only had moderate success. We beat a hasty retreat at the end saying a brief farewell to the staff we had worked with the year before. Little did we realise that we had just witnessed the last summer show to be staged in Folkestone. They are now a thing of the distant past.

Even today when I return to visit friends I'm frequently stopped in the street by ex-fans of Showtime asking hopefully if I am returning to put on the shows again and this is now 26 years later. How cool is that?

This is Nina and myself in Folkestone's final year – 1982

THE JEWEL IN MY CROWN

Leaving Folkestone by the back door was a sad moment made worse for me because Nina had decided to retire after fifteen truly happy years, most successful, since our first meeting in Sandy Powell's Starlight shows.

I was not really surprised, for the last couple of years I had persuaded her to remain with Showtime knowing full well that her mother desperately needed her help with their ever expanding dancing academy in Southsea. Readers will remember I had an inkling of the writing on the wall when my detractors began interfering with the production, or rather trying to, which had exacerbated the situation.

Because our acts had always been well received in the show's context I know Nina's departure would not have helped the show to remain intact. My detractors would have been in, like rats up a pipe.

Making my own departure also forced me to decide my own route forward. I decided to concentrate on devising, directing and choreographing. Whilst male dancers have longevity over girls, whose youth is their forte, males also should not go on forever, letting younger ones have their turn in the spotlight.

In the Autumn I had a contract to direct and choreograph a musical down in Cornwall. One day I received a phone call from the resident stage director of the Sunderland Empire theatre. Apparently Richard Condon had been searching the country to find me. He finally settled on Sunderland knowing I had worked there before. A process of elimination I surmised. Was my visit two years previously to Norwich about to bear fruit at last? It was.

Making contact with Dick, he greeted me with words I was longing to hear – was I available to work for him the following summer? *Was* I? Yes! Yes! Yes! How more fervent can one be? My guardian angel had been working flat out to secure a non-stop record doing what I loved most. Little did I know the next 20 years of my career was to be crowned with even more success than I could possibly imagine, even in my wildest dreams!

With my musical production successfully on stage in the West Country I hurried to Norwich to sign and seal my contract for the summer of 1983. Christmas of 82 I had a contract with the Triumph company to direct my twelfth pantomime for them in London's Wimbledon theatre. The subject was

'Mother Goose' starring Larry Grayson, Honor Blackman, Dilys Watling, Anna Dawson and David Morton.

Larry, a warm hearted man who during lunches in a local pub had everyone convulsed with laughter by his camp anecdotes. Unfortunately his style was not best suited to pantomime and his main contribution was his TV game show, which was not particularly well received with audiences. I believe that pantomime was his last attempt and he went into semi-retirement in the West Country. I recall seeing him shortly before his death, performing on a Royal Command show where he was sensationally successful with his original style once more on display, almost stopping the show. He eventually left this world still a star.

Honor Blackman was making her pantomime debut and was stunning as the evil Demon Vanity. I had choreographed her an opening routine, another first, singing 'I Wanna be Evil' whilst held acrobatically high by the dancing boys. Wow, she excelled. I told her she would be the one kids loved to hate and would have the greatest response in the finale walk downs. She was dubious but thrilled when it did actually happen. The hisses and boos resounding. In my private photo collection I have one signed by her. 'To Bob who taught me to be evil overnight' - good for my ego to think that Pussy Galore had written that.

Anna Dawson played a dizzy fairy. Once I knew she had had dance training in classical point work I suggested that it would be really funny if during her introductory spot and singing she entered actually on point travelling right

Early Hollywood

across the stage but gradually sinking until she reached the far side almost sitting on her crutch. She was doubtful but, bless her, practised to get her skills back. After all, actress/comediennes don't often get the chance to put point shoes on, and she scored a hysterical success which validated all her hard practising.

With Honor as a team, good versus evil, they stopped the show. Newspaper praise, very well deserved. If pantomime gets this equation right it is what its main thrust is all about. Fortunately comedy was safely in the hands of David Morton, a very experienced Dame playing the titular role. With Triumph's usual stunning sets and costumes designed by Terry Parsons it was a visual delight upholding their reputation as the premier theatrical company.

In the spring of 83 Dick Condon suggested that I travel to Norwich for a couple of days to look through the costume department and discuss my production ideas. On the first day I was to meet his resident wardrobe supervisor, Jenny. Going backstage I met the resident stage manager Jack Bowhill. He called across to the wings 'Robert Marlowe is here.' Dulcet tones screeched out, 'Tell him to f—k off!' apparently the only word this harridan had in her vocabulary. I had no intention of remaining, being used to polite society. Angrily returning to Dick's office, his secretary said that he hadn't appeared and suggested she get me a coffee. I refused, raging that I could not stay on the premises, but would return in an hour's time warning his secretary, incidentally the nicest person I'd met so far, that if Mr Condon hadn't arrived on my return I would go back to London immediately and consider my contract had been broken.

Over coffee in a restaurant I recalled an old Manx expression when working in the Isle of Man, which is 'Kick one and they all limp,' which at the time I thought was funny. Not at this moment when I was discovering it also seemed to apply to Norfolk, returning within the hour, anticipating that I may well be on my way back to London, end of story.

Dick was in his office totally conciliatory, explaining the resentment I had encountered. Apparently Yvonne Marsh had been best mates with the foul-mouthed creature who had screeched at me earlier. With Yvonne now disposed of her position in Dick's favour the old Manx saying was proving true. Dick had been busy phoning to someone else to undertake the position of wardrobe supervisor. She was coming to meet me that afternoon to explore together the skips containing past outfits available to be utilised again. Anne-Marie Miller arrived and we hit it off immediately.

She was a charming Irish lass, a skilled couturier no less. We explored with horror the sorry remnants remaining in half a dozen skips. It certainly was not what I had been used to working with. Anne-Marie explained certain remnants were given to the dancers to drape and twine round their own bras. I was appalled and left Anne-Marie to confront Dick with the situation revealed. She agreed a budget with him for costumes and the die was cast.

I couldn't understand the animosity I had received from certain staff members until Anne-Marie informed me that Yvonne and Dick's close association had broken down irrevocably and she was bitter and intent on revenge. Yvonne had assumed when we had lunch together at Dick's request a couple of years earlier that I had inveigled her departure – not true. Obviously she had persuaded others that this was the case and they conspired to give me a tricky start.

Whilst Dick was the guru and saviour of the Norwich Theatre Royal he had also persuaded the council of Cromer, a small resort on the cold North East coast about 20 miles east of Norwich, to let him stage a summer show on their historic and charming little pier. After a few little early settling in problems it had turned into a great success.

In the early days due to using his famous Norwich pantomimes as bait Dick would contract star names for both Christmas pantos and his summer season in Cromer. Names with pulling power like Milligan and Nesbit, Rosemary Squires, Joan Savage, Denny Willis etc most of whom had television shows adding to their celebrity.

However the first show I was given indeed had a star in my eyes - Les Wilson who I knew from Folkestone. Dorothy Wayne was also co-starring with Les and I must confess that I was uncertain as to how she would react towards me. She was very friendly with Yvonne Marsh who was badmouthing me. Both Les and Dorothy had worked the season of 82 and had been re-booked for the change-over year without Yvonne. I needn't have worried because after a wary start we clicked, right up to the present day. I love talented people and always do my best to demonstrate those talents to the fullest extent for a harmoniously successful production. On the opening night I was amused to receive a card from Dorothy with the following message and a gift of my favourite aftershave.

'Dear Bob,
A thank you prezzy for being so patient with me. At 27 I thought it was too late for dancing lessons. At 37 I know it was. But now at 47 I'm beginning to wonder. Come back to see us. I'm proud to be in this show and I have enjoyed working with you very much.
Luv Dottie!'

Praise from a fellow pro is always a treasure and so worth keeping.

Knowing that Les and Dorothy were heading the company after a successful 82 season I still felt as the new boy on the block that I would be on trial by the audiences if not the cast. Whilst I had selected my dancers, Dick had booked the rest, which included Barbara Ray a top ventriloquist and Syd Wright who had worked with me in other shows and was always dependable on the xylophone. A singing double Adeen Fogle and Robert Smith completed the cast. Strangely Dick's policy had been to open his show on a Monday which I thought odd. Audiences are more likely to attend theatres at the weekend especially when summer seasons have sparse audiences early in the season before holidaymakers arrive. Hang in there; you are in for a surprise.

During rehearsal all was going well except for one person, Robert Smith, Adeen Fogle's partner. He could not cope with any movement in production numbers. Both his feet were left. He could not sing and in the act awkwardly strummed one note monotonously on a guitar. Where the hell had Dick dug this one up from? I was embarrassed for him.

On Saturday I called the dress rehearsal for a 10.30 start with full make-up. Dick together with the chief executive Terry Nolan attended. Usually it is the entertainment director's job to attend. However Mr Nolan was particularly interested in theatre in all its facets. He would counsel but never interfered. A total friend of show business. John Bullock of Folkestone and Terry Nolan of Cromer were 'top of the pops' in the administration stakes and could be relied upon as far as I was concerned. Both supported me throughout my association with them and remain friends to the present day.

'Opening' scena

Back to my first show in Cromer. With Les Wilson and Dorothy Wayne leading the company I was confident that with the supporting artistes it would be successful. There was only one fly in the ointment. The overture over the curtain rose on a circus styled routine to the musical number 'Come Follow the Band'. The artistes all dressed in glittering circus costumes made a quite spectacular entrance except for one. Yes, you've guessed it – Robert Smith, not only trying to dance on his own feet but everyone else's too. Bumping and crashing around he certainly was an object of attention.

Dick arose from his seat half a dozen rows away from me and zoomed up hissing, 'Who the hell is that?' I replied 'Just what *I've* wondered for the past couple of weeks.' Dick said he had to leave but I told him to wait until after the rehearsal, because in my view the whole company would be thrown off balance and disorientated. For the rest of the first half Dick seethed and I could see the steam rising.

We sat over a coffee during a break and I told Dick I'd had misgivings from Day 1. However as he had booked the act I was in no position to question his decision. Remember it was my first show and it's not a good idea to argue with the boss until one's feet are firmly under the table. Dick's view of Mr Smith's dancing was that he looked as though he had soiled his underwear. Not that this was his exact terminology.

The second half scrambled through to the finale. Addressing the company he could not contain his irritation and frustration and let rip, pointedly looking at Robert Smith, saying there was a lot of work to do before we opened on Monday. He stormed out leaving me to pick up the pieces. John Grey the stage manager who has worked for a number of years with Dick in Norwich and Cromer told me he had never known Dick to be so angry. I replied that possibly he had never even witnessed the act, relying on an agent's sales talk. However it was an emergency that I had to resolve.

Adeen Fogle, an attractive Canadian singer, was excellent and I wanted her to remain with the show. Dick was adamant that her partner must leave and I agreed. Asking her if she would stay without him I was amazed to discover that he wasn't an artiste in any sense, he was really her agent, apparently as Dick had always booked a double act and being a creature of habit had advertised for such - unfortunately for Mr Smith who expected only to stand in the background strumming one string on a guitar – wrong. I only produced shows where everyone did everything. It had become my production trademark – no passengers allowed.

Going to Robert's dressing room he knew he was for the high jump. Dick had agreed on leaving the theatre, prior to me sorting out the problem, that I could offer him a job publicising the production, etc. In fact a backroom dogsbody. However as Adeen's agent he wanted her to remain, as was her desire also. As I have said, thank goodness we were not opening that Saturday night.

I had previously agreed that I would perform within the production numbers to fill the gap that Robert's leaving entailed, telling Dick I would only agree to do this for the ten days before the second show had to open. In the meantime Dick had to find a male dancer/singer to rehearse immediately and in time to join the company without delay.

Whilst I had choreographed the show I had no problem with that aspect, however I only had Sunday to memorise all the songs. Walking across the cliff tops on Sunday I committed it all to memory, practising putting it together. Any onlookers taking a stroll must have concluded I was a nutter.

Monday dawned and the company, including myself, spent the day working all the production numbers ready to open that evening. Fortunately all went well and Dick was greatly pleased at the after show party.

With my, by now, usual practice I am letting the critics of the papers put their views forward.

Encore
Ted Bell

This is not just another of those End of Pier Shows. The sure touch of Robert Marlowe in direction and choreography give it slickness and spectacle … Anne-Marie Miller's costumes, Ted Woodley's sets and Ian Scott's lighting all blend to make this as smart and professional a show as ever was wafted over by North Norfolk's sea breezes.

As with all successful summer shows, the secret is teamwork exemplified not only in the routines but in the general verve and dedication …

Daily Press
NH Easton

Bright and breezy and full of fun Cromer Pier Pavilion's Seaside Special 83 looks set to break all box office records.

Top comedy team, Les Wilson and Dorothy Wayne – both returning for a second season, lead a multi talented company through a slick two-hour show of music and mirth, song and dance, colour and movement, which deserves to pack 'em in right through to September … it is the biggest budget show presented this time – and it shows.

A superb production devised, directed and choreographed by Robert Marlowe … the trio of high stepping dancers, Sarah Clarkson, Laura Daltry and Sally-Ann Mathias – surely among the best show dancers outside London.

Rehearsals for the second show commenced the next day and fortunately Dick was able to recruit a male dancer singer to replace Robert Smith, who appeared a couple of days later to join the company. He had worked in West End musicals and blended well into the company. Of course I continued to play in the first show until the change-over.

A rather disturbing thing happened when we performed our first matinée on the Saturday afternoon. As the curtain rose we outnumbered the audience by one, three if you include the musicians Dennis and Tim Marriot, father and son. Les Wilson invited the eight brave souls down amongst the red plush seats to concentrate themselves in the centre front, to keep warm if nothing else.

Unbelievable they worked harder than us on stage with such enthusiasm that we all enjoyed ourselves both on and off stage. I was dismayed, taking it personally and thinking I was to blame. However the audiences improved as the season progressed and word of mouth praised the different style I had introduced. With Les Wilson and Dottie Wayne leading the comedy, especially in a hysterical take off on the National Health Service, still pertinent today 20 years later, the audiences started to create 'house full' notices, when the television companies started to take an interest, the BBC in particular.

Adeen Fogle was proving popular, minus Robert Smith who returned to

'Finale' scena

being an agent, and after the second show opened I relinquished my role to the newcomer. That was the only and last time I performed on that stage, which in retrospect I am glad I experienced, being able now to say 'I did it' as a member briefly of a show I was going to mastermind for a couple of decades.

After the success of the Cromer show and the opening night of the second programme I was whisked away to Dick's second production in Hunstanton. Although I had kept this rather quiet I had also signed a follow-on contract to devise direct and choreograph his sister show further up the Norfolk coast.

The Princess theatre, a former cinema, was rather like having to present a show on a mantelpiece - wide and narrow. Whilst the Cromer stage left a lot to be desired size-wise the Hunstanton stage was a thousand times worse, although going there now after its revamp, as I did recently, it's vastly changed, and thriving. Back in 1983 it was a director's nightmare especially choreographically.

I was picked up after Cromer's second show opening by Tom Dickinson and driven to Hunstanton to commence rehearsals the following morning. Tom had been engaged as theatre manager on behalf of Dick Condon's production company. He had offered me accommodation but it was a very small flat and although I only had ten days to the opening night I had to find somewhere else to stay. I had no intention of sharing a bed!

Asking advice re accommodation from the box office manageress, who was also assistant theatre manager, Pat Brooks an ex-actress offered me a spare bedroom in her beautiful cottage close to Norfolk's famous lavender fields near Heacham. Thank goodness for her presence and friendship, it helped me through what was to be a nightmare scenario.

Looking back it was a case of the sublime, Cromer, to the ridiculous. Not that Dick's team had let me down, nor the cast. I had the same set and costume designers and Dick had assembled an excellent company headed by Dennis Lotis, the well-known pop singer. My old friend Frankie Holmes, always successful, as the top comic, together with Gus Wilson illusionist, Gordon Glen accordionist, Sharon Wood - a very talented and beautiful young singer, Karen and Wayne a pop duo - young and good-looking, topped off by my dancers Caroline, Gillian and Dawn all supplying the long legged, slim and pretty essential of all my dancers.

The musical director, to my astonishment, was Derrick Taverner, famous for West End musicals from the Palladium to Drury Lane. I couldn't believe my luck to have this expert as my musical director. I guessed that as his home was Hunstanton it was a chance to work from home. Very rare in our profession even if only for a short period. I was now sure we would have a success on our hands and commenced the first rehearsals with enthusiasm and great expectations.

The biggest drawback however was the backstage conditions, which were diabolical. Basically a long corridor sectioned off by flimsy curtains. I had never seen anything as bad as this – where was Equity, our union? However it was a venue for performing artistes so everyone kept silent, suffering for their art. Unfortunately there was another fly in the ointment. This time a more dangerous one. All was to be revealed at a later date.

With only ten days to get the production together for the opening night it was a hard grind even for experienced performers such as these. Thank the lord that I had such comfortable digs to relax in after a hard day's slog.

The opening night was received most favourably by the local authority bigwigs, the Press and more importantly our boss Richard Condon.

I returned to my home, happy but exhausted. Two opening productions in less than six weeks proved successful by Press and public. Time to relax. I was due for a break. However a couple of weeks later a phone call from Dick requested me to return to Hunstanton and take a look at the show. This started to ring alarm bells for me. Call it a spooky premonition.

Arriving to view the show one evening I was greeted by the theatre manager, Tom Dicknson who seemed rather uneasy. Apparently Dick had rung, telling him not to tell the cast I was arriving. Those alarm bells were clanging in my head. I took my seat as the auditorium lights faded in case I would be spotted by the cast members peeping at the audience. I felt like a Mafia agent or a trouble-shooter which indeed I was destined to be.

The whole production had been revamped and now represented a down-market holiday camp show - the type of show I had avoided throughout my entire career, even refusing Mr Show Business himself, Richard Stone, when he attempted to persuade me to take on Butlins Holiday Camp shows some years before.

By the interval I was in a furious rage and stormed into the company manager's office. Tom Dickinson cowered, as using words I generally avoided I shrieked at him 'What the f—ing hell has happened here?'

He looked as guilty as hell but denied any knowledge of what I had just witnessed. Oh yeah? Trying to buy me a drink I refused and returned to my seat to simmer through the rest of the show. The finale proved to be the straw that broke the camel's back. It was a diabolical travesty of my original ideas which was to present a glittering, stylish walk down and classy finish which I was particularly renowned for.

With my suspicion as to the culprit getting stronger I hurtled backstage to confront the cast who in my view had been totally demeaned by the final cheap spectacle. As Frankie Holmes was the only member of the cast I had previously worked with under other managements, I knew he would tell me the truth – he did, also saying that it had been done under Dick's request, apparently according to Tom. This part I didn't believe but Frankie said that Tom Dickinson was the one passing the message.

I asked Frankie if they had seen Dick since the opening night. No, was the answer. Going to the stage manager I told him to call the whole company for a rehearsal at 11am the following morning, and then I rang Dick to request a meeting with him in the Norwich Theatre Royal the following afternoon.

Pat Brooks with whom I had arranged to stay overnight calmed me down with a strong gin and tonic, always my salvation, and kindly offered to drive me to Norwich the following afternoon. I wondered whether Dick had heard rumblings, that being the reason he had asked me to return to view the show.

The next morning I explained to the cast that the show had to be returned to the exact formula I had set for the opening night. There was just one dissenter who had actually benefited from the change – no name – but when I said that anyone who disagreed could not expect to work for Dick Condon again, he was subdued and acquiesced.

I had also learnt that a long serving and trusted chief usherette had been demoted and replaced by a rather camp young man to bring a more up to date atmosphere into the theatre. In 1983 this was quite obviously Mr Dickinson's idea of modernising. Oh well each to their own. However the rumblings of discontent were creating an atmosphere that had to be stopped immediately. More especially as North Norfolk was quite comfortably in a time warp.

With rehearsal over and back on track, Pat and I headed for Norwich. That afternoon with Pat present as a backup I told Dick the whole story.

Apparently Tom had developed a system of ringing Dick on almost a daily basis acquainting him of his own experience in creating the summer shows in Jersey for impresario Dick Ray, obviously in an attempt to dislodge me, especially for the future. His naivety astonished me. I thought he knew showbiz well enough to realise that in management everybody knew everybody and information was only a phone call away, which I believe Dick had already sussed out. He was nobody's fool.

Dick calmly asked Pat if she would be ready to take on full management of the theatre with all its responsibilities. Pat had been an actress all her life and was well versed in just about every aspect of it, so readily agreed.

Dick picked up the phone, ringing Mr Dickinson. He sacked him on the spot telling him to vacate immediately and to leave the keys with the box office staff.

I stayed overnight in Cromer to view the show again, it had settled in splendidly and was a credit to all the artistes. The box office tills were ringing merrily with audiences increasing weekly and returning for the second show. Always a good sign that we had got the equation right. I returned home happy in the knowledge that all was well and especially delighted with my first season in Norfolk.

I have realised that readers who have followed me this far may regard me as a know-it-all big 'ead. My defence, now I'm looking back, is that I started at square one in my chosen profession and experience was my only guideline throughout the 53 years I survived in the business.

When I first worked for Richard Condon, known as Dick to his friends, in spite of my own thirty-three years in the profession I was in awe of him for what he had achieved. So I was excited when he asked me to list for him my intentions regarding how I would go about creating his show for him. I have quite recently discovered the plans I originally presented in 1982. That allowed me to carry them out to his total satisfaction throughout the period I worked under his banner was for me sufficient praise.

He was very astute, in spite of his Irish blarney and charm, and straight to the point. I also sussed that whilst he was very shrewd he also liked to dominate his workforce. Once he did they could well finish up in the 'out' tray. As I had never occupied this tray except by illiterate connivers as in Folkestone, I now felt my own background deserved respect.

On one or two occasions in the early days Dick had tried to put one over on me. I stood my ground and he retreated so we were on an even field. He was the most charismatic person I had ever worked for. Some impresarios can be remote and god-like without any contact with the people they engage. But Dick was different. I knew right from the start that I must gain his respect and we developed a very warm and close association on both sides especially as the success of each season grew and grew.

As the shows increasingly became more successful Dick would ask me to view videos of prospective artistes sent in by their agents or even the artistes themselves and to express my view as to whether they were right for both our show or budget. We only slipped on the odd occasion, I'm happy to report.

Christmas 83, my first without Nina after her retirement, I directed, choreographed and took on the role of the Demon King in 'Mother Goose' for my twelfth pantomime with the Triumph theatre organisation. Incidentally I was playing Honor Blackman's role of the previous year – more butchly I hasten to add. This was presented in the Arts theatre in Cambridge where I had last appeared in 1961 when I was forced into playing Cyril Fletcher's role of the 'Queen of Hearts' due to his sudden indisposition. Although I had carried the role off until Cyril's recovery it was not one I wished to further, preferring by far the more rewarding evil roles which I was known for.

Next on my agenda was of course my second summer season for Cromer. I simply had to come up with the goods to prove I wasn't a flash in the pan on the distant horizon.

Once again, as you well know by now, it's comedy first to ensure a successful show. Dick took my advice and contracted the Jay Brothers, Gordon and Bunny always a sure bet. Co-starring with them was my friend Des King forming a perfect comedic alliance. For singers, my comrades from Folkestone, Freda Farnworth and Graham Trew together with the young singing duo Diane and Julian. Julian had served his time as pit drummer in Folkestone and now four years later, married to Diane, they were making their debut in Cromer.

As most of my dancers from Folkestone had gone on to pastures new I had advertised for dancers. Unfortunately only three as the budget would not extend to encompass four girls. Although I argued the point with Dick he held the financial reins. Little did I know that we had a television show for the BBC waiting in the wings. This was the catalyst that put 'Seaside Special' on an upward spiralling mega success for the next eighteen years – our glory years.

In the spring I had a phone call from the BBC TV centre with a request to meet up with Clem Vallence one of their top TV producers. Would I? You bet! Those phone calls are rarer than hen's teeth. We met for lunch in the Tate Gallery restaurant, which had a well renowned reputation. I knew I was up for scrutiny as to whether I would be ideal as a link man for the proposed coverage of 'Forty Minutes'.

'Forty Minutes' was a television show which held a well esteemed position each week on a wide range of subjects and the embryonic 'Seaside Special' had aroused the powers that be to show interest in this little theatre perched on the end of the Victorian pier which jutted out into the freezing cold sea of the North Norfolk coast. It was considered a dying art. Especially as most holidays were now taken in the warmer climes of the continent.

I felt fairly confident that I could find the secret to success especially as I already had the experience of my twelve continuous years in Folkestone which had stored up a stack of ideas I could brush up and polish even further to re-create again.

All we needed was what we were about to be granted – television exposure, especially countrywide. Once the contracts were agreed and all the artistes eagerly signed up I held auditions for my dancers at which the television cameras were present. All the auditionees were informed that the TV cameras were filming the process in case they didn't wish to be screened.

No one declined, all eager to be on the telly even if they didn't get the job. Indeed I was only allowed three dancers due to the budget restrictions. However there was quite a large turnout so at least they all had a brief moment of countrywide fame as a solace.

Turning away young dancers who in general are all very highly trained is always a heart aching moment. They all make such an effort even wearing full 'slap'. For the uninitiated that's showbiz jargon for make-up. Eventually whittling down to the final dozen, I selected identical twins Michelle and Jaynee Jordon, and Christina Shepherd. All pretty and very talented – naturally.

Once we were into rehearsals the television team of cameramen, lighting experts and gofers were all under the supervision of the director, Clem Vallence. To those of you who feel you know that name, Clem was the director more recently of the Michael Palin documentaries 'Around the World in Eighty Days'. He was calm, talented and totally professional and we've exchanged Christmas cards to the present day.

The company, however, had to ignore the cameras and concentrate on getting the show ready for the opening night. We all worked happily together and were able to watch the rushes each evening once the rehearsals were finished for the day. Like Topsy, it growed! The cameras were strategically placed around the theatre on the opening night and the audience were thrilled when shots of them were included, in particular at the first night after-show party, when certain people were interviewed for their opinions.

The actual film was not scheduled to reach the screens until December, too late for our present season but time to publicise the show of 1985 the following summer.

Yet again I will let the professional critic air his views.

SCS The Journal

END-OF-THE-PIER ENTERTAINMENT IS ALIVE AND KICKING AT CROMER THIS SUMMER

The latest in the string of thoroughbreds from Mr Dick Condon's 'Seaside Special' stable opened on Saturday, and early form suggests this colourful family show is set to provide the town with another theatrical winner.

Seaside Special 84 is as traditional as roast beef on Sunday with a strong emphasis on comedy and a well-judged musical balance. The whole production is wrapped in a bright package, brilliantly enhanced by excellent sets and lighting and an array of dazzling costumes that were a prime talking point after the show.

Heading a talented cast are comic brothers Gordon and Bunny Jay, two men with the mobile faces of music hall funny men and the wit and polish of modern day performers. They volley gags between them like tennis players at the net.

Des King, a comedian and a dab hand with the magic wand, quickly establishes a keen rapport with the audience through his strong, likeable personality. Song and dance fans are well catered for in the show, soprano Freda Farnworth can turn her pleasant singing voice from light opera to numbers from today's West End musicals, whilst baritone Graham Trew seems at home with songs from the past and present.

Diane and Julian blend their vocal and instrumental talents in a glossy, bouncy performance, which contains a refreshingly unpretentious version of the over-worked 'Amazing Grace'.

One of the strong points of 'Seaside Specials' is that the artistes are not simply dumped on stage and allowed to get on with their acts. Their performances are blended into the production with great dexterity by director Robert Marlowe who also choreographed the dance routines performed with such elegance by twins Jaynee and Michelle Jordan, and Christina Shepherd.

So ended my second season in Cromer. However 'Seaside Special' was on the brink of far greater success not just countrywide but in certain instances worldwide.

My pantomime of 84 was again 'Mother Goose', my third production for Paul Elliot's company in the beautiful little Theatre Royal in Lincoln, an historic city. It seemed that I was destined to remain up in the north eastern region of England into the foreseeable future.

Whilst directing and choreographing I was also playing the demon role, which Honor Blackman had originated in London three years earlier. This time a totally differing cast was in place.

Top of the bill was Brian Cant, perfect for panto, as he was well known on television for presenting children's afternoon shows. I had first met Brian thirty

'Sound of Music' scena

years previously when he was a teenager working in an office job in Ipswich, East Anglia. Totally stage struck he would travel every Saturday to Flexistowe where I was in my first 'Out of the Blue' company. Brian agreed he was our groupie, joining with the company when we relaxed after the show in a local restaurant. We all wondered how he returned to Ipswich and surmised that he cycled. Such loyalty!

This was the first time we worked together. His co-star was Geoffrey Davies also a TV star known for playing the sexy anaesthetist in 'The Doctors' series. Roy North, one of Basil Brush's cohorts, also starred, all of them well known for their television appearances, which was now an essential for pantomime, a sorry barometer of the way the TV ruled most people's lives.

Playing her first principal boy role was top model Jilly Johnson, a charming girl with the greatest asset of long, long legs. There had to be some eye candy for fathers and grandfathers dragooned into attending pantomimes. My dancers from Cromer, twins Jaynee and Michelle, together with Christina, joined others to form our chorus along with a team of local juveniles.

The '40 minutes' documentary on Cromer was scheduled to be screened during the 'Mother Goose' run. Backstage we had a green room with a TV screen. Green rooms in Victorian days and before were where performers coming off stage and dazzled by candles in the floats sat to accustom their eyes before returning to their dressing rooms. The walls were actually painted green, hence the name. Another little known fact is that the term 'Floats' was in Georgian times a trough filled with water in which the many candles were floated, obviously for safety.

Footlights with the coming of electricity still retained the term 'floats' to technicians. However nowadays footlights hardly exist at all as spot bars have now replaced them in general. History lesson over. Back to the plot.

The whole company of 'Mother Goose' were agog to watch the '40 minutes' show being transmitted. It was the fastest second half in panto history as the whole company sped, in their finale costumes, into the green room.

I awaited the newspaper verdicts with trepidation. It could be make or break for Cromer's future. 'Mother Goose' terminated on 7 February and the weekend of the 14th reports of '40 minutes' were reviewed by all the leading newspapers. Even though the big nationals were sympathetic to what they conceived as our plight, they nevertheless thought that we were about to wither on the vine of music hall.

The following are a brief showing of some comments.

Daily Mail
1 February 1985
Elizabeth Cowley

40 MINUTES 9.30PM BBC2

The End-of-the-Pier Show gets my vote as charmer of the month. Clem Vallence's portrait of a group of all-rounders gallantly mounting one of the last of the old-style pier entertainments at Cromer in Norfolk – doesn't miss a trick, from auditions to opening night. Howard Billingham's editing is a treat too – knowing just when to cut to a laughing old age pensioner or a wobbling headpiece on a nervous showgirl when it's ciné vérité and you haven't an interviewer, isn't easy. But these two talents made me feel I was backstage among the artistes on opening night, all thought of an eaves-dropping film crew forgotten.

Alas the Pier Show, part of what used to be a traditional British summer holiday is dwindling fast. As ex-Folies Bergere dancer and the show's producer Bob Marlowe puts it: 'With the package tour most people go abroad now, and it's so often bitterly cold here. But in spite of a budget that extends to only 3 dancers (there used to be 12) and making do with last year's costumes, he's undaunted, his singers have to dance, his comics have to sing and his top-of-the-bill act Gordon and Bunny Jay have to do everything. I can think of worse places than Cromer! says Bunny bravely.

The Daily Telegraph
Friday 1 February 1985
Sean Day-Lewis

Clem Vallence's The End-of-the-Pier Show (BBC2) the sad and funny contribution to 'Forty Minutes' last night recorded one of the last twitches of a tradition gradually weakened by the modern taste for foreign holidays in the sun..... director and choreographer Robert Marlowe cut his teeth with the 'Folies Bergere'. Running his eye over the 50 bright eyed girl dancers who attended his Covent Garden auditions, he did not tell them his chorus line – once 16 strong – is now reduced to three. 'Four would be choreographically easier' he explained to his Norwich based Irish Producer. We can only afford three came the merciless reply.

Musical director Dennis Marriot said, 'This is the last cradle for beginners.' It was a good year. The houses were half empty but also half full. Perhaps the cradle will last for 1985 as well and meanwhile the company were grateful for the work.

The Times
Friday 1 February 1985
Dennis Hackett

As we saw in 'The End-of-the-Pier Show', BBC2's Forty Minutes documentary last night, all worked hard. Everyone had to sing and dance, explained director and choreographer Bob Marlowe, an ex-Folies Bergere dancer, full of good humoured fortitude. When it went well it was like one big party. The subsequent local newspaper headline said 'Shadow cast over the Pier Show'. It really referred to the genre in general and the cast took it in their stride... but thanks to producer Clem Vallence those performers who made it last year may now claim the magic words 'As seen on TV'...

The Observer
Sunday 27 January 1985
Jennifer Selway

9.30–10.10 Forty Minutes BBC2
'THE END-OF-THE-PIER SHOW'
Off to lovely Cromer on the Norfolk coast to witness rehearsals for the old style Pier Show, where (as an economy measure) the principals outnumber the chorus girls by about two to one. The performers have a repertoire of valiant one-liners. 'It isn't the big time but then it's not the end of the line... We don't bring people into the theatre but on the other hand, we don't keep them out... a gorgeous programme.

The Daily Mail
Friday 1 February 1985
Herbert Kretzmer

We must be grateful for documentaries like 'The End-of-the-Pier Show' (Forty Minutes BBC2) because the institution it celebrates will soon, alas, be a thing of the past. Package vacations abroad have all but killed off the traditional British seaside holiday and with it the summer show at the End-of-the-Pier. Clem Vallence's programme went behind the scenes of one such entertainment in the quiet resort of Cromer on the Norfolk coast. It was, as you might expect, a shoestring affair. The director pleaded for 4 dancing girls but was only allowed 3. The cast of 10 worked like 20. Even the magician was called upon to sing. The audience loved it. Soon it will be as dead as Vaudeville and we will only have programmes like this to remind us of a vanished age.

It was claimed that over 5 million viewers watched the televised documentary and praised it. Not only in England but in other English speaking countries, verified by extra payments to all the artistes.

However after all the positive vibes about the artistes I was so incensed to read an article by Alan Coren in the Mail on Sunday, that I abandoned my practice of not replying to newspaper reports, and sent the following.

Dear Mr Coren
Re your article in Sunday's edition of the Mail
I take violent exception that you should label a group of hardworking young people struggling to make a modest living from their talents, as 'Freaks and Eccentrics'.

We had no particular wish to have the spotlight thrown onto our efforts. There was certainly little financial remuneration.

However, to be insulted by a parasite was a bonus we could have done without. Thankfully the rest of the Press were as kindly and sympathetic as Clem Vallance's treatment of our humble fight for survival. Should you ever find yourself fighting a rearguard action to survive in your chosen profession then I trust you do not have to endure the bitchy label of 'freak' and 'eccentric' which in spite of any dictionary appraisal is still regarded by most as an insult.

Yours truly
Robert Marlowe
Devisor, Director and Choreographer
Seaside Special 85

The following letter from Clem Vallence appeased me after the foregoing.

Dear Bob
Many thanks for your letter, I'm so glad and relieved that you actually enjoyed the film. It was made with affection, but there is many a slip… I don't know anyone who has seen it and not admired you and the company, your talents and sincere efforts to keep the Pier Show alive and kicking.

My kids are dying to see next summer's show at Cromer and very cross that I kept interrupting the on-stage stuff with all that boring documentary bit in the dressing rooms.

Thanks for the panto booklet I'll let you know if the idea gets any further. If you haven't managed to get a video of the Pier Show let me know and I will get one copied for you.

All the best for your immediate projects. Do keep in touch.
Regards
Clem

This show was, in fact, quite a turning point for Cromer and we have kept in touch ever since. In spite of the television coverage, which had received favourable reviews, many believed it was the last struggle of a dinosaur. They had not reckoned on the determination of Dick and myself to transform it into the gold plated success it was destined to be. Failure never entered our equation. Within a very short period the success of Seaside Special was a source of envy throughout the industry.

Many civic authorities sent their representatives to try and discover the formula. What they had not taken on board was the location. The charming little Victorian theatre set on a churning sea which when the sun shone turned it into Cinderella's transformation. Looking back it was quite amazing how many opening nights entertained the audiences with a dazzling sunset reflected in an unusually calm sea. Dick also had the innovative brainwave to offer every member of the anticipating audience a glass of sherry, served by young guys and girls smartly attired in black and white ensembles. A true sense of occasion which created a glow even before the curtain rose on the opening night.

With my job now over I relaxed, more than confident that we had selected the right cast of performers to top the show with success.

'Aviation' scena

At the after-show party Clem moved amongst members of the audience asking their opinions which were unanimous in their praises as one of the best ever, and this from people who had been attending for years, in one specific case a couple for almost 50, back to when my alma mater 'Out of the Blue' was presenting its summer shows in the 30s.

There is even archive film in the Cromer museum of Ronnie Brandon and Dickie Pounds the producers, husband and wife, in their younger years riding a tandem in a production number.

After the euphoric and exhilarating first night the company relaxed until 10.30am on the Monday when rehearsals began for the second show to be presented alternatively on a weekly basis throughout the season.

This began an arduous period for the cast having to rehearse new material by day and perform the current show by night. Until the second show opened the matinèes were put on hold. Originally only one matinèe on a Saturday was presented but with the show's increasing popularity and coach companies bringing in parties the matinées eventually increased to three - Wednesday, Thursday and Saturday, a sure barometer of success.

Prices of tickets were kept down to encourage not only visitors but locals as well - after all, the locals can be a show's ambassadors. Therefore the first week of each season gave a special concession of two tickets for the price of one for hoteliers, guest house proprietors and locals to spread the word. The reward was reflected in the percentage increased attendances.

Whilst Terry Nolan was chief executive he had vowed to hold the prices below 5 pounds. A worthy ambition. However once Terry retired the prices had to rise. With increased expenditure now needed to fund price rises in just about every aspect of merely presenting the show, and the audiences expecting each show to be more lavish and spectacular than the previous year, this had to be resolved.

When we tried to raise tickets by 50p it almost started a third world war amongst locals. Newspaper headlines condemned the rise. However we had no option but to proceed. The show still offered great entertainment on every level. After all, in life you get what you pay for.

On reflection, it seems incredible that in 1983 during my first production for Dick, when I had to step in at the last minute on the opening night due to internal problems in the casting, we had witnessed a matinée when the cast of 12 outnumbered the audience by 4. The 8 brave souls worked harder than we did on stage to enjoy the show! It puts the whole phenomenon into perspective.

Clem Vallence's television documentary was the key that opened the door to success and bridged the gap between live and filmed performances. It showed that the two mediums could cohabit happily, to each other's advantage.

As my seasons in Cromer were to extend over 20 years in total I will attempt to quickly cover them, for I have no wish to bore readers. I will endeavour to highlight certain years, which are interesting for differing reasons.

I was fortunate to be presented with a unique set of circumstances that many choreographers/directors would have given their eye-teeth for, and was able to prove my staying power in creating what the audiences expected. Luck and being in the right place at the right time is the true essence of show business. As in any success story, the downside is that one can't afford to stumble for there is always someone waiting in the shadows to take over. This was to be proved to me in quite a few instances throughout the years and by colleagues who I naively trusted. However, all life is a learning curve and I quickly learnt to fight fire with fire, and win. Dramatic, but true.

The season of 1985, due to the TV coverage of the 'Forty Minutes' programme became a foregone success. Gordon and Bunny Jay again topped the bill assisted by Chris Lloyd as second comic. Rosemary Squires, who had cornered the market in television advertising jingles, was the pop element of the production along with Barry Daniels, a singer impressionist from my Folkestone shows, always worth his weight in gold. Completing the company was a married couple, multi instrumentalists Carol and Roger Bryan.

A rumour reached my ears that Roger unfortunately had only one leg. Surely

'World War Two' scena

176

not? Dick Condon couldn't have pulled that on me knowing that all artistes had to participate in production scenes. The rehearsal day dawned and walking down the pier I recognised ahead of me the musical couple I had yet to meet. The husband strutted his stuff with no indication of an impediment in his gait. Phew! Someone had been pulling my leg, if you will forgive the pun.

Setting the opening routine, we broke for coffee, and I sighed with relief – no problem. Carol Bryan pulled me to one side whispering that Roger had a problem. The rumour was true. Carol explained that movement to the right in a routine was OK, however left moves caused difficulty. He had a partial loss of movement, so that any move to the left caused his lower limb to unscrew. I was probably more embarrassed than they were.

So going back into rehearsals I re-arranged the routine by eliminating all the left twists. I have to say Roger coped better in routines than others with no impediment. During the season, I understand, he could beat all the others on the tennis courts.

Their acts in the show proved successful and they were popular. My dancers, Sarah Clarkson, Louise Clifford and Kate Humphrey completed the cast.

The following critique appeared in the Press.

Eastern Daily Press
Neville Miller

Seaside Special 1985 is attracting far bigger audiences than last year – thanks no doubt to the publicity of a TV programme about the Cromer entertainment and its growing reputation as something special. The season, which opened last night, will obviously uphold the reputation since it gives its music and laughter at a smart professional canter and invariably looks as fresh as Spring ...

For the third season in a row Gordon and Bunny Jay were engaged yet again. They were of the old school and had such a cornucopia of material, all well tried and tested. I had known them for twenty two years since working together in Richard Stone's, 'Lets Make a Night of It' in Worthing. They certainly knew how to keep a show together. Good helmsmen.

Co-starring was Joan Savage singer/comedienne from 'The Black and White Minstrel Shows', also 'Friday Night is Music Night' and 'Music for You'.

An Australian musical act joined us and stayed for a number of years. Husband and wife Terry and Kathy known as 'Traffle' were extremely popular singers and versatile in all styles. Good movers, they also added greatly to the comedy sketches. A 17-year-old classical violinist Gary Lovini made a sensational debut. Tall and good-looking he had everything. Another newcomer joined at the same time. Only 23 but already loaded with charisma – his name? Bradley Walsh. All together a cast we couldn't afford today. Dick Condon certainly knew how to pick 'em.

Right from Day 1, Bradley gave off massive charisma. Easy going and friendly he was eager to participate in whatever was asked of him. A real treasure then - and now in the new millennium, a national one.

My dancers from the previous year Sarah and Louis were joined by newcomer Bridget Polley, to complete the cast.

I'm trying to give readers an insight into the actual workings of getting a show from first company meeting to first night, in an ever-shortening rehearsal period. There can be pitfalls, which a tactful director needs to be wary of to maintain that essential ingredient – harmony.

An amusing little charade occurred involving Joan Savage, very talented and excellent in sketches with the comics. However every artiste's contract stipulates that they supply their own music, costumes, etc for their speciality acts which are incorporated into the production.

I was somewhat surprised in the dress rehearsal by Joan's choice of costume. To say it was rather bizarre would be putting it mildly. A black lace cat suit, extra high heeled shoes and a scarlet sequinned bowler hat. Tactfully, I never said a word.

At the start of rehearsals for the second show on the Monday following the first night, Joan came to me very obviously upset, almost tearful. Apparently at the first night party on Saturday night one of the lifeboat men, from the world famous lifeboat station adjoining the theatre on the very End-of-the-Pier, had tactlessly asked Joan who she was trying to impersonate in such an awful outfit she was wearing – well, he was a braver man than I was - Gunga Din!

Poor lass, she was almost blaming me for not intervening. However I explained it was not my place to do so. Any director of a variety styled show expects the performer to know what works for them. I suggested that she show me alternate costumes that she had in her wardrobe. I realised in the outfit she had chosen that she was harking back to her glory days in 'The Black and White Minstrel Show'. However that was a while back and not particularly relevant at that time for my style of production. I persuaded her that a full-length black and silver sequined gown was becoming, especially as a side slit showed her legs off without being tarty. Donning her scarlet sequinned bowler for one appropriate number reminded the audience of her minstrel days. The sun shone and it was smiles all round especially when later in the week the candid lifeboat man popped in to see the show again, praising Joan's changes enthusiastically.

Finally with such a cast there was no question as to whether it would be successful – all the newspaper critiques forecast a resounding success which was being revealed by long queues each morning waiting for the box office to open, and in the evenings waiting patiently for returns which in many cases were not forthcoming.

The professional critics were falling over themselves with effusive praise.

Norfolk Journal
Richard Swallow

'Seaside Special' is billed as the last authentic End-of-the-Pier Show. But it is more than that. For a few months every summer Cromer takes on all the trappings of the West End as theatre lovers from near and far flock to see an evening of good old-fashioned entertainment. ... at Cromer they play to packed houses right through the summer months To witness what has become the theatrical event of the summer ... Alongside Glyndebourne and Stratford is the name Cromer.

Daily Telegraph
Maurice Weaver

Britain's biggest little seaside show, said to be the last example of 'End-of-the-Pier' classic ... has become famous as a successful box office phenomenon, a triumphal return to traditional seaside follies.

The Independent
Martin Roe

Sell-out performances 8 times a week suggest that other piers might do well to reconsider the virtues of this mix of song, dance, comic banter, sitcom sketches and something called 'Family Fun'.

Daily Telegraph
Charles Spencer

By the opening night the show had miraculously achieved slickness, almost seamless continuity and a dash of real style... I found it impossible to wipe an inane grin of happiness off my face. There are far too few evenings, which produce this effect.

The Stage and Television Today
Tony Mallion

There's a special magic about a visit to 'Seaside Special' ... to those of us who yearn to see a well-dressed, well-staged show which owes its success to sheer stagecraft, this is an oasis.

Eastern Evening News
Neville Miller

PUBLIC VOTES PIER SHOW A HIT

Now the quaint intimate theatre out in the North Sea, which was once thought the Cinderella of British resort theatres is the heart of a success story. House Full boards are now familiar on the Pier.

The summer of 86 had a great farewell last night party made more exciting with the news that Bradley Walsh had agreed to return for the summer of 87 but this time topping the bill. Never before had a debut year been followed so swiftly by a starring one, well deserved and eventually leading to countrywide fame with the stamp of royal approval when he sensationally appeared on the Royal Variety Show, shaking the whole world of show business with his presence. What a guy!

I'm jumping ahead a couple of years so back to the present year of 86. For the first time Dick had asked me to direct and write his Christmas pantomime for the Theatre Royal in Norwich. I have throughout my whole career always specialised in traditional pantomime. Dick knew that I had worked every No.1 theatre in the country and I was eager to add the Norwich 'Royal' to my list.

'Cinderella' was the subject, always a top favourite with children. Anne Aston was a delightful Cinders, Robin Nedwell, a well known comedy actor, made his debut successfully as Buttons, whilst veteran actress Avril Angers played a slightly barmy and forgetful Fairy Godmother, and I was to work for the first time with the well known drag act Burden and Moran as the Ugly Sisters.

Once again meeting them was to have long-term repercussions in my life. American Diane Soloman was Prince Charming but, what the heck, why shouldn't the Prince have an American accent? She was very pretty, with great legs, which delighted guys in the audience. Something for everyone!

Dick had also engaged Gary Lovini from the Cromer summer season and asked me to write a special part to encompass his violin skills. Writing a gypsy encampment in the forest scene I had the dancers swirling around him, which brought the house down. To say the pantomime was a great success would be boastful so I will leave it to the professional critics.

The Stage and Television Today
Peter Spalding

The Theatre Royal pantomime is very strong on music and spectacle this year... designs are bright, atmospheric and tailor-made to fit the constant ebb and flow of action directed at a cracking pace by Robert Marlowe.

Eastern Daily Press (Norwich)
Charles Roberts

... but what makes it special is the touch of class in every degree introduced by Robert Marlowe. He knows how to create the elegance of regal musical comedy and how to paint stunning pictures with his cast... And masterminds an overall flow and shape which are in every sense theatrical. He has by the way written the script too... A bright storyline with some hilarious gags... it has a warmth and appeal, which takes you to its heart, and, of course, there's class!

Charles Roberts was known as a critic who was hard to please so I found this particularly rewarding. However even more importantly was the following letter from Dick Condon, 18 December 1986.

Dear Bob
I want you to know how much I appreciate the superb end result of your efforts in connection with the pantomime, Cinderella.
In terms of scripting you have given the whole thing a new look and it zips along with speed and style. I appreciate all the effort you have put in and I am delighted that the achievement of such a splendid result is particularly appropriate for this, your first pantomime in Norwich.
I hope we can continue to work together both at Cromer in 1987 and also at the Theatre Royal in 1987/88 pantomime season. Please let me know if you are prepared to enter a commitment to do the pantomime next year for us as I would like to lay down plans for the production as quickly as possible and obviously would like to involve you in these plans from the beginning. Once again, you have done a splendid job and I want you to know how much I appreciate everything that you have achieved.
Best wishes,
Yours sincerely
Dick

This letter meant more than gold to me. It was a mutual admiration society. However the next job was getting together the summer season of 1987. With

Bradley already engaged to top the bill, Dick had also booked a double act Cadmen and Walker as the support comedy team.

From the previous season he had also re-booked 'Traffle'. Kathy and Terry had proved their worth and were tremendously popular with the audiences, which proved a great barometer for decision-making. They were indeed to appear many more times throughout the years – never disappointing.

Another great favourite Dottie Wayne came back for the umpteenth time. So much so I almost lost count. The biggest secret of this type of show is to always listen to what the audiences want and success can be almost guaranteed. Other company members were multi-instrumentalist Jon Barker and West End singer Brian Pulman.

Auditioning for new dancers, I selected Helen Saddler, Clair Wring and Claire Cheney, who had all reached the high standards I required.

During rehearsals, all went well, but an accident was waiting to happen. The dress rehearsal, in Dick's presence, augured well for the opening night and the company relaxed in readiness for our usual packed first Saturday performance. By the interval the audience were proclaiming it a winner with Bradley scoring heavily.

However, the winners of television's New Faces Show in 1986, Cadman and Walker, were scheduled for the final comedy spot. Unfortunately their material through the first half of the show had not amused the audience and I waited, with trepidation, to see how their last appearance would be received.

They came on stage exactly as in the morning's dress rehearsal and I waited, and waited, for the laughs. They didn't come and suddenly Vinny Cadmen lost the plot totally and went into the crudest and most disgusting routine I'd ever witnessed. The audience sat in stunned silence until the crashing of seats signalled their departure. As I never sat during the first night but stood at the back monitoring the audience's reactions, on this night I was almost killed in the rush.

Totally disappointed I also fled the sinking ship, or should I say pier? Sitting quietly in one of the seat shelters down on the front of the pier I listened to the departing audience's comments. Whilst I expected that the older members would be rightfully disgusted I was amazed by how many younger people were expressing their disgust also. Once the audience had departed I crept back to the theatre to find Dick and we agreed to meet the next morning, Sunday, to decide what to do.

The first night reception was a dismal affair with most departing early for their day off. I did the rounds of the cast offering comfort to them as far as their own contributions were concerned and promising all would be resolved for Monday's rehearsals for the second show. I avoided Cadman and Walker, telling them we needed to talk first thing Monday.

Going back to my accommodation I gazed at the room through the bottom of a third of a bottle of gin, with tonic I hasten to add. I had to drown my sorrows with something and coffee would not suffice at this moment. For three years I had established a reputation for squeaky clean shows and I was determined this would not destroy that reputation.

The next morning Dick and I, together with the chief executive Terry Nolan and the theatre manager, met over a coffee to decide on procedure. We all agreed on policy. Before Monday rehearsals I would confront the boys and give them a final warning that if they ever stepped over the line again it would result in instant dismissal with no compensation whatsoever. This would also incur loss of face in the business, something they could ill afford after winning TV's 'New Faces' only a year previously.

Monday arrived and talking to them alone in their dressing room, they were contrite We shook hands and continued with full company rehearsals for the next show in ten days time.

The critics were kindly in the show's appraisal giving credit to the cast who had excelled in their own rights, especially Bradley Walsh who nightly conquered his audience. Cadmen and Walker never put a foot wrong again and Dick rewarded them with pantomime the following Christmas in Norwich.

Bradley's second Cromer show – proving he could dance and sing for the first time. He joined my dancers, Helen and Claire, and he did not let them down.

The show proceeded peacefully through the rest of the summer and the boat was never rocked again.

At least Bradley Walsh's success was manifestly being underlined for ultimate big time stardom. So in spite of the tacky first night 'Seaside Special' was finally successfully put to bed in September.

My second pantomime for Dick in the Norwich Theatre Royal was next on my agenda. By a brilliant stroke of casting Dick had signed Wayne Sleep to star in 'Aladdin'. Dick asked me to write up the part of Genie of the Ring for him, which surprised me because being small I thought Wayne would have made a perfect 'Aladdin' which is usually played as a cheeky chappie anyway.

However I was able to write a suitable story line with a slant that justified his star position. Aladdin was played by Dilys Watling who I had last directed in the Wimbledon theatre in 'Mother Goose' in 1982.

Bradley Walsh was to play Wishee Washee in his first pantomime role with the certainty that the residents of Cromer would attend en-masse. Another wise stroke by Dick. A wily impresario.

The cast almost resembled the whole of 'Seaside Special'. Along with Bradley came 'Traffle', Kathy and Terry as Prince Pekoe and Lady So-Shi, the secondary love interest. Backing them came Walker and Cadman as the Chinese policemen. Beautiful Wei Wei Wong played Princess Balroubador, and being a dancer also, she and Wayne were will catered for in the dancing stakes.

Rusty Goffe was booked to play Slave of the Lamp, and I had the idea to use a hologram effect for the Slave's first appearance. This was projected almost 20 feet tall floating on the cave's wall with full facial movement as though speaking. It frightened the adults let alone the children. A booming voice offstage gave resonance to the spooky atmosphere. As Aladdin rubbed the lamp a small rock holding the magic lamp split in half and Rusty, who was barely 4 feet tall, sprang out. Racing round the cave to the children's delight, he then joined Wayne and Dilys in a song and dance routine climaxing as usual with a spectacular parade of jewels and Aladdin's escape from the cave.

With Charles West as a very Shakespearian Abanazer, opera singer George Reibbitt as a regal Emperor of China and last but not least Freddie Lees as a very different but extremely funny Widow Twanky, the panto upheld the success rate that Dick had set in motion when he took over the ailing theatre some years earlier.

Finally two speciality acts added further spectacle. A five handed acrobatic group 'The Dingbats' and the magic carpet act of Emerson and Jayne which had travelled the world with their mind blowing carpet which floated high over the audience and of course eventually carried Aladdin to Arabia and the successful conclusion to the oriental magic of 'Aladdin'.

It was a cast to die for and a pleasure to create from my point of view, as it was the most expensive pantomime to date costing £395,000. It recouped its costs and *then* some during the run.

Sadly a terrible shadow was cast over the company during the run. A situation had developed which caused a scandal when a young stagehand committed suicide. With Wayne Sleep's name used to headline the Sunday rags even though he had nothing to do with the situation it shows that having a famous name can be used by the paparazzi unjustly. Whilst the headlines writ large screamed his name they were swift to cover their own backs in the small print, which absolved Wayne from the scandal. However how many readers of the rubbish press bother with the small print when the headline suffices? Famous names are used all the time to grab attention and to hell with the morals.

There is a very important element I have not so far enlarged upon. That is the choice of musical directors. After the show director comes the musical one who must not only be a keyboard expert but have orchestral arranging ability. Pub pianists do not suffice! They must also have coaching skills to arrange full company harmonising. All dancers nowadays have to be capable of soloist quality where vocals are concerned which is second only to their dancing skills. Auditions are now held to encompass both in the final decisions of engagement. Gone are the days back in the 60s when groups could gang bang 'Happy Birthday' or 'God Save the Queen'. Quality is required, not quantity!

Colin Tarn my long-term musical director had recommended Roger Davison

'Oliver' scena

to me. Dennis Marriot and his son Tim on percussion had been the show's accompaniment since my first show in 1983 and now Dennis wanted semi-retirement, hence the change.

Roger Davison was engaged for his first season in 1988 and we were to have a great working relationship for the next 10 years. With keyboards now technically able to create every instrument in an orchestra due to computerisation, it was something that most musical directors were having to master – the ability to have a full orchestra sound with only two musicians in the pit.

Roger also had great skill in finding the performers' voices, which turned them into competent vocalists when it wasn't necessarily their first talent. This gave the shows a West End gloss, which was much commented on.

Along with the MD the next most important technician is the stage director who oversees the backstage crew. When I was first in Cromer, John Grey was the director in both the Theatre Royal in Norwich for the winter season then transferring to Cromer for the summer season. John's assistant stage manager was Lorraine Taylor who was eventually to take over and be with me right through to my final departure in 2002. Lorraine prided herself on doing a man's job for a man's pay. At times I had to remind her that even men needed assistance to prevent injury, which she reluctantly accepted. A great and loyal worker to have in the company.

Bradley Walsh's phenomenal success in Seaside Special shows of 86 87 and 88 made the casting of 89 more imperative than ever before. Conferring with Dick I brought names forward that I had worked with previously and whose success rate I could guarantee.

Neil James was to top the comedy stakes along with double act Lewis and Payne. Neil was a big, congenial guy with an easygoing nature, which audiences warmed to immediately. Ronnie Coyles in total contrast was diminutive and energetic with excellent tap dancing skills, and he and Neil could bounce off each other to great effect.

The singing department was in the capable hands and voices of Carol Sagar and Graham Hunter. A musical act 'Melody Lane', multi instrumentalists Roy and Sonia, very easy on the eye, completed the company. My dancers were Jane Syder, Lorraine Meacher, Nikki Worrall, headed by Sarah Clarkson who had been with me since my first show in Cromer. Nikki was destined to stay with me for a number of years eventually gaining West End stardom as Sandy in 'Grease'.

Yet again for those interested, the following critical review by CV Roberts, the feared Norwich Daily Press critic. Like Roman emperors he could thumbs up or down on any show in the Norfolk area which guaranteed full or empty houses.

Norwich Daily Press
CV Roberts

GOOD OLD-FASHIONED VARIETY IS AN END-OF-THE-PIER WINNER

Variety is truly the name of the game in the new Seaside Special, which opened before an exuberantly responsive gala night audience at the End-of-the-Pier at Cromer on Saturday night.

It is a thoroughly happy show, slick, beautifully dressed and ingenious in its multiple sets – (You'd never guess the stage and wings could barely park a minibus) – and with a range of material as surprising as it is entertaining, and custom–built for a holiday box office. Director and Devisor Bob Marlowe used to be a dancer and it shows, stylishly.

His 4 dancing girls – individuals all – and firmly meshed into the show as a whole, are as sure in floating ballet as they are in tap and rock. But he's choreographed for every member of the team, team being the word for a company that don't just work together well but share the work too!

For if comics and singers are not necessarily dancers, every last one of them is turned terpsichorean under Mr Marlowe's zippy direction, to produce some super routines.

On equal billing in that department is a sparkling adapted sequence from 'Oliver' which brings in a group of talented Cromer youngsters who contagiously radiate their enjoyment in what they're doing; and a neat shipboard 30s routine using the words and music of Noel Coward.

For contrast there's noisy Beatles music in the programme too, though balanced by one of their most poignant offerings 'Yesterday' which singers Graham Hunter and Carol Sager harmonise alluringly.

Out of the blue, Miss Sagar announces, 'Poor Wandering One' from 'The Pirates of Penzance' and carries it off splendidly to provide an operatic show stopper. Of comedians there are several; there's Neil James with more earthy double-entendres to the square foot than profanities in a cockney brawl... Yet never a word out of place to which Great Aunt Jemima could object.

There's Lewis and Payne, a pair who grow on you... and who reduced me to helpless merriment with a long, long shaggy dog story with the most groanworthy line in showbiz.

And pint sized Ronnie Coyles of the gob-stopper eyes and papier-mâché face, whose instant Fagin is one of the coups of the evening.

Overall, good old-fashioned end-of-the-pier variety in a great tradition, and Cromer's the last of the line. Long may it live on.

Again the box office reflected, by the season's end, yet another rung up the ladder box office wise, justifying Cromer Council's wisdom in retaining a live show on the end of their pier. So to bed went Seaside Special 1989.

My next venture was another incredible link into what has become not only long term friendship but an opportunity to escape run-of-the-mill pantomimes - not that I'm complaining about my previous pantos.

Working for the Triumph Organisation of Duncan Weldon and Paul Elliott, had brought me renown from all of the stars that they had the power to engage as well as the opportunity to play the Baddies opposite them. A learning curve for me.

However by 1989 I had decided that I no longer wished to perform, concentrating on directing and choreographing. Pantomimes at that period had runs of up to 12 weeks or more and I was quite frankly bored after the first month, once the creative juices ran out.

If you recall, I had met for the first time Burdon and Moran, a well-known comedy drag act, when I directed them as Ugly Sisters in 'Cinderella' in Norwich in 1986. I didn't know that they had formed a company with Paul Holman to produce shows themselves.

Out of the blue I had a call from Paul asking if I might be available to direct and choreograph for their company. Yet again my guardian angel had pre-empted my thoughts and a door was opening onto yet another avenue.

Paul Holman arranged to drive down to Eastbourne where I lived, to discuss the possibilities. This meeting resulted in me directing one of their Christmas productions throughout the past 15 years. The bait that lured me in 1990 was 'The Wizard of Oz'. No star names which I'd been used to working with, but, an extremely talented bunch of straight actors. Oh dear, that dreadfully divisive word 'straight' which still pertains within the showbiz hierarchy. Straight or variety, we are all performers to entertain. OK that's my little soapbox wobble over. On with the show.

I was truly excited to commence rehearsals and travelled for the first time to Barnsley where the show was being presented. Oo-er!

Arriving by train quite late I took a taxi giving the driver my hotel address, which I'd been assured was but a few minutes' walk from the theatre when I had booked it. Imagine my dismay when after ten minutes we were no nearer to finding the hotel and the driver appeared to be totally lost. He was fumbling through a street guide with no success. Appealing to me for help I suggested stopping at a phone box (no mobiles at that time) and ringing the hotel for directions. Eureka! They suggested we return to the railway station, so we set off, I began to think we were going via Scotland.

However after another ten minutes the station loomed through the darkness. The driver went to ask directions and returned with a broad smile saying we were indeed only five minutes away. Oh me of little faith. We duly arrived and I breathed a sigh of relief. Asking what I owed him, expecting a sum that could have paid off the national debt, he apologised profusely for the wild goose chase and only charged the fee from the station to the hotel. He forlornly told me that he was new to the job. I'd never have guessed! Explaining that all his life he'd been a miner but with pit closures been forced to find another way to earn a living, I could have wept for him. He wasn't young. I was overly generous with the tip and sadly bid him farewell whilst he gratefully thanked me.

As I entered the warmth of the small hotel I pondered on how many other poor guys were in the same boat. Little did we from the south realise what transformations were taking place in other parts of our own country. And so to bed, tired but warm – again.

After a good night's sleep – eventually - and a hearty breakfast in my comfortable little hotel, I was ready for battle. Enquiring as to where the theatre was I discovered it was indeed only five minutes' walk away.

However there was no indication of a theatre in sight. Perplexed I enquired of a local who pointed to a building, which in my eyes represented Colditz Castle and equally forbidding. Apparently it was the council's idea of what a theatre should look like – typical!

I had quite obviously been spoilt with theatres that all had impressive frontages. I was shortly to find out that 'Colditz' lived up to its name with a Kamp Komandant who ran the dump. Only thing missing was a swastika flag flying overhead and I expected to find gas chambers in the basement. How about that for a description? It truthfully wasn't as bad as that – it was worse. Obviously I was regarded as a snotty southerner. Oh well, you can't win them all.

Meeting the assembled company my spirits rose. Actors all, they proved to be a delight to work with. On the first read-through, almost word perfect which proved they'd done their homework. The portents were good. Furthermore the costumes and props were positively outstanding. Enquiring as to their provenance I found they had originated from the Birmingham Repertory theatre – 'nuff said. That theatre held a pole position in the theatrical firmament for excellence, which I was now experiencing first hand. My spirits were flying high.

When rehearsing a show I tend to forget to eat or even take a break although I've always given the cast their time off which Equity naturally demands. However, directors have areas that need special attention such as sets, props, costumes, etc, only resolvable once the cast take their breaks.

I found the stage manager co-operative, unlike the theatre manager who was confrontational on our first meeting. Why? I've no idea. It's my policy to foster good relations with all the staff from Day 1. Confrontation always upsets a company's equilibrium. Whilst I can be firm in what is required I do not court problems but try to solve them. Back in my chorus days I had experienced certain big name directors lose the plot and also the company's respect, which was worse. I often recalled my teacher's wise maxim – listen and learn.

Having said this I still regard 'Alice in Wonderland' as one of the most spectacular I've ever worked on, superbly cast and performed by the artistes. A rather amusing anecdote occurred which I've dined out on for years. On the dress rehearsal day I realised I hadn't eaten a crumb since breakfast in the hotel so I sought sustenance prior to the dress rehearsal at 7.30pm. Searching Barnsley, I found the only place to get a quick service was MacDonald's, not my idea of elegant eating, but needs must when the devil drives. So I grabbed something I didn't really fancy and found an empty table – not for long though.

It seemed the whole of Barnsley was descending on this place before going on to party elsewhere. Mainly groups of girls, freezing in miniskirts adorned in tinsel and baubles. Christmas was really starting early. These girls screeched up to my table asking if they could sit there. I politely agreed. Whilst noisy they were friendly which I've always found northerners to be. Suddenly one girl said, ' Eeeh – are you from Smoke?'

Harking back to my early days when I had toured the country as a chorus boy in the 'Folies Bergere' company I remembered that, 'Smoke' meant London. Replying that I was, the girl continued, 'I thought you was – you talk reel posh,' in friendly tones. 'They think nowt of oose down in Smoke even on't telly. In't weather forecast they leave oose til last'.

I rose, wishing them a nice evening and a Happy Christmas. They all waved cheerily. However the largest one blocked my passage saying, 'Eee, I'm gonna give you a Christmas plonker.' I took a guess on the word plonker saying, 'OK – let's negotiate – no tongues!' Her mates shrieked merrily, egging her on. I escaped with my life – just. It had passed an eye-opener half hour happily.

The dress rehearsal went well and I returned to my hotel for a nightcap and a good night's sleep. The following morning on entering the dining room I was surprised to find Paul Holman seated at one of the tables. He had travelled through the night to see the first performance.

Asking how the dress rehearsal had gone, I told him fine and he remarked that I seemed happy which was a good sign. My reply possibly rocked him a little, for although I praised every aspect of the production I continued by saying my happiness was the knowledge that I would never again return to this area of the country. And I never have.

However, I reiterate that I've remained proud of the show and casting to the present day, working with many of the performers in other shows for Paul's' company.

SEASIDE SPECIAL 1990

Spring 90 was now the next target to aim for. With its escalating success, my 8th production needed sure-fire casting. After the success of Neil James and Ronnie Coyles, Dick Condon and I were in total agreement that they be invited back to top the comedy, which they were delighted to accept.

We now needed a third comedy support preferably new to Cromer and remembering the Folkestone years I suggested JJ Stewart a good comedy artiste, but also an outstanding musician renowned for his skill on many instruments especially the trumpet. This brought a much wider scope into the show.

Singers Amanda Gleave and Anthony Barrett both renowned in classical opera world were joined by the lighter musical act of talented 'Capricorn' Sharon and Andrew, a good looking young couple also skilled at various musical instruments.

My head girl was again Sarah Clarks, joined by Nikki Warrall, her second season, and newcomers Grainne Goodship and Sasha Alexander. Also my first boy dancer, Andrew Stone a 17 year old who I had directed previously when he played Rolf in 'The Sound of Music' and who was destined to reach the West End with great starring success.

Critic's report as follows.

Eastern Daily Press
Neville Miller

A BIG SONG AND DANCE ON THE PIER

The opening night of Cromer's Seaside Special 90 show could have sold out three times – which says something.

Under Robert Marlowe's direction this show presented by Dick Condon's management and North Norfolk District Council looks likely to extend the success of this end-of-the-pier phenomenon.

It's a popular mixture of music, dance, spectacle and comedy beautifully packaged by Inigo Monks scenery with always a look of pristine classiness. The costume designer Diane Martin has a high point in a black and white scene following the example of Cecil Beaton in 'My Fair Lady'.

Neil James, a warm comedian with fast one liners, and Ronnie Coyles a clever man who makes the best of anything are back in the cast. They are joined by newcomer JJ Stewart, an enlivening personality who persuaded people from the audience to fool about on stage and apparently enjoy it.

The music revolves round two singers with operatic voices Amanda Gleave and Anthony Barrett and stylish modern duo Capricorn, all young and good to look at.

Four top class girl dancers Sara, Sasha, Grainne and Nikki are joined by Andrew in some spectacular routines.

Christmas 1990 and I was eagerly looking forward to my next Christmas production for Paul Holman, which was 'The Wizard of Oz', with many of the actors from the previous year's 'Alice in Wonderland'. They were all good movers so I was very ambitious in using Aaron Copeland's 'Rodeo' for the opening ballet on the farmstead, after which they all transformed into Dorothy's companions to see the Wizard of Oz.

Two actors that I became particularly close to were Jacquie Kaye and Stephen Brough, engaged to be married, both capable of playing any role in true repertory style. More of them later.

SEASIDE SPECIAL 1991

Once again it was time to return Gordon and Bunny Jay who had last appeared in 84 and 85 with audience popularity requesting them. They were eager to return, always enjoying a new challenge. Joining them we returned JJ Stewart who had scored heavily the previous year. Completing the comedy group was Bobby Bennett appearing for the first time in Cromer but known for radio and TV appearances. Strangely another Bennett, no relation, also appeared for the first time, 6' tall or more with the most fabulous voice that ensured his return many times.

Making her second appearance, delightfully elegant Carol Sager and a double act new to Cromer but very experienced – 'Spritza', Wayne and Vanessa. My regular dancers Pamela Mackenzie and Nikki Worrall were joined by Emily Waters and Lynne Sabat.

Critic's report:

Eastern Daily Press
CV Roberts

SPECIAL WINNING RECIPE

For more than a decade Dick Condon has been creating a series of End-of-the-Pier shows which have become a byword for the best in traditional summer resort theatre. With the 91 season which opened on Saturday he has crowned his decade with what has to be the best team in what is the best show in the Seaside Special Cavalcade that I can remember.

The winning recipe all along has been a stress on the solid values of good old fashioned variety to entertain and amuse. To that – and this 1991 offering is a perfect example – has been added pace, style and class, allied with first-rate design by Inigo Monk and splendid costumes by Diane Martin. In with a balanced fare of stand up comedy routines and a kaleidoscope of music and dance from showbiz to the classics.

In this new show the humour element is generous to a degree. One among many, I was repeatedly reduced to mopping up the tears or helpless laughter… in large at the instigation of Gordon and Bunny Jay. These two are of the old variety school and masters of what they do. Their double routine of a send-up of master mind followed up by a ventriloquist and dummy sketch was a little running masterpiece of peerless timing, quick fire pace and hilarious playing.

It has another sparkling comedian in Bobby Bennett, a soprano in Carol Sager who moves with equal ease from opera to swing; and the singing duo Spritza who bring distinctive style and dash to country and western.

Then there's the engaging JJ Stewart, a brilliant trumpet player who can't help being a comic; and gentle giant Laurie Bennett – 6' 4" – who has a baritone voice to make one sit up to attention – Music of the Night from Phantom of the Opera was a deserved show stopper.

Finally there are 4 girl dancers whose flair and zest meld the whole show together – one loses track of the number of their routines and costume changes, but never of the air of energy, talent and enjoyment, which surrounds them.

Seaside Special 91, which runs until September is devised directed and choreographed by Robert Marlowe. Roger Davison is the musical director.

Little did any of us involved in Seaside Special 91 realise that this was the last show Dick was destined to see.

When I first worked for him in 1983 I knew that he had had a lung cancer scare but hopes were high that he had beaten it. He had taken on a healthy regime, giving up smoking and alcohol, which he had assiduously maintained. However in the spring of 91 the symptoms had apparently returned although he did not share this news with us working on the show. Whilst I always departed once the second show had opened and only returned if needed, this hardly ever happened as I had a good team taking care of the standards.

On the last night I learned from his sister that Dick had returned to Ireland in late summer. But the cast had no idea of the seriousness of his illness. Early autumn everybody received the following card, appropriately of an original watercolour painting of the pier. I will repeat it in its entirety.

Thank you all, so much, for kindly writing to me upon my return to Ireland. Circumstances have prevented me from reading the letters personally, but my sister, Ann, has read each and every one to me. It was lovely hearing from you all and I so enjoyed receiving your messages.

I am sorry that I cannot write personally but I would ask you to please accept this card as my way of saying 'thank you'. I will treasure the memories of all my friends in Norwich and continue to recall the happy time I spent there for as long as possible.

Please continue to keep me in your thoughts.

Kindest personal regards and best wishes,

Dick Condon

Naturally I was very upset by the news for he had been such a good boss but more importantly a friend.

Dear Dick
It was with much sadness that I heard of your decision that 'Seaside Special 91' was to be your last show in Cromer.
It certainly has been quite a spectacular success this year and I'm delighted that this is so for everyone but especially for your last production.
As you will know Terry Nolan has asked if I will continue doing the same job for him and I'm pleased that I shall be able to keep the standards – hopefully – maintained that you initiated all those years ago and that I have had the pleasure of being associated with over the past 9 years.
Your confidence in my involvement has always been something that I've been grateful for and proud of. I assure you that I will endeavour to keep those standards of excellence for as long as I'm asked to do so in that beautiful little theatre of Norfolk.
Your long battle with ill health has been a trial so very bravely borne.
I have been in awe of your fight to go 'on with the show'. I know that your recent appearances have been acting masterpieces that I shall long remember.
My sincere thanks for involving me in your work over the years. Your standards and example I will always follow.
My thoughts and prayers are with you
God Bless
As ever in affection and respect
Bob

Dick actually died on 14 October aged only 54 years – far, far too young and the world lost one of its dedicated and charismatic impresarios.

Unfortunately I was working in the Isle of Man when a memorial service took place in Norwich. From reports of many artistes and technical staff and friends it was a truly fun packed service, which Dick would have enjoyed enormously. Especially when the bishop remarked that Dick would have counted the house and been delighted with every seat sold!

As the service was celebrated in Norwich I found a Manx church and gave my thanks for all the opportunities and friendship I had received from a true man of the theatre.

Christmas of 91 was destined to be my return to performing in spite of deciding two years earlier to retire from actual acting. Paul Holman had enticed me with a part I had never been offered previously in my portfolio of panto villains, not that it was basically a pantomime. It was 'Peter Pan' and Paul offered me the classic arch villain role of Captain Hook. It was an offer I could not refuse.

It was made more exciting when I found that Paul had engaged my friends Jacquie Kaye as Mrs Darling and Tiger Lily, with Steve Brough as Smee, Hook's accomplice. Of course my role was also double because Hook starts out as Mr Darling. I must confess I had the old hang up of not being a straight actor. But looking back I think we did complement each other. My panto brashness helped to broaden them whilst I took on their reality approach when playing Mr Darling.

The children and lost boys, etc were from the famous Sylvia Young School. We performed in the Seccombe theatre in Sutton and the sets were perfectly built for all the transformations the show entailed from the Darling household to Never-Never Land. Of course it's essential that Peter Pan and the Darling children fly which was accomplished with great aplomb. The press reports were favourable and I was modestly thrilled to be considered legitimate.

Forgive me but I'm now going to boast with the write-ups, beginning with the show business bible.

The Stage and Television Today
9 January
Peter Tatlow

Captain Hook and Mr Darling, the director and choreographer all rolled into one like Poo-Bah, could be too much for one person but for Robert Marlowe it was far from the case with his production of Peter Pan, so full of vitality and his loveable and debonair characterisation of the great sea dog so vivid at the Seccombe theatre... a happy and entertaining show. The sheer pace of it left the performers no option but to enjoy it themselves... The lost boys and pirates were performed by sprightly dancers to move the show along as a very lively musical.

The Croydon Advertiser
Christopher Wood

... and a pleasant couple of hours it makes too, thanks largely to director/choreographer and Captain Hookalike Robert Marlowe. Under Robert's direction the action moves at a brisk but not hurried pace and his evil pirate provides a much needed hissable villain in a show of otherwise honest, loveable and likeable characters...

As a footnote - the role of John Darling was played by John Pickard who went on to find fame on television in 'Two Point Four Children' amongst others. Sylvia Young's School has spawned many well-known pupils who've found headline fame in show business, which their training certainly enhanced.

SEASIDE SPECIAL 1992

Once a successful formula is established it is advantageous to return artistes who have proved popular so Gordon and Bunny Jay were returned for their fourth season after a three year absence. They always came in with new ideas, whilst repeating a few requests from previous years which had been memorable.

They were joined by newcomer Mike McCabe and returning for their third season solo singers, Michelle Summers and Laurie Bennett, fabulous voices both.

Finally Kathy and Terry – 'Traffle' – after a previous three-year stint were returned due to public demand and were destined for many more, being valuable and versatile in whatever I asked of them in the production scenes. My regular dancers Nikki and Pamela were joined by newcomers Elaine Seaton and Rachel Hiew. I'm going to spare you the critical reports, suffice to content ourselves with this headline.

PIER SHOW PACKS 'EM IN TO STAY AHEAD OF ITS PEERS

Each year had clocked up, breaking the previous year's figures for attendances until we finished by hitting 100% - quite an achievement.

Christmas 92/93 'Jack and the Beanstalk', Alexandra theatre, Bognor Regis. The very word Bognor always tickles me because of the well-known story about King George V and Queen Mary. During a previous illness the King had recuperated in Bognor of all places, resulting I believe in having 'Regis' attached to it. When he was sadly on his deathbed Queen Mary comforted him saying, 'When you've recovered we could return to Bognor'. His muttered reply 'Bugger Bogner!' has been associated with this quite gentle south coast resort ever since.

Unfortunately working in the theatre that Christmas I began to think the manager thought of it in the same way. He barely stayed for the opening night and we never saw him again during the entire run.

It was a splendid cast to work with. A young and very funny comic Mathew Linus Hunt played Simple Simon whilst second top was Roy Kean, who I'd first worked with in 'Alice in Wonderland' in the dreaded Barnsley, when he hilariously played the Cook, likewise in Bognor playing Dame Durden. For the first time in my career I was third top above the title - honour indeed - playing Flesh Creep the giant's henchman.

Arthur Askey's daughter Anthea played the Vegetable Fairy – a comedic chip off the old block. Jack was Julia Binns, a strikingly beautiful girl with the longest legs I'd ever seen, even when I was a dancer in the Folies Bergere. Pretty voiced Alison Cox made a delightful Princess whilst opera singer George Reibbitt, who I'd previously worked with, a regal King.

Richard Deloro was a truly frightening giant whose appearance had the children hiding under their seats whilst screaming for revenge. The music director was Will Fyffe Jnr., partner of Anthea Askey.

Paul Holman had again come up with awesome sets and I was amazed on seeing the stage for the first time to find even the walls of the auditorium were covered in beanstalk vines which gave great atmosphere right from the start.

I think 'Jack and the Beanstalk' is probably the hardest to stage - to span from

Jack and the Beanstork panto in Bognor Regis. I was the Giants Henchman – Anthea Askey was Fairy Cucumber and Richard Deloro as the Giant

the ordinary to the extraordinary, like magic, which of course is the essence of real pantomime.

The illusion was complete when Michael Brydon's Phantasie–en-Noir created an amazing beanstalk which towered into the flies. Jack's wonderful legs showed to great advantage as he climbed to the top, to the delight of dads and granddads. Hurrah for the Victorian principle of female boys.

Sadly this was to be the last professional panto presented in Bognor so I'm now going to present the critic's report, as written in the profession's bible.

The Stage and Television Today
14 January 1993

MAGNIFICENT COMEDY PANTOMIME

A happy Burden and Moran 'Jack and the Beanstalk' may be the last professional pantomime at the Alexandra theatre but what a way to finish.

The traditional story is adhered to and the moment they enter the theatre the audience is surrounded by a giant beanstalk, which has been painted on the proscenium and auditorium. 'Wish you were here' may be the original seaside postcard for Bognor Regis but the audience were full of the same sentiments watching the fast moving and fun pantomime. Julia Binns as Jack displayed not only good Principal Boy legs but a singing voice of great accuracy and charm.

Dame Durden with Roy Kean appearing in as many zany outfits as entrances provided the main comedy humour together with an unusual Simple Simon played with great gusto by Mathew Linus Hunt. Flesh Creep is the giant's henchman in the hands of Robert Marlowe who also wrote, directed and choreographed the production. He was aggressively pleasant without being frightening and put up a good fight against the rusty magic of Anthea Askey's enchanting fairy. A splendid speciality act Richard Deloro fitted well into the plot and the skills he exhibited gave great pleasure to the audience. Princess Felicia, Alison Cox, also proved to have a quality voice. Her duets with Jack of particular note. The dancers and the beanstalk babes, very lively, also responded to musical director, Will Fyffe Jnr who created a high standard. Well lit and dressed, Bognor's 'Jack' was great fun.

As we know the theatre manager had vanished on the first night, never to return. Whether his contract had finished or he had bunked off, no one appeared to know.

The theatre frames which usually would have carried photos of the show to encourage bookings remained empty yet we still had a month to run. I suggested to the cast that if they agreed I would take photos between the matinée and evening show, get them enlarged and with the help of the lady who was the undermanager fill the frames to shriek aloud to the passing public that a pantomime was still in progress.

It worked well and the houses remained quite respectable until we finished. It was a sad sight to watch the death throes of a once proud theatre.

SEASIDE SPECIAL 1993

With Dick now departed Vivian Goff was getting the company together for my 10th season. She rang me to say that she had been offered Hope and Keen to top the bill and wanted my reactions. I was amazed they were available as in my eyes I remembered them being on television in Sunday Night at the London Palladium way back before I even entered the profession. They could do everything - sing, dance and play musical instruments. Also acrobatic, they used to finish their TV act by playing trumpets and finishing on the last note by back flipping and landing on their knees – wow! It used to stop the show. Yes! Yes! Yes! was my reply.

In 1971 I had directed and appeared with them at the Grand theatre in Wolverhampton in 'Aladdin'. I know they could be testy on occasion but they were artistes and which artiste has never had a wobble? On that occasion though they were definitely in the wrong and my job forced me to confront them with a warning on the management's behalf.

In 93 I knew their worth and I don't bear grudges. So Vivian booked them to top the company. Along with them Neil James shared top. This was his third appearance since his first one in 89. Appearing for the third time in a row was Laurie Bennett - he was so popular we dare *not* engage him Also singer Susan Paule, a very elegant and glamorous performer with many West End musicals to her credit - 'Fiddler on the Roof', 'My Fair Lady', and 'Funny Girl' with Barbara Streisand - a very experienced lady. Also, back for the forth time, Traffle who we could not do without, such was their popularity. My head girl was Pam, an essential asset, with three new girls Jeanette Sugg, Cheryl McEvoy and Erica Lawrence.

Auditions for dancers were always over-subscribed as the standards required were recognised by all the top dancing academics as a valuable asset to any girl's CV once she could add the Cromer show to it.

North Norfolk News
Summer Show 93 Review
Richard Batson

The recipe masterminded by the late Dick Condon of good clean family fun lives on with a collection of singers, comics and dancers who will switch disciplines to produce a versatile cast whose enjoyment radiates right to the back row of the stalls.

Former television comics Hope and Keen lead by example from their home grown ground of quick fire gags routine to joining in sketches, songs and hoofing in the chorus line.

Local comic Neil James scores high on the split-your-sides-mograph - a very funny act. Two of last summer's acts are retained to give continuity – energetic duo Traffle and booming baritone Laurie Bennett who never fails to wow the audience with his moving ballards.

Traffle excel at breezy harmonies. Soprano Susan Paule is at her best with a Judy Garland collection bringing out the best of her cabaret roots, and the chorus line's tireless legs and smiles keep the show moving along.

Producer Robert Marlowe alternates two shows to give the cast and audiences more variety. The holiday themed show one starting with a rollicking seaside number and continuing at a brisk pace. The second show based on the world of romance is prettier and would appeal to West End style fans. Both have superb sets and costumes by Ian Westbrook and Diane Martin with an Elizabethan Court scene an absolute stunner.

Yet again the count at the season's end revealed the audience figures were in ascendancy. However when I suggested that we consider Hope and Keen, Mike and Albie, for 1994 Vivian was rather dubious. Apparently she'd had altercations with the lads during the season. She was always fair and considerate so I began to think other voices were denying them contracts – not my view at all. The only reservation I did have was that they were just too professional and also sophisticated for North Norfolk, although I do pride myself on bringing that quality to all my productions. Although I stood my ground I was defeated for the first time. Thirteen years later I still stand by my view that they should have had a second chance.

CHRISTMAS 1993

Once again Paul asked me to direct and choreograph 'Snow White' in the Civic Hall theatre, Guildford. In this instant it was a trio of presenters, Tony Cartwright, Peter Frosdick and last but not least Paul Holman, even though he was third in the pecking order.

It was a starry cast with Maureen Nolan of the Nolan Sisters, a beautiful Show White, Bobby Crush, a handsome Prince, and Paul Valentine played Muddles and was a great asset to the comedy.

Burden and Moran who I'd directed in Norwich as Ugly Sisters were cast separately. Roger was the Wicked Queen, and what a field day his friends had with that bit of casting - he got even, and how! Maurice played Maudie the Cook, Angela Jenkins a delightful Fairy, and last but certainly not least in my book, Stephen Lewis from 'On the Buses'. More of him later.

Paul had asked me to play the Queen's Henchman and I was reluctant to return to performing after I had decided to concentrate on other areas. However, my mind was changed by flattery - Maurice said he had always wanted to perform a comedy routine with me. How could I resist? And agreed to play the Henchman Egor. The comedy number we had great fun with was 'Choochi Face', ripe for send up. In retrospect I was so glad I had agreed for little did I realise 'Snow White' would be Maurice's last pantomime ever. It was very successful and played to excellent business.

An incident with Stephen Lewis was the first time in my whole career I had ever been physically attacked by a fellow artist. Stephen was odd to say the least and could not detach himself from his 'On the Buses' character, which was even odder. One afternoon after the tea break, we had a scene together to rehearse. He appeared stranger than ever and I had a suspicion he was under the influence of something. Suddenly he lurched towards me menacingly saying, 'Go and make me a nice cup of tea'. I replied 'I'm not the tea boy and the tea break is over,' turning and walking away. He suddenly flew across the stage and with a flying leap gave me a bruised thigh. To say I was astonished would be putting it mildly. This was witnessed by the entire company including the bosses who were gob-smacked to say the least.

I had photographs taken when the bruise developed into a deep purple from buttock to knee and threatened to sue him. Writing to his agent, who I knew, I revealed the whole incident only to be informed he had attacked one of the other stars of 'On the Buses' in the same way. He was dangerous and I thought he should be certified. I kept well clear of him, refusing to accept his apologies. I've always believed the pen is mightier than the sword.

At the last night party he approached me in full view of the cast and guests. I thought he was going to attack me for the last time and waited – would he dare? I took my revenge - I refused his apologies - and walked away. I recalled my mum's saying of years ago, 'Don't get mad, get even'.

I had enjoyed working with the rest of the company and the panto was financially successful for the management, which was to result in a return the following Christmas.

SEASIDE SPECIAL 1994

This was to be a lucky year, but not without a traumatic situation that developed on Sunday 14 November 1993.

A rig anchored north west of Cromer pier broke its anchor after being hit by a wave estimated to have been some 20' high. In the midst of a gale that reached storm force conditions, the barge was driven towards the pier. The storm force 10-12 with a top speed of 83 knots drove the rig right onto it. 'It cut through the pier like a knife through butter,' said one onlooker.

Severing power cables, the barge sent showers of sparks out over the sea. The monster rig, which weighed some 100 tonne cut a hole 30 metres wide through the pier, leaving the lifeboat station and the Pavilion theatre stranded. The rig finally came to rest on the beach near Overstrand but not before it smashed through the groynes, causing even more damage.

Terry Nolan rang me a couple of days later assuring me that the show would go on. Apparently the company with the contract, to show good faith in their promise to have the pier repaired, booked a number of seats for the show's opening night performance. And they were there.

On Sunday 1 May the pier was officially opened by Cabinet Minister Gillian Shepherd just six months after the storm. The sun shone and the task was complete. It took fifteen weeks to restore what took minutes to destroy.

Vivien and I had decided to return Les Wilson yet again. He was a great favourite with the audiences. Vince Lewis had gone solo, so he was invited to return as co-star in the comedy stakes. Returning for their third consecutive season, 'Traffle', whose regular pattern was to return every winter to Australia their homeland, flying back in the spring to 'Seaside Special', were very welcome. The patrons were proud to create their own stars.

It made my job especially easy in creating the production scenes. Speciality act first timers were Denny Lee baritone and Pauline Hannah a singer impressionist who had found fame on TV in 'New Faces'. Lastly Richard Deloro a fabulous juggler who tap-danced like Gene Kelly. I had directed and worked with him in pantomime, the Christmas of 92/93 and had no hesitation in recommending him for the summer show.

Pam my head dancer was returning for her forth season but my auditions had brought forward three new girls - Helen Pocock, Dee Jago and Melanie Laight. Helen and Dee were to return many times with Helen eventually taking over as head girl when Pam finally decided to retire and start a family, as her husband Tam had patiently asked her to. This was eventually crowned with success – most happily.

I had always entertained a certain guilt in persuading Pam to return year in, year out, not wanting to lose both a captain and beautiful classical dancer. It's a problem many female dancers wrestle with before it's too late. Most choreographers have a captain in waiting already versed in their predecessor's style whilst also bringing in their own. This occasionally has to be reined in slightly because any violent style change in a long running sequence of shows can alienate audiences. The Chinese expression 'softly softly catchy monkey,' works here.

Yet again Anglia Television had turned its cameras on to the rehearsals, and first night opening show. The best advertisement that any stage show can have, especially when TV audiences get a first hand account of the problems and artistes' backstage chatter. Something that usually remains a mystery and almost akin to eavesdropping, very enjoyable.

Charles Spencer, theatre critic of the Telegraph had become our number one fan, visiting us on a frequent basis. He had already arranged to pay a visit during the rehearsal period, arriving whilst the film crew were making yet another documentary. The TV director was delighted that such an illustrious critic allowed himself to be filmed whilst chatting to the performers, together with the knowledge that he intended to give a large spread in the weekend Telegraph, adding merit to all concerned. It was a long article so I will be selective, giving everyone a crack of the whip without boring readers – I hope!

Weekend Telegraph
Charles Spencer
2 July 1994

The evening of Sunday 14 November 1993 in storm force winds and heavy seas, a 25foot wave hit a 100 tonne construction rig breaking its anchor and slicing through Cromer's late Victorian pier like a knife through butter. The story made the national news and I'm not ashamed to admit that I looked at the pictures with a lump in my throat. Richard Condon, the most flamboyant impresario in the business put Cromer back on the map. Though he died a couple of years ago the Seaside Specials were by then firmly established...

For the past 12 years Seaside Special has been directed by the excellent Robert Marlowe. He began his career as a dancer in the Folies Bergere and it was those spectacular Parisian productions that influenced his whole approach, which he unashamedly describes as 'putting the show in show business'. He is a man who could teach some of our more precious directors a thing or two...

Just consider the speed at which he and his company bring the show together. The four girl dancers arrived in Cromer on Monday 6 June, principals on Thursday 9 June. As well as solo spots there are comedy sketches and a host of full company numbers, including a fully choreographed Fiddler on the Roof medley and a delirious Tamla Motown finale featuring a butch male comedian as Diana Ross. All this had to be staged for an opening on 18 June.

It is this company spirit that makes Cromer different from virtually any other summer show in the country and the only one of its kind on the end of a pier.

... at Cromer everyone has to pitch in, you would never guess the show had been licked into shape in less than a fortnight. When it opened to 'Le Tout Cromer' (and to judge from the number of mayoral chains every local authority chairman in Norfolk) it looked as if the company had been working together for months...

If there's one thing Bob Marlowe hates, it is the fact that 'End-of-the-Pier' has become a catch–all description for showbiz tat. 'Whenever critics want to denigrate something they say its 'End-of-the-Pier' which means it's sub-standard, appalling! I get annoyed and upset about that because it's just not true'... it certainly isn't true at all in Cromer. The hard-working cast exude a sense of infectious enjoyment, the dozens of costumes are stylish, the sets first-rate. More remarkably still, the production has a terrific range. The singer Denny Lee... moves effortlessly from Frank Sinatra to a knockout version of Nessun Dorma that brings the house down.

Topping the bill this year is comedian Les Wilson who cheerfully admits that he's 'unknown to millions'... He's got a marvellous act - warm, relaxed and creating a conspiracy of pure pleasure... Richard Deloro, a man who lumbers on with an Eeyore–like lugubriousness and proceeds to juggle with amazing grace... The delightful Pauline Hannah, who shines in the ensemble and reveals great gifts as both a singer and impressionist in her solo spot, has unmistakable class... I'm only sorry that space doesn't permit more than a passing pat on the back for the vocal duo Traffle, the cheeky cockney comic Vince Lewis and the heroically hard working dancers... Their resilience, good humour and talent is little short of inspirational and, as I strolled on the boardwalk in the interval dusk, with coloured lights shining down the pier and the moon rising over Cromer cliffs, I realised with a shock of happiness that there was nowhere in the world I'd rather be.

All these years later I still feel a glow of pleasure that the erudite and knowledgeable critic Charles Spencer thought so highly of the company, which obviously thrilled them all.

Looking back at all the companies I've worked with throughout my 20 years, all deserve to be included in the above, which placed Cromer's 'Seaside Special' on a pinnacle of success both financially and artistically.

Incidentally, Charles was always polite and gentlemanly. He must be nice - he married a ballerina! All dancers are nice. Oo-er, that's sweeping – well nearly all.

PANTOMIME 1994 'BABES IN THE WOOD' CIVIC HALL GUILDFORD

Once again due to the success of 'Cinderella' the previous year, Paul Holman's company were back in the driving seat with Tony Cartwright and Peter Frosdick, and I was invited to direct and choreograph. Thank goodness I did not perform in this show, which I would not have survived knowing what I know now.

A poignant situation had developed prior to the rehearsal period. Burden and Moran had been signed to play separate roles. Roger Burden as Fairy of the Leaves and Maurice Moran as Nurse Clucose. Due to Maurice's sudden and unexpected death in October, Roger took on the Nurse Clucose role whilst I suggested one of my dancers from the Cromer summer seasons, Helen Pocock as Fairy of the Leaves. This of course dramatically changed the method which in my view was an improvement, although I naturally regretted the reason that had caused the situation in the first place - Maurice's death.

However Rogers's role as Dame, not Fairy of the Leaves, which of course would have been comedic, gave me the chance to have a classical ballet in the show with Helen, whose strong point it was, and that is not a pun. I do not favour funny fairies, mainly because little girls in the audience love to see pretty dancers on tippy toes for the first time. Very important to capture them for the future as theatre aficionados – hopefully.

A happy product of Helen's engagement was yet another long term engagement and marriage to Adrian Jekylls, now one of Paul Holman and John Ogle's partners in the company, and the only one to have performed as an actor, singer, dancer in his past. A useful bonus combination when casting their productions.

Paul is of course a very skilled musician and able to talk turkey to his musical directors. I had long ago discovered, after working through many top managements, there were hardly any with these actual talents. This is almost unique.

Every company needs an executive charmer to smooth ruffled feathers when the going gets tough and that is where John Ogle shines. Pouring oil on occasional troubled waters. Having been a Squadron Leader in the Air Force he was quite obviously used to handling dodgy situations so there you have a perfect triumvirate, who also get along together as friends.

Having worked in my past with partnership companies I could tell tales in some instances when the office atmosphere could be sliced with a very large knife, or in panto terms a scimitar.

Having paid my respects to a company I've now worked with longer than any other, watching them getting more important also, I will now enlarge on the cast of the 94 'Babes in the Wood' company.

Topping the cast, unusually, were two females, Danniella Westbrook as Maid Marian and Sophie Lawrence as Robin Hood. I say unusual because it's rare to see two women topping. However as both were in 'EastEnders' and it was now imperative to top with TV stars to attract patrons, there was little option. Third in pecking order was another television star, Mark Jordon from 'Heartbeat'. A good-looking tall guy, pleasant and easygoing, who had been with the show for three years and about to film his fifth series. S a powerful panto draw.

Playing the evil Sheriff of Nottingham was former Royal Shakespeare actor Forbes Collins. I was pleased to meet up again with Mathew Linus Hunt playing Grab the Good Robber. We had played opposite each other two years previously in 'Jack and the Beanstalk'.

Playing the Bad Robber was Gary Snowden from TV's 'The Bill', with dancers and children from the Jean Day Dancing Academy and Specialties by Satori Puppets creating magical illusions. All was set up for a good show. Hopes were high, sadly to be shattered as you will soon discover.

In 1994 Danniella Westbrook's drug problems were well in the public domain. Therefore my own problems with this situation were about to impound on a group of performers whose contracts demanded sobriety to fulfil their agreements to rehearse, in an ever shortening period, to an acceptable standard for a ticket purchasing public.

From Day 1 it was obvious to me that we were in for a bumpy ride. Danniella was never ever on time for rehearsals. Throughout my entire career my first priority has always been punctuality. Most unions have rules regarding timing which involves overtime payments for extra, after hours work and rightly so. Whilst I've never been a fervent unionist I applaud this rule. To office, shop and factory workers it may appear luxurious to start work at 10am. But they never continue until 10pm and after at night.

A rigid rule in showbiz therefore is '10am on time', which I've always remained fervent about. Danniella was always late, sometimes very; therefore my only recourse was to ask my dance captain to read in for her. Fortunately dancers are always looking for an opportunity to exhibit other aspects of their talents, so no problem there. This was to eventually benefit, and very fruitfully, Sarah Day, for that was her name. Watch this space.

I was more than perturbed when Danniella did eventually deign to turn up and fell asleep on the theatre floor from which she could not be roused. Unfortunately she was at this time out of favour with the gutter press who were gunning for her, with photos of her allnight carousing, for her 'fans'.

Whilst I appreciate that artistes attract photographers when they reach the public domain the paparazzi are only interested in those that misbehave, and by her actions publicly at this time Danniella was high on that hit list, especially as her boyfriend was a member of a pop group behaving also in an unsavoury manner - a double whammy. Rumour had it that they had attacked a photographer, smashing his camera – oh dear – not a wise action if true.

Obviously I had informed my bosses of the problems we were all experiencing but you don't give a dog a bad name and hang them. The rest of the cast were becoming extremely unhappy with the situation and it was one I had never experienced before. Difficulties yes, but never of this magnitude. Especially when it was being enforced on us by the top of the bill, which the producers pay the most money for, trusting that they will bring in the punters, in this case teenagers as well as children on their first panto encounter. Always an onerous position but in this particular case – disastrous. Read on.

One surprising morning, Danniella turned up on time. Gasps from everyone drowned out the silence of amazement, not least from me. Taking a firm grasp on the moment I suggested that we started the rehearsal with her first entrance, which included her big solo. I sat open mouthed. She was amazingly good, showing all the talent that the famous Sylvia Young School had instilled in her. I finally saw what Sylvia had recognised. Wow! Unfortunately it was short lived, for she suddenly started to spout abuse at me for doubting her talent, using every profanity under the sun with the F word prolifically scattered throughout. I admonished her for using this language in front of the juveniles attending their first full company rehearsal. What was the use? She went into a further tirade. So I broke the company for an early coffee break. They were all obviously disturbed, so a 15 minute period was in order.

Sophie Lawrence approached me on her return, almost begging me to hear that she was equally upset with the whole situation. Sophie was equal top of the bill with Danniella. As they were both in EastEnders on TV She thought I might believe she was sympathetic towards Danniella's problems. She wasn't – and I didn't. Sophie had always been professional and I had, and still do, favour female principal boys in the Victorian tradition, as she had all the right ingredients, pretty, good legs, etc, and very talented.

There, I have enlightened readers on probably my worst experience in any of the 50 or more pantomimes I've had full responsibility for throughout my long career.

The opening night was not received particularly well. Danniella received no applause for one particular song – a lullaby required by the script, where she puts the babes into bed prior to them being kidnapped. I had realised that this was not in her style of vocals, however in panto it's necessary to perform in all styles. She did it in such a lacklustre way as to receive little applause. In fact mostly silence, which I had perceived sitting in the audience myself.

Danniella finally disgraced herself on New Year's Eve. She had faked illness with a certificate. Sarah Day, the dance captain, had taken on the role after standing in many times during the rehearsals and was able to substitute on New Year's Eve to great success. It was almost a replica of the well-known Bette Davis film, 'All about Eve'. Sarah has gone on ever since playing principal roles in pantomimes throughout the country. An understudy's dream come true.

I'm now in my usual way going to let the critics have the say. For the first time it's the paparazzi so hold on to your seats, you're in for a bumpy ride. This was reported in The Sun, not a paper I usually read but friends sent to me. Starting with the editorial.

The sun

MISS BIGHEAD
JUST WHO DOES DANNIELLA WESTBROOK THINK SHE IS?

Hundreds of fans have been let down by the disgraceful way she has pulled out of a panto. Her so-called bad back looked all right when The Sun snapped her at a nightclub. Must have been the best bit of acting she's ever done. At 20, she is on the road to nowhere if she doesn't change her idle, foulmouthed ways.

Little Miss Bighead should remember who pays her inflated wages.

Following this, inside the paper was a coloured photo in her Maid Marion costume. Written by Lucinda Evans in an exclusive interview.

Former EastEnder Danniella Westbrook was yesterday branded 'foulmouthed and arrogant' by cast members of her Christmas Panto.

They claimed the 20-year-old star swore at the director and yelled obscenities in front of child performers.

Many vowed never to work with her again after her 'appalling' behaviour during Babes in the Wood at Guildford, Surrey.

Danniella, pictured right, was paid £3,000 a week to play Maid Marion. But her performance was 'disappointing' according to showbiz mag 'The Stage'.

Cast members hit out after she was caught partying on New Year's Eve despite saying she had an acute back injury and was unfit to work.

One said 'That was despicable. She told us she didn't give a f—k about the show. We're disgusted with her.' Danniella, yesterday demanded to be freed from her contract due to her injury. A show boss said 'We want to wash our hands of her.'

As Paul Holman was responsible for the production the theatre management demanded Danniella be fired due to all the bad publicity.

There is finally a happy ending for Danniella. Recently I watched her being interviewed on TV's 'This Morning' programme. With her drug days now firmly behind her and a happy marriage to a wealthy man she has become a mother herself, which has brought about a total conversion. She has undergone an operation to have her nose, which she had totally destroyed by sniffing cocaine, replaced and now looks fantastic. She talked about being introduced around 12 years of age to smoking 'pot', deemed quite innocent. However as we now know pushers persuade smokers to try something stronger and incidentally more expensive – thus they are hooked. As I've said she looks fantastic. However more fantastic is her mission to tell her story to school children warning them of the perils ahead should they feel inquisitive to go down that road.

There can be no stronger advocate than someone reformed. She withholds no punches even showing the photographs that astonished everyone when displayed in the national Press. The only time they did her a favour. In biblical terms, 'Heaven rejoices with a sinner saved.' Me too. Finally a happy ending.

1995 was to prove the beginning of what was to be for me the end of my reign with 'Seaside Special' in Cromer, made even more hurtful by the betrayal of two life long friends that I had helped into prime positions in Cromer's theatrical firmament. When Dick Condon died his personal assistant, Vivian Goff had taken over running the theatre for the council. However as the position was only of six-month tenure it was insufficient financially for Vivian who previously had been Dick's right hand in Norwich's Theatre Royal on a full year contract. Although reluctant to leave she had no option. Especially when a full post as private secretary in a college in Norwich was the bait. The council were now searching for a replacement.

Nigel Stuart, who I had first met when working in Folkestone, was looking for a new position – why, I have never discovered, although there were many rumours circulating. Nigel had married one of my dancers from the Folkestone years after a rather messy divorce from his first wife. Maggie had been my head girl for five years – a truly loyal and trusted co-worker and thankfully still one of my dearest friends – unlike Nigel.

In 1982 when I left Folkestone, Nigel had remained for a couple more years there as entertainments director, a position which enabled him to re-locate eventually to Tunbridge Wells, also as entertainment director on the council there. Unfortunately scandals there involving certain high-ups led to Nigel also resigning. He took on producing entertainments in various hotels, which, with his 'booking artistes knowledge' stood him in good stead, but hardly occupied him as a full time occupation.

Therefore, when the Cromer council sought to replace Vivian Goff my first thought was for Nigel Stewart. The Cromer job was for only six months, which I thought would be perfect, as his part time Tunbridge Wells occupation was mainly a winter period one, with hotel Christmas events needing entertainment. So I arranged for Nigel to meet Cromer's chief executive Terry Nolan.

Nigel could always present an impressive front, and with my recommendation of my own 12 year association with him, he got the job. I was delighted not only for him but also Maggie and their young daughter Emma. It meant they could still live in Tunbridge Wells where Emma was at school and Maggie also taught part time in a friend's dancing academy.

Knowing what I know now I would never ever have introduced him to Norfolk, although on reflection it worked out exceedingly happily for another prime player in the drama. However I'm jumping too far ahead at this point, so back to Spring 95.

I was looking forward to working with Nigel again. The last time was in 1982 in Folkestone 25 years ago and I regarded him as one of my best pals in the profession, especially in the management stakes. We joined forces to cast the show.

Comedy top was Les Wilson a very funny man who had been in my Folkestone shows and coincidentally my first Cromer production. He could be near the knuckle but always screamingly acceptable even with maiden aunts, one of the safest bets in show business. Supporting him, though unknown to me, was Ken Wood. He had travelled the world with his ventriloquist act, which featured a full sized horse, quite brilliant, and you only saw the horse's lips move.

An illusionist, Nick Spellman had a mind-boggling act and to this day I never knew how he worked the illusions, even though my dancers assisted him. It's a showbiz rule that no one divulges the secrets – rightly so. Nick could also sing and dance in the big production scenas. Young and tall with dark wavy hair and more good looking than any guy had a right to be, he was swamped by fans after the shows. That type of popularity is what every show desires.

'Traffle', Kathy and Terry, joined us again, bringing new acts never seen before, as always. Beautifully costumed and presented and, with their acting skills, able to contribute to sketches. The audiences loved them.

Auditioning for a female singer, a stunning blonde turned up. I can still recall she wore a mini kilt and a tight fitting woollen top. All the guys present had their eyes pulled over her wool! She had a superb voice – the most important requirement from my point of view. However, all extras were in place so she got the contract. Further information that she was currently in 'Les Misérables' in London cemented the deal.

Later information given to me that she had only been a dresser in the theatre left me with the uncomfortable impression that I had been manipulated. However, her skills had won her the season. Students often take dressers' jobs, which fit in with their training. Alison Williams proved to be an asset to the show and very popular with the audiences. Looking back, with hindsight, I began to feel quite uneasy that someone was betraying me.

Denny Lee, the singer from 94 was returning for a second season. He had stopped the show in the previous year with his singing of 'Nessun Dorma' so I was more than happy with his return.

My regular dancers Pam, Helen and Dee were joined by a stunningly pretty girl, having danced with the Royal Ballet Company in Covent Garden and then trained with the Laines Arts School. Emma Stanworth sang and danced up a storm, Matching my regulars. Costumes and sets were in the expert hands of regulars Diane Martin and Ian Westbrook. The ever dependable John Grey as stage manager was assisted by Lorraine Taylor, and last but definitely not least, for their seventh consecutive year, Roger Davison and Andrew Pook took control of the musical accompaniment with their modern technique, making it sound like the Royal Philharmonic Orchestra.

I looked forward to commencing rehearsals. Yet again a Norwich based television company worked with the cast throughout the rehearsal period. They worked side by side with the company, not disrupting in any way and the cast were too busy with the actual rehearsals to even be aware of their presence, as enquiring cameras peeped over their shoulders for reactions. I warned the cast to ensure the toilet doors were locked when being used – there is a limit!

Opening night and I now let the critics have their say.

Daily Press
19 June 95
CV Roberts

MINOR MIRACLES A SPECIALITY AT SEASIDE

Once again it's the design – sets, costumes and lighting – which shares star billing with the performers at the latest seaside special.

Each year minor miracles are worked on the Pavilion's tiny stage, which somehow is made to look as spacious as an ice rink.

It works with particular style in the act one finale, a recreation of scenes from Hello Dolly! Which looks terrific with a dazzling set whose effortless perspectives suggest a glittering ballroom, gorgeous costumes and – another seaside certainty – first class choreography.

Coming up with new ideas each summer is no easy chore, but somehow devisor director and choreographer, Robert Marlowe manages to do so... For six seasons running, he's invited in Traffle, singing duo Kathy and Terry. Very wise too, they are the backbone of the show, not only in their zestful personal act, but in the innumerable scenes in which they are involved, to which without fail, each of them brings personality, brio and polish.

Les Wilson, the show's lead comic, is a humorist of the old school. A stand-up comedian with a wicked sense of timing, a finely honed razor against politicians and pomposity, and a flair for playing an audience which comes near to wizardry.

The audiences love him so much that he's a protected species. Ken Wood, ventriloquist, has for his dummy an hilarious horse named Galloping Claude, whose knowledge of the turf is such that he deserves a nomination to replace Henry Kelly on Classic FM.

Singer Denny Lee has a spotlight voice of splendid power, Alison Williams a pretty voice, and Nick Spellman pulls off a magical illusion act which will be a winner through the season.

Commendation too to the children's line-up. Great little charmers in a vibrantly colourful scene from Joseph and the Amazing Technicolor Dreamcoat, which provided yet another design coup.

North Norfolk News
Richard Batson

BIG BRIGHT AND BOUNCY PIER SPECIAL

Seaside Special launched itself on the holiday entertainment season with a splash of the spectacular. The show with a reputation for dazzling costumes and scenery exploded with a brighter than ever dose of sunny escapism.

There are no big stars in this show – just the show itself. Rehearsed in nine days, kept fresh by the ever fertile mind of producer Robert Marlowe, it is brought to life against a backdrop of stunning sets and costumes by Ian Westbrook and Diane Martin.

A rainbow rock gospel, decorative Hello Dolly scene, wonderful wing-walking dance number and some moodily mystic surroundings for some stunning illusions were among the highlights... the strength of the show, a unique survivor of End-of-the-Pier variety, is the versatility of the cast members who muck in with dance, song or comedy whatever their own speciality. Les Wilson, a superb stand up comic, armed with a gift, and a face, which can 'make 'em laugh' without even opening his mouth. His sidekick Ken Wood can do the same. But he is supposed to, being a ventriloquist. His stint with Galloping Claude the giant horse dummy doing impressions... brings a fresh angle to the show. So do the illusions of Nick Spellman, adding an extra dimension with some spectacular sets. Regular duo Traffle are the lynchpins of much of the action, having been in six Cromer shows, easily and energetically between their own harmonies, chorus numbers and sketches.

The other singers are returnee Denny Lee whose middle of the road cabaret style contrasts with one powerful show song from Jekyll and Hyde that had the audience baying for more.

Newcomer Alison Williams has quickly proved a big favourite with the audience too, with a sweet voice capable of travelling from Opera to Glochamorra.

Rounding off the cast are the Robert Marlowe dancers led by the polished Pamela McKenzie, who can turn their hands, or should I say feet, to everything from ballet to chorus hoofing... The recipe is the same box-office-busting blend of fun and fantasy, which will certainly be to the taste of Pier Show fans and casual trippers alike.

It remains an affordable family evening, set against a backdrop you would drive a long way to better. Cameras were filming the opening night and the Pier Show can be seen on national BBC breakfast television today between 7am and 9am.

The company were so proud that this little summer production attracted the television companies country wide, which brought our audiences from every corner of the British Isles to view a fast disappearing art form.

Seaside Special had by now established a cult status. No longer did we have to seek publicity – it sought us. Entertainment directors and local authority councillors were regular visitors to weigh up the possibilities for their own venues and I found myself headhunted. But by now I had so much affection for, and loyalty to, Dick Condon's enterprise all those years ago that wild horses would not have dragged me away. It was never a consideration and I welcomed the challenge to better the previous season. So ended the season of 95.

However I must now add that certain activities towards the end of 95 were causing me much concern regarding the new administration of the theatre. More especially because I was responsible for promoting the person involved as being right for the post. As he was a long standing friend this also was a betrayal I found hard to understand or cope with. Departing Cromer after the last night I hoped that common sense would prevail over self destruction. His, not mine.

The Christmas of 95/96 I had decided on a total change of format, a rather unusual departure for me. I intend to devote a separate section to another aspect of show business later on.

We now come to Spring of 1996.

Nigel Stewart's first season the previous year had made me uncomfortably suspicious that he had formed a special friendship with the box office manageress, even elevating her as his personal assistant and spending more time in Cromer, when his six month contract had terminated with the theatre's closure until the re-opening the following spring.

As devisor/director of the shows my contractual requirements are open ended therefore I had arranged auditions for local children, which necessitated my return. Nigel rented a house for his six month stint and invited me to stay for a couple of nights whilst there.

During the winter months with nothing to attract visitors entertainment-wise the population is considerably decimated therefore excitement is created with gossip, either imagined or suspected.

With Nigel's female assistant being the proud owner of a flashy white sports car, her husband was owner of garages and car showrooms, therefore had a high profile within the community. Apparently during the winter months this sports car was frequently parked overnight outside Nigel's house. Draw your own conclusions but I bet they accord with most of Cromer's populace. A gift for gossip-mongers.

Staying with Nigel I found evidence of a female presence in the house - shoes and clothes were in wardrobes. Confronting Nigel he denied any involvement. However with nagging persistence and a few drinks consumed, always Nigel's favourite occupation, not mine I hasten to add, he finally confessed to a serious involvement. With my suspicions now made concrete I begged him to terminate the affair for the sake of his family. By this time, his wife Maggie had given birth to Nigel's son, a delightful little fellow adored by everyone.

After a very uncomfortable night during which I had hardly slept a wink, I had to organise myself for the 10 o'clock auditions. Nigel was laid out in a drunken stupor on the settee in the lounge. I tried to get him sobered up with black coffee, finally giving up and walking to the theatre alone. On arrival the whole of Cromer's child population seemed to have descended on the theatre. Having children in the show was a great attraction although I only used them in the first half due to their schooling commitments.

Nigel eventually appeared bleary eyed and suffering a hangover, sadly something he was no stranger to. His assistant breezed around as though she owned the joint. Quite obviously her schemes were working out to her satisfaction. As I was now party to knowledge, after Nigel's confession, I fought tooth and nail on Maggie's behalf to break this situation up, for I resented being made an accomplice in deception.

During a short break in the audition I sought out the female concerned with the threat that if she persisted in breaking up my friend's marriage I would ensure the end of her career in the theatre.

With the auditions over I stormed out of the theatre heading for the railway station even though Nigel was supposedly to drive me back to London. In his condition there was no way I would get into a car with him.

He later told me his 'assistant' had begged him to come after me. Obviously she feared that I held the power to destroy her plans. I wrestled with my conscience because I had now been placed in the position of accomplice. However I decided not to reveal what I knew to Maggie hoping against hope that I could break up the situation. Maggie's friendship was more important to me than Nigel's, she had been my head girl in my groups of dancers for five years and a more loyal and trusted friend than I could have hoped for.

However, when the proverbial finally hit the fan I felt covered in guilt that maybe I should have confided in her. A loathsome position to be placed in. However, decisions are put in place at a time when one is confused as to the best course. In retrospect it was the right decision but a lot of heartache had to be endured in the meantime.

However the showbiz imperative that the show must go on prevailed and my main task was to form a cast for the summer of 1996. Nigel's option was for contracting the Simmons Brothers, Alan and Keith, and I have to confess it was the one decision I was eternally grateful for. Whilst I knew of them I had never seen them work and with my view that comedy was the most important element in a show the top of the bill had to be paramount.

I requested Nigel to contact their agent, the well-known and respected John Mann, and arrange for me to see them work. The most convenient venue was a Butlins Holiday Camp in Bognor on a Sunday night, not my idea of a perfect viewing platform. Unfortunately for the Brothers they were not shown to their best advantage.

The show was the brainchild of a member of a pop group I had previously worked with in Birmingham in pantomime and did not show the Simmons Brothers in their best light.

A dancing team of about 16 or 20, well ranked and experienced, seemed to top the bill in well-choreographed routines, which I as a choreographer would have delighted in. However now I was also director, my main thrust for topping any variety bill had to be the comedy element.

Every artiste has to believe their skills are the most important contribution on the bill, and they *are* of course. However, good as they may be, singers, dancers and speciality acts do not encourage brickbats flung at comedians by the critics on an opening night. The audiences demand laughter, without it failure.

Alan and Keith had definitely been failed by the director of this production.

They were sidelined and upstaged by the production group. Let me illustrate one particular scene. A flashback to wartime 40s required the boys to perform in drag as the Andrews Sisters. The third member was a girl singer, not the best choice when a send-up is the intention, it should be another guy. To make matters worse the dance group took centre stage with so much smoke effects and flashing lights as to make the Andrews Sisters group invisible. By this time the show was over. Butlins productions were usually fairly short in duration although presented probably three or four times during the day.

Leaving with Nigel I expressed doubts as to what I had witnessed, not feeling in my gut that the Simmons Brothers had the right strength to top Cromer's bill for the following summer.

Thank goodness Nigel persisted in their praises and I agreed to visit Johnny Mann's office and explain my doubts to him. Imagine my surprise on entering his office to be confronted with Keith and Alan also seated there.

I bit the bullet and explained what I had seen of them in the Butlins show, explaining my unease in making a final decision. Their agent naturally expounded on their ability, reinforced by written proof, and on consideration I agreed to their engagement. They did indeed work up a storm on the opening night, which ensured their return many times over. The audiences took them to their hearts demanding their return. I still remain indebted to Nigel Stewart for their introduction.

Backing them for his second season was another sure-fire success, Frankie Holmes, who together with comedy impressionist Mark Baylin completed probably one of the strongest comedy teams in Cromer's holiday seasons.

The ever perennial 'Traffle' flew in from Australia for yet another season. Soprano Michelle Summers again brought her delightful and wide-ranging skills into the equation. Andrew Stone, the stunning boy dancer I had introduced back in 1990, in the intervening years had his voice trained, so approached me with the request to be auditioned as the male singer in the show. His audition was astounding. With his looks and dance experience his inclusion in the season ensured for the first time ever scads of teenyboppers besieging the stage door every evening before and after the shows. We now appealed to a younger audience who persuaded their parents to bring them.

Pam and Helen my essential and experienced dancers returned again together with newcomers Marie McCullough and Melissa Fensom to uphold my demand for fabulous dancers.

One spectacular scene based on 'The Wizard of Oz' had the perfect cast to bring it to life with Keith and Alan in the roles of Scarecrow and Tin Man, whilst the Lion was played by Terry from 'Traffle'. With Michelle as Glinda the Good Fairy, Mark as the Wizard, dancer Marie as Dorothy and the children in fantastic munchkin costumes and masks created by the genius of Diane Martin, plus ever changing sets by Ian Westbrook, it was quite the most spectacular first half finale in all my years of devising the shows. That scene together with 'Hello Dolly' shared top billing for all time for both presentation and design.

Now it's time for the critics' reports.

Richard Batson

MARVELLOUS SPOT OF ENTERTAINING AT THE DOUBLE SEASIDE SPECIAL – CROMER PIER PAVILION

Another week, another show, another stir of the rich end-of-the pier recipe.

And the proof of the pudding is in the seating – with near-capacity audiences already warming to one of the strongest casts to grace the special in recent years.

Show one stunned with its Wizard of Oz and Riverdance, and Show two, which has just opened under the title of Glitzkrieg, is also at its best in the big chorus routines.

Music hall and The Mikado rub shoulders in this latest production, which will alternate weekly for the summer season. The Mikado in particular showed the kind of strength in depth many football managers would envy, with most of the cast able to add to the dancing and some brilliant singing harmonies.

But there were also some nice comic and inventive touches, including Three Little Maids who could open a lot of newcomers' eyes to Gilbert and Sullivan.

Show Two also gave comedy impressionist Mark Baylin a broader stage to air his mimicry talents, from Max Miller to Barry Manilow. His Frankie Howard, Larry Grayson and Eric Morecombe were gloriously realistic.

If seaside variety is about sending people home with smiles on their faces then the show succeeded through the combined comic talents of the Simmons Brothers and Frankie Holmes.

Alan and Keith's very visual tomfoolery and ability to win over an audience were matched by Frankie's slightly bizarre, beady-eyed style coupled with a good 'vent' act.

The singing also had a mix to please all tastes. Michelle Summers trilled from folk ballad to opera, while pier favourites Traffle's close harmonies shone in the Bee Gees', Run to Me.

Newcomer Andrew Stone's verve, voice, his stage presence and dancing skills were a boon to the line-up.

The icing on the cake was the Robert Marlowe Dancers – Pamela Mackenzie, Helen Pocock, Marie McCullough and Melissa Fensome – who were far more than just chorus girls with a performance which packed powerful singing, comedy sketches, ballet and one scene where they had three changes of costume.

All this for just over a fiver.

It is impossible to say whether show one or two is the better.

As Richard Batson had reviewed all of my shows I felt he was always honest in his reports, knowing the history of all the years prior to my shows entering the arena.

Following is a letter sent personally to me which shows an audience's reaction, as important as the professional's praise – if not more so.

12 September 1996

Dear Robert

I just had to write to compliment you on the excellent show which my husband and I saw last night.

We live 20 miles from Cromer and yesterday had been a normal working day for my husband and a rather hard one at that and I was not really in the mood for travelling to Cromer on such a miserable evening – but we were both completely transported by the truly stunning show.

I'm sure a great deal of hard work goes on behind the scenes but the result looks and sounds effortless – all performers deserved top billing, the costumes, scenery and lighting put the magic touch to the evening.

Thank you

Kathy Slade

When a complete stranger puts pen to paper like this it's worth more than gold to me, being completely unsolicited.

I always had them pinned on to the backstage notice board for the whole company to appreciate. Eventually the stage manager had to remove them to make room for others. Naturally, there were letters occasionally of complaint mainly about comics' material. I always replied – politely as we were always aware that certain people had pet hates.

Although all our comedians knew not to overstep the boundaries and they always obeyed the rules. However Seaside Show humour has always vied on the saucy. Remember the McGill postcards that always took the 'mickie', mainly with vicars and spinsters etc? In our present day one can't be too anodyne. Certain words were strictly forbidden such as the F word. I'm well aware that television is peppered with it nowadays that it's almost obligatory. However, I warned all comedians that the first time it was ever uttered on stage they would receive a warning, three strikes and dismissal would be the penalty, which could reverberate throughout the profession. Clean, funny comics are a rare breed nowadays but still in demand. No Bernard Manningisms! This was the edict of my guru Richard Condon and I wisely obeyed it even when he was no longer around.

So ended the summer of 1996. With the season now about to finish there only remained a couple or so fill-in weekly or even daily shows before the theatre closed entirely and was put in wraps awaiting its spring opening six months later. The final production week nearly always was an Ian Liston Old Time Music Hall bill. Always a popular choice for local audiences now the summer visitors had departed. Locals always felt that winter had really started once the coloured pier lights were extinguished. The promenade went dark and Cromer became a village again with inhabitants seeking their own amusements. They were soon into a field day of gossip and innuendo.

I always attended the final performance of the summer show departing on the Sunday. However little did I realise that my return was to be far sooner than expected this particular year.

I was therefore not party to the last night of Ian Liston's Music Hall Show, although eager voices who were present filled me in resoundingly in the aftermath. As I feared, it was on the cards that it would upset many lives dramatically and irrevocably.

After the final closure on the Saturday night I received a frantic phone call on Monday morning from Maggie in Tunbridge Wells who had just taken a call from Cromer telling her to go immediately to Norwich, where her husband Nigel was in hospital with a broken leg. It was totally impossible for her to drop everything with Emma in school and Bobbie only three years old.

I calmed her by offering to travel immediately and find out the circumstances and consequences on her behalf. Knowing the circumstances I also didn't want her to travel and discover just exactly what the situation had developed from.

After a three-hour journey I arrived at the hospital early afternoon. Exactly as anticipated, I walked into his ward to find him being consoled by his 'assistant' who quickly evacuated faster than a bullet from a gun at my presence.

Questioning Nigel as to how it happened I was given a veiled account which I guessed was a load of b———s. His explanation was that in the middle of the night he had gone to the toilet, slipped and fell in the dark... oh yeah!

I asked who had found him and he said his assistant eventually called at the flat when he didn't appear on the Monday morning at the theatre to finalise its closure. He claimed to have dragged himself back to the bedroom, unable any further to help himself. My final question, to which I already knew the answer, was how could anyone let themselves in without a key? The whole secret was quickly unravelling, to which I knew the answer.

Leaving Norwich I returned home ringing Maggie to inform her of the situation. This was the most difficult position I ever found myself placed in. Having no idea as to whether Maggie suspected that anything untoward was happening I kept the conversation to practical matters, assuring her that Nigel's leg had been set and that the hospital would soon be discharging him.

He was determined to close the theatre for the winter, which was part of his contractual obligations. This also was the termination of his six-month contract until the following year when it would be renewed.

Whilst briefly in Norwich I had also learned from performers in Ian Liston's music hall company that Nigel's broken leg was due to the fact that he had enjoyed himself too much at the final show party, that he required assistance back to his flat on the seafront – in other words he was pissed! Crude but true.

During my years devising the shows I based myself conveniently in a small delightful private hotel up on the cliff top facing the pier, which enabled me to exit and be in the pier theatre within five minutes. Therefore from the hotel's windows, with perfect spying facilities, nothing could take place unobserved.

This little hotel was perfectly run by George and Molly Caddy. I formed a long-standing friendship with the whole family sharing in their joys and sorrows. Unfortunately sorrow hit too soon with George's sudden death leaving Molly with the heart breaking decision as to whether to sell up or go it alone. Fortunately for my friends and myself she decided on the latter course of action.

The real reason for acquainting readers is mainly to inform them that any comings and goings around the pier and its environs could hardly remain anonymous from the lounge windows. Therefore Molly was able to tell me when she saw Nigel being pushed in a wheelchair to his office on the pier's end by his 'assistant'. This I naturally suspected but needed confirmation of.

Much later Molly recalled Nigel gazing from her lounge windows at the deserted winter pier and wistfully remarking 'I blew it all didn't I?' A sad end to both his Norfolk career and my long friendship with him. In such a situation one is forced to take sides and I remained fiercely protective of Maggie and the children.

Now for a truly happy ending. Maggie eventually was introduced by her next-door neighbours to the husband's best friend, Billy, and they formed a friendship, which turned to love and marriage.

Whilst Maggie ensured that Emma and Bobby had access to their father at all times – nevertheless, Billy is a wonderful stepfather to Bobby who treats him as a friend, an almost Barbara Cartland situation. But with more class.

I must now take you back to the finish of the 1996 season. With the show over, my next contract was in the Isle of Man, where I have directed many productions, following this I flew to New Zealand where I celebrated the New Year in the hope that personally it would prove less traumatic than 1995 had been.

Whilst away certain loose ends left behind in Cromer had been resolved. At some point Nigel had returned to his official office situated in a pretty rose garden – not the one on the pier – to find the locks had been changed and he was barred from entry. The writing was on the wall and obviously the council wanted rid of him. Whether a rumour or not, his assistant had lost her contract also and furthermore, or so the story went, had sued for unfair dismissal and won. My guess was that the council had been fed up with the whole scenario and negative publicity and called it a day. My cynical view was that if an extra-marital affair was a case for dismissal then quite a large proportion of the British Isles could be out of work.

On my return to England my main concern was for the summer season, so consulting with Terry Nolan the chief executive, we were in agreement that a replacement was needed swiftly as pier and theatre manager.

I was about to make another disastrous suggestion. Another betrayal by a friend I had known for more than thirty years, although our paths had criss–crossed fairly intermittently throughout the years. We were both very young when first we met. Paul Dayson was office boy to John Chilvers who ran the Grand theatre in Swansea for many years until his retirement when he was honoured by the Queen for his services to theatre in Wales.

My first association was playing Slave of the Lamp in 'Aladdin' for Elkan and Barry Simons, my first principal role and only my second pantomime. The Grand theatre was owned by the father of a well-known soccer player and at the time fairly run down. Council owned now, with millions spent on it, one of the premier theatres of Wales. However I'm speaking of 1958, my first experience there.

I'm going to rush readers through the years of the 90s. During the intervening years Paul had progressed as assistant to John Chilvers and eventually on John's retirement took over in the administrator and chief executive positions in the repertory and pantomime seasons.

My own career had also blossomed performance wise, which you will know all about in previous pages. By coincidence, which happens frequently in the theatrical profession, both Paul and Nigel's paths crossed in Tunbridge Wells through yet another odd set of circumstances. I should have heard alarm bells ringing, but we can always be wise after the event.

During Paul's management of the Swansea theatre it appeared to me that the council wanted rid of him by trumping up charges about usage of council property. As I was around directing the Swansea Operatic Society, more of which I will expand on later, I was well aware of the extreme conditions Paul was confined in. The theatre was virtually a building site and the office a Portakabin amongst the rubble and noise of rebuilding, so Paul had decided to take the office work to the peace and quiet of his home a couple of streets away. The council used this excuse to claim he used writing materials, postage stamps, etc, the property of the local authority, and planned to prosecute through the courts.

Paul fought back and decided on trial by jury. As Paul had always cultivated people in high places his case was won when the Mayor entered the witness box on his behalf and he was exonerated. However the council refused to reinstate him so he was looking for work. I sympathised completely so when Nigel was looking for a box office manager in Tunbridge Wells I suggested he interview Paul. He did and gave him the job. By an odd corollary both claimed me as a best friend and both betrayed me.

After Nigel's ignominious departure from Cromer I was extremely reluctant to recommend anyone at all to fill the theatre manager's post. However Paul Dayson was the only person of my acquaintance that I knew had managed a No.1 theatre and also knew the ins and outs of box office management so I put his name forward for an interview with Terry Nolan, leaving it entirely in their hands. I didn't even attend the interview.

The one quality Paul does have is charisma; he can charm birds from the trees and sells himself well. He got the job. To my everlasting regret. I even paid for his accommodation in my friend Molly's little private hotel when he travelled up for his interview.

More importantly now was getting the cast together. Paul had no idea of our past casts and this was not the sort of production he had ever been involved with previously. Terry Nolan and I conferred and it was decided to continue last year's success with the Simmons Brothers by popular demand and accompanied in the comedy field by Frankie Holmes. Simon Leigh, a popular stalwart capable of feeding comics and excellent in sketches with a great singing talent and looks to rival James Bond, was a great asset all round, together with multi talented Michelle Summers, an operatic soprano who could convert to country and western at the touch of a tonsil. 'Spritza' a double vocal act were new to the show but were to return many times; completed by speciality act Graham Scott and my usual dancing team led by Pam McKenzie and Helen Pocock, and joined by newcomers Leanne Parker and Gillian Redburn.

Eastern Daily Press
23 June 1997
Steve Down

Seaside Special burst into life on Saturday with an explosion of colour and dancing, and a liberal dose of slapstick.
This seaside summer show promises to keep audiences happy and flocking in if the first night performance was anything to go by.

Familiar faces like the Simmons Brothers and Frankie Holmes rubbed shoulders with show newcomers like Simon Leigh and Graham Scott.

The show opened with a fairground roundabout sequence, which was a perfect indication of the high standards of sets and costumes maintained throughout.

In traditional style the show then leaped from dance to song, from comedy to music and kept the audience guessing about where they would be taken next.

There was a healthy smattering of songs from shows like Annie Get Your Gun, Camelot and Showboat, while Simon Leigh chose a medley from Les Misérables, West Side Story and Buddy.

The Simmons Brothers, Alan and Keith, kept the show flowing seamlessly, helped no end by veteran comedian Frankie Holmes, whose ventriloquism was a highlight. Laced with gems was the final routine by the Simmons Brothers, who walked a tightrope between slapstick and farce and left the audience guessing whether some of their capers were scripted or accidental. Overall, the show is yet again a credit to director Robert Marlowe.

Eastern Daily Press
7 July 1997
Richard Batson

CURTON UP ON SECOND DECK OF SOMETHING SPECIAL

Whatever the weather outside there is always sunshine on the stage at the seaside special.

From the moment the curtain went up on a stunning summer holiday-style double decker bus, show two was on the road to another escapist antidote to the grey sky outside. A rainbow of costume, comedy and choreography all link up with a pot full of golden songs in the cast's second offering, which will run alternate weeks through the summer.

The Simmons Brothers working doubly hard are the undoubted stars with their brand of slick slapstick and homely audience rapport.

Another show favourite, soprano Michelle Summers, has poise and precision of voice equally at home with show tunes or a guitar – strumming sing-a-long duo Spritza's Neil Diamond medley was bubbly and smooth providing the show stopping moment their rich voices and neat harmonies promised. Young singer Simon Leigh wowed hearts with his dashing James Bond looks, he really had licence to kill in the ballad finale of an Elvis selection.

Specialty act of Graham Scott amused with his skilful playing of mandolin and broomstick.

Yet it is the stunning all-cast spectacular, the production dance numbers, that provide the lingering memories. They come jewelled with inventive costumes and superb sets. An enjoyable show… which is guaranteed a summer pick-me-up.

A letter received by the local paper was printed praising my dancers, which I'm reproducing here.

Arthur Grady
St Leonard's Road
Thorpe Hamlet

PIER SHOW PROVIDED A DELIGHTFUL AFTERNOON

Last Wednesday in the early afternoon, Cromer became very cold. People, especially children, huddled in doorways and shivered.

My wife and I escaped this brief bracing spell by buying the last two tickets (restricted view) for the variety show at the End-of-the-Pier.

I have never been conscious of what could be achieved on such a small stage until four lovely delightful and talented young dancers reproduced themselves by ebbing and flowing with faultless ease in front of a large make-believe stage mirror. It was five minutes of pure enchantment. This scene alone was worth the price of admission to the company's number one show.

Of course, when the girls left, three comedians came on and mucked about in front of the big looking glass. Well they would wouldn't?

All in all – an excellent entertainment.

So ended the season.

After the years of disastrous management of the pier, firstly by Nigel Stuart's reign followed swiftly by Paul Dayson's tenure, is it small wonder that the council decided to change their working policy? I was never even informed of this decision and frankly felt insulted.

Eventually I managed to read a list of managements who had applied through an advertisement in the Stage newspaper. Some I recognised as bona fide companies whilst others were complete strangers to me, Johnny-come-latelys in fact. With classic examples of local authority ignorance the decision was made to link up with a company titled impressively, 'Openwide International'. The dye was cast and I was finally informed by the council and asked to make contact, which I did.

I had, prior to arranging the meeting, made discreet enquiries as to the background of the company and was informed that they were basically a cruise line production group run by the managing director of Thompson's whose son was Adam Wide, hence the company name of 'Openwide International'. Adam had formed an agency to supply performers for cruise ships. Don't get me wrong, they represented some excellent artistes and I was eager to form a working relationship in the hope that the 'Stuart–Dayson' years would disappear into a new found dawn.

Making an appointment with Openwide's headquarters in an area of West Central London that I'd never before been to, I was misinformed as to the underground exit and wandered through a rather insalubrious and very foreign area.

Arriving at Openwide's premises I was half an hour late. As I've always frowned on people who do not keep appointment times I was profuse in my apologies to cover my embarrassment. The offices were palatial and I was impressed by their grandeur.

I had ostensibly come to acquaint the company with my plans for the summer show, which was to celebrate the pier's hundred years history, which I had gone to a great deal of trouble to investigate, in fact it spanned from the Elizabethan era to its Victorian heyday culminating with the present day.

I presented Adam Wide with a facsimile copy, which he discourteously cast aside without a glance and I was instead taken on a tour of the premises which I was expected to admire. I will admit they were grand – but – I was quite used to even grander theatrical premises based on Mayfair and the theatrical centre of the West End.

I was left with the unfortunate impression that I was being marginalised and virtually dismissed with no respect for my 17 years of endeavour to create the success that 'Seaside Special' enjoyed not only countrywide but, with the help of all the television documentaries that spotlighted Cromer – worldwide also.

I returned home with the uncomfortable feeling that there was no respect or even desire to co-operate with me. In fact, the company had been informed by the council that this celebration year was my final contracted one – wrong. In fact I had a contract signed for a further one to follow – to their dismay.

It had not been a good start for our collaboration. The local papers had been primed that this new company were going to bring a new dimension and further a new era of dazzling success for the theatre on the pier. To that end I was invited by Bruce Barrel, the chief executive of the council, to attend Openwide's inaugural presentation in the Cliftonville Hotel on Cromer's seafront.

I arrived and was completely ignored by the Openwide hierarchy who made no mention of my involvement. Instead a large screen lauded all the high octane successes of Openwide International self proclaimed hype. Had they no shame?

Prior to this company achieving control I had been contacted by the BBC television studios about the possibility of yet another documentary programme. Dick Meadows was an award winning and much respected director with a long line of successful documentaries to his name. He travelled to my home in Eastbourne to discuss the possibilities and was intrigued by the slowly unfolding story of the takeover of the Pier Show.

As he already had knowledge of all the previous documentaries that had featured the Cromer shows including the famous '40 Minutes' series, his attention was to obviously focus on the situation from Day 1.

Conversing with him about my own misgivings which had been apparent from the start Dick returned to Norwich fired by the possibility of an interesting documentary in the offing. His studio bosses agreed and contracts were put in place.

When Openwide discovered that an exposé might not appear in their favour they attempted to stop it. However I circumnavigated them by contacting the chief executive of Cromer, Bruce Barrel, and persuading him that any television programme would bring publicity that would have cost the council thousands of pounds to promote themselves. He agreed and informed Openwide that he wished them to cooperate. Round 1 to me on behalf of the show.

This had been a cliff-hanger of to-ing and fro-ing but on the designated first day of filming we started in the Norwich scenery workshops with set and costume designers in what was to prove another trophy success for Dick Meadows the director, and exposed the trials and tribulations which displeased Openwide and exposed the vicissitudes of show business in no uncertain terms. It would have made a good plot for a Hollywood movie.

When the programme reached the screens it was a very true reflection of what transpired and caused great interest, which brought people who had never previously visited the theatre. There is a belief that there is no such thing as bad publicity and this was proved most certainly on this occasion. In spite of the trauma I had suffered I was vindicated in this instance.

The following is of a letter I felt obliged to write to the chief executive in explanation of the position I unfortunately found myself forced into.

Mr Bruce Barrell
Chief Executive
North Norfolk District Council
Cromer
Norfolk
NR27 9PZ

08.09.01

Dear Bruce

I'm finding your replies very selective in what you choose to address so may I set the record straight?

It's becoming obvious that I'm being cast in the role of chief agitator, uncooperative, obstructive and in the words of one of Openwide's chief officers, and I quote – 'A monstrous ego they could well do without' – a slur I refute.

I was never at any time made party to your decision to enter into partnership with Openwide International until it was made a 'fait accompli' and I was informed that responsibility was being handed over 'lock, stock and smoking barrel' into their hands. That this company's main claim to fame is cruise ship floorshows and party planning with little experience in land based theatre shows was obviously of little consideration in your final judgement.

Throughout my entire career I targeted the top theatrical managements that I wished to work with and succeeded, in certain cases over a number of years. Names such as Howard and Wyndham, Derek Salberg, Triumph, Richard Stone, Bernard Delfont, Paul Holman, Richard Condon, Paul Elliot, E and B, all names high in the annals of the professional theatre but obviously unknown to you.

I'm making this point that in spite of my background with managements of this calibre I entered hopefully into cooperation with a company I had no knowledge of because North Norfolk District Council, under your guidance, required me to.

It became obvious from my first meeting at Openwide's offices that my long-standing association in Cromer was resented. That I was reluctantly forced to seek your aid on a few occasions indicates their lack of cooperation towards me rather than the opposite, as you seem prepared to believe.

I have chronicled the lack of communication, evasiveness, downright-prevarications and in general a total lack of respect for what I had achieved for NNDC, and in fact that I was eventually forced to go it alone to complete even the casting -a brief far beyond my contractual obligations. Your affirmation that I was in control of the show turned into a poisoned chalice. I find your claims that this year's auditions for dancers was at you insistence insulting. I've always held auditions for dancers, even inviting you (and Sheena) to attend, which you never do.

*I do hope that the £1,000 that Openwide spent on the full colour 'Stage' advertisement – mainly to advertise their association with 'Seaside Special' – came from their coffers rather than the show budget. More specifically, as I was asked to modify my ideas for this 'Special Year' as there were insufficient funds available, which I co-operated and did, as will be testified by the designers should my ascertation be doubted. Returning to the dancers **that I chose** – even though you did not remain for the singing audition, which was* *quite insultingly handled by Openwide in my view – the TV documentary innocently revealed their disdain for me. Do I need any further evidence of their lack of cooperation towards me?*

Your remark that the quality of this year's dancers vindicated your insistence on auditions astonishes me. I can't believe you've thought this through because it implies that previous dancers were substandard. That observation coming from an accountant whose knowledge of dancing I presume is minimal I find totally unaccountable. I am ashamed for you and to that end I enclose a cutting from the Norfolk News of 1994, long before you achieved the post of chief executive. This surely proves that there was respect and recognition for 'my' dancers in spite of your currently held and self-congratulatory views.

I've never mentioned that the unresolved ongoing problems in other areas than the show over the past three years occasioned a breakdown in my health during the summer of 2000, which resulted in seeing specialists so that even today I'm still undergoing treatment.

What is now occurring is hardly helpful with the ongoing publicity, which I'm being blamed for – unjustly. From your point of view this publicity is undesirable, however it is uncovering the true identify of Openwide's stance and lack of respect for my position and standing achieved over my lifetime in professional theatre. Can you wonder that I've resisted your intention of handing my contract over to a company that do not meet my requirements work wise?

You told me that I must make my own decision about how the future will be structured for myself – this ominously reeks of constructive dismissal. That Openwide are now in place for a further year with their feet firmly under the table begs the question 'what would my role now be?' Bearing in mind the uncooperative attitude they have created towards me I fear they could destroy my reputation and standing in show business which is high not only in Norfolk but countrywide should I be forced to bend the knee to their styled presentations. There is much to ponder on all sides, although I sense that between you and your partners decisions are already in place.

*I regret the tone of my letter especially after my long association with Cromer, but at least the professional acclaim and high audience attendance can ring in my ears well into the future should my position be untenable in Norfolk. **Not** of my making, I happen to add.*

The ball is back firmly in your court.

Yours sincerely

Robert Marlowe

Director-Choreographer

In retrospect Paul Dayson's first year in 1997 was the start of five fairly disastrous years administration wise and eventually I found myself fighting every inch of the way to achieve the show's success. It was a lonely rearguard action.

I can't make sweeping statements without justifying them. A painful process for me to live through again in the writing of it.

Whilst in his first year, Paul was only acting theatre manager, a usual situation until being made permanent. The position I had introduced him to required dignity and poise together with affability towards the patrons. All went well at first until promotion to theatre manager put his feet firmly under the table.

In the autumn of 97 I relished getting away from Cromer to get breathing space until after the Christmas season. One point I need to make clear is the fact that over all the years I knew Paul Dayson I was well aware that he had a large capacity for drink, especially spirits. However it never seemed to affect him or incapacitate him in any way, whilst his predecessor Nigel Stuart could drink for England - he would quickly become legless. Unfortunately for Paul he would always get into his car and drive without difficulty. This was to prove his downfall.

On one particular weekend he had visited me in Eastbourne to discuss the forthcoming summer season. As he was staying overnight my spirits supply soon ground to a halt. Personally my limit has always been brief. I do know when to stop. However on that weekend a litre bottle of gin disappeared. Guess where? Paul left after breakfast to return to Cromer via London where he was meeting with a friend for lunch. As the story goes – I wasn't there – lunch was long and Paul was on the road to Norfolk late evening. Unfortunately it was wintertime with heavy frost and icy roads, which can be a specialty of Norfolk, especially in the wilds. Rounding a sharp bend the other side of Holt, Paul skidded off the road into a ploughed and deeply furrowed field from which he couldn't reverse. As he was within walking distance of his rented cottage he locked his car and got home.

Apparently the farmer complained to the police and they eventually turned up taking details, when suddenly a mobile phone in the car began to ring persistently. The police know full well how to get into a locked car, so they answered it and on enquiring of the caller who the owner was got Paul's address and finally appeared on his doorstep at 1am. Paul was arrested and taken to the police station on the other side of Cromer and charged with drunken driving. He lost his case and his licence was revoked for three years.

He was in a dilemma, as his post required him to have a car. He was obliged to have help from friends and taxis. This was the first serious blot on his copybook. However more was to come. What Paul didn't realise at the time he was first engaged was that the box office staff, and especially the new manageress, promoted after Nigel's 'friend' lost her job, was heading a coterie to rid the pier of its new manager. Oh dear! A shining example of small town minds interfering in something they should have steered clear of, for their own sakes in fact. Within a year they would all lose their jobs or nearly all. Paul's days were numbered.

This episode I'm enlarging on to show that whilst showbiz can be a wonderful supporting club, on its obverse side it will also destroy if those in power don't observe the rules. Any position of trust has to give the right lead - in every walk of life. To get respect one must earn it.

I've already stated that both Nigel and Paul supposedly claimed strong friendship with me throughout many years' acquaintance. However, by their actions they were instrumental in changing North Norfolk District Council's approach to their summer show's presentation. Power politics at play in a tiny seaside town that many readers would have difficulty in finding on the map. This also was its greatest asset, a little pocket of 'Olde England' which attracted visitors from far and wide to experience its charm.

Terry Nolan had now retired from his position as chief executive and a new councillor had taken on his role, Bruce Barrel, now in overall charge and I was naturally apprehensive that the change would alter my position.

Terry had been an ardent and loyal supporter throughout and was responsible in engaging Dick Condon years before, to change the pier's fortunes. Terry was supportive but never interfered. Dick could be unexpectedly obstinate in certain ways but knew what he wanted and got it. This was what cemented Dick and myself in the beginning. Again, the old Chinese proverb 'softly softly catchy monkey' worked admirably with him. I was delighted when Terry was retained to support me as adviser and friend so that the link back to my beginning in Cromer was not severed after Dick's untimely demise a few years earlier.

In my view Paul Dayson's fatal flaw, which was soon to destroy him, was power struggling once he got his feet firmly under the table.

On one particular occasion when I was choreographing and directing Cole Porter's 'Can Can' in Plymouth, Paul was seeking comedians to top the summer show. He asked me to consider a Welsh act Powys and Jones, well known in Wales obviously but as I had never seen them perform, I asked him to find a date when they were working to view for myself.

It's quite a well-known and respected show business observance that regional comics do not travel well out of their own environment. Scots are a perfect example, only a few make it down south, likewise in reverse with cockneys 'oop north', although television has altered that maxim over the years.

On Sunday I travelled from Plymouth by train to central point where Paul was meeting me to travel together, this was before he was banned of course. We travelled on to a Pontins Holiday Camp near Paignton.

Powys and Jones met us in the bar before their appearance and plied us with drinks throughout the evening, sending a never-ending supply to our table. Paul downed them like mother's milk whilst I endeavoured to surreptitiously dispose of mine elsewhere. When Paul realised what I was going he willingly rescued them for his own consumption.

The boyos' act was slick and they had winning personalities. However most of their gags, whilst what was expected in a holiday camp, would have sunk like a lead balloon in Cromer. All their material concentrated around the crotch and reproductive organs. Most definitely a 'no go' area for Norfolk audiences.

During the evening Paul kept pestering me for my reaction so I finally said, no way did I feel I could recommend them on this viewing. Paul's reaction astonished me, vehemently telling me in no uncertain terms that I was an employee of the council and would do as I was told. I furiously reacted by asserting that whilst I worked through the council I was on contract to provide a summer show. He was thick with gin and tonics but still bombarded me with personal insults.

He was now revealing his true colours as far as I was concerned and that night ended my friendship with him. It's well known that business and pleasure don't mix. Quite a different premise when business and pleasure are its main thrust for success in show business. Powys and Jones were not considered after my report back to Terry Nolan. A wasted journey for me but a very valuable lesson.

After the holiday camp show I hurried Paul away not wanting to make excuses to the act. Paul had promised to drive me to Plymouth, as my last train back was much earlier. Even though I knew Paul's liquor consumption was way over the limit I didn't hesitate to get into the car knowing that his tolerance to drink would not endanger the journey.

He taunted me with insults about my attitude; but I remained silent all the way back. Finally reaching my hotel I departed telling him to remember that he was the office boy not the devisor, director and choreographer of the show, a position I had occupied for the past 16 years in Cromer and he was to mind his own bloody business, not mine. Slamming the car door I nearly woke the whole of Plymouth.

Paul Dayson's touchy feely approach with people of both sexes was about to become the weapon that the acting box office manageress was to shaft Paul with. She made a complaint to her employers – the council, of sexual harassment and Paul was suspended from his position. This happened during my rehearsal period and I was now left holding the fort. As if I didn't have enough to do! This was to happen two years running.

The second year even more astonishing assertions were made, thought up by the same person when Paul had invited the box office crew en-masse to a dinner party in his beautiful rented cottage near Holt. The accusations this time were of a more sinister kind, causing Paul's suspension for almost the entire season finally resulting in a council versus union investigation at the season's end when Paul was forced to bring witnesses for his defence. Keith Simmons and I together with Diane Martin, the costume designer, were called together with stage crew members etc, etc. It was turning into an Agatha Christie detective drama.

Travelling back to Cromer in the autumn witnesses were congregated in the council offices and sorted out like liquorice allsorts into small groups – who worked all this out in advance still remains a mystery – but in my estimation the local authority were about to lose the plot – which they themselves had plotted. Talk about crime and punishment!

Keith Simmons, one half of the comedy duo who had topped the bill in the show, and I were separated into an office whilst others also were divided and separated. What dark accusations and secrets were about to be unveiled? It's laughable now for it was about to turn into an Ealing comedy.

We hung around for what felt like hours. We were presented with refreshments, and Keith and I began to think sleeping bags were about to arrive, when we were all summoned to a general gathering.

Apparently Paul's union representative had conferred with the council hierarchy and in the politically correct atmosphere taking hold we were all informed that Paul had been persuaded to admit he had a drink problem. He was to work with the council officers to resolve the problem. We were all sent home but without a balloon and party pack of goodies.

What a débâcle, but how typical of local authority back-tracking and evasion. On my way home I tried to work out which mind crazed council despot had worked on the scenario. I failed – too many candidates.

2001 was the first show I was required to work with Openwide's company. A special one for this was also the hundredth anniversary of the Victorian pier's history.

I had returned Richard Gauntlett and Wink Taylor for their second year due to their great success in 2000. I had worked with Chris Harley in 'Cinderella' in Weston-Super-Mare at Christmas and was very impressed by his vocal dexterity and also that he had performed over 200 hundred times as Raoul, the romantic lead in 'Phantom of the Opera' in Her Majesty's Theatre in London. One doesn't require any further recommendation than that. He has also become a very loyal and close friend. Kerry-Jane Beddows, with a CV to die for, was the talented soprano. Maurice Kachuk, an extremely talented tap dancer to rival the top Hollywood greats of yesteryear, was a newcomer, along with Steve Galler a talented guitarist of classical and modern music.

All my dancers, Jessica Bedford, Rebecca Grant, Danielle Johns, Michaela Paladini, Nick Cooper and Gary Thatcher were new to me but all upheld my strict rules for excellence, which is the reason I've named them above. They are as equally important as the star names who top the bills.

Openwide had refused my request for my long-term dance assistant however they came up trumps with Emma-Jane Hardy, a real delight to work with and the following year she actually joined my team to perform. She proved a real asset.

The past history of Cromer, as I delved and discovered, was long and fascinating, starting with a charter granted by Elizabeth I in 1582. This is her actual recorded statement.

I hereby grant letters patent to the inhabitants of Cromer to transport 20,000 quarters of wheat, barley and malt for the maintenance of their town and towards the building of an old decayed pier there.

The Victorian era brought recognition when the rich and famous turned this small resort into a 'must visit' backwater. None more famous than the Empress Elizabeth of Austria known as Sisi, a great beauty of style and fashion envied by women worldwide. Strangely her life was echoed by our own Princess Diana and ended equally tragically. Following a 'love at first sight' encounter with Franz Joseph they married, to the disapproval of the Emperor's mother who eventually caused the estrangement of the royal couple. Sisi then became a tragic outcast shunned by the royal social circles, roaming through Europe seeking peace and anonymity. Arriving in highly fashionable Cromer the Empress rented the whole first floor of Tuckers Hotel, still visible opposite the pier's entrance.

Her fear of being poisoned saw the bizarre, daily ritual of a local cow being milked on the promenade outside the Empress's first floor windows and her staff supervising the baking of bread from a shop in Jetty Street. Sisi spent her days roaming the countryside writing poetry and painting watercolours.

Tragedy struck when her son, crown Prince Rudolf, a confirmed drug addict, shot himself in a suicide pact with his lover in Austria at Mayerling. Retreating into seclusion her untimely death came in 1898 when she was stabbed by an anarchist as she boarded a steamer in Geneva.

The extremely talented musical director James Moriarty, accompanied by Andy Pook yet again, made the orchestra pit sound like a fifty piece band with modern technology skilfully applied.

With all the foregoing in place I now had to deliver the goods especially as the BBC television company were monitoring our every move.

The opening of the show had quite obviously to portray the history and I had decided for the very first time in all my years there, that this had to remain for both show one and two. If audiences only attended once then they should see the lavish extent of its history. I started with the Elizabethan charter, moving on swiftly to the Victorian period, then into the 1920s heyday of Pierrot shows, finally coming bang up to date with 2001 dance styles.

I have detailed all of this because it eventually caused a rift in the company due to Openwide's decisions, which they waited until I was the other side of the world before implementing.

OK, maybe they had their reasons, but they could have had the courtesy to involve me. I could have created a far superior opening routine instead of the tacky result they came up with. I'll go no further than this, but the main culprit is forever imprinted in my memory. As usual now follows the critics reports, the first from the 'bible' of show business.

The Stage
Peter Hepple

A new name appears above the title of Seaside Special, that of Openwide International, best known for cruising entertainment but now equally interested in land-based shows. The company has certainly not interfered with the format, nor the director Robert Marlowe, who has once again produced a show that not only recalls the seaside glories of 50 years ago but in many ways surpasses them.

On what must be a relatively modest budget, Marlowe has transformed an unpromising theatre with a small stage into a venue which reaches West End standards, with superb settings by Jason Irons and magnificent costumes by Diane Martin.

The Pier opening sequence tells not only the story of the Pier but the town itself, beginning in 1582, but it would be a mistake to think that nostalgia is the name of this particular game.

Marlowe not only reflects the age of concert party in his production but is up to date in every respect. Particularly when it comes to musical theatre. The first half finale is a potted version of Chicago with all the major songs and the number chosen to end the show is nothing less than Sondheim's Old Friend.

Returning for a second season are the comedy duo of Richard Gauntlett and Wink Taylor… Both he and Gauntlett also have circus experience which makes them particularly effective visually.

The rest of the cast are hand picked for their musical and dancing skills. Kerry-Jane Beddows has loads of experience in the West End and Chris Harley spent three years in Phantom of the Opera. Maurice Kachuk is not only a versatile dancer but also an excellent singer and Steve Galler known best perhaps as a banjo player proves himself to be a fine guitarist including

Mozart's Ronda alla Turca in his spot. The six dancers are at home in all styles including classical ballet.

North Norfolk News
Richard Batson

TRADITIONAL FARE WITH A FRESH FEEL

A century of entertainment in just two and a half hours, even time traveller Doctor Who would be proud of it... As ever, it is the full company chorus numbers where the show really sparkles, under the direction of Robert Marlowe, aided by the vocals of Kerry-Jane Beddows and Chris Harley and a good looking line-up of dancers.

Best of the lot was the Pantomime Finale to the first half which was a stunning spectacle of sparkling costumes, dance, song and comedy – the special at it's finest... That is what makes this show special – the continual stirring of a magic mixing bowl of traditional Pier End variety into a fresh and tasty recipe every summer.

For the first time the show was reviewed by Michael Coveney of the Daily mail giving it an unprecedented four stars out of five.

Daily Mail
Michael Coveney

SEASIDE SPECIAL (PIER PAVILION, CROMER)
VERDICT: GLITTERING TRADITIONAL VARIETY IS NO NORFOLK TURKEY

Luckily there is relief waiting at the end of another pier – this time the one in the delightful Norfolk resort of Cromer, which celebrates its centenary this year with a slickly produced and traditional variety bill. This Seaside Special really is a thing of the past, but a thing of beauty as well. The sprightly comedian Richard Gauntlett even quotes John Osbourne's Archie Rice, asking us where we are performing tomorrow night so he can come and see us.

He then declares that the pier has come loose and is drifting towards the Hook of Holland.

Then we don't care. We have enjoyed a potted history of Cromer, a Pierrots Show, tap dancing, a Sinatra tribute, and extended excerpts from Swan Lake and Chicago. Robert Marlowe's production ingeniously designed by Jason

Irons is a mini marvel of high camp, low taste and suburban show business nostalgia.

Michael Coveney awarded the Pier Pavilion Bournemouth only two stars out of five and the Regents Park Open Air theatre in London only one out of five. The Cromer Company walked tall on Cloud 9 for days. receiving national praise and acclaim is always an extra bonus.

THE LAST NIGHT

Whilst I had received an invitation from Bruce Barrell on behalf of the council to attend the final night's performance I strongly objected to the contents of his letter. My reply, which I'm reproducing below, explains my angry dismay. That I would let down my successes throughout 19 years; shows just how little he knew me.

4 September 2001

Bruce Barrell – Chief Executive
North Norfolk District Council
PO Box 1
Holt Road
Cromer
NR27 9PZ

Dear Bruce
Your communication of 24 August to hand, though it only reached me on 31 August.

Having noted the contents of your letter I find them somewhat disturbing.

Just exactly what are you inferring regarding Paul Dayson? As far as I'm concerned Paul was made redundant shortly after his contract was passed over to your partners, Openwide International, and paid off by them. You must have been aware of that move.

I have never passed any comment on that action other than speaking on the phone with you when Openwide were being obstructive with me and I suggested that maybe they wished to serve the same notice on me. I remember with clarity your answer. However that is now in the past – a rather dismal past for me!

Furthermore whilst contractually I've never been obliged to return for final performances, it's been a matter of courtesy since Dick Condon's passing, for me to thank the cast, staff and audiences for their support in another successful season.

Your letter smacks of censorship as to what I 'might' say which I find particularly offensive! Regarding your comment that it would be inappropriate to speculate on next year I would remind you that I have a final year left on my contract signed with North Norfolk District Council.

I make this final point because although I was never consulted over your linking with Openwide International I would certainly never have agreed that my contract pass from the council's jurisdiction to a company that does not pass professional requirements I wish to be associated with.

Finally I have never signed a contract with Openwide International. If 'anyone' claims such a document exists — it's forgery.

I expect a reply to the question posed.

Yours sincerely

Bob Marlowe

If my letter appears harsh I have to reiterate that show business can be a jungle with predators waiting in the wings to step into your shoes. It's essential to stand firm on what you believe in.

Whilst I intended to be at the final performance to dutifully thank all concerned, this was not to be. I had signed a contract to direct and choreograph Cole Porter's 'Can-Can' in Plymouth. The company wished to bring forward the rehearsal period by two weeks, making it impossible for me to get from Norfolk to Devonshire in time for Monday rehearsals. I asked my friend Paul Holman to take up my seat and let me know how it finished.

PLYMOUTH

Arriving by train in Plymouth I expected to be met and taken to my hotel by a company member. A person I didn't recognise approached me holding a bill board, asking if I were Robert Marlowe. It transpired that he was from Westward Television on behalf of Norfolk TV There was no camera in sight for the only reason that British Rail would not allow them onto the station premises – thank God for that small mercy. I refused point blank to be interviewed across the airwaves.

Apparently the Monday morning Norfolk Papers had headlines, blazing large.

MYSTERY DISAPPEARANCE OF SHOW DIRECTOR

Talk about mountains out of molehills. Fortunately the person deputed to meet me turned up and knew how to get from the station without having to spout 'no comment' to any pursuing cameraman, thereby adding further fuel to a non existent fire.

This incident showed me how exasperated real celebrities get at being chased. Unless one happens to be a nude sex symbol – in which case, bring on the boys!

I'm going to take you back for a nano-second to my college days. At fifteen years of age my favourite lessons were history and geography and I had made a vow to myself that I would set foot in every country of the world before I popped my clogs. I have been fortunate to achieve that ambition over the years, financed by my theatrical career.

It was 2001 and I had booked to tour Thailand from top to toe. On Tuesday 7 August I was closing my case to catch the train to Heathrow when the phone rang, On answering it, James Moriarty, my musical director in Cromer, asked whether I knew that Openwide had called a meeting for Thursday to cut the show's opening. I was furious. It was now Tuesday, my time was running out, so thanking James I tried to place a call to Openwide. Guess what – answerphone machines with recorded messages.

For the first time, Thailand was more important than Cromer. I left.

I discovered later that Chris Harley, my loyal pal, had registered objections to the modus operandi of the timing. Bless him, but it didn't stop the rot. The die was cast.

24 August 2001

Bruce Barrell – Chief Executive
North Norfolk District Council

Dear Bruce
Thank you for your communication of 7 and 20 August, both of which arrived whilst I holidayed in Thailand. The financial problem was resolved into my bank account on the 11 August.

I hope that you can understand my dismay to find on my return that the opening sequence of 'Seaside Special 2001' had been slashed in half making a mockery of the pier's 100 years history which I understood was the main thrust of celebration.

That Openwide International achieved this during my absence indicates yet again the general attitude and discourtesy I have been subjected to since you empowered them to take control.

I am now being accused of creating a 'chasm' between us by Steve Cutbush, which I totally refute. I was more than eager to cooperate with your decision to bring this company in thus removing responsibility from the council.

I travelled to Cromer for Openwide's inaugural introduction to show solidarity with them, which you agreed to be a good move and funded. That they totally ignored my presence and made no reference to our joint co-operation was remarked upon by others present.

It has also been brought to my attention that the Openwide executives were particularly disappointed by the television documentary and certain 'moles' – every organisation has them – have indicated that blame is being attached personally to me.

The popular 'fly on the wall' technique was in operation during filming so the documentary speaks for itself and is indisputably correct. It occurred as it happened and it's unfortunate if seen as adverse by certain persons.

That you had to intervene and direct Openwide International to cooperate with the BBC television company indicated the council's desire for what was hoped would be a laudatory exposure for Cromer and its summer show.

However the aim of any documentary director is truth and if that exposed problems as they occurred – tough! I certainly did not write or direct this particular scenario. That responsibility rests entirely in other areas, which NNDC will have to recognise remains their responsibility totally.

My letter to you of 29 March indicated all the problems I was experiencing and the fact that I was involved with areas far beyond my personal brief – casting, etc.

I expected more support from all involved in the changed scenario I was forced to accept. That I am now feeling undermined is unfortunate after 19 years loyal service. However my consolation is the high national as well as local praise and attendances being accorded to both shows.

Yours sincerely
Robert Marlowe
Director – Choreographer

TRAVESTY

Adam Wide, the titular boss of Openwide International, now had his feet most firmly under the Cromer table. Readers who've followed me this far will be aware that from my first meeting with Mr Wide I had been treated with total disdain. However, he was canny enough to know that due to my longevity with Cromer audiences he must not put me down too soon. That was to follow later. I'm now going to acquaint you with his first letter to the audiences as printed in the lavish programmes.

> *Dear Theatregoer*
> *Well, here we are in this the pier's one-hundredth year, with yet another Seaside Special at the Pavilion theatre Cromer. Brimming with that remarkable mix of comedy, music and dance, which has made it a national institution over the years. The uniqueness and countrywide fame can be attributed to the dedication and vision of one man, Robert Marlowe.*
>
> *Single-handedly he has upheld the peculiarly British end-of-the-pier tradition with flare, humour and originality – and this year (his nineteenth!). He has once more surpassed his triumphs of years gone by. His vigour and enthusiasm are legendary, and we can only marvel at his continued success.*
>
> *Seaside Special is indeed that, special, and we at Openwide are very proud to be the present curators of this completely unique and glittering treasure, found nestled between the cliffs of the North Norfolk, coast-line. Long may it continue, and long may the inhabitants and visitors to Cromer carry on enjoying the exceptional talent and testament to hard work, that is permanently on display, in this remarkable and historic theatre... we hope it continues for at least another hundred years!*
> *With best wishes*
> *Adam Wide*
> *Chairman – Openwide International*

With hindsight that now reads so two-faced, even giving the impression that we were buddy buddies. As Adam Wide did not even attend the first show on its opening performance, I was totally bewildered, as I had thought he would attend with his boots well blacked.

Ah well, I surmised that he didn't wish to face competition in a popularity contest, especially after Openwide had been overruled by the council regarding the BBC documentary which was soon to hit the air waves, enlightening viewers with surfacing problems.

I received a letter from Dick Meadows, who directed the BBC TV documentary, echoing my surprise at the absence of Adam Wide the new boss of the Pier Show, repeated here.

Dear Bob

Just a short note to say the very best of luck for the run. It's a great show and one of which you should be enormously proud. Cromer and the company are very privileged to have someone of such talent in their midst.

Sally and I opened your kind present in the moonlight on the pier after we left the first night party and I was terribly moved by such a lovely book and the inscription. Thank you so much.

I hope I can reward you all with a good programme. It won't be for want of trying.

I must admit I was pretty astonished to hear from you that no-one from Openwide was at the first night of the show which after all is the jewel in the crown of the pier. I am being polite here!

Look forward to seeing the second show.

Warmest regards

Dick

After disdainfully cutting the historic opening of this special celebratory show, especially when I was on the other side of the world and not even consulted, I was appalled to learn that the management of Openwide International were of the opinion that audience members would be totally unaware that cuts in the pier's history would even be noticed. That just illustrates their lack of understanding where theatregoers are concerned. Shipboard audiences on holiday cruises pop in and out as the mood takes them and there are plenty of other distractions for them to sample.

I'm now going to reveal one of the many letters I received which contradicts Openwide's belief that their interference would not be noticed.

4 September 2001

The Editor
Eastern Daily Press
Prospect House
Rouen Road
Norwich

Dear Sir
Another opening, but changes at Seaside Special on Cromer pier may not see another show for its talented director and choreographer, Robert Marlowe. We were appalled to read the report in the EDP on Thursday 23 August whilst on holiday in Cromer, that a serious rift was developing between the new pier manager, Openwide International and Robert Marlowe over their apparent decision to cut 10-15 minutes from the opening in the pier's Centenary year.

Seaside Special can justly feel proud of the high professional standard it has achieved over 19 years under Robert Marlowe's sensitive direction, which has led to a worldwide reputation with the audience consisting of people from New York, Japan, Australia and Overstrand to our knowledge. This year, though, for the first time we felt the show's opening to celebrate the Centenary was extremely disappointing, especially when measured against the concluding number (the four seasons) prior to the interval in Show 1, which was brilliant and certainly there was nothing like a Dick (Richard Gauntlett) or a Dame!

We now know the reason why the opening was thin and unimaginative, especially as we were expecting something special in the Centenary year, and was a matter of comment as we left the show. How comforting to know this was no fault of Robert Marlowe and whilst Cromer itself as an ageing beauty may need a facelift, Seaside Special does not. So Openwide International, take care of your jewel on the pier in Robert Marlowe and we shall look forward to his continued success in his 20th season next year, in which in our view the opening/closing should be dedicated to the Best of Robert Marlowe and also encore in particular the very professional and talented Richard Gauntlett.
Yours sincerely
Bill and Nicola Sandal

Following this came another letter from a group who relished seeing the show after viewing the BBC documentary.

30 July 2001

Dear Mr Marlowe
I am writing to congratulate you on an absolutely superb 'Seaside Special'.

Six members of the family went along to the matinée on Wed 25 July, and we all had a wonderful time. Everything was perfect – the artistes being so very talented and professional, which was complemented by the beautiful costumes. I also wish to mention the musicians who make a valuable contribution to the show. The scenery too was excellent.

After we had bought the tickets, we saw the television programme 'Carry on up The Pier!' which made us look forward to the show even more.

Your dedication brought a marvellous result – long may you reign!
Good luck and best wishes
Yours sincerely
Peggy Martin

Even newspapers were featuring the problems as a cause célèbre.

SUMMER SHOW IS HIDING TENSIONS

On-stage fun and laughter at Cromer's pier-end summer show is masking simmering tensions behind the scenes that have taken another twist.

A chilly relationship between director Bob Marlowe and new pier managers Openwide International surfaced on a recent fly on the wall television documentary featuring Seaside Special.

Now Mr Marlowe, who has masterminded the show for 19 years, has been outraged after managers cut his showpiece opening number tracing the history of Cromer pier.

He attacked the 'discourtesy' of them axing the first part of the curtain raiser – because they needed to cut 10-15 minutes from the show – without consulting him.

Openwide hit back today saying that once the season had begun, the management of the show was down to them.

Managing director Steve Cutbush admitted there was a 'chasm' between them and Mr Marlowe, but said it was of his making.

Mr Marlowe was shocked to receive a letter telling him of the cut after returning from holiday.

'If they had any concerns they should have raised it at the start of the season. It has now been running eight weeks,' he said.

He now plans to take the matter up with pier owner North Norfolk

District Council. Mr Marlowe is keen to complete 20 seasons at the pier next year and has another year to run on his contract.

Now we leap ahead to the ridiculous situation after the last night of the season, which newspapers love to dramatise.

DISPUTE – BOSS MISSES LAST NIGHT CELEBRATION MYSTERY OF THE STAY-AWAY SHOW DIRECTOR

Mystery surrounds the future of the man behind one of the nation's most famous seaside shows after he failed to appear for the closing night.

For the first time in 19 years, Seaside Special director Robert Marlowe did not make an end-of-the-pier show speech after what has been a record-breaking season at Cromer pier.

Members of Saturday's audience, many of whom had been invited by pier owner North Norfolk District Council, were told he was working elsewhere.

Tributes were paid to Mr Marlowe, but away from the on-stage smiles he had voiced his concerns about the future of the show under the management of entertainment consultancy Openwide International.

Last month, Mr Marlowe said he had been keen to carry on to complete 20 seasons at the pier next year, but criticised the company after it cut 15 minutes from the show without telling him.

Last week, he said his future involvement with the production was uncertain, and yesterday he was unavailable for comment following his failure to appear.

Tensions surfaced during a fly-on-the-wall TV documentary earlier this year, when Mr Marlowe said he could not watch someone 'throttle my child'.

Openwide was brought in by the council in the pier's centenary year to help with running the Pavilion Theatre and the London Company has had its contract extended for another year. This season a record 46,000 people have watched Seaside Special. Council chief executive Bruce Barrell said he was saddened and surprised that Mr Marlowe had not been present to join the celebrations, despite accepting an invitation.

He did not know if Mr Marlowe would be back for another season.

'The Openwide involvement was about managing the theatre,' said Mr Barrell. 'They also have the ability and skills to put a show together if that becomes necessary.'

Openwide creative director Rory Holburn said he had been expecting Mr Marlowe for the last night even though he was directing a show in Plymouth.

'It would have been nice if Bob was here. He has done a superb 19 years,' he said.

Mr Holburn said the cut to the show had been made for 'operational' reasons and it was for Mr Marlowe to say if he wanted to return.

'We haven't discussed it with him but it does need deciding. Right from the beginning of the season the decision was always in his hands.' He added that the company was disappointed Mr Marlowe had voiced his concerns in public instead of speaking directly to its executives first.

'We have no chance of solving it unless he wants to talk,' said Mr Holburn.

'Bob has had a great deal to contribute to the community and the show. It's a shame to see anything go against us all working together'.

It appears everyone was consulted! Why did they miss the theatre cat? He could have had a good meow – if we'd had one.

Whilst working in Plymouth the only contact I had in Cromer was with Richard Batson, which he got some mileage out of in the local papers, and it helped to stir the storm in the teacup. Here follows my letter to the chief executive.

23 October 2001

Mr Bruce Barrel
Chief Executive
North Norfolk District Council
Cromer
Norfolk

Dear Bruce
Thank you for your letter of 10 October, which reached me on Friday 19 October after being forwarded.

There are many questions that need answering regarding the situation that has unfortunately developed with 'Seaside Special'.

I am disappointed after 19 loyal years of endeavouring to create the gold plated success that is now the story of Cromer's summer show to find myself marginalised at every turn.

It was by belief that you and I had forged a good working partnership since you were appointed chief executive of NNDC. However, the decisions taken by you last March to appoint an outside management company have soured that relationship by seemingly putting the blame on me for many of the problems that have arisen.

I reiterate that I did not seek the BBC television coverage. The final outcome exposed problems that were created by your liaison with Openwide International. The fly on the wall technique is a currently popular documentary formula, which unfortunately disclosed the events, as they were created.

That you and Openwide International conspired to show me as the culprit is totally unjust.

From my initial meeting with Adam Wide and his company I found myself treated with disdain and a total lack of respect for my achievements over a lifetime in the professional theatre. I now speak with certain knowledge of their background, which is singularly lacking in theatre presentation. Their main success is with cruise ships and holiday hotels abroad presenting cabaret. A far cry from the production styles presented in Cromer.

That they are experts in corporate style hype and high powered video presentation seems to have totally seduced you which astonishes and saddens me, more especially as you appear to take their word against mine.

I at no time refused to cooperate on the final night's amalgamation shows and for them to suggest such a thing is a downright lie. However, not for the first time have they chosen to denigrate me. It is all part of their power struggle and I am weary of it. That they wanted to muscle in and take over was apparent right from the start.

I am quite prepared to meet and discuss the ensuing situation. However, in the initial stage I do not want a one sided slanging match with Openwide International and request that we meet privately to straighten out problems which you have no actual knowledge of in spite of your claims to have supported me. I do not deny that you assisted me but you were never party to the major concerns that surfaced during the pre-production period.

I would be prepared to come to Cromer during November when I have finished my present production if you believe there is any mileage left in our association. I literally feel as though I have fought a battle against impossible odds. However, if the show's attendances and success is anything to go by then I equally feel I am the victor, which is of some consolation. However, if on the other hand I am now considered a thorn in Cromer's side then maybe our paths should divide.

Adam Wide has replied on behalf of my letter to Steven Cutbush in which he is of the belief that my contract with the council is now ended. This is not my belief as you are aware and I have not deigned to reply to Mr Wide on the matter but await your response as to whether the council wish to sever the relationship and renege on the contract.

I have put my accommodation address below should you wish to contact me direct as I am here until November 2nd.

Regards
Robert Marlowe
Director Choreographer

Yet again another report in the Cromer papers stirred up the mud or should I say muck. The following indicates the excitement readers obviously required to while away the autumn doldrums.

Norfolk News
27 September 2001

SUMMER SHOW ENDS ON SOUR NOTE

Cromer pier show director Bob Marlowe says he wants to be back for next summer's silver jubilee of the Seaside Special.

But his bosses have said they could not yet give any commitment about his involvement in next year's shows.

Speculation has been growing about Mr Marlowe's future after he missed last weekend's final night show.

This was at the end of a summer season where soaraway seat sales were soured by a simmering row between him and a new pier management company.

But speaking to the North Norfolk News the showbiz veteran said he was hoping agreement could be reached, adding 'I would like to do the silver anniversary show, which will by my 20th year.'

Mr Marlowe is currently preparing a show in Plymouth and said he missed the final night because of extra rehearsal demands.

He felt he was being made out to be the 'bad guy' following a television documentary, which showed tensions between him and pier managers Openwide International.

But has stressed the fly-on-the-wall programme only showed what really happened. He wanted to have talks with the council to iron out problems and prevent any recurrence of difficulties this summer.

The row centred on a cut made in the show without his knowledge. Openwide said this step was within their powers once the show's run was under way. Openwide creative director Rory Holburn said they would be 'delighted' to talk to Mr Marlowe and hear his concerns, but could not give any commitments on his involvement next summer until then.

He was disappointed that the director had aired grievances through the media rather than face to face.

District Council chief executive Bruce Barrell was pleased to hear Mr Marlowe wanted to talk, and saw his role as helping with any reconciliation – but added that it took 'movement in both directions' to make that happen.

But both he and Openwide stressed that whatever happened there would be a Seaside Special following the current successful format.

THE LAST CHANCE SALOON

Returning home after the Plymouth show's opening night I had agreed to meet Bruce Barrel to iron out the situation regarding the season of 2002. He initially wanted this meeting to take place in Openwide Headquarters but I refused. It would only have developed into a slanging match and I was thoroughly sick of all the to-ing and fro-ing, so suggested we meet privately together to thrash out our own problems and hopefully present a united front. The venue suggested was the Kensington Hilton, a very salubrious, spacious and quiet place to iron out the problems.

We met on a brisk autumnal morning over coffee and Bruce had now accepted that I did have a contract signed three years ago for the season of 2002 – the Silver Anniversary of 'Seaside Special'.

I had already informed Bruce by phone that whether or not the council wished to retain my services I would expect full remuneration, which was contractually in place and the last year of a four-year agreement. I had contacted my union, Equity, so knew I was standing on firm ground. I was adamant. Bruce was happy to concur and we toasted 2002 over a drink of something stronger than coffee.

Getting ready to depart Bruce told me that Adam Wide expected us for a light lunch in his headquarters. I refused - that was taking acceptance too far.

Suggesting that Bruce, being the senior partner via the council in the link up with Openwide International, act as my agent, I explained that during our conversation I had assured him of my devotion to create the most spectacular celebration of my 20-year finale with both Cromer and 'Openwide'.

We parted and I agreed that a meeting with Openwide's representatives should be arranged to further discuss the preparations for 2002. This took place in another Central London Hotel between Rory Holburn, Sheena Fairbairn, Morgan Van Selman and myself. We toasted, over a glass of wine, success to 'Seaside Special 2002' and departed. Looking back now Morgan Van Selman's last season was to be 2002. Why? I have no idea.

Rory and Sheena are now virtually running the artistic side of the company since Adam Wide's departure from the scene. Again I have no idea why – but I would have welcomed that move had it happened during my first acquaintance.

Never mind – as I have quoted Shakespeare previously – 'All's well that ends well.'

In spite of the spat I had with Rory, which was recorded in the documentary by the BBC. I still regard him as the only truly experienced partner on stage, in the company's hierarchy. An honest and nice guy. Whilst Sheena is expert at organisation, a useful combination. Rory and Sheena now have control of the artistic side of Openwide and are taking it successfully forward.

With the Cromer show of 2002 now a contractual certainty I breathed a sigh of relief. All the back biting, innuendos and downright lies were hopefully a thing of the recent past.

I concentrated on the pantomime season, which was fast looming. I have already written of this show in a previous chapter, so won't repeat it. Its success was like a balm to my artistic soul, after the foregoing Cromer situation, which hurt very much at the time.

However that's just another facet of showbiz. You have to fight for what you believe in from the Day 1, and my Day 1 was now 49 years ago. So readers will see I wasn't an easy pushover – ever. Tenacity is the name of the game.

Once the pantomime in Rickmansworth was up and running I concentrated on the company for my final Cromer show. I had sought a very clever young comic who I had seen for three years in my hometown of Eastbourne where he had topped the bill for the Royal Hippodrome summer season with phenomenal success.

He rejoiced in the single name of 'Tucker,' apparently a relic of his school days. Remember the name because if there is any justice in our profession he should become a star in its truest sense, to rank alongside Bradley Walsh.

I had tried for three summers to persuade him to join the Cromer show, but it suited him to remain with the Hippodrome show because it was only a four day a week season, enabling him to take on lucrative weekend work in other venues – my loss.

However in 2002 his agent apparently had persuaded him that a Cromer season could serve him well. Thank God! He signed the contract and was instrumental in helping to make that show the best one in my whole 20 years, as my finale exit.

Once Tucker was in place it was essential to find a talented second top but equally talented in a different set of skills. I knew who I felt would be ideal. Gary Lovini had worked in the show in 1986 alongside Bradley Walsh who was the second comedy lead to Gordon and Bunny Jay. Bradley was only 23 whilst Gary was 17 and that was his first season in show business. He was an astonishingly accomplished violinist both classical and modern and more devastatingly handsome than a boy had any right to be. Tall, slim and able to hold his own in singing and dancing routines, known as an all-rounder, a most useful label in our profession. Together with Bradley their personalities had the magic formula that drew audiences like a magnet. What a cradle of talent.

Sixteen years had passed and Gary had found fame more in America where he hosted his own TV programmes, etc. However I was determined to get him for my final season to co-star with Tucker because I felt the vibes would be good.

Many phone calls to America re-established our acquaintance, although we had always exchanged Christmas cards, and I cunningly made contact with his Dad who exerted his own persuasion in favour of the Cromer season.

Finally the contracts were signed through Openwide's organisation – what a coup that was and more especially because over the years Gary had become the perfect foil for comedy. He and Tucker formed an unbeatable bond, which had a great resonance with the audiences. Both of them were tremendous company artistes, also liked by all the other members, which is an added bonus and helped to create a harmonious happy atmosphere.

THE OPENWIDE AUDITIONS
FINAL SOLUTION

Rory and Sheena arranged the auditions for both dancers and singers. With my determination to encore the success of Chris Harly who had made such an impact the previous year I felt it was important to find a girl singer to equal his talent. A charming lass from Openwide's office was coordinating the auditions and there were quite a few to choose from. One or two quite possible but so far not one with the X-factor.

I was told the next applicant was Vicki Carr. To say I was astonished was to put it mildly. I gasped 'Surely not the American singer, who must be sixty at least?' I was assured that it wasn't and the door opened and in bounced a slim... young ... and pretty blonde in an explosion of confidence. Wow, she was like a tornado. Her talent left me gasping. We had to contract her. There was no other in the offing to match her. I was lucky – she wanted the job as much as I wanted her. I was to discover during rehearsals that she also possessed comedic skills, which made her a perfect foil to Tucker. The gods were already smiling on Seaside Special 2002.

I needed a speciality act to complete the cast. Unfortunately there are not too many around any more as work is scarce in the new millennium.

As I have always made it a rule to return artistes who had proved popular with the audience I had decided to bring back Maurice Kachuk the dynamic tap dancer from the previous year. Maurice is also an excellent company member capable of anything asked of him. Besides being a dancer in all its aspects he can sing and act, what is known in the profession as a good all-rounder.

Finally my dancers, the true backbone of any company. Since the 90s all dancers were required to have expertise in singing alongside their dance skills.

I was particularly delighted when my assistant of the previous year Emma-Jane Hardy expressed interest in working on stage in the group. Naturally she took on the role of head girl also. Jessica Bedford and Danielle Johns also returned from the previous season so I had an audition for one more girl and two male dancer/singers.

Victoria Tully a product of the arts educational school, which always had a high profile, was also an excellent singer. Two boys were balletically expert and capable of lift work, Gary Jackman and Dominic Coleman, more than fulfilled their audition promise. So with the cast complete, Diane Martin the costume designer and set designers and painters Jason Irons and Richard Matthews were all in place for their expert contributions to what I was convinced would be the best production of all my 20 years, and those would be hard years to beat, for certain.

I am not one to bang my own drum so here are the critics' reports which thrilled the whole company – so deserved after all their skilful expertise and dedication. Firstly from Richard Batson the Norfolk News show correspondent.

Eastern Daily Press
24 July 2002
Richard Batson

ONCE AGAIN IT'S A PIER SHOW WITHOUT PEER

If you are looking for a cure for the World Cup blues – then head to Cromer. The resort's summer show is renowned for its annual dose of pier-end Prozac, which transports audiences away from the problems of everyday life, whether it is the vagaries of English holiday weather, or losing to Brazil.

And showgoers heading for this year's splash of instant sunshine will need to slap on a high fun-factor cream to protect them from a show more dazzling than ever. A double celebration of the Special's 25th year, plus creator Bob Marlowe's 20th and probably final season, whetted the appetite even before curtain up.

Opening night revealed a slick, pacey show delivered by a cast brimming with youthful zest, and showing that you don't have to use wartime tunes to spark a variety audience sing-along - Elvis does the trick too.

Twinkling at the heart of the cast is debut comic Tucker whose single name hides a double-barrelled blast of cheeky seaside humour and a warm rapport with the audience.

Sharing top billing is violinist Gary Lovini, returning to the show after a gap of 17 years, and wowing the audience with a varied virtuosity ranging from classical and country to folk and gypsy fiddling.

Song soars from the sweet voiced and charming Vicki Carr, along with a return by Chris Harley with more scope this year to show off his powerful voice.

Another returnee is tap dancer Maurice Kachuk whose happy feet and smiling voice once again proved popular with the crowd. The Robert Marlowe Dancers get plenty of opportunities to show off their balletic and gymnastic skills. And the show's sparkle is made all the brighter by stunning costumes and some striking scenery and lighting.

This show has got all the hallmarks of one of the best yet. And its appeal should attract increasingly younger audiences, with cameo 'appearances' by Kylie and S Club 7 in a sketch based on Pop Idol – whose judges' verdict on the Special would be 'The Cromer crowds love you. You blew them away.'

Next to review the show for the second year running was the following report from the Daily Mail's theatre critic Michael Coveney who again gave us four stars out of five.

Daily Mail
Friday 19 July 2002
Michael Coveney

ONLY HERE FOR THE PIER
VERDICT – BARREL OF FUN AND FRIPPERY ROLLS DOWN THE PIER

At Cromer the summer show on the pier has a 20-year history under the direction of Robert Marlowe and is much more scenically ambitious with painted cloths and settings you rarely, if ever, see nowadays. Mr Marlowe provides an added sharpness and fluidity in a rock gospel musical sequence, the inevitable Abba tribute and a finale in black and silver with hats that would do justice to Cecil Beaton. Violinist Gary Lovini (a New Faces winner in 1980) really can fiddle for England and literally does so in his Golden Jubilee medley. We all sang along and thought it was the last night of the Proms.

The headlining comedian in Cromer is the single named Tucker from Romford, Essex, an immensely likeable performer with good material and a passing resemblance to both Brian Conley and Bradley Walsh.

Tucker said he loved Cromer, 'The beach was right next to the sea and there was so much to do.' He'd been weighed twice. They don't tell 'em like that any more, and more's the pity.

So while the sun's out, forget Tuscany and Morocco, head for the British Coast and the last of old style variety's summer wine.

BBC Radio Norfolk
Tony Mallion

DIRECTOR BOWS OUT

The secret of its success is Robert Marlowe's, the man who for 20 of the 25 years has devised directed and choreographed two Seaside Special programmes each year (they alternate through the season). That is a staggering 40 shows.

Robert is back for the very last time to bring us a vintage 25th Anniversary year. It's everything we've come to expect – a hand picked, versatile cast. Smashing sets, superb costumes and as musically strong as ever. Down the years, the Cromer show has been a springboard for the careers of young performers who've gone on to great success – among them Bradley Walsh, Darren Day and Gary Lovini.

Lovini, a dazzlingly brilliant violinist, returns after 16 years. He can sing and dance but it's his violin playing which brings the house down.

Vicki Carr is a great young singer with a superb voice, and making a welcome return for a second year is male singing lead Chris Harley. Maurice Kachuk is also back with his elegant tap-dancing.

The Robert Marlowe Dancers are Emma-Jane Hardy, Jessica Bedford, Danielle Johns, Victoria Tully, Dominic Coleman and Gary Jackman. But they are more than just dancers they can all sing. Indeed the blend of voices of the entire cast is breathtaking. It's a pity we don't get to hear more of the close harmony.

James Moriarty gets so much from the cast and is backed in the pit by Andrew Pook. But the person who holds the show together is lead comedian Tucker (it's his nickname) and is destined for great things. He's very funny, original, quick witted, and great with the audience. He's got a winning personality, which instantly has the crowd on his side.

Don't miss what could well be the last show of this kind.

There are very few, if any, directors like Robert Marlowe who can devise this sort of all round entertainment.

It would be unthinkable that Cromer, or the English summer could be complete without some kind of Seaside Special, and a similar show will go on.

But enjoy this unique style show while you can – we won't see the exact likeness again. Be thankful that Bob Marlowe and North Norfolk District Council have kept alive the dream of Dick Condon for a quarter of a century.

With my last two programmes now a reality and playing to packed houses I returned to my home in Eastbourne, bidding the cast farewell and jokingly warning them that I would return, like the second coming, and they would know not where or when. In the past, on an odd occasion, this had been necessary when I had had a couple of dodgy jokers in the pack, even colluding with a 'trustee' to spread a rumour that I was 'in on a certain night'. No such situation would have developed with my final hand picked and dedicated cast – superb pros all.

One morning towards the end of May the most exciting letter dropped through my letterbox. I gazed in amazement at the coat of arms on the back. It was an invitation to attend the first ever Garden Party at Sandringham.

My invitation By Command of the Queen was for my services to the county of Norfolk over the past 20 years.

My loyal stage director, Lorraine Taylor, had also received an invitation, having devoted 14 years at my side in presenting the shows.

It took place on a hot and sunny day on 18 July 2002. The champagne flowed like water, military bands played on the lawns and 12 huge marquees which had been erected in case of rain, remained empty as the sun beat down. My abiding memory of those marquees was the poles supporting them, which were entwined with literally thousands of roses. The perfume was quite overwhelming, and together with the champagne created a heady combination.

The Queen and the Duke of Edinburgh mingled with the guests and the radiance of Her Majesty's smile was quite dazzling, especially when directed right at you.

As her 50th Golden Jubilee coincided with that of my first show in the theatre in 1953 I felt doubly rewarded.

Writing after the event to thank Her Majesty for a wonderful occasion I enclosed the current theatre programme of my summer show in Cromer. I now have in my possession a letter from Buckingham Palace thanking me for that programme. With my last season now approaching I returned for the final night – a sad but proud occasion.

This was the last report from Richard Batson who had been a great support throughout my years.

North Norfolk News
Richard Batson

STANDING OVATION WELL DESERVED FOR TOP SHOWMAN

Showbiz is seldom shy when it comes to handing out tributes to its stars. We see hours of glitzy Oscar–style ceremonies on the telly as the industry fêtes the people in the spotlight.

At the weekend we saw the star behind the Cromer pier show for the past 20 years take what could be his final bow.

There was a short tribute from the Chairman of the District Council, and the presentation of a painting, but personally I felt the 'thank-yous' were a little low key for man who has done so much to help the show, the resort and the local economy for two decades.

I know the Pier Show is a team effort, featuring the cast, the crew, the council and the new management company – and not just the creator alone. But Robert Marlowe's influence in its development has been immense. His constant stream of fresh ideas and high standards have put the show on a pedestal. His perfectionism means it has not always been a painless process for the performers – but there is no doubt that he will be a hard act to follow. Maybe the lack of a huge farewell underlines the rumblings that he could be back in some shape or form.

But even if he does not return I'm sure his legacy will live on. Much like that of Dick Condon, whose face still smiles down from above the theatre.

It would be nice to think there was some larger or more permanent recognition of Robert's role in creating a unique show and helping put the special into Seaside Special.

But even if that final curtain was a little muted the biggest accolade Mr Marlowe could want which his successor has to contend with, was the standing ovation at the end of the season from the people who really matter – the audience. It is something I have never seen before in 10 years of visiting the show and a moment that I'm sure will also be framed in Bob's memories of his time in Cromer.

So came the end of my long reign in Norfolk.

In the programme was a page from Openwide's chairman. Adam Wide. I would like to think that he had been the author of the contents. However we had never hit it off from the start, so my gut reaction was that Rory Holburn had been the instigator, as indeed he and Sheena Fairburn had coordinated with me in all the arrangements for my final year. I'm going to now follow with that page because I heartily agree with the sentiments expressed in the two final sentences.

Dear Theatregoer

As we celebrate this 25th Anniversary year of Seaside Special I am reminded of a story from a national newspaper which suggested that the seaside theatre was a thing of the past, indeed it stated that the end of 'The End-of-the-Pier Show' was nigh. That did not take into account the amazing success of Cromer Pavilion Theatre, a true jewel in the crown of traditional English summer season theatre.

The reasons for Cromer theatre's success are complex. The die-hard fans, a superb location, the hard work and enthusiasm of the artistes and stage crew have all played their part in making Seaside Special 'special', and leading the way for the past 20 years has been devisor, choreographer and director Robert Marlowe.

An extraordinary talent and drive, Bob has single-handedly upheld the tradition of the end-of-the-pier show. Now, after 20 years of tireless dedication Bob has decided to seek new projects.

So let us celebrate this 25th Anniversary of Seaside Special and thank Bob for 20 glorious years, let's enjoy the summer season, the laughter, the song and dance, and the applause. We are proud and honoured to have worked with Bob and grateful for the legacy he leaves behind.

Cromer Pavilion Theatre and Seaside Special have, I am certain a bright future, with increasing audience numbers year on year, and with the potential to develop the theatre seating and front of house we should look forward to the coming years.

The Seaside Special of the future will have a fabulous history on which to build, performed on one of the most famous stages in England.

With best wishes
Adam Wide
Chairman
Openwide International

As I had been invited to record my memories of my 20 years in the final programme, I'm now reproducing them as printed.

Where to start on a trip down memory lane? So much talent and so little space to name all the artistes who have helped to build the phenomenon that is Seaside Special.

Comics, musicians, singers, dancers, costume and set designers, backstage technicians - an endless list.

Les Wilson stopping the show with Dottie Wayne in the National Health routine. My talented dancers excelling in all branches of dancing including classical ballet, many going on to London's West End stages in big musicals, even taking leading roles. Bradley Walsh's progress to Palladium and Royal Command fame, Darren Day's musical success. The spectacular Elizabethan Banquet scene, The Wizard of Oz with Diane Martin's amazing costume reproductions, the spectacular 'Holy Rollers' a popular compilation of religious rock opera repeated at the request of audiences.

The enthusiasm of all the Norfolk children who have tasted the bright lights with us.

The dedication of musical directors Roger Davison and James Moriarty amongst others for raising the chorale singing especially to enhance the fabulous musical show contributions. So much talent – so little space to name all the artistes who have contributed to the phenomenon that is 'Seaside Special'.

Finally my abiding memory of Dick Condon who brought me to Cromer. Long may the show reign supreme in the annals of seaside summer shows.

I deliberately refrained from going to Cromer for a couple of years, feeling that it was unfair on the new company members to have me virtually breathing down their necks as they found their own feet towards furthering the successful format already in place.

Professional friends finally entreated me to see the 2005 production, and I did. Di Cooke, an extremely talented choreographer, was now in charge of directing the show and I was most impressed. The show reporter, Richard Batson, was able to re-assert in the local press my real pleasure that Seaside Special was spiralling forever upwards.

Now in 2006 with extra resources most obviously in place Di Cooke has come up with stunning effects and ideas that I would be proud to have attached my name to. What more can I say? Except to wish for their growing success in perpetuating Dick Condon's dream of live summer shows on Cromer Pier.

THE WORLD OF PANTOMIME

Origin and Historical Development

The word 'pantomime' does not in fact actually appertain to the definition of mime. It evolved from the Roman 'pantomimus', which refers to an actor and not a type of performance. The great Roman dancers Pylades and Bathylos performed in vast arenas without using words, whilst still conveying their meaning, and thus was born the art of pantomime. Once theatres were built in the Greek style rather than arenas, actors came into their own and the spoken word ruled.

A form of pantomime was initiated by the Romans during the mid-winter Saturnalia, when men dressed as women and vice-versa. Slaves became masters and masters slaves. Thus evolved the topsy-turvy world of present-day Christmas productions with Dames, Principal Boys and Penurious Royalty – the poor becoming wealthy at the finale.

There was however a lighter side to Roman entertainment. The arenas also staged pageants of victorious battles and historical allegories, some performers even attaining fame that ranked alongside the gladiators, although less bloodthirsty. One such favourite was a Roman actor, by the name of Pantomimus. He could fill arenas with his exaggerated antics, rather in the style of our present day clowns. Hence the appellation of 'pantomime' up to the present day.

With the advent of Christianity these entertainments, which had become amoral and subversive, ceased and were discontinued for hundreds of years.

Medieval England

I am now advancing centuries to our own entertainments, which will show how the actual seeds of our present day pantos germinated way back in the mists of time.

Small touring groups of actors would travel the country to bring the 'Miracle Plays' to eager crowds. These small groups travelled with their stage, which was an Oxon drawn truck, which they set up in towns and village squares.

As the plays were of religious significance the lead actor took the role of God. He was seated centre back on the platform facing the crowd. The Spirit of Good entered on his right hand whilst Evil appeared on his left hand.

Thus the pantomime tradition evolved. Fairies always enter stage right, which is the audience's left, whilst the reverse applies to the Evil Spirit.

The other rule is that when Good confronts Evil on stage, there is an invisible line down the centre, which neither must cross during their verbal battles. Once on stage alone, the whole space becomes theirs, but they must still exit off their own side.

This still applies today in companies loyal to tradition If we dump the traditions, then dump pantomime! Which would be a tragedy in my view. Every child's first theatre visit at about five years of age, is likely to involve a pantomime. Adults remember this from their own childhood.

The Victorian Era

The Victorians realised that there was to be vast wealth obtained in presenting a Christmas production to bring cheer to the winter solstice. Thus was born the tradition of our present day pantos, which are much more robust than back in the 17th Century.

The first recorded pantomime performance was devised by John Weaver, the dancing master of Drury Lane. He claims the year to be 1702 but in all probability it was a few years later.

Until 1843 a law was in force which made it illegal to act for hire, gain or reward any spoken dramatic performance unless it had a royal patent. Monopolies were held by Drury Lane under the direction of David Garrick, and Covent Garden directed by John Riches.

Riches had made so much money from his pantomime presentations at the Lincoln's Inn Fields theatre that he leased land in Covent Garden and built his own theatre, which now competed in an intense rivalry with Drury Lane. Each vied with the other to produce more elaborate and stunning scenes and effects to draw the crowds, courting bankruptcy in the process of trying to outdo each other.

These pantomimes were very different from what eventually followed because they were based on allegorical and historical events, tied together with the characters of the Italian Commedia dell'Arte. Commedia dell'Arte later came through France to England in the form of the Harlequinade, which featured the loves and trials of Harlequin, Columbine, Pierrot, Clown, Pantaloon, etc.

Many technical items evolved with these shows are still in use today – wings, traps, and pulleys, cloud and smoke effects, and even the first naturalistically painted canvas backdrops found their birth with pantomime. These revolutionary ideas even had their own featured details exploited on the extremely verbal playbills.

To get round the lack of a royal patent, many theatres engaged musical artistes for which no patent was required. They charged for this item but then allowed their audience to remain for a dramatic performance, which was given gratis afterwards. Hence a bird whistler appeared between the acts of 'The Merchant of Venice' by this subterfuge.

In 1788 the law was minimised and theatres were permitted drama for 65 nights a year. By 1800 royal patents were held outside London by many towns and cities. In 1843 the law was totally repealed and many new theatres flourished, to the extent that most towns could boast three and sometimes four pantomimes running from Christmas until Easter.

In 1879 Drury Lane, now controlled by Augustus Harris, brought great changes. Realising the great popularity of the music halls, he persuaded its stars to play in his Christmas productions – to the chagrin of his straight actors, who deplored the arrival of the low down common variety people -a prejudice that can still be found in evidence today!. However, Harris persisted with his plans and brought the great Joseph Grimaldi to Drury Lane, with such success that even today clowns are nicknamed 'Joey' after this great artiste who died tragically young.

These artistes brought their own songs, acts and business into the shows and yet again another profound change took place in the presentation of pantomimes. Other great names working under Harris's banner were Little Tich, Vesta Tilley, Marie Lloyd and Dan Leno. Leno was one of the greatest Dames ever and is revered to this day for his playing of Widow Twanky, Mrs Crusoe and most famously Mother Goose. The Harlequinade was now mainly dropped, except for a token appearance as a prologue, and we moved into the world of the fairy tale.

Not all of these changes were applauded, and Charles Dickens complained in 1896, 'Then came the deluge – the floodgates of music hall opened and all that was agreeable about the good comic pantomime was drained out.'

However the Public did not agree, and when in 1912 King George V commanded a royal pantomime performance, the seal of approval was conferred on a branch of show business that, until then, no decent lady and certainly no child could view with ease.

I trust by now readers will realise why I'm so vehement in maintaining that pantomime with its honoured traditions is worth protecting for all future audiences and more especially for children's first, wide-eyed delight.

So began pantomime with music hall stars, which, in varying degrees, was the forerunner of today's productions, although now we introduce television personalities into the time-honoured roles and plots of yesterday's stories.

Pantomime is an art form peculiar to Britain – no other country has it. Its apparent simplicity is its greatest ploy.

And so we come to a 19th century ditty, which still applies today.

'Three things are required at Christmas time
Plum pudding, beef and pantomime.
Folks could resist the former two,
Without the latter none could do.'

During my theatrical career I have directed over 60 pantomimes with top star casts. In most cases I also played the villains - in my opinion the best roles to get one's teeth into.

On one occasion I was delighted to help Honor Blackman tackle her first panto Baddie. I told her that children loved the opportunity to shriek and boo the villain most. She was dubious but I persisted telling her that in her finale entrance she would get the biggest audience response from the youngest section, which was amply proved, to her delight. In my album I have her photograph inscribed, 'To Bob who taught me to be evil – overnight.' Not bad, eh? What an ego boost from Pussy Galore!

Theatre Superstitions

Professional performers are notoriously superstitious and many have private little rituals they must adhere to before a show for a successful performance – applying their make-up in a certain order, putting one particular shoe on before the other, etc, etc, etc. Each individual ritual to placate the anger of the gods.

Straight actors have the famous Shakespearean proscription - never to mention 'Macbeth', but only refer to it as 'the Scottish play.' Anyone doing so must be expelled from the room. Once outside they must turn three times, curse an oath and knock for re-admission to gain forgiveness. Odd maybe, but without traditions we would be a lot poorer, in my view.

There is a finale superstition that is written into all of my pantomime scripts. Once the performers take their walk-down, there is the traditional little routine of the 'couplets'. A single rhyming line is given to each principal to take a step forward and deliver, with the final line pronounced by the star.

During rehearsals the cast can deliver all their own lines but the final one is never revealed until the first night's performance, and no one knows but the star. To ignore this is regarded as bringing bad luck on the company.

I was requested recently to reply on NODA's behalf (the National Operatic and Dramatic Association), to a letter received from a certain society's secretary, telling of a series of disasters that had befallen their company during their run. Apparently their director had 'pooh-poohed' saving the last couplet line until the first night. This had resulted in some quite unexpected accidents, including the Emperor of China tripping and being taken off to the hospital during a performance. I replied, but resisted the temptation to say 'I told you so!'

Is it possible to ignore panto traditions. No! No! A thousand times No!

Finally it is well recorded that all theatres have ghosts due to all the energies released during performances going back through the centuries, and energy is the one indestructible agent in the world. I have actually witnessed such a phenomenon whilst working at the beautiful Georgian Theatre Royal in Bath which has the reputation of being the most haunted. This was verified by the cast and audience when the phantom appeared during the first performance and made contact with the star Lesley Crowther, gaining newspaper headlines for the show. Hope the ghostie got its 10 per cent! No cast member during the run wished to be the last one to leave after the show.

Pantomime Particulars

1953
JACK AND THE BEANSTALK
Producer Francis Laidler
Alhambra Theatre Bradford
Bunnie Doyle, Betty Dayne, The Seven Romas, Lorna Lee, The Storr Brothers.
My first panto as one of the Seven Romas stilt act.

1955
OLD KING COLE
Producer Tom Arrow
Theatre Royal Birmingham
Vic Oliver, Harry Shields, Sylvia Cambell, Vanda Vale, Beryl Foley.
My first principal role, as Young Prince Cole.

1956
QUEEN OF HEARTS
Producer Reg Lever
Regal Theatre Barnstable
Gene Durham, Kenneth MacDonald, Vilma La Verne, Du Marte and Denzer, Stephanie Debret, Robert Ash.
I played the Knave of Hearts

1958
ALADDIN
Producers Elkan and Barry Simmonds
Grand Theatre Barnstable
Ossie Morris, Reginald Vincent, John Cartier, Barbara Willoughby, Helene du Toit, The Five Roberts.
I choreographed and played Slave of the Lamp

1959
QUEEN OF HEARTS
Producer Cyril Fletcher
Arts Theatre Cambridge
Cyril Fletcher, Betty Astell, Billy Tasker, Eric Garrettt, Julian Jover, John Carolan.
I choreographed and played Spirit of the Woods.

1960
SLEEPING BEAUTY
Producer Cyril Fletcher
Kings Theatre Southsea
Cyril Fletcher, Betty Astell, Dennis Martin, Billy Tasker, Wally Patch.
I presented an act as a Puppet Master on stilts with all the dancers as puppets, which stole the show. Also choreographed which was headlined and caused a jealous rift with the management.

1961
QUEEN OF HEARTS
Producer Cyril Fletcher
Arts Theatre Cambridge
Cyril Fletcher, Betty Astell, Julian Jover, Billy Tasker, Eric Garrett, Howard Eastman, Jan Melvin.
I choreographed and played Spirit of the Woods.

1964
MOTHER GOOSE
Producers Elkan and Barry Simmonds
Embassy Theatre Peterborough
McDonald Hobley, Leon Cortez, Marc Fleming, Tommy Osbourne, Wendy Jones, Tony Snape, The Falcons, Jenny Vance, Zio Angels.
I was directing for the first time – choreographing and presenting an act with Jenny.

Standing tall for Mother Goose

1965
ALADDIN
Producers New Theatre Trust
New Theatre Cardiff
Tommy Trinder, Charlie Chester, Reg Dixon, Judy Kenny, Du-Marte and
Denzer, The Lynton Boys Marlowe and Vance.
I choreographed and presented our act – was asked to take over direction midway.

1966
ALADDIN
Producers Bernard Delfont and Derek Salberg
Princess Theatre Torquay
The Barron Knights, Billy Burdon, Martin Dell, Jenny Maynard, George Bolton,
Gavin Gordon, Robert Marlowe, Jenny Vance, Roselli Singers and Dancers.
I choreographed as well as presenting our own act.

1967
GOODY TWO SHOES
Producer Derek Salberg
Alexandra Theatre Birmingham
The New Vauderville Band, Jack Tripp, Chris Carlson, Fay Lenore, Jenny Vance,
Robert Marlowe, Arthur Tolcher, The 4 Kinsmen.
Jenny was Goody. I choreographed and played the Evil Spirit.

1968
DICK WHITTINGTON
Producer Derek Salberg
Alexandra Theatre Birmingham
The Dallas Boys, Cy Grant, Ted Rogers, Gordon Peters, Pat Lancaster, Raymond
Bowers, Thorey, Brandt Brothers, Claude Zola, Philip Blaine.
*Jenny had retired to start a family. I choreographed and played King Rat. My next
partner Nina Brown was Head Girl in this production.*

1969
ALADDIN
Producer Derek Salberg
Alexandra Theatre Birmingham
Michael Bentine, Donald Peers, Ronnie Stevens, Jasmine Dee, Martin Dell,
Billy Burden, Martin Lawrence. *I played Slave of the Lamp and choreographed.
Colin Tarn was in the orchestra and wrote the words and music for a stunning
'Willow Pattern Plate' ballet routine, which created quite a stir.*

1970
ALADDIN
Producer Derek Salberg
The Grand Theatre Wolverhampton
John Hansen, Hope and Keen, Billy Burden, Jasmine Dee, Ronnie Coyles, Martin Dell, Dennis Spencer.
I had total control, as director/choreographer. Nina Brown became my dancing partner, which was to continue for many years. In this panto we played Slave of the Lamp and Genie of the Ring respectively.

1971
GOODY TWO SHOES
Producers Triumph
Forum Theatre Billingham
Helen Shapiro, McDonald Hobley, Sandy Lane, Tom Mennard, Charlie Lea, Wally Thomas, Alton Douglas.
I played the Evil Spirit. I became a fully-fledged director/choreographer for the Triumph Company for the next 14 years.

1972
JACK AND THE BEANSTALK
Producers Triumph
Princess Theatre Torquay
FreddieDavis, Lynda Baron, Richard Murdoch, Bob Johnson, Rainbows End, Jumpin Jax. *I directed/choreographed. Nina and I played Good and Evil.*

1973
BABES IN THE WOOD
Producers Triumph
Richmond Theatre London
Arthur Askey, Ed Stuart, Carol Hawkins, Lynda Baron, Frank Williams, Ian Lavender.
I directed/choreographed. Nina I played Good and Evil.

1974
BABES IN THE WOOD
Producers Triumph
Princess Theatre Torquay
Bernard Breslaw, Patricia Bredin, Richard Murdoch, Peter Butterworth, James Hayter, Kent Baker, Samantha Lee, Pamela De Waal Babes.
I directed/choreographed. Nina and I played Good and Evil.

1975
ROBINSON CRUSOE
Producers Howard and Wyndham
Theatre Royal Newcastle
Mike and Bernie Winters, Old mother Riley, Pat Lancaster, Laverne Kari Grey, Loftus Burton. *I directed/choreographed and played Black Beard the Pirate. Nina was Spirit of the Sea.*

Old Mother Riley's understudy, Roy Roland. An astonishing revelation.
Robinson Crusoe, Theatre Royal, Newcastle 1975

1976
JACK AND THE BEANSTALK
Theatre Royal Newcastle
Julie Rogers – a *delightful first time Principal Boy,* Jack Douglas, George Lacey, John Gower, Leah Bell, George Truzzi, Maggie Beckit.
In this company were four singers, one of which was destined for fame - his name, Graham Cole. Graham played the front legs of the cow but now is famous for his longevity in 'The Bill' on TV.

1976
DICK WHITTINGTON
Producers Triumph
Congress Theatre Eastbourne
Anita Harris, Harry H Corbett, Dora Bryan, Deirdre Dee, Nina Brown.
This production I directed only – choreography was in the excellent hands of Denise Shaun, a delight to work with. I played King Rat, with Nina as Fairy of the Bells.

Dick Whittington – Congress Theatre, Eastbourne 1976
Starring Anita Harris, Dora Bryan and Harry H Corrbett

1977
MOTHER GOOSE
Producers Triumph
Congress Theatre Eastbourne
Patrick Cargill, Nerys Hughes, Mark Wynter, Deirdre Dee, Donald Hewlett, Michael Knowles, Dawson Chance.
I directed, choreographed and played Demon Discontent, whilst Nina played my Opposing Half.

1978
DICK WHITTINGTON
Producers Triumph
Ashcroft Theatre Croydon
Barbara Windsor, Norman Vaughan, Bill Owen, Donald Hewlett, Michael Knowles, Deirdre Dee, Reg Dixon.
I directed/choreographed and played King Rat opposite Barbara. We had a ball! Nina was Fairy of the Bells.

1979
ALADDIN
Producers Triumph
Theatre Royal Bath
Leslie Crowther, Judy Carne, John Clegg, George Lacey, Margo Harris.
I directed/choreographed, playing Genie of the Lamp to Nina's Slave of the Ring.

1980
JACK AND THE BEANSTALK
Producers Triumph
Congress Theatre Eastbourne
Basil Brush with Billy Boyle, Mark Wynter, Jack Tripp, Tommy Trinder, Anthea Askey, Alan Christie, Beverley Adams. *I directed/choreographed and played Giant's Henchman. Nina was Spirit of the North Wind.*

1981
JACK AND THE BEANSTALK
Producers Triumph
New Palace Theatre Plymouth
Basil Brush with Billy Boyle, Mark Wynter, Jack Tripp, Richard Murdoch, Anthea Askey, Alan Christie, Beverly Adams.
I directed/choreographed. Nina and I played the same roles as the previous year. In fact the cast were identical except for Richard Murdoch replacing Tommy Trinder.

1982
MOTHER GOOSE
Producers Newpalm Productions
Wimbledon Theatre London
Larry Grayson, Honor Blackman, Anna Dawson, Dilys Watling, David Morton, Cheryl Taylor, Desmond and Marks.
I staged and choreographed but did not appear.

1983
MOTHER GOOSE
Producer Paul Elliott
Arts Theatre Cambridge
Brian Cant, Donald Hewlett, Michael Knowles, David Morton, Julie Dawn Cole.
I directed and choreographed, taking over Honor Blackman's role of the previous year as the Evil Spirit.

1984
MOTHER GOOSE
Producer Paul Elliott
Theatre Royal Lincoln
Brian Cant, Geoffrey Davies, Roy North, Sheelagh Gilby, Jilly Johnson.
I directed/choreographed and repeated my role of 1983.

1985
CINDERELLA
Producer Paul Elliott
Lewisham Theatre London
Paul Henry, Jess Conrad, Brian Cant, Tracie Bennett, David Moran, Roy North, Duggie Chapman, Dawson Chance, Irene Handl.
I was director/choreographer only.

1986
CINDERELLA
Producer Richard Condon
Theatre Royal Norwich
Robin Nedwell, Diane Soloman, Anne Aston, Avril Angers, Pat Mooney, Burdon and Moran, Nicholas Nickelby, Michelle Summers, Gary Lovini - *in his first pantomime at 17 years old.*
I wrote and directed this panto. Christine Cartwright choreographed beautifully.

1987
ALADDIN
Producer Richard Condon
Theatre Royal Norwich
Wayne Sleep, Dilys Watling, Wei Wei Wong, Walker and Cadman, Bradley
Walsh, Freddie Lees, Rusty Goffe, Charles West, George Reibbett, Traffle, Peter
Whitbread, Emerson and Jane, The Ding Bats.
*I wrote the script and directed. Christine Cartwright again choreographed. This was
Bradley Walsh's first pantomime and stardom beckoned. A young, well-experienced
dancer was also destined to make his name as a top choreographer - Stephen Mear is
now well established and respected.*

A New Beginning

Now my guardian angel had another plan for me, which was about to open up
a whole new era.

Whilst I had heard of Burden and Moran and knew they were a drag magic
act, I had never met them until 1986 when they were engaged to play the Ugly
Sisters in 'Cinderella' for the Theatre Royal in Norwich. They contributed in no
small way to the outstanding success that production enjoyed.

Being the director I did not get an opportunity to socialise due to the
workload. Once the opening night was over my job was done, I left it in the
hands of the production company and departed.

A couple of years later I received a phone call from Paul Holman, which was
eventually to lead firstly to a great friendship, and secondly to the longest
association I have ever formed with a production company. It is always
flattering, no matter how experienced one is, to be sought after and the time for
me was right.

I had always accepted new challenges and was getting tired of directing the
usual pantos - 'Jack and the Beanstalk', 'Aladdin', 'Dick Whittington', etc, even
though these had brought me into contact with top star performers.

I had agreed to meet Paul and he drove to Eastbourne one weekend to discuss
possibilities. What transpired on that weekend has now endured for 15 years and
in that time an acorn has developed into a sturdy oak.

Many changes in our profession have also occurred. In the past the variety
and even the straight theatre supplied the top liners. No longer. If one does not
have a television profile, forget it! Anyone now topping a panto poster is
accompanied by their TV provenance, writ large.

I am not knocking the change because many of these performers have quality
training in their background which includes singing and dancing. However
reality TV has let a few slip through the net – disastrously in many cases. As a

director, I have been fortunate and escaped that pitfall, almost. On the odd occasion I have been able to create a disguise for the inadequate. No names, but I know who.

The first production I undertook for Burden & Moran and Paul Holman Associates was in my estimation the most exciting and spectacular of my entire career - 'Alice in Wonderland', with a mainly young cast who could do it all - sing, dance, whatever was required of them.

The only drawbacks in my view were firstly the venue - Barnsley - and secondly the multi purpose local authority hall - I wouldn't call it a theatre. However, we overcame the obstacles.

The actual book had been adapted by Malcolm Sircum, who also wrote the music and lyrics, which he had done for the Birmingham Repertory Company the previous year. The Birmingham Rep had an enviably high reputation in the theatrical firmament with quality always their goal.

When told that the stunningly beautiful costumes including all the animals had been designed by Terry Parson, one of England's top creators, I wasn't surprised, because all of the Triumph Organisation productions I had worked on for 12 years had engaged his services.

However, what did surprise me – no, astonished me - was discovering that the sets and amazing props had been specially designed by Celia Imogen, and created on site throughout the summer by Shaun King and his backstage staff. I was flabbergasted – my flabber had never been so gasted!

Prop-makers in London could not have bettered them. They were works of art fit for a museum, many of them mechanical, like the enormous mushroom which the caterpillar sat on smoking his hookah pipe, foot operated to emit spasmodic puffs of smoke. The attention to detail was remarkable. All I had to do was help create the performances to match - an easy task with this young and enthusiastic cast.

Whilst I had worked with holograms in 'Aladdin' I had never encountered laser beams, but Paul had decided to use this effect when Alice entered the rabbit hole. Suddenly a revolving beam revealed Alice dangling on a wire whilst singing an appropriate song. She didn't even get danger money – but we all suffer for our art and the effect brought gasps and applause from the audiences. What a way to start! Follow that? We did.

I intend now to credit all the cast. They were perfect in creating the individual characters.

ALICE – Lydia Watson
DUCHESS – Roy Kean
WHITE RABBIT – Neil Smye

MOCK TURTLE – Steven Brough
QUEEN OF HEARTS – Shirley Vaughan
KING OF HEARTS – David Fellows
COOK – Jacquie Kaye
CATERPILLAR – Nigel Wild
MAD HATTER – Mark Jardine
TWEEDLE DUM – Peter James
TWEEDLE DEE – Gary Kielty
HUMPTY DUMPTY – Sean Connelly
MARCH HARE – Jay Worthy

The musical director of my summer shows in Cromer and also good friend, Roger Davison, excelled. Over the intervening years I have met and even performed with some of the above cast. However showbiz is very much a case of ships that pass in the night.

It was a joy to work with all the above artistes. I'm convinced that this show could have transferred to a small London theatre in its entirety without changing a single performer and would have proved a hit. London's loss.

1990 'Wizard of Oz' The Forum Theatre Hatfield

As I had never directed 'The Wizard of Oz' I was delighted having new ground to break and also the opportunity to work again with some actors from 'Alice in Wonderland'.

A young up-and-coming actress Tara Wilkinson was excellent as Dorothy supported in other main parts by Steven Brough as the Lion, Kevin Marlowe as Scarecrow, Richard Stockwell as Tinman and Steve Aliffe as the Wizard. With only 12 actors in total there was much doubling of characters, and with children and pupils from the JJ Theatre School of Watford playing munchkins, the Ladies and Gentleman of Oz, Farmhands, etc it was a crowded and effective visual feast.

I had created an opening sequence on the Farmstead prior to the cyclone, when the main characters doubled as farmhands in an ambitious ballet danced to Aaron Copeland's 'Rodeo' which caused quite a stir, setting the standard for what was to follow.

1991 'Peter Pan' Seccombe Theatre Sutton

1991 proved to be a watershed personally for me. Whilst I had concentrated on directing and choreographing in recent years I had not performed since playing the Baddie in Mother Goose at the Theatre Royal in Lincoln.

Paul Holman seduced me with the offer to play the arch villain in Peter Pan,

Captain Hook. I didn't think twice and accepted it as a dual role, firstly Mr Darling who transforms into Hook. Mrs Darling and Tiger Lily were played by Jacqui Kaye whilst Smee, Hook's reluctant sidekick, was played by equally versatile Steven Brough. Both of these actors had worked in 'Alice in Wonderland' and were worth their weight in gold.

Young actors from the renowned Sylvia Young Theatre School played the Darling children. Sacha Flory as Wendy, Leonard Kirby as Michael and John Picard as the top hat wearing John. The latter actor went on to star in TV sitcoms. Peter was played delightfully gamin by West end star Jackie Crawford.

The lost boys, all from Sylvia's London school, were very impressive in all departments, acting, singing and dancing. I feel sure they will all have gone on to find work in the musical theatre which is what their schooling excels in, with a full roster of household names to the school's credit. Sylvia Young is a very canny lady and knows how to sell her star pupils.

A local school run by Ann Smith supplied all the other dancers and juveniles, all talented and well disciplined, who played mermaids and Indians, etc.

As I had never actually studied as an actor, concentrating on dancing in all its facets, I had learned a lot on the hoof playing opposite many straight actors, whilst still retaining my variety artiste quality. I like to think we benefited on both sides.

It was the one and only time I played Hook but I still regard it as a high spot in my career and was extremely grateful for the opportunity.

As I have always delved into historical fact, I had discovered that the original Captain Hook, Gerald du Maurier, the Victorian actor of acclaim, played the role as if his right arm were severed, so I followed his example. Not easy when one is right handed. But I always strove for authenticity.

I am now going to boast a little but you don't have to take my word for it. The newspaper critics had their say below and I was particularly pleased when the critic of the Croydon Advertiser wrote the following.

Croydon Advertiser
Christopher Wood

...and a pleasant couple of hours it makes too, thanks largely to director/choreographer and Captain Hookalike, Robert Marlowe. Under Robert's direction, the action moves at a brisk but not hurried pace and his evil pirate provides a much-needed hissable villain in a show of otherwise honest, loveable and likeable characters.

Living out my childhood in Thornton Heath, the Croydon Advertiser was our local paper, so to the neighbours who remembered me I had finally made it.

The Stage and Television Today
Sutton January 9 1992
Peter Tatlow

PETER PAN - SUTTON

Captain Hook and Mr Darling the director and choreographer all rolled into one like Poo-bah, could be too much for one person but for Robert Marlowe it was far from the case, with his production of Peter Pan so full of vitality and his loveable and debonair characterisation of the great sea dog so vivid at the Seccombe theatre.

1992 'Jack and the Beanstalk' Alexandra Theatre Bognor

Yet again Paul Holman had persuaded me to appear as the Giant's Henchman, a role I'd played many times previously. This was the first ever pantomime of my career for Francis Laidler's company in 1953 although then I appeared on stilts as one of the Giant's Children – seven in all.

I have already written in more detail about this. It was a delight to work opposite Anthea Askey, Arthur's daughter, who played the Vegetable Fairy.

1993 'Snow White and The Seven Dwarfs' Guildford

This I've already described. It starred delightful Maureen Nolan, Bobby Crush, Burden and Moran, Paul Valentine, Angela Jenkins and Stephen Lewis from 'On the Buses', who physically attacked me in front of the entire company. I was on the verge of suing him. There were plenty of witnesses and Equity would also have agreed with me. However, I did get my revenge.

1994 'Babes in the Wood' Guildford

This was the disastrous Danniella Westbrook saga already recorded in great detail. However, it did have a happy ending, as should all pantomimes.

As I had other contracts elsewhere for 1995 and 1996 Paul and I parted company to return again in 1997.

1997 'Aladdin' Arts Link Theatre Camberley

Paul gave me my first opportunity to play Abanazer the arch villain, who had escaped me, although I had performed in many Aladdins previously but always as the Slave of the Lamp. Simon Bright, another pupil from Sylvia Young's stable, had already starred as Gavroche in 'Les Misérables' in London and had his own television programme. He made a perfect Wishee Washee.

Emma James was Aladdin, very experienced, and as my combatant a real pleasure to work with, also fulfilling my preference for females playing Principle Boys – a Victorian tradition which is, in my view, real pantomime. I know I keep on about this and today's practice substitutes males. There are certain pantos which are more apt such as Robinson Crusoe.

My friend Mark Wynter who started his career as a pop singer is a perfect example of male Principal Boys. Mark and I have worked together many times. Now of course he is regarded not only as a musical performer but also as a straight actor and I first met Mark when he was in Shakespeare's Romeo and Juliet. Back to the Aladdin company.

Yet another Sylvia Young protégée, Natalie Searles, was a beautiful princess. Mark Monero, with a television CV to die for, was stunningly athletic as the Genie of the Lamp. Widow Twanky was played in true robust tradition by Roy Alvis who commanded the stage. Anthony Cable was impressive as the Emperor and the cast was completed in true bouncy style by the Chinese Policemen Andy Collins and Richard Moody.

I was to work for the first time with the musical director James Moriarty who was to eventually take over the musical direction of my productions in Cromer's summer seasons for the following four years.

As usual I had directed/choreographed and written the script so there was no excuse for not knowing the lines.

The press reports were extremely complimentary and rightly so because the cast gave their all and we played to good business.

1998 'Aladdin' The Playhouse Weston-Super-Mare

This starred Australian Stefan Dennis well known for his role in 'Neighbours', playing the Baddie – Abanazar - for the first time. Co-starring was Gladiator, Rocket, as Genie.

Brian Tracey played Wishee Washee and we were destined to work together many times after this. He certainly knew how to work the audiences up and they loved him. His partner in comedy was Roy Alvis as Widow Twanky.

I had worked with Roy the previous Christmas so I knew his strengths, having played opposite him. A fantastic group of international gymnasts and acrobats – the Acromaniacs – besides performing their breathtaking stunts also played the Chinese Policemen and the Emperor of China.

The Princess was Jane Horn whilst my long-term dancer in the Cromer shows Helen Pocock was Slave of the Ring. There were others of my Cromer Dancers, Gillian Redburn and Marie McCullogh, who played So-Shi.

Last but certainly not least, as he played the titular role of Aladdin, was Lewis Rae, a very experienced and versatile performer with all the skills.

'The Stage' reporter gave the following critique.

The Stage
Jeremy Brian

Paul Holman Associates has spared no expense in mounting one of the most lavish pantomimes seen in the resort for years. For once it is not the players who win the loudest applause but the sparkling costumes in the Enchanted Cave and Royal Wedding Procession scenes. The top of the bill was former Australian soap star Stefan Dennis who brings an unexpected dignity to the role as Abanazar as well as a fine delivery. His Genie of the Lamp is the Gladiator Rocket and there is excellent support from an unusually large strong cast. Brian Tracey as Wishee Washee and Roy Alvis as Widow Twanky work hard and successfully for the laughs while Lewis Rae and Jane Horn are full of personality, as well as possessing strong singing voices, as Aladdin and his Princess.

The comedy acrobats – Acromaniacs – double as the Chinese Policemen and Emperor whilst Marie McCullough (So-Shi) and Helen Pocock (Slave of the Ring) complete a line-up enhanced also by the Phantasie-en-Noir puppets.

1999 'Snow White and The Seven Dwarfs' The Playhouse Weston-Super-Mare

There is a very amusing story attached to this production. Whilst working on the Cromer Summer Show Paul Holman rang me regarding the Christmas Pantomime.

'Bob, how would you like to return to Weston-Super-Mare again?'
'I'd love to, the expert stage manager and crew are such a delight to work with, which makes my task easier and it's a well-run venue.'
'There is an extra inducement.'
'Not more money?'
'No, I already pay you too much. Something better than money. The biggest female star in the world.'
(Thinking it could not be Tessie O'Shea as she was no longer in this world) 'Is it Liza Minelli?'
'No, bigger than her!'
'Not Barbara Streisand?'
'Bigger even than her.'

'I am already on my knees in supplication. Relieve my excitement. Who?'
'Madge.'
'Madge who?'
'Madge Bishop!'
'I'm no wiser. Who the hell is Madge Bishop?'
'Madge from 'Neighbours'.'

I thought to myself, oh gawd! I'd only ever watched one episode in abject horror and thought how boring and awful it was. If the cast sat round a table they all sat in a straight line - facing front. In my early opinion it was a perfect example of Hicksville, never to be viewed again.

Paul enthused about how lucky he was to get her, as she would be an enormous draw. So the deal was done.

'Snow White' was not a panto often performed. In my entire career, now spanning 36 years, I had been asked only once to direct/choreograph and play the Wicked Queen's Henchman at Guildford in 1993. I still think it's a good Christmas show and children love it so I was tempted in spite of my disappointment that it wasn't Liza or Barbara. I agreed to take it on.

Now I had to watch 'Neighbours' (again!) to fathom out who Madge actually was. My friend Molly, who owned the private hotel I stayed in whilst in Cromer, told me that it was repeated at lunchtime every day, as if once weren't enough.

So during a lunch break I grabbed a sandwich and dashed back to watch it on Molly's TV. I sat like a rabbit facing a cobra, watching a couple of extremely young actors chosen for their youth and looks. Eye candy for the viewers of all ages and predilections obviously, because in my opinion they didn't even have the talent to get into a theatrical training college.

Surely the female wasn't Madge – please! Suddenly a doorbell jarred my nerves and the girl dashed off scene to return with – yes, you're already ahead of me – Madge!

I truthfully could not make out what she was screeching, not being familiar with the Aussie patois. So this was the actress cast to play the Wicked Queen in 'Snow White'. I couldn't believe my ears. However the die was cast, she was the lady I was to direct. The character she was playing I assumed was a rough hick, hardly my idea of a beautiful Queen who demanded of her magic mirror on a daily basis 'Who is the most beautiful woman in the land?' Blimey, what a hope, I thought. Anyway, forget it for now, I told myself with the opening night of my summer season fast approaching.

Now I'm going to jump you all to the first rehearsal of 'Snow White' in Weston-Super-Mare. I had learned by now that Madge's real surname was not Bishop, but Charleston – I was ready to dance!

Others in the cast who I already knew, were Helen Pocock who was one of my Cromer girls playing Fairy Snowdrop and Mark Monero who I'd shared a dressing room with when we both performed in 'Aladdin' in 1997. Mark was to play Henchman to the Queen. Brian Tracey played Muddles, and we had worked together the previous year in 'Aladdin' in the same theatre. Rosie Jenkins played the titular role with style and grace and had the required beauty to make her, 'The fairest of the land'.

Phil Haze played the Dame along with Michael Waring as the Prince, a product of the famous Betty Laine School which specialises in musical theatre. Again the dancers were provided by the local dancing school with high professional standards run by Tina Counsell and her mother – a real pleasure to work with. Phantasie-en-Noir provided the black magic sequences essential in creating real magic.

I have kept the next surprise till last. The first get-together of the entire cast is when Paul or a member of the management greets the assembled cast over a coffee prior to the read-through of the script. To my surprise I was meeting Anne Charleston for the first time, a tallish, slim and most attractive lady. Where had Madge disappeared to? Gone were the rasping, glass shattering, screeching vocal contortions I had heard – only the once I must add, and in its place a most mellifluous sound to rival Peggy Ashcroft or any of our Royal Shakespeare leading ladies. My heart rejoiced - she was going to be good. No, excellent. And she was. She was always on time and thoroughly professional in every way. One little incident gives an indication of Anne's popularity with the fans which came quite close to home, my own home in fact.

Living in a large Victorian house, one of the only six flats was occupied by one of the top theatrical hat makers in England, Simon Dawes. Naturally, both being in showbiz, we had become firm friends. A photo of Anne in the leaflets which advertised the pantomime depicted her in a headdress that in my view did not truly represent the Disney image in the Hollywood film.

I had previously mentioned this to Simon who was a fan of 'Neighbours' and Anne Charleston in particular. He offered to make her something similar to the Disney headdress, as a gift, which he created perfectly, even sending one of his employees by train to Weston, in a last minute cliff hanger!

Anne was thrilled with it. It pays to have talented friends. I offered to create a ballet for Simon in exchange. He's never taken me up on it – too busy is his excuse.

The 'Stage' critic gave his verdict.

The Stage
Jeremy Brian

SNOW WHITE AND THE SEVEN DWARFS - WESTON-SUPER-MARE

With 27 professional versions of this show playing in Britain this Christmas dwarf actors have been scarce. Producer Paul Holman has solved the problem by casting children in the roles for his show at The Playhouse. Towering sets, gorgeous costumes and a burst of fireworks at the finale frame a well chosen cast led by Australian soap star Anne Charleston as the evil Queen Griselda.

She is matched by Mark Monero as her Henchman, while it would be difficult to imagine a more attractive pair of lovers than Rosie Jenkins making her delightful pantomime debut as Snow White and Michael Wareing as the Prince.

Comic action fizzes along in the lively hands of Phil Haze, Dame, and Brian Tracey making a return to Weston as Muddles. The production's strong dance line-up is co-ordinated by Helen Pocock who also plays Fairy Snowdrop.

2000 'Cinderella' Playhouse Theatre Weston-Super-Mare

This production featured Andrew Lynford, Adele Sylva, Jack Douglas, Postman Pat, Darrock and Howe, Chris Harley, Patrick Jamieson and Vivian Russell.

Andrew Lynford an 'Eastenders' star and Adele Sylva from 'Emmerdale' filled me with foreboding, being soap stars. However, my fears were proved wrong when I read their CVs. Adele was from Sylvia Young's College of talent whilst Andrew's background was impeccable and both proved to be panto stars. In fact Andrew turned out to be the best Buttons I had ever directed. Jack Douglas I had worked with previously. I knew his foibles and circumvented them.

My first Christmas production with Darrock and Howe confirmed them to be one of the best and funniest Ugly Sister combinations, to rival well known others. Vivien Russell was a delightful Fairy Godmother.

Finally I was to meet Chris Harley, playing Prince Charming. Chris had all the requirements for the romantic lead, looks physique and a superb singing voice. He had played the role of Raoul in Phantom of the Opera in London for 200 performances, which needs top vocal prowess.

I harassed him in one area alone - trying to improve his dancing, especially when it was required in the Ballroom sequence with Cinderella. He became frustrated with my persistence, which I understood. He was a perfectionist, as also am I, so I would not let him off the hook. He finally achieved what I required, but it was like getting blood out of a stone at that period.

Chris had got the false impression that I didn't like him. How wrong he was and after the first night I approached him asking whether he would be interested in joining my company next summer in Cromer. He still maintains his complete surprise at being asked.

Jumping ahead I can reveal that he was cast as the male singer for my last two productions of 'Seaside Special' but more of that later. We are firm friends to the present day, which goes to illustrate that perfectionism is necessary to create a perfect artist.

Being the choreographer also, I was always pleased that Paul insisted on hiring professional dancers. They cost more than local dancing schools, who liked to have their young pupils gain experience. They learn a lot from performing with the professionals, which also encourages the standard for them to go into the theatre as a career - if they are lucky. The competition is fierce.

Now the critic for our pro paper.

The Stage
Jeremy Brian

Paul Holman Associates' third annual pantomime ... is the most spectacular yet. Robert Marlowe's production decorates the traditional pantomime with gorgeous costumes and scenery, a generous line up of dancers, a delightful transformation scene involving genuine Shetland ponies, and Phantasie en Noir puppets for good measure. The cast is not bad either.

The biggest bonus is that the two soap stars who inevitably top the bill are both excellent. Andrew Lynford, ex-Eastenders, immediately makes his mark with the youngsters as cheeky Buttons, whilst Emmerdale's regular Adele Silva is by no means just a pretty face in the title role.

Lynford is the heart of the action highlighted by the back projected giant screen car chase, there is strong comedy back-up from the experienced Jack Douglas as Baron Hardup, and a particularly gruesome pair of Ugly Sisters from Roger Darrock and Stephen Howe.

Chris Harley (Prince Charming) Patrick Jamieson (Dandini) and Vivian Russell as the Fairy Godmother all display pleasant voices and personalities to match. Rest assured bookings will not go unrewarded.

2001 'Jack and the Beanstalk' Watersmeet Theatre Rickmansworth

Frazier Hines, Peter John, Ed Littlewood, Rosie Jenkins, Sean Cook, David Bradshaw, Amanda Burdett, Nick Cooper, Dancers from the Maria Studio and the spectacular star puppets.

Frazer Hines started as a child in films alongside Charlie Chaplin, Omar

Sharif, Michael Caine and Michael York, eventually finding TV fame in 'Emmerdale'. Peter John, a well known Dame and music hall artiste, is one of England's top panto artistes. Rosie Jenkins, a skilled musician, actress and dancer played the princess. Ed Littlewood playing Jack was a product of the Royal Academy of Music. Sean Cook as villainous Fleshcreep, Amanda Burdett a delightful Fairy and finally Nick Cooper who had been a dancer/singer in my Cromer season, played a fearsome Giant as well as dancing in the production numbers.

Altogether a distinguished cast complemented by the Maria Studio dancers and the Phantasie of the Star Puppets which created the UV spectacular necessary to take the cast up the beanstalk.

Now the professional critic's review.

It is a sign of our eco-friendly times that the standard Good Fairy here was replaced with the Organic Katie Cucumber (Amanda Burdett) – 'All carrot dress and sprouting goodness everywhere'. That is just one example of the thought that has gone into this Watersmeet Theatre show.

Top billed Frazer Hines breezes through as Simple Simon with kids and adults immediately warming to his relaxed and engaging style, while Peter John as Dame Durden is exceptional throughout. When it comes to fun at Christmas time there ain't nothing like a good Dame to wake everyone's stupor and John did it with great aplomb, supported by an ever bubbly Jack (Ed Littlewood) and perfectly cast Princess Amelia (Rosie Jenkins). While the Goodies are very good, top Baddie Sean Cook as Fleshcreep is their impressively nasty foil, being hissed and booed with great enthusiasm. The surprise elements came from two spots of UV puppetry.

Like so many seasonal shows it is the costumes that grab the plaudits and even Daisy the Cow milked plenty of applause. But it was the hugely impressive Giant Blunderbore (Jane Crockford) that stole everyone else's thunder. A perfect end to a quality show that had all the trimmings including fine dancing, courtesy of Marie Anderson Studios, plenty of feel-good songs and for the sponsors plenty of name drops.

2002 'Aladdin' Oakengates Theatre Telford

Starring Joe Inglis, Brian Tracey, Robert Marlowe, Steve Heather, The Renleah Experience and Jane Horn.

Brian Tracey played Wishee Washee and had the audiences eating out of his hand. He knew exactly how to involve the kids who cheered his every entrance. A great asset in pantomime. I have heard recently he has now left the business – a sad loss to the profession when skilled artistes quit.

The starring role of Aladdin was played by the 'Vets in Practice' television programme's Joe Inglis. This was his first season in panto and Paul had asked me to consider the role of Abanazer again, feeling that as most of Aladdin's scenes are mainly with Abanazer, my past experience in playing Baddies would help Joe to bounce off me in our scenes together. Although I had previously decided to retire from performing, concentrating on directing and choreographing only, I agreed.

Joe was an eager Aladdin. Although rather tall, as Aladdin is supposed to be an urchin, Joe's height gave him a commanding presence. However, I had a tall hat and could dominate. That old expression, 'If you can't fight, wear a big hat', proved the point.

'Aladin' – Oakengates Theatre Telford.
I came out of performing retirement to play opposite the Vets in Practice TV star

Joe arrived at rehearsals almost word perfect (I'll leave out the singing) and was to prove a perfect foil to me. As he was the vet on 'Blue Peter' the children flocked to the stage door every night for his autograph. Paul Holman had a canny choice in engaging the 'buzz' performers of the moment and this proved true in Joe's case.

Whilst the other soap stars and TV personalities could disappoint in performance, and I have the mental scars to prove it, this was not so as far as Joe was concerned.

When the season finished I suggested that singing lessons could prove a profitable asset if he was to continue performing. He had the looks and physique, including height. I have not heard anything further since, so maybe he decided not to advance his talents in performing arts.

I'm now going to recount an unexpected dilemma, which proved the theatre adage that the show must go on.

The opening performance was on Friday 20 December. I had rented a charming cottage within 20 minutes' walk to the theatre. On Saturday 21 December with two shows to perform I had decided to stock up for Christmas food-wise, as it was virtually impossible for me to get home. A large Sainsbury store was my nearest place to get the Christmas fare I wanted. This was on the other side of a six-lane motorway. However a short cut had been pointed out across a pedestrian bridge, so starting out I found the route left for me by the cottage's owner, who was in Spain for the duration.

Finishing my purchases and loaded down with essentials and Christmas goodies I started back, as time was getting short towards the matinée. I decided to shortcut to the pedestrian bridge, which was to prove a near fatal mistake. The Sainsbury store was up high on a ridge and I decided to leave the curving paths I had first negotiated, to save time.

Telford at that time had had horrendous rainstorms and the slope I had decided to take was a muddy quagmire. With both hands loaded with shopping I started down. After half a dozen steps I realised I was in trouble. To retrace back to the path was impossible so with no other option I continued down. It was now starting to pour again. Suddenly I was on a slide from which I could not recover and I fell head over heels, crashing against hidden rocks, all my bags' contents scattering with me.

Picking myself gingerly up I retrieved my packages. With no option other than to carry on I fell yet a second time. This time I was nearing the footbridge so I virtually crawled onto terra firma. Heading back along the road I realised I was bleeding profusely from my hand. It was still pouring down and eventually I reached my cottage. This was one of only three and not attached.

Opening the door with difficulty I quickly rushed to the kitchen sink to stem the blood. As the water turned scarlet I realised I would have to get to hospital quickly. The house was like a slaughter yard. I had no car as I'm not a driver, so calling the theatre manager I explained my predicament. I could not enlist help from the neighbours even though I had knocked on their doors they were not in, so I sat awaiting one of the theatre staff who were going to get me to a hospital. The time was now past midday and our matinée was at 2pm.

After 15 minutes the box office assistant arrived and holding a blood soaked towel round my hand we made off for the local hospital, only to find there were no staff who could attend to me. We then had to drive to another one quite a few miles away where there were doctors who could deal with it. Arriving there I explained that in 75 minutes I was expected on stage in Telford's theatre and as I was first on in the prologue, I begged them to fast track me if possible.

The staff were sympathetic and did their utmost but it still took time. First an injection against lockjaw then a charming Indian doctor, after examining my hand found that my thumb was exposing the bone so he needed an X-ray to be sure it wasn't broken. Blood was still pumping out, covering the X-ray equipment.

Cutting this gory story short, we were eventually heading back to Telford. My driver friend had already warned that I would be a bit late. A bit? That was hopeful. Arriving at the theatre I hurried to my dressing room.

I should explain that as we had opened only the previous evening there were no understudies to take on my role. As I also did magic tricks in the prologue I needed my hands –both - to perform these intricate stunts. With my thumb now covered in bandages that made it look like a truncheon, I called for the first aid people to remove the bandage and apply an Elastoplast. Thankfully they had used invisible stitches at the hospital so the bleeding was staunched.

The stage manager had brought me a coffee sickly sweet with sugar, which a nurse had said was good for delayed shock. With help I got dressed in my elaborate costume and as the overture commenced 15 minutes late it was a case of - on with the show!

I will never know how I got through it frankly as the first half was by far the toughest - I was hardly ever off. Doctor Theatre worked his magic and I finished the matinée totally exhausted.

We had a couple of hours before the evening show so I laid on the floor under the make-up benches and slept until the half hour call prior to the evening performance. I can honestly now claim that 'the show must go on' is in every performer's psyche - that come hell or high water they can't let their fellow actors down.

Fortunately directly behind the theatre was an extremely large medical centre with all the facilities on hand and the theatre manager arranged for me to have my wounds examined and re-dressed every day before the shows.

They still bandaged it up like a truncheon but the first aid lady dutifully re-dressed it with an Elastoplast and whilst the medical practice nurse thought I might be scarred for life, I fortunately am not. The invisible stitches dissolved and hey presto – Doctor Theatre had worked the miracle.

Christmas Day dawned sunny and frosty and I cooked my rescued Christmas goodies, enjoying the day quietly watching what television has to offer.

Boxing Day had two performances in store so with most of the company rushing to get home and back in only one day I was probably the most refreshed and 'up for it' member of the company.

Lisa and Steve of the Renleah Experience had a couple of amazing acts, one of fire-eating performed by Lisa as the Genie of the Ring whilst Steve her partner, besides being the Emperor of China, also had his head chopped off in their second act. Not only that but Steve was also company manager, dutiful and honest with all. Sadly though with work diminishing many are having to go abroad or find other occupations.

Steve Heather playing Widow Twanky was extremely experienced, this being his 42nd panto. He was so easy and natural to work with. I looked forward to our scenes together where we could bounce off each other with insults galore, which the audience appreciated. In panto when artistes are having a good time the audience respond likewise.

Jane Horn was a beautiful and graceful Princess with a great, classically trained voice. She had been understudy for Eponine in 'Les Misérables' many times in the West End. A product of Sylvia Young's famous school her CV would occupy the rest of the page. Starlight Express, Joseph and the Technicolor Dreamcoat, The Rocky Horror Show are but a sample.

The Dancers were supplied by Nicola Carmichael and whilst her juveniles were disciplined and behaved perfectly, I had recourse to berate some of he older girls who were bolshie 15 year olds – typical of their time and age. One day during our tea break I had reason to enter their dressing room to find them sprawled in their costumes whilst their changes were lying all over the floor.

I sarcastically asked if they owned the frocks. They looked at me as though I had just dropped in from Mars. They gazed sullenly without replying. I told them that if Mr Holman had come in he would be furious and dismiss them. I gave them 10 minutes to replace them on hangers and lounge around in their practice clothes rather than the show costumes.

Returning in due course they had done a total spring clean and were dutifully seated on chairs instead of the floor as previously. I warned them that I would unexpectedly knock and enter, and if I found a similar situation during the run, I would report them to Nicola their head teacher, who they were very respectful of. Nicola had trained at the most famous Midlands college The Hammond School of Chester, whose pupils I had engaged during my career. The lesson was learned and they never mistreated their costumes again.

In show business that is a crime, especially when one knows what they cost to design, make and maintain. Costumes have to earn their keep and are expected to last through a few seasons.

Completing the rest of the cast were, last but certainly not least, the Chinese Policemen, Ping and Pong, played expertly by Sean Cook and Ahmet Ahmet. Both proficient in singing and dancing, adding greatly to the full ensemble work.

The professional critic gave the following review.

Corny Jokes, glittery costumes and a lot of audience participation are the essential criteria for a good panto – and Aladdin has all that and more.

A resident madman who can get the audience truly involved with the whole show also helps and in Brian Tracey, Oakengates has found an expert playing Wishee Washee. He is the perfect foil to Joe Inglis (Aladdin) but it is Tracey who drives the action along helped in no small measure by Steven Heather as Widow Twanky. If you are going along expect to get involved!

Joe Inglis the vet who made his name in a docu-soap… including resident vet in Blue Peter, is the Wise to Tracey's Morcambe. He is the straight man who is not afraid to send himself up and has a persona that appeals to all ages – kids love the easy way he talks to them and your granny will think him a charming young man.

Sean Cook and Ahmet Ahmet playing Ping and Pong, The Chinese Policemen, provide the slapstick so essential in pantomime. Jane Horn is a good Princess with a nice singing voice and a good chemistry with Aladdin.

Leah Hanman is excellent as the all singing, all dancing Genie who can also eat fire and chop off her partner's head in a cameo magic act. The Carmichael School of Dance turn in remarkably polished performances with Grace McKee and Elizabeth Hamson who combine their dancing duties with excellent performances as Slave of the Ring and So-Shi the Lad-in-Waiting.

Robert Marlowe not only wrote and directed the show but stars as the evil Abanazer, the excuse they need to boo and hiss.

2003 'Cinderella' Spa Theatre Bridlington

Bobby Knutt, Stephanie Dooley, Carlton Gronon, Darrock and Howe, Peter Kort, Peter McCrohon, Nicky Sweeny, The Collette Tyler School of Dance, George Gold's Shetland Ponies.

Barbara Theakston

This has to be the most delightful family pantomime to be presented at this theatre… In the all important role of Buttons, Bobby Knutt plays with typical Yorkshire style and he is magic with the children. Carlton Gronow as Prince Charming and Peter McCrohan as Dandini work well together in vocal duets. Stephanie Dooley is a pretty Cinderella whose powerful singing voice belies her delicate appearance while Nicky Sweeny choreographer and Fairy Godmother is equally successful, her impressive speaking voice providing a promising opening show. Ugly Sisters Stephen Howe and Roger Darrock do not come more grotesque, delighting in the response of the children and parading a series of zany costumes. A well dressed production that deserves an enthusiastic response.

2004 'Snow White and The Seven Dwarfs' Spa Theatre Bridlington

Starring Bobby Knutt, Nikki Kelly, Saira Alice Bell, Colin Roberts, Justin Giles, Nicky Sweeny, Peter McCrohen.

Barbara Theakston

The sound of children clapping along to the overture got this delightful pantomime started before the curtain rose. They loved to boo the Wicked Queen, Nikki Kelly, whose commanding stage presence, powerful speaking voice and dramatic gestures make for a great performance. While her rather less wicked partner in crime Egor, Peter McCrohan, also evoked well deserved disapproval.

Chief good guy, was comedian and actor Bobby Knutt, a popular Yorkshire character who posseses that magical way with children that is essential to this type of role. As Dame Dumpling Colin Roberts was responsible for much of the laughter with his bizarre costumes and antics.

Saira Alice Bell as Snow White and Justin Giles as Prince Richard sings extremely well in solos and duets. Choreographer and Fairy Snowdrop, Nicky Sweeny excels in both capacities. This is a truly traditional family pantomime.

2005 'Snow White and The Seven Dwarfs' Watersmeet Theatre Rickmansworth

Starring Bernie Clifton, Nikki Kelly, Colin Roberts, Hannah Spicer, Nicholas Maude, Peter McCrohan and Helen Morrish.

This was the first time I had ever worked with Bernie Clifton and I was particularly thrilled to have the opportunity to do so. A delightfully modest but hugely talented man. Most people only recall him riding his ostrich and when he has tried to drop that character the audiences refuse to allow him to. He found a way to placate them by having small ostriches made for children identical to his own. Coming on solo he then brings on half a dozen children following in line to satisfy his audience.

In pantomime, as I was to discover, he has a fantastic array of enormous blow-up giant sized objects ranging from deep sea divers through to an enormous sausage – I do mean enormous. This he staggers on with and then hurtles into the audience where the children, to screams of delight, turf it over their heads to the back of the theatre, returning it on the opposite aisle to the stage where Bernie wrestles with it into a much smaller shape – brilliant in panto.

To round up his comedy he has an astonishing singing voice, very unexpected. When Snow White lies poisoned on a catafalque in the forest and he poignantly sang 'On my own', from Les Misérables, there wasn't a dry eye in the theatre.

Nikki Kelly again excelled as the Wicked Queen working well with Bernie, and yet again the Maria Anderson Dancing School provided the well trained children who wore Paul Holman's fantastic dwarf costumes which are the best I have ever seen or worked with. They genuinely represent Disney style dwarfs but are not copies. This is essential when true born humans of limited height are in short supply – no pun intended!

The Disney organisation jealously guards its original concepts and will not even allow the original names to be used so circumnavigation is the order of the day. Any transgression is noticed by spies and reported back to base, as I know from past knowledge, when working at the Theatre Royal in Norwich. If anyone should disobey, lawsuits will follow as sure as night follows day.

After working in pantomime throughout my entire career and being honoured to have directed most of the famous comics in the profession I take pleasure in placing Bernie Clifton in the top echelon. No, I am not his agent, just an admirer.

This now concludes my section on pantomimes, and I reiterate – the most important area of show business in my view, as the very first introduction of children to theatre. Capture them at this age and hopefully showbiz has got them for life.

THE FINALE

At long last I have reached the finale.

Like all productions one starts off with high intent and great enthusiasm – 'This will be my greatest success!' Next follows realisation of the enormity of the project. Then in creeps the self doubt. Why, oh why did I embark on elucidating more than fifty years of desire, determination and downright struggle? The answer of course is the glamour, glitz and the shining star of show business which lures thousands into its clutches.

It was ever thus, and continues, with television reality programmes acting as the trap of public humiliation and despair for many wannabees, used as showbiz battle fodder for TV audiences addicted to watching public tears and sorrow - similar to our ancestors watching burnings and hangings at Tyburn, and Victorian Sunday afternoon jaunts to Bedlam, to taunt the unfortunates who were incarcerated there. A sorry reflection on humanity. 'Enough!' I hear you cry, of this sermonising.

Firstly the stars. Whether actors, singers or comics, this is the most exhilarating yet also frightening position to occupy. At every performance you are judged on this highest level, rather like the Roman arenas when Nero's thumb turned up or down decided one's fate. I have seen comics in particular almost suicidal after coping with an unresponsive audience. It is no wonder they can command the highest renumeration when successful. It is well deserved.

My own philosophy has always prevailed that no matter how much the singers, speciality acts and dancers excel, if the comedy fails, you ain't got a show.

Next I must bring forward for due praise all the unheard and unsung of the theatre world – the technicians. Without them the performers would look pretty drab. The electricians, sound technicians, set designers and painters. Last but certainly not least, the costume designers and seamstresses. All add the glamour and glitz which enhance the performers who reap the public acclaim, and we should never forget it.

Finally my top award goes to the backbone of every show, the Chorus. Years ago the Chorus consisted of two separate groups, singers and dancers, and never the twain should meet except to combine their talents. Singers regarded themselves as the most important whilst dancers maintained the top dog position was theirs.

During the years however all that has changed dramatically with the coming of American musicals, 'Annie Get Your Gun', 'The King and I', 'Oklahoma', etc. Chorus members were expected to be expert in both singing and movement, and auditioned accordingly.

When I auditioned dancers back in the 60s, the chosen number were required to sing en-masse – either 'Happy Birthday' or the national anthem. This required volume only, to ensure their contributions didn't sound like mice on fire. Nowadays girls and boys turn up with their own backing tapes at auditions. The quality is astonishingly high, as are their dance standards. Unfortunately unless a show is destined for London or Broadway with enormous financial backing, the budgets for smaller productions limit the chorus numbers drastically.

In the distant past 12 or 16 dancers were the norm - all girls. Boys were far harder to find, as it was not considered a manly occupation. Even working for top management companies I would have to abandon hope of finding enough boys to fulfil the requirement. In the past 20 years however, more boys have come forward to be trained but they can still hold out for the top jobs. I speak form experience. In the new millennium girls still outnumber the boys by a ratio of 20-1.

Training schools such as Betty Laines, Arts Educational, etc, when holding their passing out parade shows, still find their boys snatched up by all the top managements, leaving little selection for the smaller shows. The film 'Billy Elliott' which spawned the West End stage show and groups such as 'Tap Dogs' have now encouraged males to consider a career in dancing.

Mathew Bourne the innovative choreographer made headway with his all male 'Swan Lake' and a balletic adaptation of the music from the opera Carmen into an extremely forceful ballet deliberately entitled 'Car Man', about drivers rather than Spanish bullfighters, even involving an all male nude shower scene. This new scope in dancing has encouraged more men to consider it a profitable vocation.

Classical ballet has always attracted young boys towards training for their companies. However the selection is rigorous and many fail the final requirements in strength, physique and ability.

However, the variety theatre benefits from the rejects because these lads take up what is usually termed modern ballet, a very different style which their previous balletic training enhances. The best of both worlds in fact, so all is not lost.

Whilst my autobiography is dedicated to Jenny Vance and Nina Brown, my erstwhile dancing partners, I would finally like to include all of my dancers, male and female, who have over the years performed with skill and dedication, and greatly enhanced the shows they have graced.

As Tiny Tim would say in 'Scrooge', 'God bless 'em – every one.'

Modelling for a knitting pattern

MONEY, MONEY, MONEY!
FILL-IN JOBS

Back in the 50s with music halls still flourishing there was plenty of work available for dancers. Each week 'The Stage' publication had advertisements requiring artistes for musicals or variety bills.

The singer John Hansen was appearing in productions of 'The Desert Song', 'Rose Marie', ' The Student Prince', all of which required singers and dancers. Sue Pollard even appeared in one of these musicals when young, as his serious leading lady.

Music halls, which existed in every city and town, usually with two or three venues, presented stars of radio and films in lavish revues. 'Old Mother Riley', Arthur Askey with Richard Murdoch, Tommy Trinder and Tommy Handley - the list was endless. Dance teams proliferated – Marie de Vere girls, Buddy Bradley's groups, The Jack Billings Dancers, Tiller Girls, etc - far too many to list here.

Television was in its infancy but about to explode into everyone's home. This also presented variety bills and large scale revues. 'Sunday Night at the London Palladium' was about to burst onto the screen, making a star of Bruce Forsyth and mixing both classical and variety artistes into a star studded entertainment eagerly awaited by the viewers.

In the theatre, some tours were rated No.1s, which required artistes of the highest calibre, attracting dancers of high ability and standards. As the rating went higher, oddly the standards went lower and most dancers steered clear of anything labelled second or third rate. This usually included the nude revue, although artistes like Phyllis Dixie and Jane of the Daily Mirror had raised standards even in that genre.

On one occasion I was introduced to a comic who was venturing to stage his own revue starring himself. His name was Billy Shakespeare - whether his real name or not I never knew. He was looking for a couple of boy dancers and we met in the Salisbury pub, in London's Charing Cross Road, where many pros conducted business over a pint. As Billy enthused over his ideas for his revue, which were to be titled 'Won't you powder my back for me?' with nudes sitting in bath tubs for the opening. He talked me out of even considering it. I bade goodbye and I phoned him later with an excuse, thanking him for nothing. I had decided on the standards I aspired to and nothing was going to deter me.

The lower rated productions, unfortunately in my view, attracted mediocre artistes prepared to work for less. Whilst the theatrical unions had been in existence for a number of years, Equity and the Variety Federation still touted for members. The strongest union was the Musicians, of course. One could not put on a musical without music so this gave them an edge, and even a reputation for bolshie attitudes. Variety theatres still boasted of pit orchestras with a dozen local musicians, some of which even had other daytime jobs. The musicians had varying degrees of excellence. Screeching violins were quite frequently the butt of music hall jokes by the comics.

Young dancers, of which I was one, soon realised the need for raising their own standards to get top quality jobs. Whilst there were, and still exist, excellent schools throughout the country, most dancers focused their attention on London for extra curricular training with top schools and academies there, mainly because the principals had personal access to the large and important production companies.

Much later in my career when I needed to hold auditions for dancers for my own productions, I decided to hold an audition up in Manchester so that northern dancers didn't have to travel south, putting an advertisement in 'The Stage' newspaper for dancers on the same day in London, which was taken by my dance partner Nina, whilst I personally waited in a Manchester studio.

I waited in vain with a rehearsal pianist and not a single dancer turned up. Nina, however was crowded out and could have filled my requirement 10 times over. Lesson learned. Dancers preferred congregating in London, especially in the spring when summer shows needed literally hundreds of dancers, because in the 50s and 60s every resort had three or four shows to cast.

Foreign holidays were soon to decimate audiences for many of these productions. Girls would travel to London and stay for as long as it took to get a job, staying with friends and relatives or at the theatre girls' club in Greek Street, Soho, a very strictly run hostel that protected the young dancers with curfews, to their families' delight, if not the girls.

The double audition north and south was a costly experiment, which I never attempted again.

Back to my training days. In the 50s boys did not become dancers. It was not considered a proper job. Therefore I was basically a late starter in my early teens, having to fund my own training from the meagre apprentice wage I received as a dental technician.

Attending a local dancing school with an excellent reputation, I quizzed the Principal about London schools for further advanced training, aware that as a late starter I needed to get into the schools with access to production companies.

One of the top schools was run by Joan Davis in West Street off Cambridge Circus, right in the heart of theatre land. Miss Davis was also a director/choreographer of London revues and musicals. Borrowing money from my reluctant parents, I booked private lessons with Miss Davis mainly to get her opinion of my embryonic talent – if any. After half a dozen classes she assured me I had talent enough to continue training.

As my parents had already funded me through college for a conventional education, they were not in a position to do so again. Where to get the cash to further my long held desire for a theatre career?

There was an agency for part time work in Charing Cross Road which on investigation proved totally unsuitable. However, speaking with other students I discovered areas that I would not have remotely considered - photographic and cat-walk modelling, film extra and various other one-off occupations, some decidedly insalubrious, which happily I avoided.

Most boys, unless devastatingly handsome, which I wasn't, did not even consider photography or modelling work. When I was a young schoolboy I would question my mother by asking if I was good looking, to which she would reply 'You'll pass in a crowd.' Hardly encouraging. However conceit is not attractive and when it shows it is downright ugly.

Joan Davis instructed me to get professional photographs taken, as they acted as one's agent when arriving on producers' desks. This I found to be sound advice when I undertook a part time job in an agent's office. Any photos that appeared to have been taken in the would-be artiste's back garden or lounge were binned immediately as not being worthy of consideration.

When I was 16 and taking part in a local amateur revue group I had been introduced to a photographer who I thought of as a local, but was to discover he was actually one of London's top fashion photographers like the late Lord Lichfield and Tony Armstrong-Jones. Getting him to take some professional photos for my portfolio, he informed me that I had a lucky gift. I was apparently one of those types known as 'photogenic'. The camera loved me - wow!

Taking advantage of this gift from the gods I sent photos to all agents who specialised in work that would fit in with my expensive dance training. I mention expensive because at that time the American choreographers and dance instructors were flying the Atlantic to bring modern techniques to London. Joan Davis employed these gurus and I was determined to study these new skills.

With George Erskine-Jones I studied floor work and knee slides which every male dancer had to achieve – the buzz moves of the 50s. These skills were later to assist me in getting my first principal role.

Another American teacher was Richardina Jackson, a member of the Harlem Ballet Company of New York - all arms and legs - essential assets for any dancer. As she stretched hers I gazed in admiration and copied her avidly.

Miss Davis also employed a soloist of the Royal Ballet. Anne Negus danced lead roles such as the Bluebird Pas-de-Deux, etc. A pretty little creature who I heard, after retiring, had married a farmer and settled in Cornwall. A total contrast to her glamorous past.

As I had never studied classical dance I took private lessons to acquaint myself with the basics which stood me in good stead when I became a choreographer. At least I knew the terms if I wasn't expert in the practice. However in retrospect it must have sufficed because I gained a reputation in my revue work for classically styled ballets.

I studied another balletic style under the tuition of Sigurd Leeder, an ex-principal dancer of the Ballet Joos. Kurt Joos and his company had escaped Nazi persecution back in the 30s and started a school down in Devon teaching his modernistic style, which was based on the classical barre, but more free style. His most famous creation, still referred to even today, was 'The Green Table' based on the collapse of the League of Nations which was formed to bring world peace after the First World War. I took only evening classes with Sigurd's group but left when I felt it was all too precious. Being told to create a solo routine around being a foetus? I couldn't remember!

Writing to the Ballet Rambert Company I was given a two-week course, rather like an elongated audition, to assay my chances. These classes with Madame Marie Rambert, a renowned ballerina in her day, were a fantastic tour-de-force, which money could not buy and I was getting it for free. I was actually offered a scholarship but without any financial assistance it proved impossible for me to take up. Frankly I also realised it was too late. By the time I had trained I would have been nearer to retirement. As far as the classical world was concerned. I still wish that I could have had that training back in my childhood. However 'know thyself' is a maxim I've always stood by.

With my photographs in hand, I approached modelling agencies in Charing Cross Road. Getting onto the books of Bridges and McCausland, and Betty Jacoby who specialised in one-off, occasionally highly paid work of short duration, which didn't interrupt the more important dance training. After one or two fashion shots for – of all things – knitting patterns, I was elevated to cat-walk modelling which were mini shows in themselves where the carriage and grace of dancers was an asset.

A most thrilling contract brought me into the presence of a famous Hollywood film star. Vivian Blaine had starred as Miss Adelaide opposite Frank Sinatra as Nathan Detroit in 'Guys and Dolls', alongside Jean Simmons and Marlon Brando. She had starred in the same role on Broadway and was now in London, repeating her success. Arriving by taxi she entered the studio carrying a case which she set up to reveal a mirror surrounded by mini lights and proceeded to expertly apply false eyelashes and perfect make-up. She had entered the studio as a pretty woman and now, before my fascinated gaze, became a stunningly beautiful movie queen.

Compare that with the stars of today - Madonna, JayLo, Britney - who arrive with their entourage of managers, secretaries, make-up stylists, hairdressers, and 'gofers' - a veritable army to present one personality.

My own contract along with a young girl dancer appearing in a West End show was to represent teenagers -own clothes - which we were, who rode Raleigh bicycles, which we didn't. It was only still shots thankfully. With Vivian Blaine, Sam Levene and Stubby Kaye starring in the Coliseum production of 'Guys and Dolls' still running in London, the advertising catch phrase was to read 'Even guys and dolls love Raleigh bicycles'.

Strangely I never saw a published advertisement. However that's the trade. Money to waste or tax fiddle? Who is to know? At least we kids got well paid. More dance lessons for me.

THE TELEVISION MIRACLE

Television is now such an institution with most homes housing at least two or three sets, some as big as cinema screens. However it never really took off until the late 40s or 50s. It was around before the Second World War on a minute screen set in an unwieldy casing that occupied an entire corner, in a small lounge or 'front room', as it was usually called.

However, to own one was something to swank about and condescendingly allow less fortunate neighbours to watch. Our next door neighbour did own one and during the War, when there were no transmissions, it was wrapped in swaddling rugs in the air raid shelter. Whatever else was destined for destruction it was not the TV set!

I do recall quite vividly my first sighting. It was probably around 1946. Invited into our neighbour's house with about half a dozen other visitors we all crunched around the postage stamp screen to see a special programme relayed across the channel between England and France, an outside broadcast and filmed, I believe, in Boulogne. The first shots took us into a nightclub owned by a well-known cabaret artiste who during her song would snip the end of a gentleman's tie, whilst a waiter attached it to the ceiling. It was a gimmick, which was obviously considered an honour, because the ceiling looked like a forest of half ties – extraordinary.

I can't really recall what took place on our side. Probably either Gracie Fields or even Petula Clark. Anyhow, it was enough to boast about to one's school friends, especially the staggering firework display that ended the show.

My first ever appearance was in 1955 in my second pantomime at the Theatre Royal in Birmingham. An outside broadcast, as it was termed, it was filmed previously during an earlier performance. It was transmitted on a Sunday afternoon during the run and my parents boasted to the neighbours, showing them the 'Radio Times' which actually had my name in it. That copy is still in my theatrical treasure chest. Proof indeed of a pioneering occasion for me.

With TV sets now as essential as refrigerators, deep freezers and microwaves, it must be hard to remember that its emergence is well within living memory of many folk, and it's important to record this living moment. Too much is taken for granted nowadays.

For dancers television was now a tremendous bonus. It enabled one to fill in the awkward periods between the summer seasons and pantomimes, especially for girls who until now had done 'temping' in an office or the harder occupation of waiting on tables in restaurants. Male dancers fared much better because there were never enough around to fill the vacancies. Even so, the higher one's standard, the better the job.

My first big engagement, which placed me quite securely into the TV firmament, was a six weekly live performance entitled 'Dreamtime with Barbara', the Barbara in question being the daughter of Bebe Daniels and Ben Lyon, the American team I've already written about on radio.

Barbara fancied her chances as a pop singer and with influential parents – as always – no problem, the six-week run was assured. My agent had put me forward and after auditioning I was cast alongside Bruce McClure and a young girl dancer Carole Keith. We formed the dancing trio to back Barbara Lyon. Bruce, a Scot, was to arrange the dance routines, a renowned choreographer of Howard and Wyndhams Scottish productions 'Wish for Jamie' and pantomimes.

The television director was an up-and-coming whiz-kid, Russell Turner, making quite a name for himself in this medium. The running storyline was that Barbara was seen preparing herself for bed. Through her window she saw a young man's shadow cast on his curtains in the house opposite, playing drums. Fantasising about him, she then dreamt romantically each week, with the actions taking place in varying situations - 'Paris in the Spring', 'Cloud Cuckoo Land', etc. It sounds rather trite now but it was a novel idea at the time.

The young drummer was Jack Parnell, related to Val Parnell who ran the London Palladium Theatre. Jack did not appear until the final episode, bringing fantasy to fact. Well, it was late night TV not being transmitted until 10pm after the news - nothing too cerebral for that time of night.

Ben Lyon, Barbara's father, would appear in the studio on transmission day making suggestions, which didn't appear to go down too well with the director, and tense situations arose. However, we dancers kept a low profile. We had enough on our plate. We were only allowed three days rehearsal time, which took place in various freezing church halls dotted around central London. The television centre was still a dream in the making.

On the Friday we went into the studio for the first time when, to our dismay we encountered scenic and space problems, which in some cases meant rearranging the routines at the last minute. As shows were transmitted live it really was panic stations, not like today with most programmes pre-recorded.

The very first screening turned out to be a day fraught with drama. I've never really worked out whether it was a plot that got out of hand or not. We broke for lunch in the BBC canteen and many folk came up to wish us luck. Suddenly

Russell appeared with an armful of newspapers grinning happily with the remark, 'Get this!' We did.

Each differing paper had the same blurb, and we were astonished to see that Barbara and Russell were announcing their engagement. That it was coinciding with the first episode was obviously timed to get the most publicity.

Russell was a director destined for great things – very charismatic - and had an entourage of girlfriends eager to get better acquainted. Even Carole Keith had been a part of his past. We crowded around with everyone else to offer our congratulations when suddenly a plate full of lunch came hurtling the length of the table to crash on the floor.

Russell's female assistant fled the restaurant in tears. She obviously had no previous knowledge of the breaking news and was visibly upset. We all kept quiet and returned to the studio. Putting two and two together we surmised that she nurtured hopes that were not going to be fulfilled. As I have said, Russell was charismatic. Oh well, on with the show!

After the lunchtime débâcle the show was transmitted live that night and was received favourably by the press, and my mum and dad.

In the period about which I'm writing, television was extremely experimental. Firstly it was rationed. Twenty-four hour transmission was not even on the horizon. There were period breaks when it closed down completely. There was no choice, you took what you got.

'Dreamtime', with six episodes planned, had problems which today would never enter the equation. Firstly was lack of rehearsal space, so the aforementioned church halls and even rooms over pubs – fatal! - all over London made a lucrative trade for anyone with space. This presented difficulties and there were no mobile phones. Any urgent problems, and there were many, lost valuable rehearsal time which was limited anyway, and a lack of liaison was endemic. Finding pennies for phone calls and then finding a phone box were irritations unheard of today.

Our studio manager, when he eventually found the place we were rehearsing in, would mark out our dancing space on the floor, which could be very confining anyway. We, however, had no idea of the set until we arrived in the studio on the day of transmission.

Set designers have by way of tradition always been a law unto themselves. When I eventually became a director I would bring this faction on board in the earliest stages of planning, thereby reining in some of their extreme flights of fancy. In any creative situation it is important to liaise with all the departments involved - costumiers, choreographers, stage directors and musical directors - creating the team that is responsible for the ultimate production.

I well recall a couple of hazardous situations in 'Dreamtime'. One thankfully did not reach the viewers while the other unfortunately did.

The second episode was set in Paris in the spring and arriving in the studio on production day, Bruce had discovered to his dismay that the centre of our dance area was occupied by a huge three-dimensional blossom tree, which was designed to shed petals like snowflakes during our routine - an idea which assumed dominance. Bruce and I had rehearsed a lift, which floated Carol high above our heads in a long run so that she appeared to be high in the sky. You've probably guessed by now! Our first attempt left Carol clinging to the branches whilst the studio floor was flooded with petals – ouch! Especially for Carol up on a branch. It seemed like the Third World War was about to take place!

Russell liked the idea of both set and routine. However a compromise had to be reached before we went on the air that night. Verbal battles ensued. Russell arbitrated and his final decision was that the dancers should moderate the flight in length and height, whilst the dominating tree was placed further back in the set.

Peace reigned. However if Bruce and I appeared uneasy that night on screen the real reason was obscured from the viewers, as Carol floated lower than intended and did not finish up a tree.

The fourth episode was a total disaster. We were now moving towards the end of the series. Russell's fame for innovation was spreading and his ideas getting more ambitious. The fourth show was to represent 'Cloudland'. Barbara's chosen song, a current favourite, was 'Love and Marriage', the second line of which was 'Go together like a horse and carriage'. The designers had presented Russell with a life-sized horse with wings representing Pegasus, who pulled a carriage with Barbara sitting in it, pretending to control the reins. So far, so good. The painted background was fluffy pink, white and lilac clouds, very romantic. We dancers were just as romantically attired and the opening shots were very classical in interpretation.

As the lead into the song commenced, Barbara entered and we were supposed to sink down into the clouds. Russell wanted a real cloud effect to operate. However in that period it hadn't been invented. Nowadays, we have very sophisticated electrical machines that achieve that effect and those who have seen 'Les Miserable' and 'Miss Saigon' among others will be aware of how excellent a contribution it can be.

The studio manager together with the technicians came up with a brainwave. They placed buckets of dry ice all around the set, keeping it off camera. At the given moment the crew poured boiling water into the buckets. As dry ice will roll across the surface only, the addition of the boiling water causes it to rise and drift into a cloud formation. Hurrah! We were in business.

The night of transmission we danced our classical ballet, appearing to float on top of the clouds sinking down to the floor, as Pegasus and Barbara entered.

The effect intended was that as we sank below the clouds, Barbara rose to float on high.

What the technicians had not taken into account was that the powerful studio lighting had already created a high temperature, which together with the boiling water completely obliterated the set, and Barbara was a ghostly voice permeating what had turned into an excellent interpretation of a London 'peasouper' - if anyone today remembers what they used to be like.

What we need to remember also is that years before, sound radio had gone through what we were trying to achieve in the 50s, and look where TV is now.

Russell Turner was at the forefront of trying to break new ground and the whole series gained praise for being a watershed of what was to come. For Barbara, unfortunately, it didn't prove to be a ladder to success in the pop world. Neither did her eventual marriage to Russell, which ended in divorce.

Television in the 50s was becoming most households' main source of entertainment and whilst I was glad to be part of this prolific work source as a stop-gap, I was concerned that many of London's theatres on the outskirts of the West End were closing their doors and after interior reconstruction emerging as television studios with audience capacities for outside broadcasts. Theatres such as Chelsea Palace and Holburn Empire for example had their stalls boarded over to enable the cameras to track in for close-ups. With variety now regarded as a dead duck, I guess we had to be grateful that a use was being found – progress.

On TV the Black and White Minstrels became so popular that it spawned a stage show that ran for years in the Victoria Palace, making stars in the process. A friend of mine, John Boulter, who had been a member of the 'Out of the Blue' company of Brandon and Pounds with whom I started my own career, found fame worldwide through this particular door, proving that with variety now in its dying stages television was going to be the new route for performers to gain fame and fortune.

Whilst acknowledging this phenomenon, I still considered myself a live theatre performer, making use financially of the TV medium but always keeping my priority for live shows right through to the present day.

The impresario Jack Hylton put his name to TV Saturday Night Spectaculars, which were lavish returns to variety enabling viewers to stay indoors for their entertainment. Thus was the subtle change taking place for a previous theatre-going public. For good or bad, only time was to tell.

One particular television show I was proud to be part of was 'Beat up the Town'. A musical production directed and choreographed by Jack Billings, it had a host of stars, some in the making others already made. Cyril Fletcher, Terry Thomas, Bob Monkhouse, Vanessa Lee and an up-and-coming, pretty ingénue Jill Day. We actually rehearsed this show on the building site of the White City

Television Centre, now coming to fruition after years of planning, the building sounds deafening us during rehearsals.

One particular production number taken from a Broadway show which originally made a star of Eartha Kitt some years before, was based on an American murder case – not, one would think, suitable for this type of show. Titled 'Fall River Legend' it told the story of Lizzie Bordon who killed her parents with an axe. A song titled 'You can't chop your mamma up in Massachusetts' became a hit through the treatment invented on Broadway, and now re-invented for London.

The action took place in the courtroom during the trial and the local hicks and their gals, disappointed that their annual hoedown usually held in the courtroom had been cancelled, agreed to attend the trial on condition that the hoedown was still held. A hilarious situation! Combining both trial and dance.

All the stars took the main parts whilst the dancers joined in the high jinks. Of course Lizzie Bordon was reprieved and went off with her defence attorney.

How true this old tale was I really don't know but its success rocked the show – they don't make 'em like that any more.

I used that same scena many times when I became a director of my own productions – a fantastic romp that always brought the house down. Now, probably 50 years on from its original conception, I would take a bet it would still cut the rug.

A small sample of the chorus:

Lizzie Bordon took an axe
She gave her mother forty whacks
And when she found what she had done
She gave her father forty-one!

In complete contrast to the above, was my next television appearance, or I should say appearances, because it was a very long running series.

'Music for You' was the brainchild of Eric Robinson who conducted the BBC concert orchestra and attracted stars from opera, ballet, concert platforms and Broadway musicals such as Howard Keel, Margot Fonteyn, Yehudi Menuin, Joan Hammond, Isaac Stern, Hilde Guedan, - the list was endless as the show's popularity grew. Transmitting on a weekly basis it introduced many viewers to areas of entertainment they might have considered too highbrow for their liking.

Audiences attracted to Broadway musicals found that excerpts from popular operas such as 'Madame Butterfly' and 'La Bohème' contained music they had heard previously without realising it was classical.

One of the first episodes I danced in contained a serious of sea shanties, set on a replica pirate galleon. On this set I first made the acquaintance of John

Lawrenson, who featured regularly on radio's, 'Friday Night is Music Night' as the leading baritone. John was to eventually marry my first dancing partner, Jenny Vance. That was way in the future at this moment.

It was during this particular scene that I nearly had my ear bitten off by a beast of the forest! I volunteered when the director asked for someone who was fond of animals. Little did I realise I was to be partnered with the ship's monkey. We first met on transmission day. His trainer informed me that whilst he would happily sit on my shoulder, if he became excited I was to pacify him with a piece of banana.

The rehearsal for my particular shot took longer than anticipated and the studio heated up with the lighting necessary for shooting the bridge scene. My own excitement at getting a soloist shot was obviously communicated to my 'mate' who was sitting perilously close to my ear with chattering teeth. I slipped a piece of banana up to pacify him, which he quickly crammed into his jaws. This exercise required a few takes and I ran out of banana. The trainer replenished me and I continued stuffing my little friend.

What I didn't know until the trainer told me was that monkeys have a capacity for storing food within them until later when they can re-digest it. Now he tells me! With the transmission time approaching, excitement was mounting amongst all connected in the production. This was obviously being transmitted

Starlight – Eastbourne – 'The Lizzie Borden' scena

to little 'Chico' whose rather pointed little teeth were chattering, too close for comfort, to my ear.

Oh why had I volunteered?! I didn't need stardom with a dangerous animal. In my vivid imagination I was already in a hospital having my ear stitched back on. Oh gawd!

The shanty song to accompany my solo promenade started, and walking towards the camera armed with a small chunk of banana I nervously offered it to 'Chico', who pushed it aside with his paw whilst excitedly chattering with those teeth.

That night at home getting my parents' reaction to their son's 'starring' moment they laughingly told me that I looked slightly deformed with my head at a strange angle, and was that the director's requirement for my appearance as a cripple?

I said, 'Yes,' lying through my teeth. They said I did it perfectly. Lesson learned – never volunteer, not even for television.

Once a dancer or singer was known for their talent their name was put on a roster and it became like a club that you could drop in or out of as other commitments took over. Very useful for keeping a full date book.

On another occasion I had the opportunity of studying at close quarters the stunningly beautiful soprano Hilde Guerdan as Hanna Glavari in 'The Merry Widow'. Dancing in close proximity it enabled me to observe and appreciate the qualities necessary to reach stardom. No matter how perfectly trained the voice, or even the feet of star ballerina Margot Fonteyn, the keynote to fame is personality. It is such an ephemeral quality it can't be taught. One either has 'it' or not.

Strangely television, now a major force in most households, has the capacity to turn personality into a plus or minus situation. How often does one hear the comment 'I can't stand so and so.' Some chat show hosts become much admired and can last for years, whilst others can hardly survive through their own lunchtime.

One name springs immediately to mind – Michael Parkinson, who because of his approach has the truly famous queueing up to be interviewed. He does his homework, asks the right questions and generates a relaxed atmosphere which appeals to the viewer. Personality is the X factor.

In the new millennium the rash of programmes where viewers phone in to eliminate the contestants they dislike the most now proves this.

Having been a performer in the experimental period of TV when it was exciting to be at the sharp end, I feel that we have lost more than we have gained. How often does one hear the cry 'There's nothing worth watching on the telly'.

As an optimist I'm hoping audiences will return to live theatre. However I won't hold my breath.

I'm sure that by now readers will have ascertained that I'm a man of the theatre, not television. However I have taken advantage of it, for which I will be eternally grateful.

THINGS THAT GO BUMP IN THE NIGHT

Throughout previous pages I have written of my guardian angel. I now intend to substantiate my beliefs with reasons why. Guardian angels are not ghosts, they are purely to guide and protect you, and if you believe, everybody has one.

You may well think I am a crank but I have also been in her presence, therefore refer to 'her' rather than 'he', because she actually appeared to me in female form, and I was scared initially. I shall not share any more of this experience with readers for it's far too personal. However throughout my whole career, as one door shut, almost without pause, another opened. In some instances, against seemingly impossible odds. So I'm a true believer, and grateful for her protection.

However, getting back to ghosts, and due to scepticism, I shall start with a ghost story that unfolded before my eyes and many others' and reached headline proportions in newspapers.

In 1979 I was contracted to direct/choreograph and appear as Slave of the Lamp in 'Aladdin' in the beautiful Georgian Theatre Royal in Bath, my eighth production under the 'Triumph' banner of Duncan Weldon and Louis I Michaels.

Heading the cast as Wishee Washee was Leslie Crowther with veteran Dame George Lacey playing Widow Twanky. Incidentally I had worked with George in 1976 in Newcastle's Theatre Royal when his temperamental attitude had been a problem, which I had to solve.

However in 1979 George had sent me a card prior to rehearsals, humorously welcoming me back as the prodigal son returning to mother's arms. He behaved himself beautifully. He had no option as I was performing in the panto this time and knew how to forestall problems in the embryonic stage.

Aladdin was played by Judy Carne who had starred on American television in 'Rowan and Martin's Laugh-In' where she was the butt of all their mishaps – deliberately.

Judy, an English actress, had returned to England after marrying and divorcing Burt Reynolds, the Hollywood star. Due to other unfortunate circumstances she had returned to England wearing a metal head cage because of a broken neck, which occurred in a horrendous car crash. The newspapers had a field day flooding the papers with quite gruesome pictures.

This now was her first pantomime engagement since returning from the States, although she had previously starred in London revues in the past under a different name. She had problems, which was sad because occasionally her original talent shone through.

The Bath theatre had a quite ghostly reputation as one of the few theatres haunted by two ghosts from different eras. One walked on the floor that no longer existed and had reputably been seen on many occasions. The other was grounded and traversed the corridor behind the dress circle. The story I'm unfolding started in the theatre's Victorian period.

A scenic designer and painter was commissioned to create a backdrop for a ballet in the pantomime depicting giant flowers and butterflies. Working at the top of a rickety ladder he unfortunately plunged to his death. This tragedy must have cast quite a dampener on the season's production that Christmas. From this incident grew up the story that if a butterfly appeared on stage during any current production its success would be ensured.

Like all good pantomimes, after the prologue came the opening scene set in Peking. All the characters made their introductory entrances and the audience awaited the star's turn. The orchestra went into its razzmatazz which introduced Leslie Crowther as Wishee Washee. Guess what? As Leslie rushed towards the footlights a butterfly fluttered down from the fly–tower and settled on Leslie's shoulder. Remember we are talking December, not a period usually associated with butterflies. The local press writ large 'Phantom Butterfly Brings Success to Aladdin'.

A further incident had occurred during the rehearsals that year. I had kept the dancers back for an extra couple of hours into the evening, informing the stage door keeper that we would finish 8pm. I offered to lock the stage door for him so that he could have an early break, with which he was happy to agree.

Finishing the rehearsal I gave the dancers 10 minutes to change and waited on stage to count them out. At that time – probably the same today – the dressing rooms were concentrated on one side of the stage and artistes departed across the stage to the pass door, then exiting through the stage door.

I counted all the dancers through and was about to depart myself when I heard distinctive footsteps traversing the corridor behind the dress circle. Exasperatedly I called out 'You can't get out that way – come back across the stage.' The footsteps rattled down the spiral steps towards the stalls, but no one appeared. I could feel the hairs on the back of my neck bristling as I beat a hasty retreat. I departed the theatre convinced that I had counted all the dancers through. Although I had not seen anything I was relieved to lock the stage door behind me and leave whoever it was to their haunting.

Recounting this story the following day to the stage manager he told me of another incident he had encountered on a previous pantomime. Some years ago pantomimes used to have canvas stage cloths that were stretched across the wooden boards and painted to match in with the subject matter being depicted. Paving stones for 'Cinderella' and 'Dick Whittington', forest grasses for 'Babes in the Wood', a sandy base for 'Robinson Crusoe' and so on.

This painting was the responsibility of the stage manager, usually undertaken prior to the final dress rehearsal. On the occasion being described to me Martin had dismissed his staff to accomplish the task on his own, starting at the footlights - a quaint old–fashioned terminology now as modern lighting designers no longer have any use for footlights - a mistake in my view because they did have their uses in certain areas. Shin Busters is the new term, which do exactly that! Ah well, progress …

Back to Martin. He patiently covered his stage cloth in the desired effect, gradually working to the back of the stage. Pausing when he reached the pass door to survey his handiwork and ensure that every inch had been filled, he passed through to lock and exit by the stage door. Remember, it's the stage managers job to make sure that nobody is in the theatre when he finally locks the building up.

You have probably guessed by now if you are at all spookily inspired that when Martin unlocked the theatre the next day he found footsteps all over the stage cloth. Just footsteps. As I'm now recounting many occasions which pose questions with no answers I'm going back to my very first pantomime in 1953/4 at the Alhambra theatre in Bradford.

The theatre digs list supplied addresses to the artistes and about eight or nine of us were housed in Leazes Terrace, a short run from the theatre. One Sunday night we all got involved in what probably everyone has indulged in at some point in their lives - the moving glass that answers questions put to it.

Writing every letter of the alphabet onto small squares of paper which we placed in a circle on the table, with a down-turned wine glass in the centre, we all sat around with our index fingers poised lightly on the base, waiting for the first tremor of movement.

Only one member of our group had previously experienced this and we all obeyed her instructions. Our 'expert' had found a couple of candles. This, she told us, was essential in creating the necessary atmosphere to try and encourage an 'entity' to appear.

She also explained the importance of an extremely light touch from all, to enable the glass to travel smoothly across the polished surface. Any force used would upset the fine balance. All of us engaged in this game sat owl-eyed in expectancy. Correction, I shouldn't have said 'game' for it was certainly not that, as we were about to discover.

Suddenly the glass gave a slight tremble, the atmosphere became quite charged, I guess with our silent excitement. Our expert asked 'Is anyone there?'. Slowly and smoothly moving, it spelt out 'Yes'. Questioning if it had a message for anyone present, it again spelt out 'Yes' before returning to its centre.

On being asked to spell the name of the person whose attention it sought, the glass started to tremble then slowly moved into a gentle circle, spelling out the name of one of the girl dancers. Once the name had connected, its speed of pace increased until most of us lost contact with it.

Suddenly the young girl whose name it was burst into tears, leaving the room, followed by her friend. The rest of us sat, silent and confused, whilst our expert doused the candles and switched on the lights.

We later learned that the girl who first fled the room had lost someone she was close to quite recently, hence her dismay.

That was the only time I was ever involved and have since learnt via informed and reliable experts that it is an opportunity for mischievous and evil spirits to gain entry into a group of amateurs, excited to play with the spirit world. There is an ongoing fascination in the world at large to believe and experience strange happenings, but one must remain balanced, otherwise health can be seriously put at risk.

Throughout my life, even as a small boy, I have experienced strange happenings which I have not necessarily sought. *They* have found *me*. When I was about eight years old I had an out-of-body experience. We lived in a large Victorian house with a big kitchen. One morning reading my 'film fun' comic I suddenly found myself high up near the ceiling and actually gazing down at myself reading my comic. I was on a level with a large water tank which boiled water from a kitchen range. Now, 50 years or so later, I can still remember it. This is recognised as an experience typical of the very young. Thankfully I grew out of it.

I am sure that many readers will have knowledge of near death experiences, either personally or via a friend or relative.

My father was a good man but not particularly religious, attending church only on special occasions such as weddings, christenings and funerals. However, whilst in hospital in London he was very seriously ill and found himself travelling through that notoriously dark tunnel towards the brilliant white light. He told me that he heard familiar voices welcoming him forward and indeed wanted to reach them. However, fate decreed that it was not his time to take that journey. He found himself being reluctantly drawn back into our world.

Naturally once back and recovering he was grateful not to have left the family. However, he maintained, right up until his time to depart, his belief in an afterlife. It is my belief that he is now with my mother and others he loved.

SPIRITUALISM

I shall now reveal my own cornerstone of belief in an afterlife. When my mother died far too young by today's standards I was working in pantomime in Birmingham. It was very sudden and unexpected, although on three previous occasions I had premonitions, well in advance, concerning my mothers health. We had always been close and thought alike in many instances – almost telepathic.

The first foretold breast cancer, which three months later proved true. In the final one I foresaw her death a week in advance, to the very moment. It happened in the form of a cocoon of brilliant white light in which I was trapped in a pitch dark surround. Each occasion I was terrified but well aware it concerned my mum and not good news. I don't know how else to explain it – sinister premonitions which came true.

Mum passed over a week before Christmas, which was harder to bear being the usual time of joy. However the discipline of show business came to my rescue. My mother was so proud of my theatrical achievements and I knew she would have wished me to go on. Yet again Doctor Theatre assisted me.

After the New Year I sought solace at the instigation of a close friend to attend a spiritualist church in Birmingham. I needed comforting. It was a total disaster from the moment I entered. It reeked of charlatans and fraud. All flickering candles and wobbling incantations. A most soulless and unbelievable experience, never to be repeated.

Had it been a theatrical first night it would have folded before the interval! With bad reviews. Strangely I had a dream, only once, and saw my mum which comforted me. It never occurred again but no matter, once was sufficient.

However, once back in London my musical director friend Colin Tarn suggested that we attend a real spiritualist meeting in Knightsbridge. The author Conan Doyle had left his rather grand house to perpetuate the spiritualist movement and promised that he would return after death to prove continuity. He never has.

I believe he was not allowed to. We all have to achieve our own beliefs privately. However that particular evening lacked all the ghastly mumbo-jumbo of the Birmingham fiasco. There were no dimmed lights and stupid sepulchral whisperings on this occasion.

It was conducted in a large, well lit room, packed with quite ordinary looking people of all ages. Prior to starting a lady pianist played a selection from various showbiz musicals.

Colin and I felt completely at home. We desisted from singing along. The meeting was hosted by a respected male medium and whilst I had hoped my mother would appear for me, she didn't. But I was totally comforted by the evening's revelations for others present. Their emotional responses convinced me of sincerity and I've never felt the need to attend another meeting all these years later. In the words of Vera Lynn's famous song:

We'll meet again
Don't know where
Don't know when
But I know we'll meet again
Some sunny day

Strangely a few years ago I met a female 'sensitive' who told me that I could develop the 'power', whatever *that* is. But I've no wish to pursue it.

There's finally a rather spooky revelation that occurred on that Knightsbridge occasion. During the interval – yes, they do have one - refreshments were available for the visitors. Descending to the hallway to partake in them, there was also a bookstall. Perusing the books, I was startled to recognise a photo on one book of an actor I had shared a dressing room with during 'Mother Goose' at the Embassy Theatre, Peterborough in 1965. He worked under the name of Ian Sinclair and played the villain, Demon Glum.

He had never revealed that he was head of his Scottish clan and not only that but a spiritualist medium highly respected within the movement. He toured America giving lectures also. Purchasing his book I learnt of the Seven Stages of man, women also I trust, and was enlightened by the revelations within.

In show business we are rather like ships that pass in the night. I've never met up with Ian since. However he stays in my mind, well remembered. A few years ago I actually recognised him on television dancing a Scottish reel at Hogmanay. Guess who he was partnering? The Queen mother! I guessed he was also representing his clan, of which he was the head.

Finally I'm now going to relate the most revealing and astonishing situation that happened in 1956 during my second pantomime, 'Old King Cole' in Birmingham.

This was the first show in which I had a small principal role and during the run I befriended Beryl Foley who played the Princess. She had far more experience than I, even playing Mrs Snow in the musical of 'Carousel', and I was impressed. We shared coffee breaks, and our hopes and fears together.

One Sunday Beryl had invited me to tea at the suggestion of the mother and daughter whose house she was staying in. Beryl had already told me that the daughter, a mature lady well into her 60s, read palms and foretold the past and future – if she liked you! It was a hobby apparently, and I had high hopes she would like me and oblige.

Arriving at 4pm on the doorstep of an impressively large Victorian house I was made most welcome. So far – so good. A very genteel afternoon tea was served, delicate sandwiches and a silver cake stand with small but delicious delicacies atop.

Beryl and I chatted away about showbiz, exchanging gossip and theatrical scandals which fascinated our listeners, who were all agog. It was a world far removed from their sedate existence. I could always talk for England, adding spice and amusement like salt and pepper. Suddenly the daughter asked whether I would like my palm read? Would I? I was gagging for it!

I must apologise for the fact that I cannot now recall their names. However what transpired that day has resonated throughout my life and become the foundation of my belief in survival after death.

The Hereafter

Taking my left hand my new found friend explained that the left revealed my past whilst the right foretold my future. She scored on many details in my past, even a nervous breakdown through bullying when very young. Other revelations convinced me she knew what she was talking about. Bolstered by the 'left' revelations I eagerly proffered my right hand when prompted.

Firstly she told me that I had an exceedingly long life line with good health, which was comforting. However my career line was to divide eventually. My present as a dancer would achieve much acclaim and success, but I was destined for greater fame as a choreographer and director of musicals, etc, etc, etc. Wow! With hindsight it has all proved true, as readers who haven't skipped whole sections, will know.

I was also told that both hands were ablaze with colours. Very important to me, as I eventually painted in oils and watercolours, so this also turned out to be proved correct.

Thanking her profusely I prepared to leave, not wishing to outstay my welcome. Her mother, who had remained quietly attentive throughout, asked me whether I was expected back at my digs. I wasn't as I was only in bed and breakfast accommodation. On learning that, I was invited to stay a little longer and join them for coffee and sandwiches later. What was to happen then was truly incredible.

This lady I had surmised must be in her 80s at least, if not older. Her daughter I had already guessed to be in her 60s, remembering my own grandmother. I've always had a knack for guesstimating ages which proved useful when auditioning dancers later in my career.

Mother, on further revelation, had trained as a doctor and was in America when the San Francisco earthquake exploded. She had helped in rescuing survivors. What a lady, she had all her marbles and was most interestingly erudite. Besides tea, I was having a first hand history lesson – always my favourite subject at college.

After further refreshment I felt I should make my reluctant farewells, it had been a fascinating visit.

Suddenly Mother asked me if I had something personal in my possession that only I had owned. Puzzled, I asked why.

Whilst mother did not 'do' spiritualism or palms, she was apparently expert in psychometry – I believe that was the name of what was to provoke a rather perplexing mystery in my life.

The object required, so she said, had ideally to be a signet ring or cigarette case which no one else had possessed. My parents had wanted to give me such a signet ring for my 16th birthday. It was something I had pestered them for since age 14. Back in the early 50s, 18 carat gold was unobtainable except for dental treatment. However, as I was pursuing a very brief apprenticeship as a dental technician, my boss agreed to cast me a ring and and I helped him do so, according to my own design. How more personal can one get than that? I had worn it solidly for at least five years. It had a small shield with my initial engraved in the centre.

Apparently, inanimate objects like this took on personal vibrations which could be picked up and interpreted by a skilled and sensitive medium.

Mother took the ring firmly in the palm of her hand, telling me that once she connected with the power she would ask questions and I must reply with only Yes or No, nothing else. Beryl and I sat transfixed. The atmosphere in this large Victorian House seemed to increase and after what seemed an eternity, Mother, who seemed to be in a trance, said 'A young man in an air force uniform is approaching.'

Beryl and I glanced nervously around – nothing.

She continued 'He wishes to connect with you. Do you recognise or have knowledge of him?'

'No,' was my reply.

She carried on, 'He's telling me he was shot down over Germany at the beginning of the Second World War. Does that help?'

'No.'

'He's asking me to be more explicit in his appearance and claiming a family connection. He has a mop of curly red hair, very distinguishable. Do you recognise him now?'

'No!', emphatically.

She carried on, 'Oh dear, he's so disappointed and his spirit is slowly leaving.' With that, Mother gave a long sigh and opening her eyes, asking 'Did you receive any messages?'

I was somewhat surprised, not realising, as was now explained, that a spirit has to be recognised in its new form – if not, then no contact is possible.

The whole afternoon and evening had been a most exciting occasion, even the latter episode which had appeared not to work satisfactorily.

I said my goodbyes and returned to my digs, still clinging to my palm-reading episode which I wanted to come true, but with strong doubts about the psychometry episode.

The pantomime still had about six weeks to go to its finish when we all bade our fond adieus. Sadly mine and Beryl's paths were never to cross again, but that's showbiz.

Once I returned to the parental home I got caught up in the usual hunt for another job, also filling in time attending classes to keep in trim for auditions. Fortunately for me I never had to wait too long. Once in London I would stay at classes all day, returning on the last train back home.

My mother always waited up until I was safely back home - something mothers do, or did then, Also she wanted to share a last coffee and chat over my day's doings.

It was now more than a month since my return and suddenly I remembered I had not told Mum about my various encounters with the occult. She was interested in my palm readings, hoping they would prove correct.

However, a most strange expression took over when I started on the story of the RAF boy who tried to make contact.

She asked 'Do you remember my cousin Auntie Elsie?'

Did I? You bet! When my brother and I were still attending junior school Mum would collect us and we would walk to have tea with Aunty Elsie, who lived a few streets away from us. She always had shop bought cakes that were far more exciting than Mum's home made ones, which is a shabby thing to recall now, because my mother was a fabulous cook, especially where cakes were concerned. But that's kids for you, ungrateful.

Anyway the most important part of this conversation was about to unfold. Aunty Elsie had a son in the RAF who was killed at the beginning of World War II and more importantly had striking red/gold hair, much commented on.

I felt a cold shiver down my back for here was a second cousin trying to make contact with someone he'd never met, who didn't even know about him. It's now apparent to me that he probably wanted to get a message of comfort to his mother, who was still alive.

Now, whenever I'm questioned about the hereafter, I'm highly hopeful that it does exist, otherwise how could this entire incident have occurred? We were related but had never met. There has to be more to life and death.

Finally for all interested ghost hunters, London is a fantastic location for hauntings. You can join ghost walks with experienced guides who will take you all over, with stories to make your flesh creep.

The Tower of London, as expected, is loaded with them, notoriously Anne Boleyn, described by Stanley Holloway in his music hall song 'With her head tucked under her arm, she walks the Bloody Tower'. Don't think I would relish seeing that!

Drury Lane theatre has a ghost that frequently appears in the upper circle watching over new productions. Must be a long departed director counting the house!

Finally, on the ghost walk one is taken to an alleyway by the side of the Adelphi Theatre in the Strand, which leads up to Covent Garden, past the stage door where history records, in Victorian times the leading man of the play was stabbed to death whilst entering the stage door, by his understudy.

That strikes me as a bit extreme, no matter how much one wants the part! Anyway the alley is reputed to be truly haunted and I personally would not take a short cut on a winter's night.

Sleep well!

SHIPBOARD CABARET

In the autumn of 1963 I had first heard of work available to dancing acts onboard ships. Making enquiries I discovered the main agency for these contracts was through the offices of Gerald Bright, known famously as the Bandleader – Geraldo.

Contacting him with photographs and CVs, which by now were fairly impressive, of the various acts that Jenny and I had presented in pantomimes and summer seasons, we were excited to receive a letter giving us an appointment.

His office was situated at the top of Bond Street adjoining Regent Street. Readers who have seen the film 'The Producers' will recall that office with its stained glass, half-moon windows reaching to the floor. Gerry's mahogany desk was huge and monopolised the whole space. His assistant, office boy and Jack-of-all-trades was crunched up in a tiny corner, but obviously within shouting distance. His name was Keith Salberg, nephew of the famous Derek Salberg.

When I say 'shouting distance', I mean it. He was treated like a dogsbody and I felt truly sorry for him being treated with such disdain in other people's presence. However, he remained quite phlegmatic at all times for which I admired him.

Gerry agreed to put us on his books for future engagements and I had obviously explained that our availability was limited to seasons in the spring and autumn as fill-in work between theatre shows.

Now in the new millennium with many theatre shows sadly in decline, most artistes can find work only on cruise ships which present full scale musical shows as well as revues.

If you like work at sea then all's well. If you don't, there aren't many other options available. However, back in the 60s the only engaged personnel entertainment–wise was a dancing act and a soloist singer, plus three separate orchestras - chamber, light orchestra and dance.

Whilst most boats now are one class, back in the days of yore three were obligatory - first, cabin and tourist. First was exactly that – for theatre stars, landed gentry and the rich, rich, rich. Cabin was the intermediate zone – the almost rich and wannabees - whilst tourist was distinctly higher than that of

Titanic notoriety but mainly for Brits leaving to start anew in other lands with governmental monetary aid. Also young backpackers discovering a world far beyond their own family backgrounds. An exciting time to be part of, even if only spasmodically in mine and Jenny's experience.

Crossing the North Atlantic to the New World could be rather like purchasing a lottery ticket, as far as the weather was concerned. It also depended on the depth of your purse. If first class, you were located in the part least harassed by weather temperament. Cabin class had its ups and downs, whilst tourist was mostly all downs. If a good sailor – OK, if not then on your knees in the loo throwing up and praying for salvation.

I'm not knocking tourist class because back in 1954 I took my first Atlantic crossing to seek work in Canada, and tourist was all I could afford. When the weather was fine all was right with the world – when rough it was hell.

The food was good and could be likened to dining in Lyons Corner House – The Brasserie naturally, which most working class families regarded as a treat in London. My mum and dad always took my brother Peter and myself there for celebrations. The Brasseries had waiter service and a small orchestra playing during dinner – very posh. So that is the comparison with tourist class on ships back in the 60s.

Now that Jenny and I were on Geraldo's agency we had been assured that first class accommodation was an inclusive part of the agreement. This came also with the responsibility of hosting a table in the dining room, which wasn't a hardship as any professional artiste travelling the Atlantic would be seconded to our table, making for many interesting encounters.

But I am jumping the gun again. We still had to get our first contract. Getting an agent, even a top one, is only the key in the door.

Christmas of 1964 we were working in pantomime in the Embassy Theatre, Peterborough in 'Mother Goose' which I have already written about in the pantomime section. That season was memorable for two things, firstly Winston Churchill's funeral and secondly, rather more tritely, our first contact through Geraldo's office. And what a contract!

It was for Montreal, and whilst I had lived and worked in Canada for six months previously, Eastern Canada was new territory for me whilst for Jenny, it was especially exciting being her first trip there.

With our pantomime now terminating, we packed our theatre skips with costumes and props and headed for Liverpool and the Canadian Pacific ship the 'Empress of England'.

Crossing the North Atlantic we were to encounter sea–sickness, oo-er, and we were naturally expected to perform in cabaret – our reason for being there

However a remedy was at hand. My cabin steward told me that the doctor would give an anti-histamine injection which was the antidote to sea-sickness.

Apparently sufferers from hay fever taking anti-histamine were not troubled by sea sickness, hence a rescue procedure was formulated.

We met up with the ship's doctor Bob Thomas – a lively and likeable character who was to become a particular friend to Jenny and myself, especially when showing us around both Quebec and Montreal on our first visit.

Whilst Jenny didn't suffer with sea-sickness I most definitely did so had the injection. The nurse explained that I had to go immediately to my cabin as I would experience sleepiness and must lie flat straight away, but must ask my steward to wake me after half an hour, when I must go on the open deck and walk around to gain my sea legs. Eureka! It worked and more importantly I would not need another injection whilst working on board the ship for the duration of the contract, which was for a couple of months. Usually at a time during this period we would cross and re-cross the North Atlantic at its roughest periods of the year, spring and autumn.

This was unavoidable for us, as we regarded this work as a fill-in between our theatre season of summer revues and pantomime. Whilst cabaret was OK we always considered ourselves theatre performers within a full company.

Back in the 60s cabaret consisted only of a dance duo and a singer who were expected to fill a thirty minute spot between them. This was performed in two separate classes of the ship. As there were three classes to entertain we performed over only three nights. There was no cabaret on first or last nights by ship rules, the reason being that passengers had not unpacked on the first night and on the last night were packed ready for disembarkation the following morning.

At that time a dress code existed as below.

FIRST CLASS
Men Dinner Suit
Ladies Optional Full Length or Cocktail Dress

CABIN CLASS
Men Optional Dinner Suit or Smart Suit with Tie
Ladies Optional Cocktail or Smart Day Dress

TOURIST CLASS
Men Casual (but expected Tie)
Ladies Optional (Trousers discouraged but this was usually ignored)

Jenny and I brought two separate acts with us. The first one, to cause an impression, consisted of four full costume changes in full view, starting à la Astaire/Rogers in full evening attire, transforming to French Apache which in turn changed to 1920s Charleston, etc, finally going into lavish Latin American.

The latter was deliberately to inspire the audiences to attend our half hour dance classes, which were an integral part of our contract. These classes were at 11am when we taught the basic steps of both ballroom and the latest dance crazes such as the Cha Cha Cha, Bossa Nova, etc. Some brave participants even requested, for a laugh, the intricacies of the 1920s Charleston, Black Bottom, etc. Most collapsed in fits of giggles on the floor. Fun was the object of the exercise.

If your mathematics are correct you will have surmised that we were hardly overworked on the five day crossing. With a twice a day, half hour dance session and two 15 minute cabaret spots on only three days, the total only amounted to nine hours a week.

The young pursers' workload was extreme, consisting of front desk work answering questions on immigration, etc by the day and participating late into the night with all the entertainments. No wonder they were envious of Jenny and myself, especially with our first class contracts, being waited on hand and foot. Would you believe our contracts also gave us a special tipping allowance for the staff? We jokingly taunted them en route to 'Watch it!' or they'd have regrets.

The ship's hostess who was in charge of organising all the activities for the passengers was a delightful young and pretty girl, Christine Whiteford, who became another particular friend of ours along with Bob Thomas the ship's doctor.

We offered to help Christine by judging competitions - beauty, talent, fancy dress, etc, which was a help for her and also enabled us escape the boredom with too much time on our hands.

After crossing the North Atlantic, especially in October, and coursing through rough seas whilst on occasion being unable to walk on the open decks, it was quite a relief to enter the St Lawrence Seaway into calmer waters and most interesting to pass through the various locks towards our first docking in Quebec, for passengers whose destination it was.

This also enabled us to explore ancient Quebec together with other passengers for a few hours before continuing to the final destination, Montreal. Quebec was very French and was having problems at that time with other provinces in the Western States whose allegiance was not to France.

On another occasion Jenny and I were stranded in Quebec due to a horrendous accident so had evidence which caused us to sympathise totally with the Western States' views. However, more of that story later – don't miss it.

Back to our first time in Montreal, a beautiful and very cosmopolitan city. As we were returning with the Empress of England we had a couple of days to explore and were able to use the ship as a hotel. This was quite a spooky experience, for without the bustle of hundreds of passengers it felt like being on the 'Marie Celeste'. We could return for our meals whilst in dock. However, with much to explore we only bothered with a hurried breakfast, grabbing a sandwich on the hoof at lunchtime, but returning exhausted to shower and enjoy a relaxed dinner in the company of the ship's officers, as only a couple of tables were in operation in the first class restaurant in dock.

Obviously below decks all the staff and crew were working full out preparing for the ship's return to England and the next influx of passengers. The crew were lucky to get even a few hours ashore, which they made hilarious use of. There is no second guess as to where they headed. Passengers usually started arriving mid morning so a certain amount of sobering up crew-wise, was the order of the day.

The ship suddenly awoke from its gentle slumber as its life-blood – the passengers – started to explore. It's something only sailors or shipboard personnel can relate to on transatlantic crossings, for cruise ships are alive and fully operational throughout their entire voyage.

Whilst on the subject of cruise ships I must now enlarge on the present day diversification of show business. With summer shows almost in terminal decline trained singers, dancers, comics and speciality acts have no option than to seek work at sea, which has now evolved beyond all recognition, culminating in revues and full scale musicals set in what pros call 'proper' theatres, with all the various stage devices that their land based counterparts have enjoyed for years.

No longer does the singer or dance duo have to perform in the ballroom or cramped low-ceiling tourist bars, where there was little to enhance their performance. I am sure that the cruise lines are now the largest area of employment for all branches of the theatrical profession.

Back to the 60s, when shipboard entertainment was in its embryonic stage.

If any reader has never seen the 'fall' season of eastern Canada, known to us as autumn, do consider the trip. Whilst Jenny and I eagerly anticipated it, words failed us. As the ship progresses up the river the view is ablaze with every shade of yellow, gold and orange to deepest crimson. It has to be the 8th Wonder of the World. Even skilled artists would find it impossible to re-create the luminosity of the landscape.

On this first contract we traversed the North Atlantic about four times, each trip taking approximately two weeks, which enabled us to snatch a couple of days back home before joining the next crossing.

I have already mentioned our friendship which developed with the ship's doctor Bob Thomas. He had written a best selling book about his life in the Antarctic called 'Dew-Line Doctor', when he had been stationed with the Eskimos.

'DEW' stood for distant early warning when the world was anticipating another atomic bomb atrocity. No change there, then! He cared for American personnel stationed there but also gave succour to the Eskimos, and became a local hero. A fascinating read.

On this first visit to Montreal, Bob and Christine, the social hostess, showed us around the beauty spots and clubs, etc - so hectic that we were glad to get back to the shipboard routine of the homeward journey. Jenny and I considered our shipboard work as a paid holiday - something that never came into our land based show business contracts.

In the 60s many families were emigrating to Canada. The government gave them virtually free passage to help them get started in their new lives. Jenny and I found the embarkation scenes in Liverpool too much to bear, with sobbing relatives saying their final goodbyes. Friends and relatives had permission to tour the ship prior to departure, including walking round the outer decks. Naturally they were on the brink of tears when the deck stewards walked through with their hand bells and the loudspeakers boomed 'All ashore that's going ashore!' Then the tears fell, as grandparents hugged the little ones, promising to visit once the family was settled in.

It was a sad scene. However once at sea, optimism surfaced and all joined happily in the various activities – deck games, bingo and our dancing classes, etc. Young children were looked after in cribs so mothers had a real holiday.

During the next three crossings, Geraldo and his wife said they would take a trip to see us work. We were perfectly happy as the shipboard reports of our acts and willingness to muck in with the entertainment staff were favourable. He was our boss and we were pleased when he said that any time we wanted to do a few crossings, just let him know.

However one of our Canadian Pacific trips turned into a complete disaster, which was reported in England on television and in the newspapers, although we didn't know it at the time. Even our parents anxiously rang the Canadian Pacific offices to make sure we were OK.

It had been an ordinary winter crossing after our summer season had finished, although it was to be our last one in late November as our next job was pantomime in Cardiff, Wales.

Reaching the sanctuary of Quebec we went ashore for our usual two or three hours, wandering through its historic streets, returning in time to set sail for Montreal. During dinner we were suddenly shaken so vigorously as to send plates swirling across the tables, whilst wine glasses crashed and shattered all over the floor. Quite a violent smack in fact. Seeing the waiters' faces we realised that something truly untoward had occurred.

Over the Tannoy system passengers were asked to report to the purser's office immediately. The information was that as we took off from Quebec with a threatened snowstorm materialising, our ship had collided with a tanker and the prow had received severe underwater damage.

We limped back to the dock and passengers were told to ready themselves to travel by rail to Montreal immediately. Jennie and I watched them departing.

However, as honorary ship's officers, according to our passbooks we were obliged to remain with the ship whilst it was towed to a dry dock across the other side of the St Lawrence Seaway, where repairs would take place.

It was truly like a ghost ship now. Jenny and I were the only occupants in the first class section of the ship. It was snowing fast and my steward was very worried that if the river started to freeze up they would all be trapped until the spring, when it would again become navigable.

Meeting with the purser, he told us it was hoped to repair the gashed-out prow in a week, when we would then limp back to England, but without passengers as the insurance would only allow crew to return, which included *us*. The orchestra members were still with the ship but their accommodation was down in the tourist end so they were not allowed into the first class section, even under these unusual circumstances. The formality of that period was unbelievably rigid.

Jenny and I rattled around, lonely and fed up. Being in dry dock, no toilets or showers were usable so we had to trek, off the ship and through deepening snow, to land based toilets. Even in the middle of the night! Yet again meals were served, along with the other officers, in the first class dining room. At least the rest of the crew had company down in the bowels of the ship in their own pub.

To relieve boredom Jenny and I, together with a few of the band boys, would travel each day by bus and ferry across to Quebec and this was where we encountered the bloody-mindedness of the French Canadians who refused to speak English to us. Incidentally, the archaic French that Canadians continue to speak would not be understood in present day France.

I wanted to buy some boots as I had not anticipated being snowed in, so I clumped into a shoe shop and conversed in plain English, totally ignoring their French replies. They wanted the sale of course, so were forced to serve me, regardless. I found what I wanted and stormed out, feeling inclined to 'two-finger' them, but not wishing to sink to their level, did not do so. Now I fully understood how the rest of Canada despises the Eastern French Canadians with their separatist agenda.

One night Jenny and I, together with a couple of the lads from the orchestra, went across to Quebec to see a programme by 'Les Grands Ballets Canadiens' which required no spoken word, naturally. As classical ballet has its own sign language, Jenny and I were perfectly at home with it.

Within the week we were informed that the repairs were going according to plan and hopefully we would be returning to Liverpool. The chief purser asked us if we would be prepared to give a couple of shows to the crew as there would be no passengers to entertain, which we readily agreed to do, only too thankful to be returning home, even in limping mode so as not to stress the temporary repairs.

So on Saturday night we left freezing Quebec. I was woken the following morning by my steward bringing me breakfast on a tray. His first words startled me.

'Have you looked out of your window, Sir?'

At the tone of his voice I leapt out of bed, to gaze at land, not the open sea as expected. My God, how slow were we travelling! By morning we expected to be in the open sea. Apparently we had reached the Atlantic in the middle of the night only to have the repaired prow smashed apart by the heavy seas, and were trailing back to the dry dock in Quebec yet again. Apparently the crew had been frantically blocking up the doubly-damaged hull by stacking all the mattresses from the tourist cabins, in order to prevent us sinking to the bottom of the ocean. Otherwise – Titanic, 'Here we come!'

Now I knew for certain we could never get back to England for our next contractual obligation, so I made an appointment immediately with the chief purser and later that morning confronted him, demanding that arrangements be made to fly Jenny and myself back. He was adamant that we held ship's officer status and were obliged to remain with the ship. My response turned the air purple

I explained that our contract was with Geraldo's office and contained a definite return date which had already been broken. Therefore our union, Equity, would uphold any forthcoming compensation claim. I then demanded that a senior officer of the Canadian Pacific company be contacted, otherwise legal proceedings would be set in place. This was now Saturday and we were tied up on the dockside in Quebec.

That night during dinner on the ghostly stricken ship a message came that a director of the company was to meet me the following morning. There had been no sign of the ship's captain since the original collision almost ten days beforehand and the superstitious seamen were adamant that he had jinxed the ship. He had never been popular since we had left Liverpool on this ill-fated crossing and had been relieved of his post.

The Empress of England was now in the hands of the second-in-command. Obviously he was not responsible for the faulty repairs which had brought us back to Square 1. Were the French Canadians responsible for the work in hand, making an anti Brits gesture, I wondered?

My main aim now was to get us back to England. A call to my cabin on Sunday morning around 11am saw Jenny and myself in confrontational mode, ready to meet the chairman of the company. He at first appeared doubtful about flying us back as I was requesting. I persisted regardless.

He of course knew that with the freezing up of the St Lawrence Seaway the ship was in danger of having to remain in Canada until the spring thaw. I told him that in two weeks time we were due to start rehearsals in Cardiff for their

Christmas production of Cole Porter's 'Aladdin', that I was contracted to choreograph the show, that I had already engaged 12 dancers and that we, also, were to appear. The extensive publicity had been in place for weeks. If he didn't get us back I was more than prepared to sue the Canadian Pacific Company, together with Geraldo's company, for loss of earnings and my professional reputation, which counts for a hell of a lot in the theatrical world. I left it for the chairman to ponder my claims. He explained that he had to put it to the directors and await their decision. We parted.

That evening during dinner in the ghostly restaurant the purser informed us that we were to travel in the morning by train to Montreal and fly back to England via Holland that night. The reason it was via Holland was because the Canadian Pacific Airline Company did not have a franchise to land in England. Oo er! Was there another CP disaster in store?

Jenny certainly thought so. When waiting in the Montreal departure lounge we saw the huddled figure of the dispossessed ship's captain waiting to board the same flight. She recalled the sailors' talk of jinx. However, I placated her with the thought that lightning never strikes twice. I did cross my fingers though!

We arrived early morning in Amsterdam and had arranged to fly on to London that evening. As neither of us had visited the Dutch capital we took a coach trip for the whole day, visiting all the interesting places the city had to offer.

Arriving back at our respective homes with traveller's tales, we prepared ourselves for our pantomime season in the capital of Wales, where the local papers garnered publicity for the pantomime with headlines writ large, 'Panto Stars in Sea Drama', and so on. We basked in the glow of reluctant fame.

THE FABULOUS QUEEN ELIZABETH AND QUEEN MARY

With the experience of the Canadian Pacific Company in the bag, I decided to approach the Cunard Company. When I had travelled to America in 1954 it was as a passenger on the Queen Elizabeth in tourist class. The only glimpse of first class had been prior to arrival in New York when immigration officials had boarded the ship and all passengers had to assemble in the main first class ballroom to get passports stamped for entry.

America has always been stringent as to who they let in since the mass European immigration in the 30s, when passengers were virtually incarcerated on Ellis Island for de-lousing and suchlike procedures, plus a background investigation into their past, before being allowed to so much as set foot in New York proper. Many were turned away and sent back, as the museum now portrays in poignant pictures displayed throughout those very processing halls, which lie within the shadow of the Statue of Liberty – a symbol of irony for the unhappy rejects.

Anyway my memory of being granted permission for a six month stay in the Grand Ballroom of Queen Elizabeth, now fuelled my desire to present our own dancing acts in that grand setting. Jenny and I likened it to perhaps dancing in Westminster Abbey – not that we had done that!

Approaching Cunard offices situated in Trafalgar Square in London I was directed to their department dealing with entertainment. They had mainly used ballroom exhibition couples, but I knew a dance act similar to our own, who had worked for the company, so with photographs and recommendations from Geraldo's officer I procured our first engagement - a crossing to New York on the Queen Elizabeth. The dream had become reality and this time it was to be a first class one.

Readers who travelled on Queen Elizabeth will recall what a monumental credit it was to British workmanship. In the 30s plastic was almost unheard of, marble and fabulous woodwork flourished throughout. Cabins in first class had amazing marquetry panels set into the walls. The ballroom where we performed in the first class section had four huge marble fireplaces which burnt logs. With enormous leather sofas and armchairs, it rather resembled a Pall Mall gentlemen's club. However, there were rather more intimate and comfortable lounges around, together with well appointed reading and writing rooms.

A huge swimming pool and 'keep fit' area even had mechanical horses for the equestrian orientated clients, who obviously could not bring their horses with them. Dogs travelling with their owners had their own kennels and exercise areas. They were not allowed to be walked on the open decks for obvious reasons. Once I had established a rapport with the kennel master he allowed me to exercise any dog travelling alone. I had a boxer dog who was my constant companion when touring with theatre shows. I missed him, so was more than happy to briefly befriend any lonely travelling pooch.

I can still recall a beautiful Irish wolfhound called Emily, all silver grey and white. She was nervous of being alone and excitedly happy when I walked her in the exercise area. One stormy night with lashing rain and high winds I was concerned for her. The dogs all had individual small box kennels with mesh doors for air out on the top deck. I got out of bed, dressed and made my way up, to find her cowering at the back of her kennel, shivering with fright. Crawling in beside her she snuggled up and we both dozed off together, rocked by the motion. Thankfully storms at sea can soon abate. This did and I returned to the comfort of my own cabin. The final day on arrival in New York I stroked

Jenny and I leaving New York with the
Statue of Liberty between us in the background

goodbye to Emily, to be reunited with her owners who had flown the Atlantic. All three classes on the ship had facilities for pets.

Back to the real reason – our work load. It was very similar to the Canadian Pacific company ship's routine. We did the same number of shows and dance classes in each category - first, cabin and tourist. Having travelled as a passenger ten years previously I knew exactly what to expect in the cramped tourist section, and nothing had changed.

Jenny and I had an adagio act, some spectacular lifts with Jenny spinning above my head, which had we attempted would have found her straddling the fire extinguishers! So all of those parts of the act had to remain earthbound. All was OK in the cabin and first class lounges. The first class lounge ceiling was three floors high. We could have arrived by plane!

There were three orchestras and we were given a choice as to which one we would like to play for us in our cabaret spot. This meant they would accompany us to the relevant class each night. We chose the cabin class group, which was funkier, for our needs. They were fun to work with also, which always helps, audience-wise. Rapport is a tangible asset.

The company also put at our disposal a private studio for passengers wishing

Jenny and I photographed on the Queen Elizabeth when appearing in cabaret

to have private dance lessons. There was no obligation on us to do so but it was a lucrative opportunity and we certainly had plenty of time on our hands to let our feet earn extra dosh. We set our own fees and the ship's office asked for 25 per cent. Fair enough – they supplied the studio and cleaned and polished the floors, etc.

On one trip Lord and Lady Astor of Hever Castle travelled with their only son John and their eldest daughter Bridget. John Astor was, I believe, about 17 years old and Bridget, the eldest of three girls, was 15.

It was their first visit to New York and they were as excited at the prospect as almost anyone else making their first visit. Their father Lord Gavin Astor asked me if Jenny and I could teach John and Bridget social dancing, as they had apparently expressed a wish to learn the latest Latin American dance crazes sweeping the world.

Obviously it was part of our service to keep ahead with all the trends so we had studied in London with the top Latin masters to acquire these new fangled rhythms. Now was the chance to recoup our original outlay, so Cha Cha Cha and Bossa Nova - there we were!

Bridget and John had great fun and were soon making good progress. After they had seen our act during one evening in which we demonstrated the styles of the 20s – Charleston, Black Bottom, etc - the young couple asked for lessons in that also and became really quite good. Apparently most of their mates hoofed around, performing not very expertly, at Hunt Balls, etc, so John and Bridget looked forward to getting the opportunity of showing off their prowess on the next occasion.

That was many years ago and the family title Lord Astor of Hever has now passed to John himself. In 2003 friends visited me in Sussex where I live and wanted to visit Hever Castle, which is steeped in history. Anne Boleyn had resided there and Henry VIII wooed her, as well as her older sister, back in the mists of time.

Whilst the Astor family still own Hever they do not actually live there. However, visiting with my friends I felt the urge to contact John again. I asked one of the guides whether a letter sent to Hever would be forwarded and she assured me that it would, when I explained my connection with the family some forty years ago previously.

About ten days later a letter arrived from the House of Lords from Sir John, thanking me for evoking happy memories of years gone by. As I had written in my letter to him, if nothing else, everybody always remembers their first visit to New York. He said that he had forwarded my letter to his sister Bridget, who was also delighted that we had remembered them. How polite was that? I had not taught many lords to dance the Charleston, nor the Bossa Nova.

Jenny and I had first class accommodation, serviced by our own steward and stewardess. Our contract also requested that we hosted the entertainers' table in the palatial dining room each evening. This was not a hardship as we met many theatrical performers travelling to perform on Broadway or to film in Hollywood.

Showbiz people always have a special empathy – it's a hazardous profession, with comedy and tragedy in equal measure - for dinner table conversation. So whilst the host and hostess ate frugally – we had two cabaret sessions to perform and dancers never eat before a show – we looked forward to dinner time for the above reasons. Our table was always the merriest, viewed with envy by other nearby diners.

One couple I remember because when I was a student I recalled seeing them regularly on television in 'Sunday Night at the London Palladium'. Joy and Serge Ganjou had a spectacular adagio act, three brothers and Joy who I believe was called 'Juanita' in the act. They were elegantly attired in Georgian costumes with white powdered wigs and Joy was thrown through the air and caught acrobatically in mid flight. It always brought the house down. They had fascinating tales to tell.

Besides our own adagio act there was always one other performer with us, either a singer or comedy speciality entertainer. On one crossing we met Pat Lancaster for the first time, oddly enough during lifeboat drill which took place immediately the ship set sail. We had noticed her without knowing she was also part of the cabaret performance. Pat always had, and still does, great style – not flashy – but perfect for the elegance required on the Queen Elizabeth. Still young, she already had an enormous theatrical reputation behind her - West End revues, a regular radio programme - the list was endless. We have remained friends throughout the years - quite an achievement when in many instances we can be like ships passing in the night.

Some years later when Jenny had retired from show business to start a family and I was a director/choreographer, Pat and I were to work in pantomime. This was for Howard and Wyndham in the beautiful Newcastle Theatre Royal. Pat was contracted to play Principal Boy in 'Robinson Crusoe'. At this time I had a new dancing partner Nina Brown who played Spirit of the Sea, whilst I played Blackbeard the Pirate, together with Mike and Bernie Winters as Captain and Mate.

I have yet again jumped too far ahead which is inevitable when introducing new characters. So back to Jenny and myself still with the Cunard Company.

We worked many times on the Queen Elizabeth but eventually got the opportunity to cross on the Queen Mary. Each of them had its particular identity and whilst the Elizabeth was grander, the Mary was the one that most of the crew members preferred to travel with, considering it more homely. I think I could understand the differences, but we ourselves liked both, for differing reasons.

The Cunard fleet had many smaller cruise ships when cruising had not reached the mega proportions of the present day. All of these smaller ships had by tradition names ending in 'nia' - Lucitania, Carmania, Franconia, etc.

The theatrical profession has numerous superstitions which you break at your peril, but sailors have even more, as we were to discover.

These smaller ships did the Mediterranean and Scandinavian cruises and we enjoyed many sailings in calmer waters and warmer climes than the North Atlantic routes. We were especially honoured to be asked to perform at the Cunard inaugural service between New York and Bermuda. This was a weekly service which entailed leaving New York on Saturday lunchtime and arriving in Bermuda first thing Monday morning, when we had two days to enjoy this island, a British possession, with its English police uniforms and red pillar-boxes for posting cards, et al. Jenny and I hired motor scooters as did most people and we bombed around discovering all its semi-hidden treasures.

Leaving at Wednesday lunchtime we arrived back in New York on Friday morning, docking during the night in fact, so that we had a whole day and a half to see the top Broadway shows before departing again at Saturday lunchtime. What a job to land! We felt as if we were in paradise – the best of both worlds - New York bustle and excitement which never wavered, and the peaceful beauty of Bermuda.

However we can vouch for the terror of the Bermuda triangle, because we experienced it! Out of a calm sea and a clear sunny sky, whilst seated at Sunday lunch, the ship suddenly juddered alarmingly, sending plates, dishes and glasses crashing and smashing in an absolute orgy of self destruction, some passengers even tipping backwards to the floor.

Everybody, including the waiters, was badly shaken. However the sea which had appeared to boil calmed almost immediately. It still remains one of the world's mysteries, and not one I would like to ever experience again, especially when one recalls the stories of planes being sucked from the sky to disappear forever.

Back to the Atlantic. Crossing it on the famous Queen Elizabeth or Queen Mary, there used to be a weekly ritual, for which all the passengers were happy to abandon their lunches. It happened each Saturday when the two ships literally passed each other at the midpoint, obviously a something no longer to be seen, but treasured by all who were lucky enough to witness it. Both ships arriving towards each other through the autumnal mist and hooting their sirens in joyful recognition and greeting – truly a sight to behold. It can never, ever be repeated. Two magnificent ships of such fame and grandeur – true romance of the sea.

Another little anecdote worth mentioning was meeting up on quite a few crossings with the famous British actress Hermione Gingold. Most may now remember her for starring opposite Maurice Chevalier in the Hollywood film of 'Gigi'. She was however also a famous star of British stage and radio. Terrified of flying, she was in demand on both sides of the North Atlantic and became a great favourite of the ship's staff. Jenny and I met her on many occasions and she often wanted us to share afternoon tea with her, which always developed into hysterics with the crew and other passengers. She should have received an entertainment fee! A much loved character.

The Queen Elizabeth had a most exclusive private restaurant available to the first class passengers only, called the Veranda Grill, open till late at night. As we had cabaret to perform we would only eat a very light meal at dinner time - it's impossible to dance on a full stomach - so we were made honorary members of the Veranda Grill, enabling us to have something after the show when we were literally starving! The solo cabaret artiste did a late night show up there, but it was impossible to perform our own act, with its high above my head lift work - it would have had Jenny suspended on the sprinkler fire alarm system.

On one crossing I heard that Tommy Cooper and his wife were travelling in cabin class. Jenny and I had never worked with him but we had mutual friends in the profession so made acquaintance. I approached the purser for permission to take him up one night to the Veranda Grill because I knew the staff and waiters were dying to see him. One evening we accompanied Tommy and his wife, and whilst fairly quiet and shy, once surrounded by fans he went into overdrive. The Veranda Grill came to a hilarious standstill and even the pursers crept in as everyone queued for his autograph. It was a happy moment.

His death, too early, was in full view of a theatre and TV audience, who imagined it was part of his act and laughingly applauded. Very sad, but what a way for a comedian to go, amidst laughter. Once more there is mirth in Paradise.

On another occasion I had the opportunity to approach an actor I had long admired. It was very early morning on the Queen Elizabeth approaching New York. I had seen Alec Guinness as he was then, before being knighted. Notorious for his shyness, he apparently always had his meals alone in his cabin. I had seen him previously hastening round the open deck exceedingly early before most people were even up.

On this particular morning few people were promenading and he had stopped and was gazing out to sea. Taking my courage in both hands I made apologies first then spoke of my admiration of his work from his early years in 'Great Expectations', through the 'Lavender Hill Mob' and including his tour de force when he played every character in a family which included a dowager, 'Kind Hearts and Coronets'. Even speaking briefly of his classical stage roles.

He appeared surprised at my knowledge of his career and shyly thanked me. I swiftly left and never saw him again – respecting his solitude.

These are some of the memories I treasure from my showbiz life at sea.

Ria Jones and the author

THE WORLD OF AM-DRAMS

For the uninitiated, that stands for Amateur Dramatics, and the next story I am embarking on defines drama in no uncertain terms. Firstly I need to reveal how I got involved.

It was my first pantomime for the Triumph Organisation up in Billingham's amazing Forum theatre in 1971. This town had been created by ICI, and as its centrepiece had an Olympic size swimming pool, ice skating rink and exceedingly well appointed theatre. The Forum was a launch pad for full-scale musicals destined for London's West End. It also possessed exceedingly modern, fully functioning workshops, with mechanical painting frames, enabling the staff to create everything that straight plays or musicals required.

During this time when I was directing and choreographing 'Goody Two Shoes' starring Helen Shapiro, friends from Darlington, who were heavily involved in the amateur theatre, came to see a performance. One of them played many of the leading roles, and I was to hear for the first time about an organisation called NODA -National Operatic and Dramatic Association. This was formed to assist amateur artistes in achieving professional standards, and almost unique in England. My friends told me that NODA frequently sought professional directors, for the larger societies who could afford them, to take on their shows for brief periods. I expressed interest, so they gave me the London address.

Writing to Brian Clark, the administrator, I offered my services when available. My main interest was the opportunity to work with large casts in the more modern musicals, newly available for amateur companies. This was, unfortunately, a thing of the past with professional companies, where new financial Equity agreements were in place, making a large chorus unaffordable, unless it was a Lloyd-Webber musical, destined for London and Broadway.

Brian agreed to put me on NODA's books, more especially when I told him it was really dependent on my availability between professional commitments, which he thought was a good selling point for amateur societies. Brian was, at that particular time, trying to clean out the Stygian stables of certain useless amateur directors who had been brought to his notice, in an effort to streamline the organisation. As he ruefully remarked, it was akin to starting the Third World War.

I was to work on my first amateur production sooner than expected. A phone call asked if I would be prepared to take on a production of 'The Merry Widow', which was already halfway into its rehearsal period, because the director had walked out. Why, I had no idea at the time. This was being presented in the Oswald Twistle Town Hall, up in Lancashire. All my pro friends shrieked with laughter at the thoughts that venue conjured up – clog dancers et al.

I had only two weeks left to pull the production together for the opening night. The principals were talented and well on with the libretto. However, being a choreographer I felt the show needed more 'zizz'. They were eager to have a go - so we did. I was ambitious for them, and the final result was simple, but effective.

I was on a learning curve though, and about to discover a leading lady prepared to ransom the whole company for her own selfish ego - even walking out in a tantrum on the dress rehearsal. She had talent and was certainly, as far as I could see, the right person vocally for the demanding role of the Merry Widow. It was imperative to get her back. She would have enjoyed being pleaded with and persuaded, but I was definitely not about to go down that route. No, cunning was the order of the day, so I conferred with the chairman about finding another local society within a reachable distance, who had performed the Merry Widow during the past year or so.

The tantrum had occurred because of a missed photo call for the local papers which had been arranged for 2pm on the Sunday afternoon. I had allowed photographers half an hour, so that we could start the full dress rehearsal promptly at 2.30, as it is essential to be on time, with paid musicians in the pit and ready to go. All the cast had assembled in costume and full make-up, dead on time. However, no sign of the leading lady. This was not unusual, as I had already discovered during rehearsals. With time getting short, I wanted the famous shot of the Widow's entrance at the top of the ornate staircase, with all the men, in full evening dress and military uniforms, greeting her.

Still no leading lady. So I selected one of the young chorus girls of the same height and figure, to put on the Widow's costume, together with the famous hat which had originally created a fashion statement, copied by stylish ladies back when the show had its first professional production. The young lady took her place at the top of the stairs with the male chorus and principals grouped around her. The Press got their shots and departed. With minutes to go to the overture, our leading lady finally put in an appearance. When she found that the photographs had been taken, she stormed out, followed by her husband and young son, screaming protests all the way.

So we were now back to our search for a replacement. The chairman had found another singer, who was on her way. She had played the role a couple of years previously. I had broken up the cast until she arrived. Conferring with the musical director I suggested she sat in the pit with the musicians and sang the required numbers. I also asked the girl who had substituted for the photographs to perform the on-stage moves. All chorus members are ready to step in when an opportunity occurs, but I knew that vocally this girl was not up to the role. I did know what I was doing. I suggested that the chairman confide in the best friend of the absent prima donna.

Well, faster than a rat up a pipe, she was back in the building. I refused to stop the rehearsal. I knew full well she would be in place for the opening night and she knew I knew, so she sat seething through to the first interval, when I magnanimously agreed that she could do the rest of the rehearsal. What a palaver. Biter bit.

I was leaving after the first night, but I did have one last prod at the tempestuous leading lady. I had discovered, much to the chagrin of the rest of the company, that her husband had always presented her with an enormous floral display across the footlights - she always played the lead. So I asked the theatre manager to hide the flowers away, determined to frustrate her ego trip. I watched from the back of the stalls as father and son searched frantically, and unsuccessfully, for the ostentatious display. They had been hidden where no male could find them – in the ladies toilet.

All went well on the opening night and it was universally agreed to be a resounding success. The company presented me with a most artistic book, containing hand-drawn, hysterically funny sketches by one of their artistes. It is still in my treasure chest. This show was the only time I ever experienced such shenanigans with an amateur company, until much, much later.

During my work with various amateur groups right across the country, many have achieved high standards that even professionals would envy. As always though, there are others not up to scratch, with many lacking the background organisation necessary to ensure success.

Whilst I shall not name or shame certain societies, I have on occasion refused to continue working when the company has not fulfilled its side of the contract. If I had a pound for every time I have heard the line, 'Everybody agreed that Doris Nobody was far superior to Barbara Streisand in our 'Hello Dolly',' I would be very wealthy. Likewise, a pound for each time I have heard that, 'Everyone said our production of 'Chicago' beat the West End show to shreds.' What planet do they inhabit? Hey ho! Never mind, they don't get paid for performing, so I guess they need some form of boosting, as opposed to boasting.

The times I have been asked by amateur performers if I thought they could make it in the profession is uncountable. My response has always been the same, even with the very talented. If you have a family and a well paid job guaranteed 52 weeks a year, don't throw it away for a dream, which may now be virtually impossible for even experienced professionals to realise.

Attending open auditions, you may find yourself competing against hoards of young, professionally trained aspirants, which can prove very daunting. I am not saying it can not be done, because many of today's top names did start in the amateur theatre. But times have changed and it is now more of a risk, with less work available. If you have no family ties and are under 30 years of age, by all means have a go. But - like boy scouts - be prepared. Even some of my pro dancers are now finding that their temporary jobs are of longer duration than their professional ones.

Having said all the foregoing I'm now going to turn all I have written on its head. During my work with amateurs I encountered four performers that I agreed to help become professionals, which they all did with resounding success.

Firstly, working with the Swansea Musical Society, I met Menna Trussler when I was engaged to direct 'Camelot', Not one of the easiest musicals to stage. The committee had cast the show and Menna was the evil witch Morgan Lefay. She was outstanding.

When I first started directing amateur societies I was given the cast on arrival. That had to stop. I was the professional, expected on occasion to make a silk purse out of a sow's ear. I was getting fed up with being expected to turn the chairman or other official's wives or girlfriends into acceptable performers, because they had always taken the leads - no recommendation, as I had found to my cost. According to their thinking, why engage a professional if they could do it themselves?

'Camelot' requires a leading lady as the Queen with a powerful, trained voice and excellent acting ability and in Jean Thorly-Davis they indeed had the right performer. The role of the King also requires powerful acting. He only has one song, which is semi-sung, and David Thomas was well cast. A young and extremely handsome young man, Peter Llewellyn, undertook the role of Sir Lancelot whose godlike beauty and skills has to be strong enough to topple the throne. Peter fulfilled the requirements with style, easy charm and an excellent singing voice. He could have found fame in the profession I felt sure but he was a solicitor. All these years later he is a respected Judge, so he took the right road in life.

'Camelot' was a great success for the society and the following year I was asked to direct 'Calamity Jane'. And this is where I can prove the point I have made earlier, the committee had cast the show – again – and in their belief that they knew how to cast, had given the two female roles to Jean and Menna without any regard as to whether they were right for the very different characters.

Obviously to their way of thinking, once a leading lady – always a leading lady!, 'The chairman's wife' ethos prevailed. Jean had made a magnificent Queen in Camelot but was totally unsuited to the Calamity Jane role, which required a much rougher quality of singing, as opposed to her operatic soprano, whilst

Menna would have played and sung the hoyden Calamity Jane perfectly, something I had realised during the first run through. After the first week's rehearsal I was far from satisfied and approached the committee with the request to reverse the roles before it was too late, but Jean refused to even consider it.

Calamity was the lead. It's a situation that has spoilt many a talented group. So I had no alternative but to continue with the show as they had cast it. I still think it would have been a better show recast. However my mind was now made up - I would never direct another amateur show that I had not auditioned or cast. I could not afford to let amateurs ruin my professional reputation.

Later I was to direct 'Hello Dolly', and Menna Trussler played the titular role to perfection. Once her daughter had become an adult, Menna asked whether I thought she could make it as a mature professional actress. I was certain that she could, but first came the Equity hurdle. Without a card it was difficult. Writing to Equity on her behalf they replied that the best route would be via a repertory company, which the Grand Theatre in Swansea, under John Chilver's direction, ran very successfully.

Menna approached John who agreed to engage her as assistant stage manager, which was to eventually gain her enough credit for the valued Equity card. She is now a most successful actress, even starring in a Welsh-speaking soap for a number of years, laughingly confessing that although Welsh born, she had to speak the part in parrot-fashion Welsh to begin with. I am sure the number of years it's been running she is now fluent. In 2006 she became a stalwart in 'Little Britain' on national TV, famous across the country, as a Welsh *ladee*.

Returning to Swansea to direct 'My Fair Lady' I was determined to have a final say in the casting. No committee was going to override my choice, I was the person paid to deliver the show and no one was going to ruin my professional reputation.

A battle was in view when the chairman, new to me, said I would be guided by a panel of 12 appointed officers. Oh yeah? Wait and see, I thought to myself, and I already knew who would win.

All societies expected the director to supply the pieces required for auditions which is absolutely correct as the director should know the show inside out and sideways.

First things first, the role of Eliza. Many had put their names forward to audition. It was a desirable role. Some too old others not able to cut the rug vocally. As in any musical, singing is the first priority. I wanted that first, and dialogue second. My choice song-wise was first the more operatic 'I Could Have Danced All Night' when Eliza goes to the ball as a lady, secondly 'All I Want Is A Room Somewhere' as the cockney flower girl.

A pretty, dark-haired girl entered. So far I had not been too impressed with the forerunners. It's a very, very demanding role. This girl had a full length black

Finale of Les Miserable

*This is Julia Worsly   This is Ria Jones
as Eponine   as Fonteyn*

*Julia and Rea – backstage of the Palace Theatre, Manchaster. The first national
tour after a long run in Lonon*

skirt on with a demure white blouse. Her hair was piled elegantly on top of her head, she looked very sophisticated, with poise. She had obviously had dancing training, which to the trained eye is very easy to pick up. Her voice rang throughout the room with great melodic power.

Once finished, I had to stop myself from applauding – not the done thing at an audition. Requesting the second number I watched her go into the corner where she had a small bag. She took out a ragged shawl and removed pins from her hair which, with a quick shake, cascaded to her shoulders. She then hitched up her skirt, wrapped the shawl round her shoulders, and lo and behold there stood the flower girl – amazing.

What a performance. Here was my Eliza. No one else who followed could hold a candle to her. In dialogue she also excelled, had learnt the small sections required by heart which was more than one or two others had even prepared. There was no competition.

I was totally dumbfounded when the chairman said the board didn't want her to play the role as she had let the company down a couple of years before, when they had done the 'King and I'. Also she was far too young to play the part.

What a load of balderdash. I was incensed. Being told that the girl's mother was waiting outside, I asked her to come in. She was upset on hearing that the society didn't want her daughter and explained that she had been the one who forgot to bring her to one rehearsal. She had only been playing one of the Siamese children. I could not believe that the girl was shortly to have her 15th birthday. She had a maturity far beyond her years.

I rounded furiously on the chairman, pointing out that one of his auditioning committee was a traffic warden, by day a worthwhile occupation, but at night in the society she couldn't sing, dance or act so how dare she vote against this talented young girl standing before us?

I gave him my ultimatum - this girl would play Eliza or I would tear up my contract and refuse to direct the show. I won, and Ria Jones went on to be a fantastic success in the show, turned professional and starred in many West End productions. She famously re-created the role of Fonteyn in Les Misérables in its long London run. In 2006 she appeared in 'High Society', in London's West End again, gaining great plaudits in the press. A true 'star is born' story. She is a lovely and extremely talented girl who never forgets her beginnings.

With my experience of working and directing amateur actors expanding, I was able to pick and choose who I wished to work with because I only regarded it as fill-in work between my professional shows.

My dancing partner Nina had extolled the virtues of her local society to me, the Portsmouth Players, so when the opportunity came I took it eagerly. They were a basically young group of very talented performers and my first production with them 'Jesus Christ Superstar' was a sensational success, which cemented our liaison for many years to come. Under my guidance they made all the costumes themselves. I had never liked the professional productions set in American Ball Parks, even used-car parking lots and so on. I strongly felt it should be firmly back in the times of Christ, which together with the avant garde music would find extra response with modern audiences. I was proved right.

The costume department advertised for old sheets and blankets, dying them in natural colours that would have been correct for the period and turning them into the biblical garments of the period. We hired the priests' garb and centurion uniforms, and the single permanent set with temple steps and palm trees truly helped to create the period of Christ's final days on earth.

With local church groups screaming abuse before they even saw the production, ticket sales escalated and the box office was inundated before we opened. The mainly youthful company rose to the occasion, the principals experienced, and success was ensured. A near professional presentation, which received high praise and set the standard for the future.

Auditioning the company for 'Kiss me Kate' a young girl had joined for her first audition. She held a good job down as a PA for a large firm with a good salary and company car, but had ambitions to become a professional performer.

She auditioned for the second female lead, Lois Lane, which I was happy to give her for her superb singing quality. I believe she had sung with a semi-

Jesus Christ Superstar

professional group as their singer doing local gigs, but she definitely had a personality and quality that demanded attention.

Eventually she went on, under my direction, to play the leads in 'Sweet Charity' and Fanny Brice in 'Funny Girl' where she stole the reviews. There was no stopping her. She was so determined to turn pro, that I introduced her to a small semi-pro group touring the West Country, which enabled her to clock up the essential work-load to gain an Equity card and then audition for professional productions.

The next surprise came when she got the role of Eponine in the London production of 'Les Misérables' and found herself playing opposite Ria Jones. So both my original discoveries joined forces in friendship. Truth is stranger than fiction, I was delighted that I had been instrumental in opening doors for them. However, once through, it is their talent that carries them to the next level of achievement – fame.

Julia next went to Hollywood, where she played Madonna's sister in 'Evita'. A special quartet was written into the score of the film when the director found that Julia had a powerful singing voice. Watch this space for future fame and remember the name Julia Worsley.

Finally the last of the quartet I helped gain professional status was a young boy, Andrew Stone. Working with the Norwich Operatic Society on the 'Sound of Music' Andy auditioned for the role of Rolf, the young Austrian post boy who turns Nazi. He had had extensive dance training and was quite brilliant. The role calls for him to dance with Lisl, so he was perfect, also just 16, which approximated Rolf's age. The die was cast, he got the part.

As Andy was anxious also to make dancing his career I was also in a position to offer him the chance of an Equity card. Working through a local authority who only presented one professional show a year – their summer one – gave me as director the right to bring two newcomers into the profession.

So I offered Andy a dancing position for the Cromer season, gaining him official status. A couple of seasons later when I was holding auditions for singers for the Cromer season, Andy had rung me in advance asking whether I would now consider him as the principal male singer for the summer season. I replied that he could turn up by all means but warned him that competition was fierce amongst males for that role. In my mind he was only an excellent dancer.

However on audition day he turned up. Always a good-looking boy, he had matured and had dedicated the past couple of years to vocal training. I thought that with his physical appearance and youthfulness it would encourage a younger audience also. So I decided to take a chance. There are many facets of a show's composition and they all worked beautifully that summer.

Andy had already danced in the musical 'Grease' so the image, whilst a departure from the norm, worked. The matinées began to fill with schoolgirls who waited for Andy's autograph. He was a local star. I had never had a male singer with such dancing skills either. In the evenings more teenagers with their parents were in the audiences. The second cohort had arrived.

So there are the four amateurs turned into successful professionals - Menna Trussler, Ria Jones, Julia Worsley and Andrew Stone.

Andy went on to work in many West End shows, mainly as a dancer I believe, although he was signed up for the production of 'Showboat', where he understudied and performed the role of Mr Snow. As Mr Snow was given to a black actor/singer in line with political correctness, I puzzled as to why they had given the understudy role to a white boy. Having said all this, neither could I understand, frankly, why a black actor had been cast in the first place, as the 'Showboat' story rests entirely on America's Black v White cultural paradigm, which it attempts to resolve. The music is of course fabulous but my feeling is that it is now better performed exclusively at concerts.

Working for Basingstoke Operatic Society when they wished to present 'Showboat' I told the committee that we had to resolve the casting by putting advertisements in the local papers asking for black performers to take on the roles that are required. As Basingstoke is very industrial, quite a lot of black people live and work there so I thought we might be in with a chance. For two separate nights we waited in vain. Not one turned up. I had hoped at least we might have had an aspiring black singer for the role of Joe who sings 'Old Man River', a powerful song about the plight of the black population of America.

As the show revolves around the black/white situation, the white performers had to black up to maintain the ethos of the show. There were no complaints and with the fabulous songs, each well known and well sung, the show packed out the theatre. No problems with race relations.

Some years later the National Theatre put on a professional production with the required black and white casts. However I felt the show lacked the theatrical zizz that the appearance of the Showboat itself should have provoked. I left at the interval for this reason - the only time I have ever done that at a professional show.

Whilst I have worked for many amateur societies through the years, my favourite ones are the Portsmouth Players and the Manx Operatic Society who I have directed for over 14 or 15 years each. The Manx Operatic Society has always had an over-abundance of young males and must be the envy countrywide of all other societies, who sometimes struggle to find enough for their requirements.

With the Isle of Man being a banking island, many young University lads live and work there and a number take part in the University drama groups, hence the abundance.

That was the only society throughout my 20 odd years of directing amateurs that I have ever agreed to direct and choreograph 'West Side Story' which requires two teams of able movers to play the Jets and the Sharks. Their production was outstanding and could have rivalled any professional company in my view, and I am the harshest critic of my own work, which doesn't always help. However, most societies realise that if *I* am pleased *they* are pleased.

One cannot play at theatre, which sounds an odd thing to say, but I am sure readers will understand. I have worked with a couple of societies that I have walked out on because they did not treat their hobby seriously whilst still charging their audiences to watch them 'messing' about.

There endeth the lesson, and also my chapter on amateur theatre. Good luck to all who take it seriously.

Sadly, I no longer work with amateurs since doing so very recently with a society formed only for the glorification of the husband and wife foundation members. I was rudely criticised and pronounced unworthy of my contracted fee, which they refused to pay. You only need one lousy apple in a barrel to turn the rest, so why risk getting another barrel of rubbish? I am not going to name the company, they know who they are and can rot in hell, for all I care. I have no need of their money, nor patronage.

By welcome contrast, here are two recommendations from my long term, favourite societies, which I am proud to have received.

31 Fastnet House
South Parade
Southsea
Hants
PO5 2JG

Dear Bob
I was most surprised to learn from your recent telephone call that you were having problems with an allegation of 'unprofessionalism' from an Amateur Operatic Group for whom you had directed. As you know, I was chairman of Portsmouth Players, a well known and successful Amateur Operatic Society on the South Coast who present musicals at the Kings Theatre, Southsea three times a year, when we play to audiences of some 8,000 for a week's run.

I was told a few years ago by Eileen Dobson, a member of Portsmouth Players and past president of NODA, that we had the highest annual turnover among the 2,000 plus amateur musical societies in the UK. The importance of engaging top class professional directors has to be of paramount importance if we are to maintain a high standard.

You will recall that the first of the many shows you directed for us over a period of 11 years was 'Jesus Christ Superstar'. We were very proud that The Really Useful Group, who released the show to a very select group of accredited societies for a period of a few months only, chose us as a worthy society. The show, you may remember, played to local and national acclaim.

Other productions you have directed for us included 'Calamity Jane', 'The Gondoliers', 'Mr Cinders', 'Kiss Me Kate', 'Gigi', 'Funny Girl', 'Sweet Charity' and 'Charlie Girl'. Every one has been a great success and this was evidenced by the fact that we continually asked you back to direct.

I must admit that I am very surprised by this allegation and I hope you are able to sort out any problems arising from it.

I hope you keep well.

With kind regards

Yours sincerely

John Lindsey

Robert Marlowe
Director/Choreographer

I first met Robert Marlowe in 1983 when he arrived on the Isle of Man to commence rehearsals for the Operatic Society's production of 'The Merry Widow'. Such was Bob's enthusiasm coupled with an artistic vision and a professionalism rarely seen in amateur dramatic circles, that his services were retained for the next 15 years.

During the majority of those years I was the Chairman of the Society and I'm pleased to be able to report that with Bob's guidance the Manx Operatic Society gained a reputation as one of the finest and most 'professional' amateur musical societies.

Bob directed 15 musicals and 2 pantomimes for the Society and we were rewarded with almost 30 NODA awards during his time with us. These awards included Best Show, Best Production (twice) and Best Choreography (4 times). The musicals he directed showed a diversity of repertoire ranging from 'Jesus Christ Superstar' to 'Chicago' and included such classics as 'West Side Story' and '42nd Street'.

His professionalism and dedication reached heights that most would fail to achieve and he established standards that could only be an aspiration for the majority of amateur musical societies.

Maurice E Mawdsley
Life Member
Manx Operatic Society
Isle of Man

ALL CHANGE – AND ON WITH THE SHOW!

'Times are changing', we hear it every day. I'll rephrase that, 'Times have changed', and nowhere more so than in the world of amateur musicals. Now why? After all, excellent musicals were presented in times gone by with superb singing voices.

There are many varying factors and one is the change in styles. Modern musicals require singers to have a brasher quality. Gone is the operetta voice with its articulated vowels - a retrograde step, many will undoubtedly claim. However, one cannot stop the progress of changing fashion.

Nowadays every member of the audience is a critic, whether they realise it or not. In the past a visit to the theatre or cinema was an occasion. One dressed up and departed with the intention of enjoying oneself, no matter what the shortcomings. With entertainment at the touch of a button, even the uncritical become blasé and unimpressed. Is this a bad thing? I think not. It means one has to make an even greater effort to please, and the pursuit of excellence is always a worthwhile project.

I refuse to differentiate the category 'amateur'. That makes me see red. So were Torvill and Dean, yet they captured the world with their skills. In my career I direct top professionals as well as amateurs and do not differentiate between the two. We are all in the business of entertaining and charging money from our audience for doing so. They therefore deserve similar skills and dedication from both. Chorus members have to be proficient in singing, dancing and acting. No longer will merely one of these talents be sufficient to enable you to become one. The days have long gone when the singing chorus stood in a semi-circle belting out the words, whilst the dancing chorus rushed into the centre to compete in a 'who is best' competition, and never the twain did meet. This change has applied to the professionals since 'Oklahoma' hit the scene and whilst it has taken a little longer in the amateur theatre, it is now expected that their productions replicate the standard of the originals.

We are bombarded daily in newspapers and magazines to pursue image by slimming and making ourselves as attractive as possible. This has a knock-on effect in what is expected in our viewing entertainment. No longer can overweight 60 year olds masquerade as 20 year olds in fast moving routines requiring skill and pace. By the same token I would not cast a 20 year old in a part requiring maturity. Every age has its requirements and there is room for everyone, but please – be your age!

It is essential to attract the young and talented for they are the life-blood of all societies wishing to survive into the next decade. This will wipe out completely the sometimes lingering impression amongst the general public that amateur societies are made up of elderly ladies and adolescent schoolboys, a very unfair assumption in these changed times. In view of the foregoing, gird up your loins! And on with the show!

This article was reproduced in quite a few of the programmes for shows that I directed for the amateur movement, who agreed with all the sentiments expressed.

With shows like 'West Side Story', 'Jesus Christ Superstar' and 'Chicago' becoming available for amateur performance, younger people were eager to join the societies.

Gone are the 'Rose Marie', 'Desert Song' and 'Chu Chin Chow' of yesteryear, good as they were. Of their time, but now museum pieces. Only Gilbert and Sullivan still find an audience, although when the 'Mikado' was given a different slant a few years ago in the London Coliseum starring Eric Idle, many Gilbert and Sullivan fans objected. I personally loved it. Oh well, to each his own.

EPILOGUE

Well there it is, two and a half years in the writing, in an effort to give readers a first hand account of theatrical entertainment throughout the past 50 years. Every aspect except one, the circus.

Even as a child the clowns terrified me and I was afraid the lions would escape and eat me. I have never relished seeing magnificent wild creatures made to perform contrary to their natural inclinations.

Domestic pets are a different matter. Dogs, especially poodles, have a natural tendency to perform and please their owners. Jenny and I witnessed a troupe of performing dogs of differing breeds when we joined a variety tour. Their excitement before their performances was infectious.

One new style of circus is the Canadian Cirque du Soleil, an astonishing troupe of performers and not an animal in sight. It's an artistic tour de force of acrobats, singers, dancers and actors in spectacular settings and lavish costumes, touring the world to great acclaim.

With this final paragraph I hope I have completed the show business circle, in your eyes, and that you have been suitably entertained by this peep behind the scenes – with the laughter, the comedy and the tragedy.

Me and My Gals

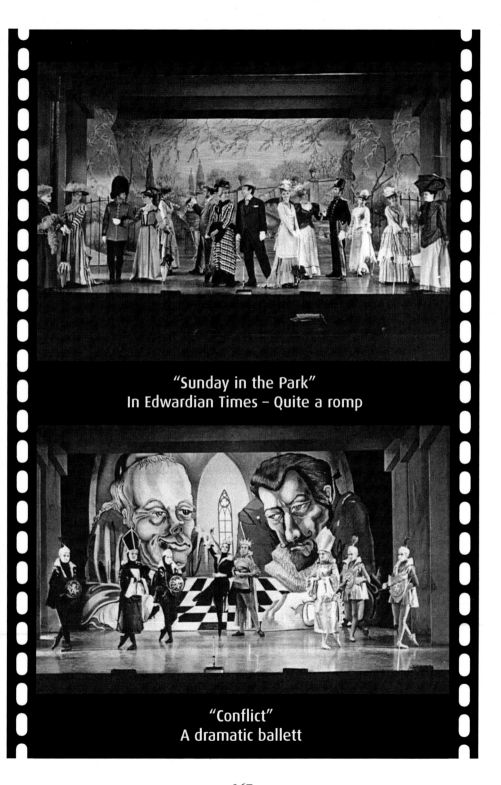

"Sunday in the Park"
In Edwardian Times – Quite a romp

"Conflict"
A dramatic ballett

"Pianomania"
Moments of Melody

The last production at the Marine Pavilion – Folkestone
including all stage crew and administrators

Opening scene taken from the Broadway show "Follies"
The title said it all:
Hats off, here they come, those beautiful girls.

A Scene from "Song of Norway"

A Dutch scene which started in a forest of Daffodils.
These were placed on darts which the dancers picked until
none were left - very effective!

Finale for the Queen's 25th Silver Wedding Anniversary.
Frankie Holmes starred - a very versatile comic.

A Cuban scene. This starred Les Wilson, a droll comic whose style raised the roof

A Swiss scene

A Wild West scene with Les Wilson as Buffalo Bill

A tribute to ABBA

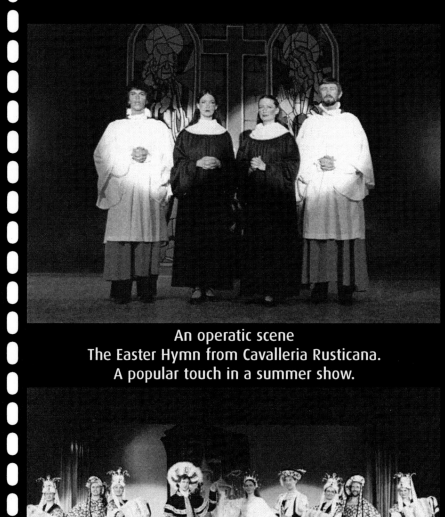

An operatic scene
The Easter Hymn from Cavalleria Rusticana.
A popular touch in a summer show.

"Camelot" which had a full stage snowfall at the end

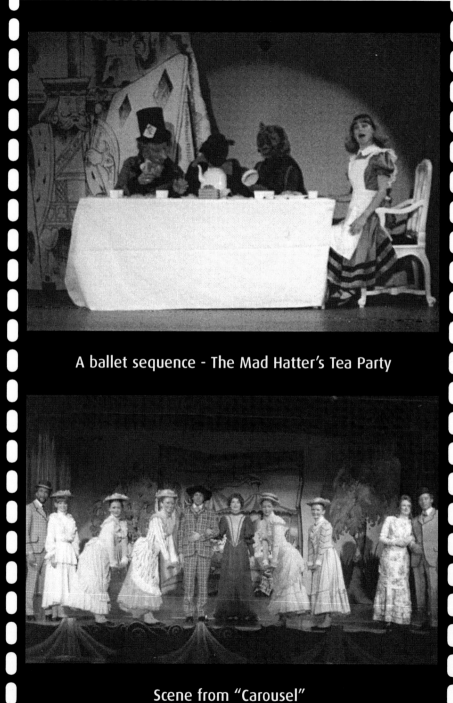

A ballet sequence - The Mad Hatter's Tea Party

Scene from "Carousel"

"The Sound of Music"
The departure over the mountain scene

"Latino"
Red hot and sexy

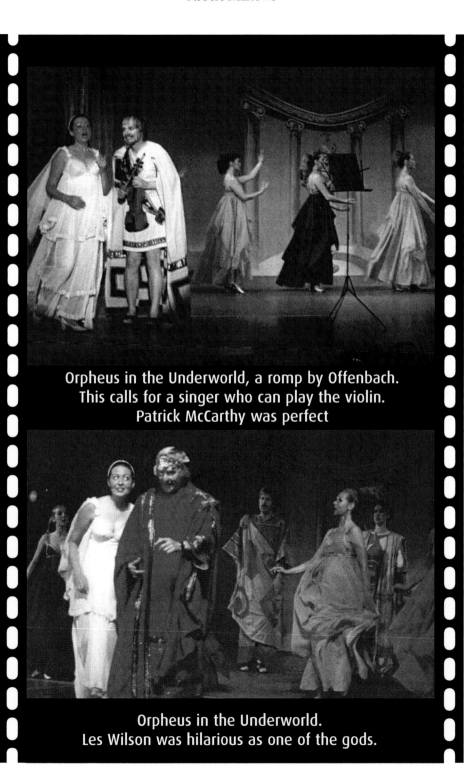

Orpheus in the Underworld, a romp by Offenbach.
This calls for a singer who can play the violin.
Patrick McCarthy was perfect

Orpheus in the Underworld.
Les Wilson was hilarious as one of the gods.

A Highland scene with a water effect and pipers leading the company over the falls down to the glen.

"Pantomime"
with all the men as dames and girls as principal boys

"The Sound of Music"

A ballet sequence
"La Boutique Fantasque"
Where dolls come alive at night and enjoy the dance

"Orpheus"

"Orpheus"
The famous can-can in hell

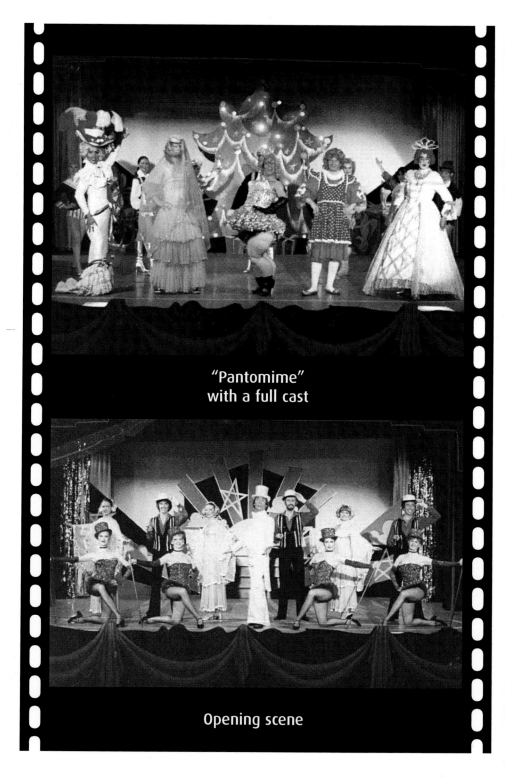

"Pantomime"
with a full cast

Opening scene

Finale

"Doctor Dolittle" with fabulous costumes by Rosemary
Waters who dressed all the Folkestone shows over my
12-year tenure - we remain friends to the present day

The hunting scene from the Broadway musical "Mame"

The finale of "Mame"
with spectacular horses for the dancers to 'ride'!

"Oliver"
I had a ball playing Fagin

"Oliver"
with the boys

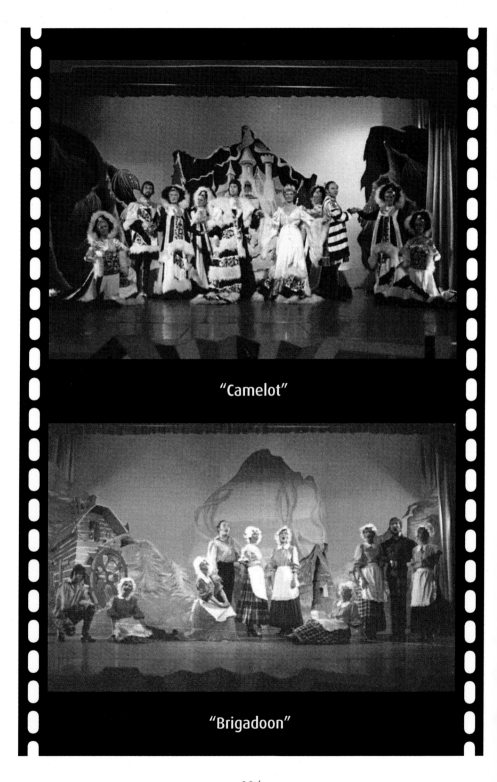

"Camelot"

"Brigadoon"

"Fiddler on the Roof"

"Spanish Fiesta"

"Jesus Christ Superstar"

"In Old Vienna"

"Sail Away"

The ballet "Coppelia"

The Roaring Twenties

The musical
"Song of Norway"

A tribute to Noel Coward

"James Bond"

"Slap That Bass"
Starring Gordon and Bunny Jay

"A Tribute to ABBA"

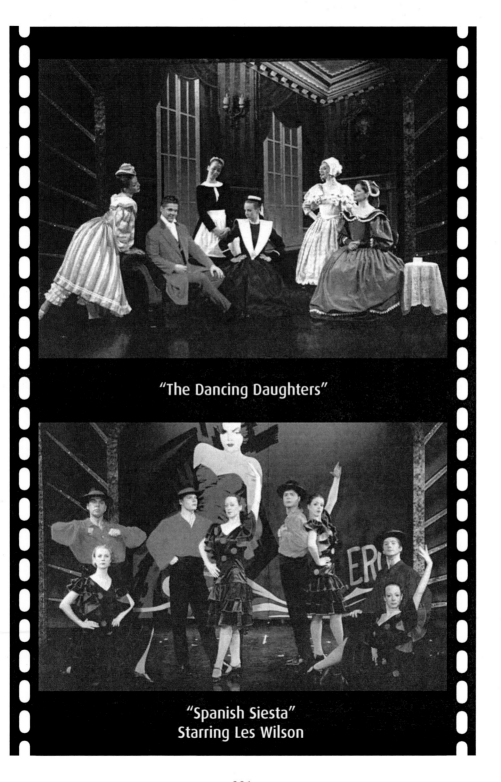

"The Dancing Daughters"

"Spanish Siesta"
Starring Les Wilson

Full company in "Greece". A young comic starred
Multi talented – he should be famous!

Ian Adams and Vivienne McMaster
in their show-stopping act

Cromer finale with puppets

All the backstage crew with their heads poking through
the seaside postcards set

A Dresden ballet scene.
Dancers as figures on a clock and candlesticks

A scene depicting the dangers of smoking and drinking

"Hello Dolly"
The opening scene

"Hello Dolly"
The full company in the finale

Quartette with ventriloquist horse

Scene from "Lizzie Borden"
who killed her parents with an axe. A hoedown romp!

Saucy sketch with Les Wilson and Kathy from Traffle

The finale of "Jesus Christ Superstar"
with local children representing the world

Opening scene which started in London and finished in
Cromer with travel effects

"One Singular Sensation"
Danced by the entire company

A Christmas opening (in summer?) entitled:
"We Need a Little Christmas"

"My Fair Lady"
The scene at Ascot

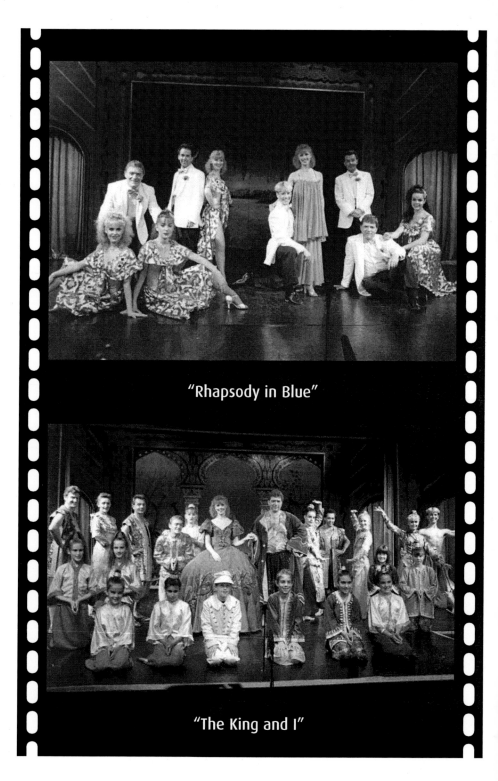

"Rhapsody in Blue"

"The King and I"

The cast taking a bow at the end of the show

The full company in "Tamla Motown" scene

Stagedoor scene depicting various decades: Victorian,
Twenties and Mod Rockers, Godron and Bunny Jay

"Fidler on the Roof"

Nick Spellman with his amazing illusion act

My dancers in the aviation scene
Pam, Helen, Dee and Emma

My dancers
Pam, Helen, Dee and Melanie

Richard Deloro
Tap dancing juggler